Linguistic Atlas of the Middle and South Atlantic States

Fascicle 1

CONTENTS

Raven I. McDavid, Jr.
Raymond K. O'Cain

The University of Chicago Press, Chicago and London

Linguistic Atlas
of the
Middle and South Atlantic States

Linguistic Atlas of the United States and Canada

Hans Kurath
Director

Linguistic Atlas
of the
Middle and South Atlantic States

Raven I. McDavid, Jr.
Editor-in-Chief

Raymond K. O'Cain
Associate Editor

George T. Dorrill
Assistant Editor

†Guy S. Lowman, Jr.
Principal Field Investigator

Volume I

Sponsored by The American Council of Learned Societies

The University of Chicago Press

Chicago and London

Preparation of this volume was made possible
in part by a grant from the Research Materials
Programs of the National Endowment for the
Humanities

The University of Chicago Press, Chicago 60637
The University of Chicago Press, Ltd., London
© 1980 by The University of Chicago
All rights reserved. Published 1980
Printed in the United States of America

Library of Congress Cataloging in Publication Data

Main entry under title:

Linguistic atlas of the Middle and South Atlantic
    states.

    (Linguistic atlas of the United States and Canada)
    Sponsored by the American Council of Learned
Societies.
    Issued in parts.
    1. English language in the United States—
Dialects—Middle Atlantic States—Maps.
2. English language in the United States—
Dialects—Southern States—Maps. I. McDavid,
Raven Ioor. II. O'Cain, Raymond K. III. American
Council of Learned Societies Devoted to Humanistic
Studies. IV. Dorrill, George T. V. Series.
G1246.E3L5   912'.1'427974   79-24748
ISBN 0-226-55742-1 (fasc. 1)

To Edgar H. Sturtevant, Edward Sapir, and Leonard Bloomfield,
whose interest, encouragement, and advice made it
possible for Hans Kurath to carry out this project.

A WORD OF WELCOME

One can safely predict that the *Linguistic Atlas of the Middle and South Atlantic States*, along with the *Linguistic Atlas of New England*, will be of fundamental value to the student of American English for generations to come. Taken together, they constitute the first systematic sampling survey of usage in the Atlantic States where the chief varieties of our English developed during the colonial period, dialects that were carried westward in the nineteenth century.

The analysis and interpretation of some of the field data from this extensive area by Hans Kurath, Raven I. McDavid, Jr., and E. Bagby Atwood have shown that the Atlantic States are divided into three major dialect areas: the *North* (New England and New York State), the *Midland* (Pennsylvania and the Southern Upland), and the *South* (the plantation country from Chesapeake Bay to Georgia). Each of these three major areas has sub-divisions reflecting its colonial history, such as Eastern New England, the Philadelphia area, the Piedmont of Virginia, and South Carolina.

The achievement of this perspective on the character and the history of our English in the Eastern States led scholars to undertake field surveys in various parts of the Midwest and the Far West and to trace regional features current in these derivative settlement areas to their homeland on the Atlantic slope. Thus Albert H. Marckwardt surveyed the North-Central States, Harold B. Allen, the Upper Midwest; Carroll E. Reed and David W. Reed, the Far West; E. Bagby Atwood, the state of Texas; William R. Van Riper, Oklahoma; Gerald R. Udell, Missouri; Marjorie M. Kimmerle, Colorado; and now Lee A. Pederson is engaged in a survey of the Gulf States.

As far as vocabulary is concerned, Frederic G. Cassidy's nation-wide survey for his *Dictionary of American Regional English* will add substantially to our stock of information. But for phonological and grammatical features the *Linguistic Atlas of the Middle and South Atlantic States* and the *Linguistic Atlas of New England* will remain for some time to come our only source of reliable data.

The publication of the wealth of the field data from the Middle and South Atlantic States will be welcomed by all students of our language, whether they are concerned with the usage of the cultured or the folk in that area or with the regional and social dialects of the derivative areas to the west. All of us who have had a share in this enterprise feel grateful to Raven I. McDavid, Jr., and his staff for their determined effort to bring this about.

Hans Kurath

The publication of the *Linguistic Atlas of the Middle and South Atlantic States* (*LAMSAS*), beginning with this fascicle, completes the editorial responsibilities assumed in 1929 by Hans Kurath, Director of the Linguistic Atlas of the United States and Canada.

The first regional survey, the *Linguistic Atlas of New England* (*LANE*), proceeded smoothly. Field work was completed in two years, 1931-3; the first volume appeared in 1939 and the third and final volume in 1943.

The next survey was to be a Linguistic Atlas of the South Atlantic States (Delaware to northeast Florida), but the depression and the scanty resources of Southern institutions curtailed operations. Only Guy S. Lowman, Jr., who did the largest share of work in New England, was kept in the field. After a preliminary South Atlantic survey (1933-4) and a systematic investigation of Virginia and North Carolina (1935-7), Kurath could find no funds for work further south. He arranged for Lowman to investigate parts of southern England (1937-8), to complete work in Delaware and Maryland, and to begin the survey of the Middle Atlantic States (southern Ontario to West Virginia). All but southern Ontario and upstate New York had been covered when Lowman died in an automobile accident in the summer of 1941.

To complete the Atlantic Seaboard survey Kurath chose Raven I. McDavid, Jr., now Editor-in-Chief, who had studied with Bernard Bloch and Kurath at Linguistic Institutes. Despite the suspension of field work during World War II, McDavid finished the survey of southern Ontario, upstate New York, South Carolina, eastern Georgia, and northeastern Florida by June 1949, thus completing Kurath's basic scheme for the Middle and South Atlantic States. Later incorporated into the Atlantic Seaboard archives were a few field records made by McDavid in the 1950's for Albert H. Marckwardt's Linguistic Atlas of the North-Central States in Ontario (3), Ohio (6), and Kentucky (20), along with several Ohio records made for Marckwardt by Frederic G. Cassidy (2), Alva L. Davis (3), Cassil Reynard (1), and W. Edson Richmond (4). Still later (1965-74), a number of records were added-- principally of old-fashioned speech--from Ontario (5), upstate New York (7), South Carolina (7), Georgia (40), and Florida (2).

All of these last records--by Gerald Udell, Raymond K. O'Cain (now Associate Editor), Lee A. Pederson (now

Director of the Linguistic Atlas of the Gulf States), and several of Pederson's students, particularly Grace Reuter and Barbara Rutledge--were recorded on tape and transcribed by McDavid. Less than one percent of the records for *LAMSAS* represent transcriptions by field workers other than Lowman or McDavid. The work of the various investigators is identified in the Table of Informants by Types (pp. 6-13).

II

Editorial work began on the South Atlantic materials in 1940, Kurath being assisted by Bernard and Julia Bloch and several graduate students, notably Jane Daddow (Hawkins), Jeanette Dearden (Denning), Phyllis Jones (Nixon), and Elizabeth Gardner. As linguists were drawn into the wartime language program, editorial operations slowed until they ceased on Kurath's departure from Brown University to the University of Michigan in 1946 to become editor of the *Middle English Dictionary*. By that time list manuscripts had been drafted for about 300 items for the area from southern New Jersey through North Carolina.

The cessation of editorial work at Brown coincided with two major decisions by Kurath on the format.

(1) There would be only one regional Atlas, embracing both the Middle and South Atlantic States.

(2) It would not be published as overprinted maps like *LANE* but as lists, printed by photo-offset from typed copy. This would permit less costly publication and produce volumes easier to use and store.

III

It was hoped that the University of Michigan would help fund further editing. For various reasons this help was not forthcoming, though there was support for three broad-guaged interpretive volumes: Kurath's *Word Geography of the Eastern U.S.* (1949), E. Bagby Atwood's *Survey of Verb Forms in the Eastern U.S.* (1953), and Kurath and McDavid's *Pronunciation of English in the Atlantic States* (1961). There were also a number of monographs and articles published, but no systematic work on the basic material. Following Kurath's retirement (1962), Dean Robert Streeter of the Humanities Division of the University of Chicago arranged to transfer the Atlantic Seaboard materials to Chicago (1964); McDavid became Editor-in-Chief, and Alva L. Davis, of the Illinois Institute of Technology, Co-Editor.

IV

With half time available for editing, McDavid spent the
next decade adjusting editorial practices to the new
scheme, incorporating the last field records into the
collection, and preparing additional list manuscripts.
By the summer of 1974 about two-thirds of the first stage
of editorial work was complete.

Davis hoped to utilize the facilities of IIT to
complete the editorial process and prepare copy for the
printer. However, his activities were restricted by a
lack of released time and by heavy administrative responsibilities. Mary Lee Al-Azzawi, a research assistant
funded by the National Council of Teachers of English
(1971-4), aided Davis in formulating editorial plans.
However, Davis and IIT ceased active participation in 1974.

The major advance at IIT was the solution of the
problems of preparing copy. Composition by VariTyper had
been envisaged, but no funds were available to develop
appropriate shuttles. In 1966, Martin Tytell prepared a
phonetic typewriter from a design by Davis and McDavid,
but it required the transfer of paper from one machine
to another. The development of the IBM Selectric typewriter solved the technical problems, but there was no
suitable phonetic element. Finally, Davis and McDavid
designed an element for the Atlas, and in 1974 arranged
with Camwil, Inc., of Honolulu to manufacture it, an
undertaking largely supported by contributions from
interested individuals and organizations. The editors
cannot overemphasize their gratitude.

V

The most important step toward publication was the 1974
decision of the University of South Carolina to provide
support. Responsible for this participation are:

(1) the interest of Milledge B. Seigler,
senior professor in the University, and John R. Welsh,
Head of the English Department and later Vice-President
for Instruction;

(2) the presence at South Carolina of O'Cain,
a former student of McDavid; and

(3) the cooperation of Kenneth E. Toombs,
Director of Libraries of the University.

It was arranged that McDavid be invited as visiting
professor to oversee the beginning of editorial work at
South Carolina. In 1974, half the archives were moved
there, the remainder in 1976. South Carolina is providing
housing and work space, supplies and equipment, released
time for O'Cain, and funds for student assistants. To

date, George T. Dorrill, Hugh D. Brown, Molly E. Daniel,
Linda L. Barnes, Nell H. Huffman, and David Fischer have
participated in editing; the work of composition was
begun by Karen M. Garrison, and continued by Linda K.
Lineberger and Sara L. Sanders.

In the meantime at Chicago, Richard C. Payne, a
former student of Marckwardt, joined the editorial staff.
Royalties from the reprinted *LANE* (1972) and the second
edition of the *Handbook of the Linguistic Geography of
New England* (1973) supported two editorial assistants,
Nancy Hopkins and Glenda Pritchett. The staff at Chicago
completed list manuscripts for the territory through North
Carolina, and provided initial proofreading; at South
Carolina the staff are adding data from South Carolina
through Florida, giving final proofreading and editorial
revisions, and preparing copy. Audrey R. Duckert of
Massachusetts (who prepared the word-index for the second
edition of the *LANE Handbook*) and David R. Carlson of
Springfield College will prepare an index with the cooperation of the Computational Center at the University of
Massachusetts. The index should be ready by the time the
last fascicle goes to press.

The National Endowment for the Humanities granted
McDavid a Senior Fellowship for the year 1975 to assist
in preparing the *LAMSAS Handbook*. Since 1977 NEH has also
contributed substantially to the support of editorial work
at South Carolina.

VI

It is impossible to offer an exact timetable for a work
of this scope, involving the responses of more than 1200
informants to a questionnaire of some 840 items. At no
time, however, will accuracy be sacrificed to speed.

A full list of those who have helped to support the
project will appear with the final volume. At this time
we must specifically acknowledge the continuing interest
of the American Council of Learned Societies, which
sponsored the project at the beginning, provided material
help at all stages, and has been a constant source of
moral support. Even more important is the contribution
of Hans Kurath, who conceived the plans for the original
Atlas and has participated actively in it for nearly half
a century. He continues to offer both counsel and
inspiration.

Raven I. McDavid, Jr.
Editor-in-Chief

INTRODUCTION
I. ARRANGEMENT OF THE LISTS

The *Linguistic Atlas of the Middle and South Atlantic States* (*LAMSAS*) will complete the publication of the full phonetic record of the primary dialect survey of the area of American colonial settlement begun by the *Linguistic Atlas of New England* (*LANE*). *LAMSAS* follows in most details the methodology outlined in the *Handbook of the Linguistic Geography of New England*; an analogous interpretive volume for *LAMSAS* is in preparation. Until that volume appears, the following remarks should, in accompaniment with the *LANE Handbook*, generally serve to guide the user of these materials.

The 1216 principal field records made for *LAMSAS* from Ontario to Florida have been arranged in 518 numbered *LAMSAS* communities. Each *LAMSAS* community is identified by the state or province abbreviation and a number: Ont 1-10, NY 1-64, NJ 1-21, Pa 1-67, WVa 1-54, Ohio 1-18, Ky 1-7, Del 1-6, Md 1-27, DC 1, Va 1-75, NC 1-75, SC 1-44, Ga 1-44, Fla 1-5. In general, *LAMSAS* communities correspond to counties (rather than townships, as in *LANE*), except that in a few cases there may be two or more *LAMSAS* communities in a single county (as NY 33 and 38--Herkimer county) or two counties may constitute a single *LAMSAS* community (as Ky 1--Carter and Rowan counties). The locations of the *LAMSAS* communities are shown on the accompanying base map.

Usually two informants of contrasting age and social background were interviewed in each community, often at different locations within the county. (See Lists 1, 2, and 3 for names of the locations and counties.) Informants are identified by the community number and a lower case letter beginning with *a*, except that no letter follows if there is only one informant in the community, or in the case of Negro informants, who are designated by the community number preceded by *N* (or *2N* for a second Negro informant, i.e., Md 2N22, SC 2N11, Ga 2N37). Cultured informants are designated by underscoring.

The data are presented in lists rather than on maps. The most effective way of examining the distribution of linguistic features is to make charts on copies of the accompanying base map. The University of Chicago Press has given permission to make copies of the base map for charting; the customary acknowledgements should be made in any publications.

The order of presentation of the responses of the informants is the same in every list. Communities are arranged in the geographical order given above. Within each community, the order of informants is by social rank, in ascending order from the least cultured to the most cultured.

The Table of Informants by Types (pp. 6-13) provides the social type, age, sex, year of interview, and field worker for each principal informant. More detailed information on the informants will be provided in the *LAMSAS Handbook*.

In addition to principal informants, there are also auxiliary informants in some communities. These are either informants whose interviews were not completed for various reasons, or persons--often relatives or neighbors--who happened to be present at the interview of the principal informant and who provided responses to certain questions. Responses from auxiliary informants are preceded by * (or ** for a second auxiliary informant) and follow the responses of the principal informant. Vitae for auxiliary informants appear in the *LAMSAS Handbook* following those of the corresponding principal informants.

The topical order of presentation follows that of *LANE*, which generally follows that of the work sheets, with certain exceptions; for instance, place names and topographical terms are presented first, and most grammatical items are gathered at the end. Topical divisions may be introduced by headnotes applicable to all the lists within the division.

Before each list there is an explanatory headnote containing such information as the manner of elicitation, any special conventions of presentation, and other matters bearing on the interpretation of the item investigated. Reference numbers to the work sheets (WS) and the map in *LANE* are provided for each item systematically investigated. Following each list is a commentary containing significant comments of informants or field workers, amplifying information, or related forms. Sometimes subsidiary lists (e.g., 4a, *Eastern States*) will follow the main list.

Where two or more successive informants offer responses identical in every respect, the inclusive numbers are consolidated and the response is entered only once. Non-responses are indicated by ---; successive non-responses are also consolidated. Lists of items not investigated systematically contain only the responses recorded; non-responses are not indicated.

II. PHONETIC ALPHABET

The responses are presented in Kurath and Bloch's modification of the International Phonetic Alphabet, which, with other signs and symbols, is described in Chapter IV of the *LANE* and *LAMSAS Handbooks*. The phonetic alphabet and other symbols in *LAMSAS*, typewritten from specially designed elements, sometimes differ slightly from the hand-drafted characters in *LANE*.

1. CONSONANTS

	BILABIAL	LABIODENTAL	DENTAL	ALVEOLAR	PALATALIZED ALVEOLAR	RETROFLEX	ALVEOLO-PALATAL	PALATO-ALVEOLAR	PALATAL	RETRACTED PALATAL	ADVANCED VELAR	VELAR	GLOTTAL
STOPS	p b		ṯ ḏ	t d	ţ ḑ	ṭ ḍ			c ɟ	č̓ ɟ̓	k̓ g̓	k g	ʔ
NASALS	m	ɱ	ṉ	n	ņ	ṇ			ɲ	ɲ̓	ŋ̓	ŋ	
LATERALS			ḻ	l ɟ ł	ļ	!			ʎ				
FLAPS			ſ̣	ſ ⌐	ſ̦	ſ̣							
FRICATIVES	Φ β	f v	ṣ ẓ θ ð ⊥̣ ɾ̣	s z ⊥ r ʁ	ṣ̦ ẓ̦ ⊥̦ ſ̦	ṣ̣ ẓ̣ ⊥̣ ſ̣	ʃ ʒ ʃ̣ ʒ̣	č̣ ƚ	ç ʝ	ç̓ ʝ̓	x̆ ɾ̆	x ɣ	h ɦ ɦ̦
FRICTIONLESS CONTINUANTS	(ɥ) (w)	F ʋ	ſ ʁ		ſ̣				ʝ ɥ	ʝ̓ ɥ̓	w̆	w	

2. VOWELS

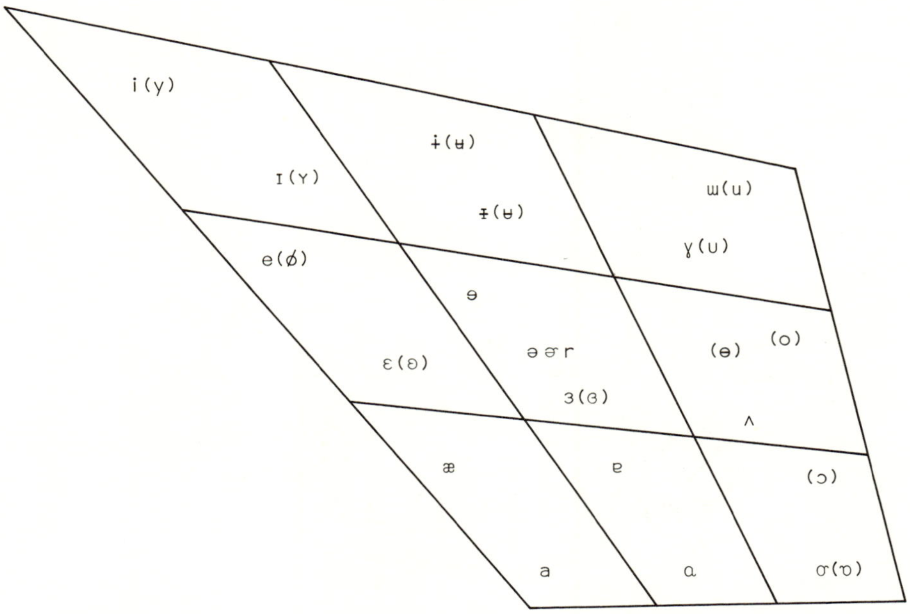

Symbols for rounded vowels are enclosed in parentheses.

3. DIACRITICS

<	ə< k̂	fronting	~	ə̃ r̃	nasalization	,	ə̢	pharyngealization	‘	‘p p‘	aspiration
>	ə> c̆	backing	̯	ə̯ r̯	rounding	–	m̶	velarization	·	o·	long
^	ə^	raising	_	u̱	spreading	̪	t̪	dentalization	:	o:	overlong
˅	ə˅	lowering	∘	ə̥ d̥	unvoicing	_	t̠	lenis	˘	ə̆	short
.	ə̣	*r*-color	ˬ	t̬	voicing	⌒	b̑	implosive		ʔt̯ ɹ̯	coarticulation
.	ṭ	retroflexion	’	ə̉ ’t	glottalization	‿	r‿	linkage			

Diacritics may be used in various combinations. They are described fully in Chapter IV of the *LANE* and *LAMSAS Handbooks*.

III. STRESS, SYLLABIFICATION, WORD DIVISION

Primary stress is indicated by the superior stress mark ˈ: thus [ˈhotɛl] *hotel*; secondary stress is indicated by the inferior stress mark ˌ: thus [ˈæˌdɹɛs] *address*. Often only exceptional stress patterns are marked in the lists. The headnotes explain the unmarked regular patterns.

A vertical stroke below certain consonants (typically [m,n,l,r]) indicates syllabic function where it is not otherwise apparent: thus [laɨtn̩ɨŋ] *lightening*, but [laɨtnɨŋ] *lightning*.

Where not otherwise apparent vowel symbols not intended to represent a diphthong are separated by the hyphen -: thus [bæ-ɨl] *barrel*. (See p. 133 *LANE Handbook* for exceptions.)

When a phonetic entry is a phrase containing two or more words, the words are normally separated by spaces for the sake of convenience in reading. However, when the final consonant of one word and the initial consonant of the following word are completely assimilated, the words are not separated: thus [poɚt̬əˈɬʉʒʉ>zɨ^] *Port*

Dalhousie. When the field worker indicates that the final consonant of a word belongs also to the initial syllable of the following word, this is indicated by the linkage ‿ : thus [prɪn'tsɨz æ·ᵊn] *Princess Anne.*

When the field worker indicates that the stress of the second word sets in before or together with the final consonant of the first word, so that this consonant belongs phonetically to the following syllable, the words are divided according to the syllable division: thus [ˌsɪn 'tɪnɨgəz] *St. Inigoes.*

It is sometimes difficult or impossible to decide where the boundary between two words should be drawn. In such cases the words are usually not divided: thus [jʊstə] *used to.*

IV. LABELS

Various labels indicate the manner in which a response was secured, the informants' reactions to an item, and their opinions of its currency and status. These labels-- as well as the evaluations of the practices of the field workers, the background and personality sketches of the informants, and the observations in the commentaries-- serve to aid in interpretation of the responses.

Elicited forms are unmarked, though labels from (2) below may be affixed. Normally the field worker described a work sheet item and the informant responded with its name.

The labels are of two general types:

(1) Labels that apply to all following forms unless cancelled by another label of this class (or by a semicolon in a combined list).

  cv recorded from the informant's unguarded conversa-
      tion, not in response to a line of inquiry.

  s   suggested by the field worker and repeated by the
      informant. A suggested response is not recorded
      by the field worker unless he has reason to be-
      lieve it represents the informant's natural
      usage, a question that cannot always be decided
      instantaneously; therefore suggested forms are
      generally to be regarded as less trustworthy
      than others.

Conversational forms follow elicited forms. Suggested forms follow conversational forms. All three cate- gories may have forms with labels from (2) below. Responses from auxiliary informants are included only where they provide additional information and they follow all responses from the main informant. The order of elicited, conversational, and suggested responses is repeated for as many auxiliary infor- mants as offered responses.

(2) Labels that apply only to the form to which they are affixed. They sometimes are used in combination with certain other labels.

(a) labels preceding the forms:

  f   forced, secured by repeated questioning or
      insistence on an answer.

  cr corrected spontaneously by the informant; such
      forms usually follow immediately the initial
      response.

  r   repeated at the field worker's request; such forms
      usually follow immediately the initial response.

  :   denotes hesitation on the part of the informant,
      whether from uncertainty or disinclination to
      utter a word or phrase.

  ?   denotes doubt on the part of the informant, as to
      the meaning, pronunciation, or naturalness of a form.

  !   denotes amusement on the part of the informant,
      caused by the pronunciation, meaning, or broader
      subject matter of the form.

  ⊥   heard; reported by the informant as heard from
      others but not his own usage.

  N   judged by the informant as Negro usage; forms from
      languages other than English will be identified as
      warranted.

  †   judged by the informant as old, out of date,
      obsolete, or heard only from an older generation.

  →   judged by the informant as recently introduced, or
      heard only from a younger generation.

(b) labels following the forms:

  (?) indicates doubt on the part of the field worker.
      Where the field worker is uncertain of his tran-
      scription, the doubtful segments are identified in
      the commentary: thus (main list) [†ʃɨ'mʌˇŋg (?)],
      (commentary) [†]: doubtful.

  (√) indicates certainty on the part of the field
      worker. Where the field worker indicates con-
      fidence about his transcription, the segments
      that he marks as certain will be labelled in the
      commentary by *sic*: thus (main list)
      ['waˀɛoᵁnɨŋ (√)], (commentary) [-n-]: *sic*.

V. SUBSTITUTE SYMBOLS

A number of signs are used to avoid the repetition of
identical words or parts of words in a single entry
These are listed below, as well as certain other symbols
used regularly in the lists. Additional signs, symbols,
and conventions will occasionally be used in the lists
and will be explained where they occur.

~   replaces a word repeated without change in an
entry: thus [ˈkuʂuˤpɚ ˌstɹiˇit, ˈkupɚ ~]
(to repeat the word [ˌstɹiˇit]). If more than
one word is repeated, ~ is used for each word:
thus [cv dʒeˑmzɨˤz ˈkˤɟɔˇˑᵊs ˌroˑᵊdz
⊥ɴ ˈdʒiˑᴶmzɨˤz ~ ~] (to repeat [ˈkˤɟɔˇˑᵊs
ˌroˑᵊdz]). If the repeated word differs only
in initial stress, ~ is used in combination with
stress marks: thus [cv ˌnɟɥˑ ˈɪˆŋləˆn,
ˈ~ ˌ~]. Sometimes the symbol ~ is used in the
commentary to refer to a form on the main list,
giving the context in which the form was recorded.
It is not to be regarded as a separate instance
of the form: thus (main list) [cv ɪŋləˆn,
ɪŋlɨʃ], (commentary) *England* people [ˈ~
ˌpiˑᴵˆpəˆɬ], *English* sparrow [ˌ~ ˈspɑˤrəˆ].

-   replaces a phonetic symbol or sequence of symbols
(usually a syllable or group of syllables) repeated without change from a preceding word: thus
[wɛˤləˆn cv wɛ-] (equivalent to [wɛˤləˆn
cv wɛləˆn]). If more than one form is repeated,
the hyphen refers to the immediately preceding

word: thus [ˈæɟɨˤnˌdeˑl, -ˌdeˑᵊɟ, ˈæˑlɨn-]
(equivalent to [ˈæɟɨˤnˌdeˑl, ˈæɟɨˤnˌdeˑᵊɟ,
ˈæˑlɨnˌdeˑᵊɟ]). Additional segments may be
included to aid in the unambiguous identification
of what was repeated: thus [fɹɨədɛɬfjə,
ˌf-ˈd-] and [ˈbrukˌheˇɨvən vɪɬɨdʒ; ˌb-ˈ-].

+   following a form indicates that an identical
response was recorded from the informant's free
conversation: thus, [wɛləˆn +] is equivalent
to [wɛləˆn cv wɛləˆn].

=   is used after a semicolon to indicate that all
the forms preceding the semicolon in the entry
are to be repeated after it. The semicolon is
used on lists that combine two or more separate
work sheet items. Thus, on the list that com-
bines work sheet items 11.3 (*drove*) and 11.4
(*driven*), the following uses of = are possible:
[droʂuv; =] (preterite and participle the
same); [droʂuv, drɪˑᵊv; =] (preterite both
drove and *driv*, participle the same); and
[dɹoˤuv; =, dɹɪv̆n] (preterite *drove*,
participle both *drove* and *driven*).

---   indicates that no response was secured. If a
response was obtained from an auxiliary informant but not from the primary informant, * (or **)
appears before the first response.

Δ   indicates a cross-reference to another list.

VI. CONVENTIONS USED IN THE COMMENTARIES

In the commentary, references are made to the main list in
several ways. Labelled forms are identified by the affixed label. Where a phonetic transcription is necessary
to refer to a form (or one or more of its segments), it is
enclosed in brackets [ ] unless the phonetic form consti-
tutes the whole commentary. Where references can be made
in normal spelling, the cited form is written in italics.
No identification is used if the reference is to an entire

entry. Any specific abbreviations, conventions, or symbols
used in a commentary will be explained at its beginning.

Definitions and comments of the informants reproduced
verbatim are enclosed in quotation marks unless a phonetic
transcription is also supplied. Comments by the editors
are signed (Ed.). The comments of the field workers and
their paraphrases of the remarks of the informants are
entered without distinguishing marks.

To study social differences in speech or trends in usage, one must consult Ch. VI, *LAMSAS Handbook*. For ready reference the following rough tabulation of all main informants by type, age, and sex should prove serviceable. The field workers are identified as follows: B--Bloch, C--Cassidy, D--Davis, L--Lowman, M--McDavid, O--O'Cain, P--Pederson, Re--Reynard, Ri--Richmond, Rr--Rueter, Rt--Rutledge, U--Udell, S--[student]. Records made since 1965 were transcribed by McDavid from tape.

Type I: Little formal education, little reading, and restricted social contacts.

Type II: Better formal education (usually high school) and/or wider reading and social contacts.

Type III: Superior education (usually college), cultured background, wide reading, and/or extensive social contacts.

Type A: Aged and/or regarded by the field worker as old-fashioned.

Type B: Middle-aged or younger and/or regarded by the field worker as more modern.

Formal education and self-education through reading and association with others are more significant for the character of the informants' speech than mere age. In other words, the difference between social groups is usually greater than between successive generations of the same social group. For this reason, the age groups are treated as subclasses of the social groups. Within each community the informants are listed in ascending order of sophistication. Underscored numbers designate cultured informants, whether Type II or Type III.

	TYPE	SEX	AGE	DATE	FW
ONT					
1a	IB	M	78	68	U
b	IIB	F	58	68	U
2a	IA	M	82	49	M
b	IIA	M	74	49	M
3	IIIB	F	59	49	M
4a	IIA	M	74	68	U
b	IIB	F	66	68	U
5	IA	F	88	49	M
6	IIIB	M	33	52	M
7	IB	F	85	68	U
8a	IA	M	80	49	M
b	IIA	M	70	49	M
c	IIA	M	64	49	M
d	IIB	M	64	49	M
9	IIIB	M	42	50	M
10	IIA	M	77	50	M
NY					
1	IB	M	53	33	L
2a	IA	M	63	33	L
b	IA	M	85	33	L
c	IIA	F	80	33	L
3a	IA	M	71	41	L
b	IA	M	70	41	L
c	IB	M	50	41	L
d	IB	M	48	41	L

	TYPE	SEX	AGE	DATE	FW
NY					
4a	IA	M	69	41	L
b	IA	M	79	41	L
c	IB	M	51	41	L
5a	IB	F	70	41	L
b	IB	M	62	41	L
c	IIB	F	51	41	L
d	IIB	M	64	41	L
e	IIA	F	82	41	L
f	IIB	M	53	41	L
g	IIB	M	50	41	L
h	IIIA	M	68	41	L
i	IIIB	M	54	41	L
6a	IA	F	76	41	L
b	IIB	F	48	41	L
7a	IB	M	45	41	L
b	IB	M	39	41	L
c	IB	F	43	41	L
d	IIA	F	79	41	L
e	IIB	M	63	41	L
f	IIB	F	67	41	L
g	IIB	F	55	41	L
h	IIB	M	38	41	L
i	IIA	M	85	41	L
j	IIIB	F	59	41	L
k	IIIB	M	60	41	L

	TYPE	SEX	AGE	DATE	FW
NY					
7l	IIIA	F	76	41	L
m	IIIB	F	62	41	L
8	IA	F	83	41	L
9a	IA	F	75	41	L
b	IA	M	77	41	L
c	IIB	F	55	41	L
10a	IB	M	59	41	L
b	IIIA	F	63	41	L
11	IIB	F	42	41	L
12a	IA	F	67	41	L
b	IIB	F	55	41	L
c	IIIA	F	65	41	L
13a	IA	M	81	41	L
b	IIIA	F	68	41	L
14a	IA	M	78	41	L
b	IIB	M	46	41	L
15a	IA	M	84	41	L
b	IIB	M	49	41	L
16a	IA	M	66	41	L
b	IIA	M	61	41	L
17a	IA	M	77	41	L
b	IIB	M	45	41	L
18a	IA	M	82	41	L
b	IIB	M	49	41	L
c	IIIA	M	84	41	L

	TYPE	SEX	AGE	DATE	FW
NY					
19	IB	M	52	41	L
20a	IA	M	77	41	L
b	IIB	M	35	41	L
21	IA	M	73	41	L
22	IIB	M	51	41	L
23a	IA	M	84	48	M
b	IA	M	74	48	M
c	IIA	M	75	48	M
24a	IA	M	74	41	L
b	IIB	F	61	41	L
25a	IA	M	75	48	M
b	IIA	M	68	48	M
26a	IA	M	82	48	M
b	IIA	F	77	48	M
c	IIB	M	54	48	M
27a	IA	M	74	48	M
b	IIA	F	82	48	M
c	IIA	M	72	48	M
28a	IB	F	54	48	M
b	IIA	F	87	48	M
29a	IA	M	84	48	M
b	IB	M	67	48	M
c	IIA	M	70	48	M
30a	IA	M	82	48	M
b	IA	M	87	48	M

NY

	TYPE	SEX	AGE	DATE	FW
30c	IA	M	85	48	M
d	IA	M	77	48	M
e	IIA	F	75	48	M
31a	IIA	M	94	49	M
b	IIA	M	76	49	M
32a	IA	M	77	49	M
b	IA	M	71	49	M
33a	IB	M	52	48	M
b	IIB	M	50	48	M
c	IIB	M	57	48	M
34a	IA	M	85	49	M
b	IA	F	c65	49	M
c	IIA	M	81	49	M
d	IIIA	M	81	49	M
35a	IA	M	78	41	L
b	IIB	F	45	41	L
c	IIIB	M	62	41	L
36a	IA	M	78	41	L
b	IIB	M	52	41	L
37a	IA	F	80	41	L
b	IIB	M	42	41	L
c	IIIB	F	52	41	L
38a	IA	M	81	41	L
b	IIB	M	54	41	L
39a	IA	M	79	41	L
b	IIB	M	43	41	L
40a	IA	M	79	41	L
b	IIB	M	51	41	L
41	IIB	M	47	41	L
42a	IA	M	63	41	L
b	IIB	M	45	41	L
43a	IA	M	80	41	L
b	IIB	M	41	41	L
c	IIB	F	47	41	L
44a	IIA	M	78	41	L
b	IIB	M	38	41	L
45a	IA	M	72	49	M
b	IA	M	75	49	M
c	IA	M	70+	49	M
d	IIIA	F	72	49	M
46a	IA	M	82	49	M
b	IA	M	72	65	P
c	IIA	F	73	65	P
47a	IA	M	57	49	M
b	IIB	M	40	41	L
48a	IA	M	78	49	M

NY

	TYPE	SEX	AGE	DATE	FW
48b	IA	M	76	49	M
c	IIA	M	63	49	M
d	IIB	F	60	49	M
49a	IA	M	87	49	M
b	IB	M	44	41	L
c	IIA	M	80	68	U
d	IIB	F	c50	68	U
50a	IIA	F	92	49	M
b	IIA	M	75	49	M
51a	IA	M	80	49	M
b	IIA	M	87	49	M
c	IIA	M	75	49	M
d	IIA	F	70+	49	M
e	IIIA	M	89	49	M
52a	IB	F	49	49	M
b	IIA	F	77	49	M
c	IIB	F	47	68	U
53a	IA	M	85	49	M
b	IIIA	F	80	49	M
54a	IA	M	74	68	U
b	IIB	M	50	68	U
55a	IA	M	84	49	M
b	IIA	F	85	49	M
56a	IA	M	77	49	M
b	IIA	M	84	49	M
57a	IA	M	73	49	M
b	IIA	F	79	49	M
c	IIIA	F	83	49	M
58a	IA	M	72	49	M
b	IIA	M	81	49	M
c	IIB	M	63	49	M
d	IIIB	F	60	49	M
e	IIIB	F	65	49	M
f	IIIB	F	62	49	M
59a	IIA	M	71	49	M
b	IIB	M	44	41	L
60a	IA	M	87	49	M
b	IIIA	M	74	49	M
61a	IA	M	82	49	M
b	IIA	M	77	49	M
62a	IA	M	89	49	M
b	IA	M	85	49	M
c	IIA	M	85	49	M
d	IIIA	F	73	49	M
63a	IA	M	70	49	M
b	IIA	M	83	49	M

NY

	TYPE	SEX	AGE	DATE	FW
63c	IIB	M	47	41	L
d	IIIA	M	72	49	M
64a	IA	M	81	49	M
b	IIA	F	80	49	M
c	IIIB	F	65	49	M

NJ

	TYPE	SEX	AGE	DATE	FW
1a	IA	M	70	39	L
b	IIB	M	52	39	L
2a	IA	M	80	39	L
b	IB	M	42	39	L
3a	IA	M	86	39	L
b	IIB	M	55	39	L
4a	IA	M	70	39	L
b	IB	M	53	39	L
5a	IA	M	75	39	L
b	IB	M	58	39	L
6a	IA	M	75	41	L
b	IB	M	47	39	L
7a	IA	M	72	39	L
b	IIIB	F	49	41	L
8a	IA	M	77	41	L
b	IIB	M	57	41	L
9a	IA	F	76	41	L
b	IIB	M	56	41	L
10a	IA	M	78	41	L
b	IA	M	68	41	L
c	IIB	M	49	41	L
d	IIIB	M	59	41	L
11a	IA	M	82	41	L
b	IIB	F	57	41	L
c	IIB	M	41	41	L
12a	IA	M	80	41	L
b	IIB	M	49	41	L
13a	IA	F	80	41	L
b	IB	M	47	41	L
14a	IA	M	78	41	L
b	IIB	F	44	41	L
15a	IA	M	70	41	L
b	IB	M	46	41	L
16a	IA	M	75	41	L
b	IIB	M	45	41	L
17a	IA	M	82	41	L
b	IIA	M	66	41	L
18a	IIA	F	68	41	L
b	IIB	F	58	41	L
c	IIIB	F	57	41	L

NJ

	TYPE	SEX	AGE	DATE	FW
18d	IIIB	F	54	41	L
19a	IA	F	75	41	L
b	IIA	F	65	41	L
20a	IIA	M	80	41	L
b	IIB	M	61	41	L
21a	IA	M	71	41	L
b	IIB	M	55	41	L

PA

	TYPE	SEX	AGE	DATE	FW
1a	IA	M	68	39	L
b	IB	M	43	39	L
c	IIA	F	68	39	L
d	IIA	M	66	39	L
e	IIIA	M	68	39	L
f	IIIB	M	62	39	L
g	IIIA	M	70	39	L
h	IIIB	F	59	39	L
2a	IA	M	70	39	L
b	IIB	M	57	39	L
3a	IA	F	91	39	L
b	IA	F	67	40	L
c	IIB	M	58	40	L
4a	IA	M	80	39	L
b	IIIB	M	48	39	L
5a	IA	M	79	39	L
b	IA	M	82	40	L
c	IB	M	57	39	L
d	IA	M	67	39	L
e	IIIB	M	49	39	L
6a	IA	M	75	39	L
b	IA	M	67	39	L
c	IB	M	49	40	L
d	IIIA	M	69	39	L
7a	IA	M	80	39	L
b	IB	M	53	39	L
c	IIA	M	65	39	L
d	IIIB	M	39	39	L
8a	IA	M	65	39	L
b	IIB	M	46	39	L
c	IIA	M	66	40	L
d	IIIA	F	62	39	L
9a	IA	M	78	39	L
b	IB	M	57	40	L
c	IIIA	F	68	39	L
10	IA	M	66	39	L
11a	IA	M	73	39	L
b	IIB	M	37	40	L

PA

	TYPE	SEX	AGE	DATE	FW
12a	IA	M	67	39	L
b	IIB	F	47	39	L
13a	IA	M	74	39	L
b	IIB	M	47	39	L
14a	IA	M	76	40	L
b	IIB	M	36	39	L
15a	IA	M	69	39	L
b	IIB	M	44	39	L
c	IIIB	M	62	39	L
16a	IA	M	69	39	L
b	IIB	M	39	39	L
c	IIB	M	50	39	L
17a	IA	M	72	39	L
b	IIA	M	74	39	L
18a	IA	F	69	39	L
b	IIIB	M	60	39	L
19a	IA	F	70	39	L
b	IIB	M	49	39	L
20a	IA	M	75	39	L
b	IIB	M	44	39	L
21a	IA	M	72	39	L
b	IIB	M	56	39	L
22a	IA	M	85	39	L
b	IIB	M	48	39	L
23a	IA	M	87	39	L
b	IIB	M	51	39	L
24a	IA	M	74	39	L
b	IIB	M	42	39	L
25a	IA	M	80	39	L
b	IIB	M	52	39	L
26a	IA	M	83	39	L
b	IIB	M	51	39	L
27a	IA	M	70	39	L
b	IB	M	50	39	L
28a	IIA	M	72	39	L
b	IIIB	F	50	39	L
29a	IA	M	60+	39	L
b	IIB	M	42	39	L
30a	IA	M	73	39	L
b	IIB	M	48	39	L
31a	IA	M	75	40	L
b	IB	M	54	40	L
32a	IA	M	80	39	L
b	IB	M	40	39	L
33a	IA	M	77	40	L
b	IIB	M	46	39	L

PA

	TYPE	SEX	AGE	DATE	FW
34a	IA	M	79	39	L
b	IIB	M	37	39	L
c	IIIA	F	75	39	L
35a	IA	M	67	39	L
b	IIB	M	46	39	L
36a	IA	M	73	39	L
b	IIB	M	50	39	L
37a	IA	M	76	40	L
b	IIB	M	40	40	L
38a	IA	M	70	39	L
b	IIB	M	42	39	L
39a	IA	M	85	40	L
b	IIB	M	41	39	L
40a	IA	M	77	40	L
b	IIB	M	36	39	L
41a	IA	M	70	40	L
b	IIB	M	58	39	L
42a	IA	M	59	40	L
b	IB	M	51	40	L
43a	IA	M	79	39	L
b	IIB	M	51	39	L
44a	IA	M	75	39	L
b	IIB	M	51	39	L
45a	IA	M	81	40	L
b	IIB	M	43	40	L
46a	IA	M	61	40	L
b	IIB	M	45	40	L
47a	IA	M	90	40	L
b	IIB	M	49	40	L
48a	IA	M	89	40	L
b	IA	M	70	40	L
c	IIB	M	44	40	L
49a	IB	M	72	40	L
b	IIB	M	44	40	L
50a	IA	M	80	40	L
b	IA	F	70	40	L
c	IIB	M	47	40	L
51a	IA	F	74	40	L
b	IIB	F	c50	40	L
52a	IA	M	76	40	L
b	IIIB	M	48	40	L
53a	IA	M	78	40	L
b	IIB	M	43	40	L
54a	IA	F	83	40	L
b	IIB	M	53	40	L
55a	IA	M	85	40	L

PA

	TYPE	SEX	AGE	DATE	FW
55b	IIB	M	40	40	L
56a	IIA	M	87	40	L
b	IIB	M	44	40	L
57a	IA	M	75	40	L
b	IIB	M	53	40	L
58a	IA	M	84	40	L
b	IIB	M	42	40	L
59a	IA	M	87	40	L
b	IIB	F	41	40	L
60a	IA	M	77	40	L
b	IB	M	40	40	L
61a	IA	M	84	40	L
b	IIB	M	40	40	L
62a	IA	M	87	40	L
b	IB	M	40	40	L
63a	IA	M	74	40	L
b	IIB	M	36	40	L
64a	IA	M	77	40	L
b	IIB	F	43	40	L
65a	IA	M	74	40	L
b	IIA	M	51	40	L
66a	IA	M	81	40	L
b	IIB	M	50	40	L
67a	IA	M	76	40	L
b	IIB	M	37	40	L

WVA

	TYPE	SEX	AGE	DATE	FW
1	IIIA	F	71	39	L
2	IIB	M	54	39	L
3	IA	M	78	39	L
4a	IA	M	80	39	L
b	IA	M	76	34	L
5	IB	M	38	39	L
6a	IA	M	87	39	L
b	IIB	M	45	39	L
7a	IA	M	72	39	L
b	IIB	M	55	39	L
8a	IA	M	89	40	L
b	IIB	M	56	40	L
9a	IA	M	85	40	L
b	IIB	M	52	40	L
10a	IA	M	72	40	L
b	IA	M	76	40	L
c	IIB	M	51	40	L
11a	IA	M	69	40	L
b	IIB	M	59	40	L
12a	IA	F	80	40	L

WVA

	TYPE	SEX	AGE	DATE	FW
12b	IIB	M	42	40	L
13a	IA	M	71	40	L
b	IIB	M	36	40	L
14a	IA	M	72	40	L
b	IIB	M	42	40	L
15a	IA	F	79	40	L
b	IIB	M	58	40	L
16a	IA	M	66	40	L
b	IIB	M	56	40	L
17a	IA	M	80	40	L
b	IIB	M	53	40	L
c	IIA	M	73	40	L
18a	IA	F	75	40	L
b	IIB	M	47	40	L
19a	IA	M	70+	40	L
b	IIB	M	40	40	L
20a	IA	M	70	40	L
b	IIB	F	46	40	L
21a	IA	M	80	40	L
b	IIB	M	49	40	L
22a	IA	M	85	40	L
b	IIB	M	34	40	L
23a	IA	M	82	40	L
b	IIB	M	51	40	L
24a	IA	M	74	40	L
b	IIB	M	39	40	L
25a	IA	M	72	40	L
b	IIB	M	39	40	L
26a	IA	F	82	40	L
b	IIB	M	43	40	L
27a	IA	M	75	40	L
b	IIB	M	52	40	L
28a	IA	F	74	40	L
b	IIB	M	43	40	L
29a	IA	M	87	40	L
b	IIB	F	34	40	L
30a	IA	M	68	40	L
b	IB	M	49	40	L
31a	IA	M	63	40	L
b	IB	M	49	40	L
32a	IA	F	69	40	L
b	IB	M	45	40	L
33a	IA	M	67	40	L
b	IIB	M	55	40	L
34a	IA	F	67	40	L
b	IB	M	46	40	L

	TYPE	SEX	AGE	DATE	FW
WVA					
35a	IA	M	68	40	L
b	IIB	M	49	40	L
36a	IA	M	65	40	L
b	IIB	M	63	40	L
37a	IA	M	79	40	L
_b_	IIIA	F	69	40	L
38a	IA	M	72	40	L
b	IB	M	37	40	L
39a	IB	M	58	40	L
b	IIB	M	54	40	L
_c_	IIIB	F	45	40	L
40a	IA	M	74	40	L
b	IIB	M	45	40	L
41a	IA	M	75	40	L
b	IB	M	49	40	L
42a	IA	F	72	40	L
b	IIB	M	54	40	L
43a	IA	M	74	40	L
b	IIB	M	35	40	L
44a	IA	M	71	40	L
b	IB	M	52	40	L
45a	IIA	M	72	40	L
b	IIB	M	42	40	L
46a	IA	M	73	40	L
b	IIB	M	48	40	L
47a	IIA	M	68	40	L
b	IIB	M	36	40	L
48a	IA	M	75	40	L
b	IB	M	50	40	L
c	IB	M	45	40	L
d	IIB	M	42	40	L
49a	IA	M	65	40	L
b	IB	M	36	40	L
50a	IA	M	88	40	L
b	IIB	M	51	40	L
51a	IA	M	66	40	L
b	IIB	M	47	40	L
52a	IA	M	68	40	L
b	IIB	F	36	40	L
_c_	IIIA	M	70	40	L
53a	IA	M	79	40	L
b	IA	M	61	40	L
_c_	IIB	M	43	40	L
54a	IA	M	70	40	L
b	IB	M	41	40	L

	TYPE	SEX	AGE	DATE	FW
OHIO					
1a	IA	M	88	40	L
b	IIB	M	57	40	L
_c_	IIIB	F	53	40	L
2a	IA	F	68	40	L
b	IIB	M	46	40	L
3a	IA	M	74	40	L
b	IIB	M	52	40	L
4a	IA	M	73	40	L
b	IIB	M	35	40	L
5a	IA	M	84	39	C
b	IA	M	73	40	L
c	IIB	M	48	40	L
6a	IA	M	78	40	L
b	IIB	M	52	40	L
7a	IA	M	70	40	L
b	IB	M	53	40	L
8a	IA	M	77	40	L
b	IA	M	79	39	C
c	IB	M	52	40	L
d	IIB	M	59	40	Ri
_e_	IIIA	F	70	40	L
9a	IA	M	80	40	L
b	IA	M	74	40	Ri
c	IIB	F	43	40	L
d	IIA	M	64	40	Ri
10a	IA	M	68	40	L
b	IIB	M	44	40	L
11a	IA	M	65+	40	L
b	IIB	M	39	40	L
12a	IA	M	71	40	L
b	IIB	M	51	40	L
c	IIB	M	35	40	L
d	IIB	F	50	40	L
13a	IIA	M	82	33	Re
b	IIB	F	57	50	D
c	IIB	M	53	40	Ri
14	IIA	M	88	53	M
15a	IA	M	87	51	D
b	IIA	F	70	51	D
16a	IA	M	75	56	M
b	IA	M	74	56	M
c	IIA	M	71+	56	M
17	IIA	M	84	53	M
18	IA	M	78	53	M
KY					
1a	IA	M	76	53	M

	TYPE	SEX	AGE	DATE	FW
KY					
1b	IIA	F	85	53	M
2a	IA	M	96	54	M
b	IA	M	70	54	M
c	IIA	M	68	54	M
3a	IA	M	89	54	M
b	IA	F	101	54	M
c	IA	M	98	54	M
d	IA	M	74	54	M
e	IIA	M	78	54	M
4a	IA	M	71	54	M
b	IIA	M	76	54	M
c	IIB	F	65	54	M
5a	IA	M	84	54	M
b	IIA	M	80	54	M
6a	IA	M	74	54	M
b	IIA	M	86	54	M
c	IIB	F	65	54	M
7a	IA	M	86	54	M
_b_	IIIB	M	55	54	M
DEL					
1a	IIA	M	70	39	L
b	IIB	M	63	39	L
_c_	IIIA	F	62	39	L
2a	IIA	M	73	34	L
b	IIB	M	37	39	L
3a	IA	M	75	39	L
b	IIB	M	38	39	L
_c_	IIIA	M	66	39	L
4	IA	M	82	39	L
5a	IA	M	77	34	L
b	IIB	M	38	39	L
6a	IA	M	70	39	L
b	IIB	M	53	39	L
MD					
1a	IA	F	95	39	L
b	IIB	M	58	39	L
2a	IA	M	82	39	L
b	IB	M	48	39	L
3a	IA	M	73	39	L
b	IIB	M	43	39	L
4a	IA	F	85	39	L
b	IIA	M	80	39	L
c	IIB	M	53	34	L
5a	IA	M	69	39	L
b	IIB	M	48	39	L
6a	IA	F	79	39	L

	TYPE	SEX	AGE	DATE	FW
MD					
6b	IIB	M	58	39	L
7a	IA	M	73	39	L
b	IB	M	44	39	L
_c_	IIIB	M	55	39	L
8a	IA	M	70	39	L
b	IIB	M	51	39	L
N9	IA	F	70	34	L
9a	IIA	F	68	39	L
b	IIB	M	42	39	L
10a	IA	M	82	39	L
b	IIB	M	41	39	L
11	IA	M	77	39	L
12a	IA	F	87	39	L
b	IB	M	52	39	L
13a	IA	F	70	39	L
b	IB	M	45	39	L
c	IIB	M	55	39	L
_d_	IIIA	F	70	39	L
_e_	IIIA	F	76	34	L
_f_	IIIB	F	c50	39	L
14	IIB	M	52	39	L
15a	IA	M	71	39	L
b	IIB	M	42	39	L
16	IA	F	c60	34	L
17a	IIA	M	77	39	L
b	IIB	M	39	39	L
18a	IA	M	65	39	L
b	IIB	M	49	39	L
19a	IA	M	78	39	L
b	IB	M	38	39	L
20a	IA	M	68	34	L
b	IIB	M	46	39	L
_c_	IIIB	M	33	39	L
21a	IA	M	85	39	L
b	IB	M	48	39	L
N22	IA	M	92	39	L
2N22	IA	M	83	39	L
22a	IA	M	76	34	L
b	IIB	M	54	39	L
_c_	IIIA	F	65	39	L
23a	IA	M	79	39	L
b	IA	M	70	39	L
c	IIB	M	39	39	L
24	IA	M	82	39	L
25	IIB	M	48	39	L
26a	IA	F	70	39	L

	TYPE	SEX	AGE	DATE	FW
MD					
26b	IIA	M	80	39	L
27a	IA	M	76	39	L
b	IIB	M	39	39	L
DC					
1a	IA	M	87	34	L
b	IIB	F	50	39	L
VA					
1	IIIB	F	c50	35	L
2a	IA	M	84	35	L
b	IA	M	77	35	L
3a	IA	M	73	35	L
b	IIB	F	50	35	L
N4	IA	F	89	35	L
5a	IA	M	64	35	L
b	IIB	F	55	35	L
6a	IA	M	81	35	L
b	IIB	F	53	35	L
7a	IA	M	71	35	L
b	IIB	F	54	35	L
8a	IA	M	83	34	L
b	IIA	M	71	35	L
c	IIIA	F	62	35	L
9a	IA	M	73	35	L
b	IIIA	F	71	35	L
10a	IA	M	77	36	L
b	IIB	F	60	35	L
11a	IA	F	83	36	L
b	IIB	F	52	36	L
N12	IA	F	80+	36	L
12a	IA	M	73	35	L
b	IIB	M	51	35	L
13a	IA	F	74	35	L
b	IIB	F	57	35	L
14a	IA	F	88	34	L
b	IB	F	57	35	L
c	IIB	F	46	35	L
N15	IA	M	94	36	L
15a	IA	M	73	35	L
b	IIB	F	45	35	L
16a	IIA	M	70	35	L
b	IIB	M	44	35	L
17a	IA	M	64	36	L
b	IIB	M	46	36	L
18	IA	M	81	36	L
19a	IA	M	67	36	L
b	IIA	F	61	36	L

	TYPE	SEX	AGE	DATE	FW
VA					
19c	IIIB	F	55	36	L
20a	IA	M	79	36	L
b	IIA	F	63	36	L
N21	IA	F	75	36	L
21a	IA	F	80	36	L
b	IIB	M	56	36	L
22	IA	F	86	36	L
23a	IA	F	90+	36	L
b	IA	F	73	34	L
24	IIA	F	64	36	L
25	IA	M	76	36	L
26a	IA	M	82	34	L
b	IA	F	78	36	L
c	IIB	F	47	36	L
27	IA	F	88	36	L
28a	IA	M	84	36	L
b	IIB	F	60	36	L
29	IA	M	75	36	L
30a	IA	M	79	36	L
b	IIIB	F	c50	36	L
c	IIIA	F	85	34	L
d	IIIA	F	83	36	L
e	IIIB	F	50	36	L
31a	IA	M	70	36	L
b	IIB	M	55	36	L
32	IIIA	F	70	36	L
33a	IA	F	73	36	L
b	IIB	F	47	36	L
34a	IA	F	66	34	L
b	IIB	F	45	36	L
35a	IA	M	75	36	L
b	IIB	F	44	36	L
36a	IA	M	75	36	L
b	IIB	F	55	36	L
37	IA	M	76	36	L
38	IIB	M	43	34	L
39	IIIB	F	47	36	L
40a	IA	F	81	36	L
b	IIB	M	18	36	L
41a	IA	M	80	36	L
b	IIB	M	54	36	L
42a	IA	M	75	35	L
b	IIB	F	61	35	L
N43	IA	M	86	36	L
43a	IA	M	68	36	L
b	IIA	M	64	36	L

	TYPE	SEX	AGE	DATE	FW
VA					
44a	IA	F	74	35	L
b	IIA	M	63	35	L
45a	IA	F	67	34	L
b	IIB	M	54	35	L
N46	IA	M	c70	34	L
46a	IA	F	72	34	L
b	IIIB	F	c55	35	L
47	IA	M	80	35	L
48a	IA	F	66	35	L
b	IIA	F	62	35	L
49a	IA	M	62	35	L
b	IIB	F	48	35	L
50a	IA	M	76	36	L
b	IIB	F	58	36	L
51a	IA	M	82	36	L
b	IIA	F	62	36	L
52a	IIA	M	71	35	L
b	IIB	F	50	35	L
c	IIIB	F	55	35	L
53a	IA	M	82	35	L
b	IIB	M	56	35	L
54a	IA	M	62	34	L
b	IIB	M	44	35	L
55a	IA	M	72	34	L
b	IIB	F	62	35	L
56a	IA	M	71	35	L
b	IIB	F	54	35	L
57a	IA	F	79	35	L
b	IIA	F	64	35	L
58	IA	M	73	35	L
N59	IA	M	80	33	L
59a	IIB	F	46	35	L
b	IIIB	F	54	35	L
60	IA	M	80	35	L
61a	IB	M	53	33	L
b	IIB	M	54	35	L
62a	IA	F	77	35	L
b	IIB	M	55	35	L
63a	IA	M	80	35	L
b	IA	F	73	35	L
64a	IA	F	83	35	L
b	IIB	F	59	35	L
65a	IA	F	70	33	L
b	IIB	M	56	33	L
c	IIIB	F	35	35	L
66a	IA	F	70	35	L

	TYPE	SEX	AGE	DATE	FW
VA					
66b	IIA	M	52	35	L
67a	IA	M	83	35	L
b	IIB	F	c50	35	L
68a	IA	F	79	35	L
b	IIB	M	52	35	L
69a	IA	M	76	35	L
b	IIB	M	52	35	L
70a	IA	F	61	34	L
b	IIB	F	48	35	L
71a	IA	M	75	35	L
b	IIB	F	51	35	L
72a	IA	M	82	35	L
b	IIB	M	45	35	L
73	IA	M	63	35	L
74a	IA	M	77	35	L
b	IIIB	F	56	36	L
75a	IA	M	74	36	L
b	IIB	M	52	36	L
NC					
1	IA	F	66	36	L
2a	IA	M	65	34	L
b	IIB	M	41	36	L
3a	IA	M	79	36	L
b	IIB	F	37	36	L
4a	IA	M	83	36	L
b	IIB	F	38	36	L
5a	IA	F	74	36	L
b	IIB	F	44	36	L
6	IIIB	F	57	36	L
7a	IA	F	74	34	L
b	IIB	F	43	36	L
N8	IA	M	80	37	L
8a	IA	F	70	36	L
b	IB	F	41	36	L
9a	IA	M	71	36	L
b	IIB	F	60	36	L
10a	IA	M	76	34	L
b	IA	F	70	36	L
c	IIB	F	41	36	L
11a	IA	M	82	36	L
b	IIB	F	39	36	L
12a	IA	M	77	36	L
b	IIB	F	46	36	L
13a	IA	M	75	36	L
b	IIB	F	40	36	L
N14	IA	M	77	37	L

NC

TYPE	SEX	AGE	DATE	FW
14a IA	M	70	36	L
b IIA	F	75	34	L
c IIIA	F	67	36	L
15a IA	M	74	36	L
b IB	F	53	36	L
16a IA	F	74	36	L
b IB	M	44	36	L
17a IA	M	66	36	L
b IIB	M	48	36	L
18a IA	M	71	37	L
b IIA	F	61	37	L
19a IA	M	69	36	L
b IIB	M	51	36	L
20a IA	M	69	34	L
b IA	M	72	36	L
c IIB	F	42	36	L
21a IA	F	71	37	L
b IIB	M	45	36	L
22a IA	M	68	34	L
b IIB	F	43	37	L
23a IA	M	75	37	L
b IIB	F	46	37	L
c IIIB	F	48	37	L
d IIIB	F	55+	37	L
N24 IA	M	89	37	L
24a IA	F	70	37	L
b IIB	M	45	37	L
N25 IB	F	60	34	L
25a IA	M	73	37	L
b IIA	M	68	34	L
26a IA	F	70	37	L
b IIB	F	57	37	L
c IIIB	F	37	37	L
27a IA	M	70	37	L
b IIB	F	47	37	L
28a IA	M	73	37	L
b IA	M	67	37	L
c IIB	F	40	37	L
29a IA	M	78	34	L
b IIB	F	43	37	L
30a IA	M	89	36	L
b IIA	F	65	36	L
31a IA	M	68	36	L
b IIB	F	59	36	L
32a IA	M	73	34	L
b IIIB	F	59	36	L

NC

TYPE	SEX	AGE	DATE	FW
33a IA	F	68	36	L
b IIB	F	40	36	L
34a IA	F	70	36	L
b IIB	F	61	36	L
35a IIA	F	80	34	L
b IIB	F	44	37	L
N36 IA	M	77	37	L
36a IA	M	76	37	L
b IB	M	43	37	L
37a IA	F	65	36	L
b IIB	M	52	36	L
N38 IA	M	81	37	L
38a IA	M	70+	37	L
b IIB	F	58	36	L
39a IA	M	77	36	L
b IIIB	F	45	36	L
40a IA	F	68	34	L
b IIB	M	58	37	L
41 IIIB	F	54	37	L
42a IA	M	84	37	L
b IIB	F	44	37	L
43a IA	F	80	37	L
b IIB	M	41	37	L
44 IIB	M	49	37	L
45 IA	F	80	37	L
46a IA	M	83	37	L
b IIB	M	44	37	L
c IIIB	F	48	37	L
47 IA	F	76	34	L
48 IIA	M	52	37	L
49 IA	F	79	37	L
50a IIB	M	45	37	L
b IIIB	F	38	37	L
51a IA	F	76	37	L
b IIB	M	49	37	L
N52 IA	F	90	37	L
52a IA	F	77	37	L
b IIB	M	48	37	L
53a IA	M	82	37	L
b IIB	F	42	37	L
54a IA	M	79	34	L
b IIB	F	41	37	L
55 IA	M	86	37	L
56a IIB	F	60	37	L
b IIIB	F	45	37	L
57a IA	M	81	37	L

NC

TYPE	SEX	AGE	DATE	FW
57b IIB	M	36	37	L
58a IA	M	72	36	L
b IB	F	39	36	L
59 IA	F	86	34	L
60 IIB	M	41	37	L
61a IA	M	74+	37	L
b IIB	F	40	37	L
62a IA	M	76	36	L
b IIB	F	52	36	L
63a IA	F	74	36	L
b IIB	F	52	36	L
64a IA	M	86	37	L
b IIB	M	39	37	L
65a IA	F	66	37	L
b IIA	F	64	34	L
66a IA	M	75	37	L
b IIB	F	53	37	L
67a IA	M	84	36	L
b IIA	M	81	34	L
68a IA	F	67	37	L
b IIB	F	42	37	L
69a IA	M	77	37	L
b IIA	F	57	34	L
70a IA	F	71	36	L
b IIB	M	16	36	L
71a IA	M	78	37	L
b IIB	M	54	36	L
c IIIB	F	49	36	L
72a IA	M	74	37	L
b IIB	F	45	36	L
73a IA	F	86	36	L
b IIA	M	77	34	L
74a IA	M	76	36	L
b IIB	F	57	37	L
75a IA	M	83	36	L
b IIB	F	52	36	L

SC

TYPE	SEX	AGE	DATE	FW
1a IA	F	81	37	L
b IIB	F	56	37	L
2a IA	F	70	37	L
b IIB	F	48	37	L
3a IA	M	72	34	L
b IA	M	80	47	M
c IIIA	F	67	47	M
4a IB	M	55	46	M
b IIA	F	81	46	M

SC

TYPE	SEX	AGE	DATE	FW
4c IIB	M	55	46	M
5a IA	M	79	48	M
b IIA	M	80	46	M
c IIB	M	61	46	M
d IIIA	F	71	46	M
N6 IA	M	77	46	M
6a IA	M	60	34	L
b IA	F	79	48	M
c IIIA	F	68	48	M
N7 IA	M	83	46	M
7a IIA	M	75	46	M
b IIA	M	85	46	M
c IIIA	M	78	46	M
d IIIB	F	50	46	M
8a IA	F	74	47	M
b IA	M	58	47	M
c IIA	M	67	47	M
9a IA	M	75	47	M
b IA	M	65	47	M
c IIIB	M	c50	47	M
d IIIA	M	73	47	M
10a IB	F	53	46	M
b IIIA	M	85	48	M
c IIIA	F	64	48	M
N11 IB	M	58	34	L
11a IIA	M	86	46	M
b IIB	M	57	65	P
c IIB	F	58	46	M
d IIA	M	83	46	M
e IIA	M	76	46	M
f IIB	F	48	46	M
g IIIB	M	24	46	M
2N11 IIIB	M	44	46	M
11h IIIB	M	52	46	M
i IIIB	F	51	34	L
j IIIB	F	69	46	M
12a IA	M	80	47	M
b IIA	F	70	34	L
13 IIB	M	52	48	M
14a IA	M	84	34	L
b IIB	M	51	47	M
15a IA	M	83	47	M
b IIA	M	68	47	M
c IIA	M	85	47	M
N16 IA	M	68	46	M
16 IB	M	69	67	O

SC

	TYPE	SEX	AGE	DATE	FW
17a	IA	F	76	46	M
b	IA	M	68	46	M
c	IIA	F	88	46	M
d	IIA	M	78	46	M
N18	IA	M	75	46	M
18a	IB	M	68	46	M
b	IIB	M	62	46	M
c	IIIB	F	61	46	M
N19	IB	M	53	34	L
19a	IIB	F	51	46	M
b	IIB	M	70	65	P
c	IIB	F	68	46	M
d	IIIB	M	67	48	M
20a	IA	M	80	48	M
b	IIA	M	76	48	M
c	IIA	M	72	48	M
d	IIB	M	53	48	M
21a	IA	F	70	37	L
b	IIA	F	66	37	L
N22	IA	F	65	34	L
22a	IIB	M	62	47	M
b	IIA	F	65	34	L
c	IIIA	M	74	47	M
23a	IA	M	81	47	M
b	IA	M	72	47	M
c	IIA	M	66	47	M
d	IIB	M	66	47	M
e	IIIA	M	75	47	M
N24	IA	M	82+	46	M
24a	IA	M	67	65	P
b	IA	M	84	46	M
c	IIA	M	65	46	M
d	IIIA	M	86	46	M
25a	IA	F	78	34	L
b	IIA	M	77	47	M
c	IIIB	F	30	47	M
26a	IIA	M	72	47	M
b	IIIB	M	55	47	M
27a	IB	M	71	65	P
b	IIA	M	75	47	M
28a	IA	F	78	47	M
b	IIB	M	39	47	M
c	IIB	M	44	47	M
d	IIB	F	19	47	M
29a	IA	M	78	47	M
b	IIA	M	87	47	M

SC

	TYPE	SEX	AGE	DATE	FW
29c	IIA	M	82	47	M
30a	IA	M	63	34	L
b	IIA	M	79	46	M
c	IIIA	F	73	46	M
31a	IA	M	64	47	M
b	IIA	M	86	47	M
32a	IIA	M	80	47	M
b	IIA	M	86	47	M
c	IIB	M	55	47	M
d	IIIA	M	78	47	M
33a	IA	M	75	34	L
b	IIA	M	75	47	M
34a	IA	M	75	47	M
b	IIA	M	73	47	M
c	IIA	F	80	47	M
35a	IB	F	59	47	M
b	IB	M	37	47	M
c	IIA	M	76	67	O
36a	IA	M	73	46	M
b	IA	F	76	46	M
c	IIA	M	73	46	M
d	IIIA	M	80	46	M
37	IB	M	66	65	P
38a	IA	M	94	46	M
N38	IIA	M	73	46	M
38b	IIB	M	66	46	M
c	IIIA	M	75+	46	M
d	IIIB	F	59	46	M
39a	IA	M	62	46	M
b	IIIA	M	84	46	M
40a	IA	M	63	41	M
b	IIA	F	78	41	M
41a	IA	F	79	34	L
b	IIB	M	58	41	M
42a	IA	M	70	41	M
N42	IB	F	54	41	M
42b	IIB	F	67	46	M
c	IIIA	M	58	41	M
d	IIIB	M	26	37	B
e	IIIB	M	52	64	M
43a	IA	M	100	41	M
b	IA	M	66	41	M
c	IIIA	M	69	41	M
44a	IA	M	70	41	M
b	IIA	M	85	41	M

GA

	TYPE	SEX	AGE	DATE	FW
N1	IB	F	40	72	S
1a	IB	M	72	46	M
b	IA	F	77	72	Rr
c	IIA	F	90	46	M
d	IIA	M	76	46	M
e	IIB	F	36	46	M
f	IIIA	F	78	34	L
g	IIIA	M	76	46	M
h	IIIB	F	60	45	M
N2	IA	M	67	46	M
2a	IA	M	78	46	M
b	IIB	M	43	46	M
3a	IA	M	80	34	L
b	IA	F	83	48	M
N4	IB	M	53	34	L
4a	IIA	M	77	47	M
b	IIA	M	72	47	M
c	IIIB	F	58	47	M
5a	IIB	M	57	47	M
b	IIB	M	60	47	M
c	IIB	M	66	47	M
d	IIA	M	80	47	M
e	IIB	M	61	47	M
6a	IA	M	79	47	M
b	IIIA	M	78	47	M
7	IA	M	87	47	M
8a	IA	F	86	47	M
b	IIB	F	50	47	M
9a	IB	F	c70	72	Rr
b	IB	M	c60	72	Rr
10a	IA	M	67	34	L
b	IIA	M	84	48	M
N11	IB	F	60	72	S
12a	IIB	M	54	46	M
b	IIIB	M	61	68	Rr
13a	IA	M	69	34	L
b	IIIA	M	83	47	M
14a	IA	M	76	46	M
b	IA	M	70	46	M
c	IIA	F	88	46	M
15a	IA	M	83	34	L
b	IA	M	92	48	M
16a	IA	F	61	47	M
b	IIA	F	85	47	M
c	IIB	F	72	70	S
d	IIIB	F	54	47	M

GA

	TYPE	SEX	AGE	DATE	FW
N17	IB	F	48	65	P
17	IIB	M	71	65	P
18a	IA	M	82	72	Rt
b	IA	F	70	72	Rt
19a	IA	M	71	47	M
b	IA	M	72	47	M
20a	IA	M	77	47	M
b	IA	M	75	47	M
21a	IA	F	71	71	Rr
b	IA	F	74	47	M
22a	IB	M	c60	65	P
b	IIA	M	75	47	M
23a	IA	M	55	47	M
b	IIA	F	80	72	S
c	IIB	F	58	72	S
d	IIIA	F	62	47	M
e	IIIB	F	67	68	P
f	IIIB	F	24	72	S
N24	IA	M	68	70	S
24a	IA	M	64	34	L
b	IA	M	66	47	M
N25	IA	F	71	72	S
26	IB	M	49	71	Rr
27	IIIB	M	48	65	P
28	IIA	M	80	65	P
29a	IA	M	87	47	M
b	IIA	F	67	47	M
30a	IB	M	71	46	M
b	IIA	M	77	46	M
c	IIIA	M	77	68	Rr
31	IA	F	73	71	S
32	IB	F	61	68	P
33a	IA	F	75	72	S
b	IB	F	62	72	S
N34	IA	M	75	47	M
34a	IIA	F	65	34	L
b	IIB	M	62	47	M
N35	IA	F	80	71	S
N36	IA	M	69	72	Rt
N37	IA	F	82	71	S
37a	IA	M	95	47	M
b	IIA	M	75	47	M
c	IIB	F	45	70	S
2N37	IIIB	M	55	68	P
37d	IIIB	M	59	68	P
e	IIIB	F	53	70	S

GA	TYPE	SEX	AGE	DATE	FW
37f	IIIA	F	84	47	M
g	IIIB	M	51	47	M
h	IIIA	M	73	47	M
i	IIIB	F	59	68	P
38	IA	M	79	66	P
39	IIA	M	66	68	P
40	IA	F	72	70	S

GA	TYPE	SEX	AGE	DATE	FW
41	IA	M	81	74	S
42a	IA	F	74	47	M
b	IIA	M	73	47	M
43	IA	M	85	34	L
44a	IA	M	91	47	M
b	IA	M	80	47	M
c	IA	M	72	47	M

GA	TYPE	SEX	AGE	DATE	FW
44d	IIA	M	70	47	M
e	IIA	M	72	72	S
FLA					
1	IA	F	70	47	M
2a	IA	F	69	47	M
b	IIB	M	58	70	S

FLA	TYPE	SEX	AGE	DATE	FW
2c	IIIA	M	85	47	M
3a	IA	M	65	47	M
b	IIA	M	77	47	M
4	IB	M	56	74	Rt
5a	IA	M	74	47	M
b	IIA	M	75	47	M

LAMSAS includes field records made for all or parts of four regional linguistic atlases. First, *LAMSAS* is the combination of the formerly autonomous surveys of the Middle Atlantic States (MAS) and of the South Atlantic States (SAS). It also includes records made for *LANE* and for the Linguistic Atlas of the North-Central States (NCS).

The makeup of the work sheets for these four atlases is not always the same. (For a detailed comparison see Alva L. Davis, Raven I. McDavid, Jr., and Virginia G. McDavid, eds., *A Compilation of the Work Sheets of the Linguistic Atlas of the United States and Canada and Associated Projects*, 2nd ed. (Chicago: University of Chicago Press, 1969).) While the differences for particular items will be summarized in the headnotes of the *LAMSAS* lists, the following table (as well as the vitae in the *LAMSAS Handbook*) will enumerate the field records according to the work sheets used.

In general, the MAS work sheets were used from Ontario to West Virginia and the SAS work sheets were used from Delaware to Florida. The NCS work sheets were used in Ontario, Ohio, and Kentucky. The preliminary SAS (PSAS) work sheets were used from Delaware to Georgia. Records made after 1964 were taped and generally used combined work sheets. Four incomplete PSAS records used as auxiliary records for later SAS records are marked with *.

MIDDLE ATLANTIC STATES WORK SHEETS
1939-41, 1948-9

Ont:	2ab, <u>3</u>, 5, 8a-d
NY:	3a-64<u>c</u> (except 1965-74)
NJ:	6a, 7<u>b</u>-21b
Pa:	1a-67b
WVa:	8a-54b
Ohio:	1a-12d (except NCS)

SOUTH ATLANTIC STATES WORK SHEETS
1935-9, 1941, 1945-8, 1964

NJ:	1a-5b, 6b, 7a
WVa:	<u>1</u>-7b (except PSAS)
Del:	1a-6b (except PSAS)
DC:	1<u>b</u>
Va:	<u>1</u>-75b (except PSAS)
NC:	1-75b (except PSAS)
SC:	1a-44b (except *LANE*, PSAS, 1965-74)
Ga:	N1-44e (except PSAS, 1965-74)
Fla:	1-5b (except 1965-74)

NORTH-CENTRAL STATES WORK SHEETS
1939-40, 1950-6

Ont:	<u>6</u>, <u>9</u>, 10
Ohio:	5a, 8b, 8d, 9b, 9d, 13b-18
Ky:	1a-7<u>b</u>

NEW ENGLAND WORK SHEETS
1933, 1937

NY:	1-2c (= *LANE* 50-51.3)
Ohio:	13a
SC:	42<u>d</u>

PRELIMINARY SOUTH ATLANTIC STATES WORK SHEETS
1933-4

WVa:	4b
Del:	2a, 5a
Md:	4c, N9, 13<u>e</u>, 16, 20a, 22a
DC:	1a
Va:	8a, 14a, 23b, 26a, 30<u>c</u>, 34a, 38, 45a, N46, 46a, 54a, 55a, *58, N59, 61a, 65ab, 70a
NC:	2a, 7a, 10a, *12a, 14b, 20a, 22a, N25, 25b, 29a, 32a, 35a, 40a, 47, 54a, 59, 65b, 67b, 69b, 73b
SC:	3a, 6a, N11, *11a, 11<u>i</u>, 12b, 14a, N19, N22, 22b, 25a, 30a, 33a, 41a
Ga:	*1a, 1<u>f</u>, 3a, N4, 10a, 13a, 15a, 24a, 34a, 43

TAPED INTERVIEWS (COMBINED WORK SHEETS)
1965-74

Ont:	1ab, 4ab, 7
NY:	46bc, 49cd, 52c, 54ab
SC:	11b, 16, 19b, 24a, 27a, 35c, 37,
Ga:	N1, 1b, 9ab, N11, 12<u>b</u>, 16c, N17, 17, 18ab, 21a, 22a, 23bc, 23<u>ef</u>, N24, N25-28, 30<u>c</u>-33b, N35-N37, 37c, <u>2N37</u>, 37<u>de</u>, 37<u>i</u>, 38-41, 44e
Fla:	2b, 4

COMMUNITIES INVESTIGATED

1. COMMUNITY NAMES IN NORMAL SPELLING

Names of the locations of the *LAMSAS* communities and informants are given below in conventional spelling. The 518 numbered communities generally correspond to counties, the names of which appear in capitals above the community numbers. In twenty-six instances there are two or more *LAMSAS* communities in a single county (e.g., Frontenac, Ont 3, 4); in seven instances two counties constitute a single *LAMSAS* community (e.g., Glengarry and Stormont, Ont 1).

Following the names of the counties the locations for each informant within the county are given. Semicolons separate the three classes of names: (1) the usual designation of the informant's locality (neighborhood, settlement, environs, etc.); (2) the post office; (3) the township (or district, parish, etc.).

Identical names in different categories are not repeated. Commas indicate changes of residence or different ways of referring to locations. Names given by auxiliary informants, if different, follow the principal informant's entry. The vitae in the *LAMSAS Handbook* provide details on these matters.

The spelling and location of each name have been checked in the best available sources, both historical and contemporary. Names of minor civil divisions have sometimes been supplied by the editors. In general the names represent the situation at the time of field work. Subsequent changes, e.g., the abandonment of many rural post offices, or changes in political status or boundaries, are not represented.

Following the list is an index of county names to community numbers which includes the names of several important cities.

ONTARIO		
GLENGARRY and STORMONT		
	1a	Martintown; Charlottenburgh
	b	Cornwall
LEEDS		
	2a	Fairfield East; Elizabethtown
	b	Spicers Hill, Outlet, Warburton; Lansdowne
FRONTENAC		
	3	Kingston
	4ab	Wolfe I.
LENNOX AND ADDINGTON		
	5	Amherst I., Bath; Ernestown
YORK		
	6	Toronto
LINCOLN		
	7	St. Catharines
WELLAND		
	8a	Rileys Bridge; Welland; Wainfleet
	b	Quaker Road; Welland;

ONT (WELLAND)		
	(8b)	Thorold
	c	South Wainfleet; Wainfleet
	d	Port Colborne; Humberstone
WATERLOO		
	9	Riverside; Galt; North Dumfries
BRANT		
	10	Echo Place; Brantford
NEW YORK		
SUFFOLK		
	1	Orient; Southold
	2a	East Hampton
	b	Sagaponack; Southampton
	c	Georgica, Bridgehampton; East Hampton, Southampton
	3a	Brookhaven Village; Brookhaven
	b	Huntington
	c	Coram; Brookhaven
	d	Fort Salonga; Northport; Huntington

NY		
NASSAU		
	4a	Old Brookville; Glen Head; Oyster Bay
	b	Freeport; Hempstead
	c	East Meadow; Hempstead
KINGS (BROOKLYN) and QUEENS		
	5a	Flatlands; Brooklyn
	b	Brooklyn
	c	Brooklyn, Ozone Park
	d	Brooklyn
	e	East Brooklyn, East New York, Flatbush
	f	Brooklyn, Queens
	g	Flatbush; Brooklyn
	h	Brooklyn Heights
	i	Flushing
RICHMOND		
	6a	Huguenot, Annadale; Staten I.
	b	Tottenville; Staten I.

15

NY

NEW YORK (MANHATTAN)

   7a–m New York

BRONX

   8   West Farms, Westchester;
          Bronx

WESTCHESTER

   9a   Tarrytown; Greenburgh

   b   Middle Patent; Bedford;
          North Castle

   c   Crossover; Bedford

ORANGE

  10a   Mt. Salem; Unionville;
          Greenville

   b   Goshen

PUTNAM

  11   Putnam Valley

DUTCHESS

  12a   Pecksville, Peck Slip;
          Holmes; East Fishkill

   b   North Clove; LaGrangeville;
          Union Vale

   c   Poughkeepsie

ULSTER

  13a   Mt. Marion; Saugerties

   b   The Mountain Road; Hurley

SULLIVAN

  14a   South Hill; Grahamsville;
          Neversink

   b   Monticello; Thompson

GREENE

  15a   Goshen St.; Jewett

   b   Jewett

COLUMBIA

  16a   Clermont; Germantown

   b   Blue Stores; Hudson;
          Livingston

RENSSELAER

  17a   Petersburg

   b   South Schodack; Schodack

ALBANY

  18a   Filkins Hill; East Berne;
          Berne

   b   Altamont; Guilderland

   c   Albany

SCHENECTADY

  19   Duanesburg

NY

SCHOHARIE

  20a   Pine Grove; Middleburg;
          Broome

   b   Sharon Springs; Sharon

MONTGOMERY

  21   Salt Springville;
          Fort Plain; Minden

FULTON

  22   South Mayfield;
          Gloversville; Mayfield

SARATOGA

  23a   Corinth

   b   Bacon Hill; Schuylerville;
          Northumberland

   c   Schuylerville; Saratoga

WASHINGTON

  24a   North Hartford; Hartford

   b   Fort Edward

WARREN

  25a   Weverton; Johnsburg

   b   Warrensburg

HAMILTON

  26a   Lake Pleasant

   bc   Speculator; Lake Pleasant

ESSEX

  27a   Crown Point, Ticonderoga

   b   Hague Road; Ticonderoga

   c   North Ticonderoga;
          Ticonderoga

CLINTON

  28a   Plattsburg

   b   Chazy *Champlain

FRANKLIN

  29a   Brainerdsville; Belmont

   bc   Malone

ST. LAWRENCE

  30a   East Hill; South Colton;
          Colton

   b   Fort Jackson; Hopkinton

   c   Hopkinton

   d   Fort Jackson; Hopkinton

   e   Hopkinton Village;
          Hopkinton

JEFFERSON

  31a   Stone Mills; Watertown;
          Orleans

   b   Theresa

NY

LEWIS

  32a   Highmarket; Constableville

   b   New Bremen; Lowville

HERKIMER

  33ab Old Forge; Webb

   c   Big Moose; Webb

OSWEGO

  34a   Fruit Valley; Oswego

   b   Oswego

   c   Pulaski; Richland

   d   Oswego

ONONDAGA

  35a   Kakatt; Elbridge

   b   Oran; Manlius; Pompey

   c   Syracuse

MADISON

  36a   Fenner Corners; Cazenovia;
          Fenner

   b   Peterboro; Smithfield

ONEIDA

  37a   Lee Center; Lee

   b   Maynard; Marcy

   c   Utica

HERKIMER

  38a   Columbia Center; Ilion;
          Columbia *Paines Hollow;
          Mohawk; German Flats

   b   Ilion Gorge; Ilion;
          Litchfield

OTSEGO

  39a   Elliot Hill; Worcester;
          Decatur

   b   Schuylers Lake; Exeter

DELAWARE

  40a   Lee Hollow; Bovina Center;
          Bovina

   b   Walton

CHENANGO

  41   Plymouth

CORTLAND

  42a   South Hill; Cranes Mills;
          Truxton

   b   East Homer; Cortland; Homer

BROOME

  43a   Whitney Point; Nanticoke

   b   Centerlisle; Lisle

   c   Binghamton

NY

TIOGA

44a Red Brush, Owego;
     Lounsberry; Nichols

b   Halsey Valley; Barton

CHEMUNG

45a Dun Hill; Elmira; Big Flats

b   Tompkins Corners;
     Horseheads; Catlin

c   Big Flats

d   Elmira

SCHUYLER

46a Monterey, Barkers Mill;
     Painted Post; Orange

b   Reading Center;
     Watkins Glen; Reading

c   Townsend; Watkins Glen; Dix

TOMPKINS

47a Windy Knob, Cooper St.;
     Newfield *Caroline
     Center; Caroline

b   Dryden

CAYUGA

48a Cato

b   Meridian; Weedsport; Cato

c   Bentons Corners; Ira

d   Victory; Cato

SENECA

49a Romulus

b   Fayette

c   Waterloo

d   Seneca Falls

WAYNE

50ab Sodus

ONTARIO

51a West Richmond; Livonia;
     Richmond

b   Geneva

cd   Naples

e   Geneva

YATES

52a West Italy; Naples; Italy

b   Penn Yan; Milo, Benton

c   Barrington, Milo; Penn Yan

STEUBEN

53a Unionville; Bath

b   Bath

54a Canisteo

NY (STEUBEN)

54b Hornell; Hornellsville

ALLEGANY

55a Rushford

b   Hardys Corners; Cuba;
     Rushford

WYOMING

56ab Arcade

LIVINGSTON

57ab Livonia

c   Beecher Road; Lima; Livonia

MONROE

58a Brighton; Rochester

b   Pittsford

c   Rochester

d   Bushnells Basin; Pittsford;
     Perinton

ef   Rochester

GENESEE

59a Le Roy; Bergen

b   Bethany Center;
     East Bethany; Bethany

ORLEANS

60a Lyndonville; Yates

b   Albion

NIAGARA

61a Olcutt; Newfane

b   Lockport, Olcutt; Newfane

ERIE

62a Clarence

b   Eden

c   Delaware Park; Buffalo

d   Orchard Park

CATTARAUGUS

63a Willoughby; Great Valley

b   Randolph

c   Elkdale; Salamanca;
     Little Valley

d   Salamanca

CHAUTAUQUA

64abc Westfield

NEW JERSEY

CAPE MAY

1a   Goshen; Middle

b   Beesleys Point; Marmora;
     Upper

CUMBERLAND

2a   Robinstown; Port Norris;

NJ

(2a) Commercial *Dorchester

b   Mauricetown; Commercial

SALEM

3a   Harmony; Salem; Quinton

b   Hancocks Bridge;
      Lower Alloways Creek

GLOUCESTER

4a   Almonesson; Sewell;
      Deptford

b   Oak Grove, Repaupo;
      Swedesboro; Logan

CAMDEN

5a   Brooklawn; Sicklerville;
      Winslow

b   Cedar Brook; Winslow

ATLANTIC

6a   Port Republic

b   Steelmanville;
      Pleasantville; Egg Harbor

BURLINGTON

7a   South Park; Chatsworth;
      Tabernacle

b   Rancocas; Burlington;
      Willingboro

OCEAN

8a   Warren Grove;
      Little Egg Harbor

b   Barnegat; Union

MONMOUTH

9a   Union Hill; Englishtown;
      Manalapan

b   Tennent; Englishtown;
      Manalapan

MIDDLESEX

10a   Perth Amboy

b   Prospect Plains; Cranbury;
      Monroe

c   Cranbury

d   Highland Park;
      New Brunswick

MERCER

11a   Federal City; Flemington;
      Hopewell

b   Trenton

c   Rosedale; Princeton;
      Lawrence

NJ

SOMERSET
- 12a   Neshannic Station; Branchburg
- b   New Center; Somerville; Hillsborough

HUNTERDON
- 13a   Snydertown, Lynvale; Ringoes; East Amwell
- b   Copper Hill; Flemington; Raritan

WARREN
- 14a   Piersons Corner, Union Brick; Blairstown
- b   Vienna; Independence

SUSSEX
- 15a   Stillwater; Newton
- b   The Plains; Augusta; Frankford

MORRIS
- 16a   Jacksonville Road, Kinnelon; Towaco; Pequannock
- b   Jacksonville Road; Towaco; Montville

UNION
- 17a   Union Center; Union
- b   Elizabeth

ESSEX
- 18ab   Nutley
- c   Newark
- d   Orange

HUDSON
- 19ab   Jersey City

BERGEN
- 20a   Park Ridge
- b   Oradell

PASSAIC
- 21a   Wayne
- b   Lower Preakness; Paterson; Wayne

PENNSYLVANIA

PHILADELPHIA
- 1a   Kensington; Philadelphia
- b   Philadelphia
- c   Frankford; Philadelphia
- de   Philadelphia
- f   Germantown; Philadelphia

PA (PHILADELPHIA)

- 1g   Philadelphia
- h   Germantown; Philadelphia

BUCKS
- 2a   Lurgan; New Hope; Upper Makefield
- b   Aquetong; New Hope; Solebury

MONTGOMERY
- 3a   Norristown, Trooper; Lower Providence
- bc   Spring House; Lower Gwynedd

DELAWARE
- 4a   Pennington Heights; Wilmington (Del); Bethel
- b   Chester

CHESTER
- 5a   Uwchland; Upper Uwchlan *Birchrunville, Bonnie Bray; West Vincent
- b   Marshallton; West Chester; West Bradford
- c   Eagle; Uwchland; Upper Uwchlan
- d   Cochranville; West Fallowfield
- e   Elkdale; Elkview; New London

BERKS
- 6a   Bethel
- b   Reading
- c   Hamburg; Tilden
- d   Reading

LANCASTER
- 7a   Cherry Hill; Peach Bottom; Fulton
- b   Chestnut Level; Quarryville; Drumore
- c   Fairmount; Ephrata; West Earl
- d   Lancaster

YORK
- 8a   Slate Hill; Delta; Peach Bottom
- b   Delta; Peach Bottom
- c   Shermans Valley; Hanover; West Manheim

PA (YORK)

- 8d   York

DAUPHIN
- 9a   Manada Hill; Grantville; East Hanover
- b   Linglestown; Harrisburg; Lower Paxton
- c   Harrisburg

LEBANON
- 10   Heilmandale; Lebanon; North Annville

NORTHUMBERLAND
- 11a   Turbotville; Lewis
- b   Northumberland; Point

MONTOUR
- 12a   White Hall; Anthony
- b   Danville; Valley

COLUMBIA
- 13ab   Greenwood Valley, Rohrsburg; Orangeville; Greenwood

SCHUYLKILL
- 14a   Valley View; Hegins *Pitman; Eldred
- b   Ashland

LUZERNE
- 15a   Mooretown; Sweet Valley; Ross
- b   Muhlenburg; Shickshinny; Union
- c   Kingston, Wilkes Barre

CARBON
- 16a   Little Gap; Palmerton; Lower Towamensing
- b   Mauch Chunk
- c   East Mauch Chunk

LEHIGH
- 17a   Kuhnsville, Chapmans; Allentown; Upper Macungie
- b   Allentown

NORTHAMPTON
- 18a   Mt. Bethel; Upper Mt. Bethel
- b   Pierce; Easton

MONROE
- 19a   Marshall Creek; Middle Smithfield
- b   Cresco; Barrett

PA

PIKE

20a   Long Meadow, Dingmans
     Ferry; Milford; Delaware

  b   Dingmans Ferry; Delaware

WAYNE

21a   Scott Center; Starucca;
     Scott

  b   Laurella; Honesdale; Berlin

LACKAWANNA

22a   Fleetville; Dalton; Benton

  b   Hack, Fleetville; Dalton;
     Benton

SUSQUEHANNA

23a   Harford

  b   Heart Lake; New Milford

WYOMING

24a   Fox Hollow, Jenningsville;
     Mehoopany; Windham

  b   Roger Hollow; Mehoopany

SULLIVAN

25a   Bethel, Estella;
     Forksville; Elkland

  b   Elkland Ch., Estella;
     Forksville; Elkland

BRADFORD

26a   Warren Center; Warren

  b   Camptown; Wyalusing; Herrick

TIOGA

27a   Cherry Flats, Whitneyville;
     Mansfield; Covington

  b   Niles Valley; Wellsboro;
     Middlebury

LYCOMING

28a   Huntersville; Hughesville;
     Wolf

  <u>b</u>   Williamsport

CLINTON

29a   Loganton; Green
     *Beech Creek

  b   Mackeyville; Lamar

POTTER

30a   West Bingham; Genesee;
     Bingham

  b   Fox Hill; Ulysses

CAMERON

31ab   Rich Valley; Emporium;
     Shippen

PA

CENTRE

32a   Holts Hollow, Johnsons Run,
     Milesburg; Bellefonte;
     Boggs

  b   Wingate; Boggs

BLAIR

33a   Blueknob; Portage;
     Greenfield

  b   Baughman Settlement;
     Tyrone; Snyder

HUNTINGDON

34a   Nossville; Blairs Mills;
     Tell

  b   Cassville; Cass

  <u>c</u>   Huntingdon

MIFFLIN

35a   Irishtown; Mattawanna;
     Bratton

  b   Ferguson Valley; McVeytown;
     Oliver

UNION

36a   Allenwood; Gregg

  b   White Deer Valley;
     Allenwood; Gregg

SNYDER

37a   Troxelville; Adams
     *Port Ann

  b   Independence;
     Port Treverton; Chapman

JUNIATA

38a   Spruce Hill; Port Royal

  b   Lost Creek Valley;
     Mifflintown; Fermanagh

PERRY

39a   Eshcol, Ickesburg;
     Millerstown; Saville

  b   New Bloomfield; Center

CUMBERLAND

40a   Newburg; Hopewell

  b   Mount Hope; Newville;
     Upper Mifflin

ADAMS

41a   Hunterstown; Gettysburg;
     Straban

  b   Fairfield; Hamiltonban

PA

FRANKLIN

42a   Oak Grove; Chambersburg;
     Letterkenny

  b   Criders Ch.; Chambersburg;
     Hamilton

FULTON

43a   Buck Valley; Hancock (Md);
     Union

  b   Pigeon Cove; Warfordsburg;
     Bethel

BEDFORD

44a   Clearville; Monroe

  b   Clear Ridge; Everett;
     West Providence

SOMERSET

45a   Humbert; Confluence;
     Lower Turkeyfoot

  b   Boone, Shanksville;
     Friedens; Stony Creek

FAYETTE

46a   Greenbriar, Ohiopyle;
     Dunbar; Stewart

  b   Brownsville, Dawson;
     Luzerne, Lower Tyrone

GREENE

47a   New Freeport; Freeport

  b   Waynesburg; Whitely

WASHINGTON

48a   Burnsville; West Finley

  b   Buffalo; Hopewell

  c   Sugar Run; Eighty-four;
     Nottingham

WESTMORELAND

49a   Crisp; Rector; Cook

  b   Mansville, Stahlstown;
     Ligonier; Cook

ALLEGHENY

50a   Elizabeth

  b   McKeesport; Elizabeth

  <u>c</u>   Elizabeth; Forward

51a   Wilkinsburg

  b   Greentree; Pittsburgh

BEAVER

52a   Cannelton; Darlington

  <u>b</u>   Darlington

PA

LAWRENCE

53a   Weller Hill, Princeton;
       New Castle; Slippery Rock

b   Weigleton; New Castle;
       Slippery Rock

BUTLER

54a   Nixon; Butler; Penn

b   Brownsdale; Butler; Penn

MERCER

55a   Leesburg; Volant;
       Springfield

b   Pleasant Valley; Mercer;
       Findley

VENANGO

56a   Hannasville; Cochranton;
       Canal

b   Nickleville; Emlenton;
       Richland

CLARION

57a   Kissinger Mines;
       Rimersburg; Madison

b   East Brady; Madison

ARMSTRONG

58a   Brickchurch; Kelly Station;
       Burrell

b   Brickchurch; Ford City;
       Burrell

JEFFERSON

59a   Anita; McCalmont

b   Mt. Pleasant; Summerville;
       Beaver

INDIANA

60a   Crete; Indiana; Center

b   Jacksonville; Blairsville;
       Blacklick

CAMBRIA

61a   Summerhill, South Fork;
       Sidman, Lovett; Croyle

b   North Ebensburg; Ebensburg;
       Cambria

CLEARFIELD

62a   Fairview; Morrisdale;
       Graham

b   Salem; West Decatur,
       Blue Ball; Boggs

ELK

63a   Winslow Hill; Benezett

PA (ELK)

63b   Kersey; Fox

MCKEAN

64a   Jander Run, Shinglehouse;
       Little Genesee (NY);
       Ceres

b   West Eldred; Eldred

WARREN

65a   Fairview, Yankee Bush;
       Warren; Sugar Grove

b   Tidioute Creek Road,
       Tidioute; Torpedo;
       Triumph

CRAWFORD

66a   Conneaut Lake;
       East Fallowfield

b   Conneaut Center;
       Linesville; Conneaut

ERIE

67a   Arbuckle; Wattsburg;
       Venango

b   Wattsburg; Amity

WEST VIRGINIA

JEFFERSON

1   Shepherdstown

BERKELEY

2   Martinsburg; Hedgesville

MORGAN

3   Rock Gap; Omps

HAMPSHIRE

4a   Augusta; Hanging Rock;
       Sherman

b   Romney

MINERAL

5   Burlington; Welton

GRANT

6a   Jordan Run; Union

b   Petersburg; Milroy

PENDLETON

7a   Swedeland; Milam; Bethel

b   Brandywine; Bethel

8a   Carr Schoolhouse;
       Mouth of Seneca; Union

b   Circleville

PRESTON

9a   Fellowsville; Newburg; Reno

b   Cuzzart; Pleasant

WVA

MONONGALIA

10a   Foley Run; Blacksville;
       Clay

b   Dalton; Morgantown; Clinton

c   Morgantown; Morgan

MARION

11a   Dents Run; Mannington

b   Davis Ridge; Farmington;
       Lincoln

HARRISON

12a   Isaacs Creek; Wilsonburg;
       Sardis

b   Lost Creek; Grant

TAYLOR

13a   Belgium; Grafton;
       Booths Creek

b   Meadland; Flemington;
       Booths Creek

BARBOUR

14a   Meadowville; Belington;
       Glade

b   Fox Hall; Philippi;
       Pleasant

TUCKER

15a   St. George

b   Horseshoe; Parsons;
       St. George

RANDOLPH

16a   Wymer; Dry Fork

b   Beverly

UPSHUR

17a   Queens; Washington

b   French Creek; Meade

c   Black Lick Run, Abbott;
       Buckhannon; Meade

LEWIS

18a   Bablin; Duffy;
       Collins Settlement

b   Weston; Courthouse

BRAXTON

19a   Crites Mtn.; Little Birch;
       Holly

b   Morrison Ch.; Sutton; Holly

NICHOLAS

20a   Craigsville; Beaver

b   Muddlety; Summersville;
       Hamilton

WVA

WEBSTER

21a Gauley River, Bolair;
      Jerryville; Fork Lick

  b Browns Mtn.; Replete;
      Hacker Valley

POCAHONTAS

22a Elk; Marlinton; Edray

  b Hillsboro; Little Levels

GREENBRIER

23a Smoot; Meadow Bluff

  b Renick; Falling Spring

MONROE

24a Dutch Corner; Caldwell;
      Second Creek

  b Sinks Grove; Second Creek

SUMMERS

25a Bargers Springs; Talcott;
      Greenbrier River

  b Lowell; Talcott

RALEIGH

26a Toneys Fork; Clear Creek;
      Clear Fork

  b Surveyor; Trap Hill

FAYETTE

27a Russellville; Nuttall

  b Hawver; Hico; Nuttall

BOONE

28a Gordon; Crook

  b Low Gap; Washington

MERCER

29a Christians Ridge; Elgood;
      East River

  b Bent Mtn., Athens;
      Princeton; Plymouth

WYOMING

30a Bear Hole Fork; Pineville;
      Center

  b Oceana

MCDOWELL

31a Trace Fork; Panther;
      Sandy River

  b Crane Ridge; Bradshaw;
      Sandy River

MINGO

32ab Naugatuck; Hardee

LOGAN

33a Crawleys Creek;

WVA (LOGAN)

(33a) Chapmansville

  b Mitchell Heights;
      Henlawson; Logan

LINCOLN

34a Hamlin; West Hamlin;
      Carroll

  b Hamlin; Carroll

WAYNE

35a Maynard Branch; Kiahsville;
      Grant

  b Wayne; Union

CABELL

36a Merritt Creek; Salt Rock;
      McComas

  b Tom Creek; Barboursville;
      McComas

MASON

37a Tribble; Union

  <u>b</u> Henderson; Arbuckle

PUTNAM

38a Lanham; Poca; Pocatalico

  b Heizer; Poca; Pocatalico

KANAWHA

39a South Charleston

  b<u>c</u> Charleston

40a Grapevine; Sissonville;
      Poca

  b Upper Pinch; Pinch; Elk

CLAY

41a Bickmore; Pleasant

  b Mountain Home; Clay; Henry

CALHOUN

42a Katys Run; Annamoriah;
      Sheridan

  b Sycamore; Millstone;
      Sherman

JACKSON

43a Sandyville; Ravenswood

  b Parchment Valley; Ripley

WIRT

44a Lynn Camp; Palestine;
      Tucker

  b Reedy Creek; Palestine;
      Elizabeth

WOOD

45a Crum Hill; Belleville;
      Harris

WVA (WOOD)

45b Murphytown, Loomis Ridge;
      Parkersburg; Clay

PLEASANTS

46a Clay Point; St. Marys;
      Union

  b Schultz; St. Marys;
      Jefferson

RITCHIE

47a Racy; Petroleum; Grant

  b Hushers Run; Pennsboro;
      Clay

DODDRIDGE

48a Buckeye; Salem; Grant

  b Blandville; New Milton

  c West Union

  d Sugar Camp; Blandville;
      New Milton

TYLER

49a Pursley; Sistersville;
      Lincoln

  b Tyler; McElroy

WETZEL

50ab Jacksonburg; Grant

MARSHALL

51a Cameron Ridge; Cameron;
      Liberty

  b Big Run; Cameron; Liberty

OHIO

52a Potomac; West Alexander
      (Pa); Liberty

  b Waddles Run; Short Creek;
      Richland

  <u>c</u> Leatherwood Lane,
      Woodsdale; Wheeling;
      Triadelphia

BROOKE

53a Genteel Ridge; Wellsburg;
      Buffalo

  b Colliers; Weirton

  <u>c</u> Tent Community; Colliers;
      Cross Creek

HANCOCK

54a Hardins Run;
      New Cumberland; Clay

  b Langfits Run;
      New Cumberland; Clay

OHIO

ASHTABULA

1a   Eagleville; Jefferson;
     Austinburg

b   Center Harpersfield;
     Geneva; Harpersfield

c   Jefferson

TRUMBULL

2a   Wildare; Cortland; Champion

b   Champion Heights; Warren;
     Champion

MAHONING

3a   East Goshen Ch.; Beloit;
     Goshen

b   Ellsworth; Berlin Center

COLUMBIANA

4a   Scotch Settlement;
     Wellsville; Madison

b   Lisbon; Center

JEFFERSON

5a   Richmond; Salem

b   East Springfield;
     Bloomingdale; Salem

c   Red Ridge; Smithfield

BELMONT

6a   Armstrongs Mills;
     Washington

b   St. Clairsville; Richland

MONROE

7a   Straight Fork; Graysville;
     Washington

b   Graysville; Washington

WASHINGTON

8a   Pine Ridge; Fleming;
     Watertown

b   Oak Grove; Marietta;
     Muskingum

c   Barlow, Vincent; Marietta

de   Marietta

ATHENS

9a   Brooks; Albany; Alexander

b   Shade; Lodi

c   Whitehall; Athens

d   Athens

MEIGS

10a Stiversville; Portland;
     Lebanon

b   Sutton Ch.; Racine; Sutton

OHIO

GALLIA

11a Thivener; Northup; Harrison

b   Bidwell; Raccoon

LAWRENCE

12a Scottown; Windsor

b   Arabia; Wilgus; Mason

c   Dobbston; Scottown; Windsor

d   Platform; Scottown; Rome

PORTAGE

13a Hiram

b   Ravenna

c   Streetsboro; Kent

TUSCARAWAS

14   New Philadelphia; Goshen

MUSKINGUM

15ab New Concord

GUERNSEY

16a Old Concord; Senecaville;
     Richland

b   Greenwood; Senecaville;
     Richland

c   Lore City; Richland

MORGAN

17   Hopewell; Malta; Penn

VINTON

18   Vinton Station, McArthur;
     Elk

KENTUCKY

CARTER and ROWAN

1a   Hayes Branch; Morehead

b   Grayson

JOHNSON

2a   Boons Camp

b   Winifred

c   Oil Springs

OWSLEY and BREATHITT

3a   Old Steele Graveyard;
     Booneville

b   Scoville

c   Larose

d   Athol

e   Cow Creek; Eversole

LESLIE

4a   Simmon Fork School;
     Big Rock

b   Hyden

c   Dryhill

KY

LETCHER

5a   Linefork

b   Kingdom Come; Oscaloosa

HARLAN

6a   Crummies

b   Harlan

c   Cawood

BELL

7a   Buckeye Ch.; Ingram

b   Middlesboro

DELAWARE

NEW CASTLE

1abc Wilmington

2a   Red Lion; New Castle
     **Harris Corner

b   Hockessin, Marshallton;
     Mill Creek

KENT

3a   Willowgrove; Wyoming;
     Murderkill

b   Bethesda Ch.; Hartly;
     West Dover

c   Dover

4   Milford Neck; Milford

SUSSEX

5a   Georgetown

b   Sunnyside School;
     Bridgeville; Nanticoke

6a   Newfound; Frankford;
     Gumboro

b   Sandy Landing; Dagsboro;
     Baltimore

MARYLAND

CECIL

1a   Battle Swamp; Port Deposit

b   Rising Sun

KENT

2a   Skinners Neck; Rock Hall

b   Blacks Station; Millington

QUEEN ANNES

3a   Dominion, Kent I.; Chester

b   Prices Station;
     Church Hill

CAROLINE

4a   Williston; Denton

b   Burrsville; Denton

c   Preston

MD

TALBOT

5a	Tilghman I.; Tilghman
b	Easton

DORCHESTER

6a	Wingate *Fishing Creek
b	Salem

WICOMICO

7a	Mt. Pleasant; Willards; Dennis
b	Upper Ferry; Salisbury
c	Salisbury

WORCESTER

8a	West, The Forest; Eden; Atkinsons
b	Mile Post Farm; Snow Hill

SOMERSET

N9	Princess Anne
9a	Deal I.
b	Wellington; Princess Anne; Dublin

HARFORD

10a	Hickory; Forest Hill
b	Benson

BALTIMORE

11	Blue Mount; Monkton
12a	Boring
b	Whitehouse; Upperco
13ab	Baltimore
c	Govens; Baltimore
def	Baltimore

CARROLL

14	Silver Run; Westminster; Myers *Union Mills

HOWARD

15ab	Florence; Woodbine

FREDERICK

16	Middletown
17a	Frederick
b	Yellow Springs; Frederick; Tuscarora

MONTGOMERY

18a	Layhill; Silver Spring
b	Norwood, Sandy Spring; Rockville

PRINCE GEORGES

19a	Ritchie; Bennings; Kent
b	Aquasco

MD

ANNE ARUNDEL

20a	Shady Side
b	Tracys Landing; Nutwell
c	Annapolis

CALVERT

21a	Dares Beach Road; Prince Frederick
b	Barstow

ST. MARYS

N22	Beachville; St. Inigoes
2N22	Three Notch Road, Ridge; St. Inigoes
22a	Mattapony Farm; Pearsons; Hillville, Patuxent
b	River Spring; Avenue
c	Leonardtown

CHARLES

23ab	Nanjemoy
c	Gallant Green, Pomfret
24	Gallant Green; Waldorf

WASHINGTON

25	Keedysville
26a	Sideling Hill; Hancock
b	Hagerstown

GARRETT

27a	Dry Run; Swanton; Altamont
b	Sand Flats; Deer Park; Altamont

DISTRICT OF COLUMBIA

1a	Washington
b	Georgetown; Washington

VIRGINIA

ARLINGTON

1	Alexandria

FAIRFAX

2a	Herndon; Dranesville
b	Colchester; Woodbridge; Mt. Vernon

LOUDON

3a	Point of Rocks Road; Lovettsville *Irish Neck
b	Goose Creek Meeting; Lincoln; Mt. Gilead

PRINCE WILLIAM

N4	Hickory Grove; Haymarket; Gainesville

VA

FAUQUIER

5a	Carters Run Valley; Dudie; Marshall
b	Warrenton; Center

MADISON

6a	Nethers; Robertson
b	Madison; Robertson

LOUISA

7a	Bells Crossroads; Louisa
b	Moreland; Louisa; Mineral

SPOTSYLVANIA

8a	Alsop; Livingston
b	Post Oak; Berkeley
c	Fredericksburg

STAFFORD

9a	Rectory; Aquia
b	Aquia Ch.; Stafford Courthouse; Aquia

CAROLINE

10a	Whites; Naulakla; Madison
b	Mulberry Place; De Jarnette; Bowling Green

HANOVER

11a	Cold Harbor; Henry
b	Western View; Hanover; Ashland

WESTMORELAND

N12	Oldhams; Copie
12a	Smith Mount; Horners Mill; Washington
b	Blenheim; Oak Grove; Washington

LANCASTER

13a	Corotoman; Weems; Whitestone
b	Mollusk; White Chapel

NORTHUMBERLAND

14a	Callao; Hyacinth; Lottsburg
b	Remo; Wicomico
c	Wicomico Ch.; Wicomico

ESSEX

N15	Dunnsville; Rappahannock
15a	Brays; Central
b	Wares Wharf; Dunnsville; Rappahannock

VA

KING AND QUEEN
   16a   King and Queen Courthouse;
          Stevensville
    b   West Point; Buena Vista

KING WILLIAM
   17a   Central Garage; Venter;
          Aquinton
    b   Beulahville; Mangohick

MIDDLESEX
   18   Saluda

GLOUCESTER
   19a   Guinea; Severn; Abingdon
    b   Friends Ch.; Achilles;
          Abingdon
    c   Zanoni; Ware

MATHEWS
   20a   Winter Harbor; Onemo;
          Chesapeake
    b   East River, Ware Point;
          Port Haywood; Chesapeake
          *Mathews Courthouse;
          Westville

CHARLES CITY
   N21   Holdcroft; Chickahominy
   21a   Gillams; Providence Forge;
          Tyler
    b   Ruthville; Tyler

JAMES CITY
   22   Diascund; Powhatan

YORK
   23a   Messick; Poquoson
    b   Grafton

WARWICK
   24   Denbigh Plantation;
          Oyster Point; Denbigh

ACCOMACK
   25   Tangier I.; Tangier; Lee
   26a   Craddockville; Pungoteague
    b   Lee Mont; Justisville;
          Metomkin
    c   Accomac; Lee
   27   Chincoteague I.;
          Chincoteague; The Islands

NORTHAMPTON
   28a   Dalbys; Cape Charles;
          Capeville

VA (NORTHAMPTON)
   28b   Chatham; Bridgetown;
          Eastville

HENRICO
   29   Deep Run Ch.; Richmond;
          Tuckahoe
   30a-c   Richmond

CHESTERFIELD
   31a   Beach; Matoaca
    b   Midlothian

DINWIDDIE
   32   Centre Hill; Petersburg
   33a   DeWitt; Rowanty
    b   Aspen Hill; Dinwiddie;
          Rowanty

PRINCE GEORGE
   34a   Prince George; Bland
    b   Newville; Disputanta;
          Brandon

ISLE OF WIGHT
   35a   Mills Swamp; Smithfield;
          Hardy
    b   Whitleys Store; Windsor

SOUTHAMPTON
   36a   Drewryville; Boykins;
          Capron
    b   Courtland; Jerusalem

NANSEMOND
   37   Holland; Holy Neck

NORFOLK
   38   Deep Creek
   39   Norfolk

PRINCESS ANNE
   40a   Back Bay, Pleasant Ridge;
          Pungo
    b   Back Bay; Pungo

GOOCHLAND
   41a   Hadensville; Byrd
    b   Tabscott; Kents Store; Byrd

BUCKINGHAM
   42a   Wingina; James River
          *Slate River
    b   Mt. Tabor; Scottsville;
          Slate River

CUMBERLAND
   N43   Cumberland Courthouse;
          Madison
   43a   Çaira; Guinea Mills; Madison

VA (CUMBERLAND)
   43b   Guinea Mills; Madison

APPOMATTOX
   44a   Wesley Chapel; Appomattox
          Depot; Southside
    b   Evergreen; Southside

PRINCE EDWARD
   45a   Throck; Darlington Heights;
          Hampden
    b   Rice; Lockett

CAMPBELL
   N46   Altavista; Otter River
   46a   Lynch Station; Otter River
    b   Lynchburg

LUNENBURG
   47   Keysville; Pleasant Grove

PITTSYLVANIA
   48a   Pullens Old Store, Climax;
          Chatham; Pigg River
          *Danville
    b   Concord Ch.; Chatham

HALIFAX
   49a   Scottsburg; Roanoke
    b   Younger Store; Halifax;
          Meadville

MECKLENBURG
   50a   Reeks Mill; Chase City;
          Buckhorn
    b   Finchley; Boydton

BRUNSWICK
   51a   Ebony; Meherrin
    b   Gholsonville; Meherrin

FREDERICK
   52a   Chestnut Grove;
          Gainesboro
    b   Brucetown; Stonewall
    c   Opequon; Shawnee

SHENANDOAH
   53a   Stony Creek; Basye; Ashby
    b   Mt. Jackson; Ashby

WARREN
   54a   Brown Town; South River
    b   Rockland; Success;
          Cedarville

ROCKINGHAM
   55a   Harrisonburg; Central
          *Dayton; Ashby
    b   Harrisonburg

VA

HIGHLAND

56a Crabbottom; Blue Grass

b Pisgah; High Town;
Blue Grass

AUGUSTA

57a Sherando; Lyndhurst;
South River

b Stuarts Draft; South River

GREENE

58 Shiflett Hollow;
Mission Home; Monroe
*Doylesville; White Hall

ALBEMARLE

N59 Batesville; Samuel Miller

59a Cismont; Rivanna

_b_ Dunlora; Charlottesville

BATH

60 Burnsville; Williamsville
*Dry Run

ROCKBRIDGE

61a House Mtn., Whistle Creek;
Kerrs Creek

_b_ Lexington

NELSON

62a Dutch Creek; Elma; Rockfish
*Saunders; Lovingston

b Nellysford; Rockfish

CRAIG

63a Craigs Creek; Barbours
Creek; Newcastle

b Paint Bank; Newcastle

BEDFORD

64a Battery Creek; Big I.;
Charlemont

b Red Lands, Peaks Road;
Bedford; Central

ROANOKE

65a Cave Spring

b Upper Back Creek; Salem

_c_ Roanoke

FRANKLIN

66a Shooting Creek; Endicott;
Long Branch

b Sydnorsville; Rocky Mount;
Snow Creek

PULASKI

67a Max Creek; Hiwassee

VA (PULASKI)

67b Draper; Newbern

FLOYD

68a Eastview; Floyd

b Alum Ridge; Sowers

HENRY

69a Spencer; Horse Pasture

b Ridgeway

BLAND

70ab Bland; Seddon

GRAYSON

71a Chestnut Hill;
Independence; Elk Creek

b Independence; Elk Creek

BUCHANAN

72a Stone Coal Branch; Stacy;
Grundy

b Loggy Bottom Branch;
Whitewood; Garden

RUSSELL

73 Dortons School; Castlewood;
Copper Creek

WASHINGTON

74a Meadowview; Glade Spring

_b_ Abingdon

LEE

75a Thompsons Settlement,
Bishops Store;
Jonesville; White Shoals

b Morgans Store; Jonesville;
White Shoals

NORTH CAROLINA

CURRITUCK

1 Knotts I.; Fruitville

2a Point Harbor; Poplar Branch

b Moyock

CAMDEN

3a Belcross, Old Trap;
Courthouse, Shiloh

b Belcross; Courthouse

GATES

4a Fort I.; Eure; Hall

b Trotville; Hunters Mill

PASQUOTANK and PERQUIMANS

5a Okisko; Elizabeth City;
Mt. Hermon

b Winfall; Parkville

NC

CHOWAN

6 Edenton

BERTIE

7a Trapp; Colerain

b Askewville; Windsor

MARTIN

N8 Old Cotten Plantation,
Oak City; Hobgood;
Goose Nest

8a Holly Springs; Williamston;
Griffin

b Holly Springs; Williamston;
Williams

TYRRELL

9ab Columbia; Alligator

DARE

10a Kitty Hawk; Atlantic

b Rodanthe; Kenekeet

c Manteo; Nags Head

HYDE

11a Englehard; Middletown;
Lake Landing

b Tiny Oak; Swan Quarter

BEAUFORT

12a Beaver Dam; Washington;
Long Acre *Blounts Creek

b Washington

PAMLICO

13a Folly Road, Florence;
Whortonsville

b Merritt *Bayboro

CRAVEN

N14 Cahoque; Havelock

14a Ernul

b Vanceboro

_c_ New Bern

PITT

15a Shelmerdine; Greenville;
Chicod *Bethel

b Winterville

GREENE

16a Arba; Snow Hill; Hookerton

b Snow Hill; Hookerton

WAYNE

17a Emmaus Ch.; Dudley;
Indian Springs

b Mt. Olive; Brogden

NC

DUPLIN

18a   Chinquapin; Cypress Creek

b   Friendship; Warsaw; Faison

JONES

19a   Pleasant Hill; Kinston;
        Tuckahoe

b   Trenton; Beaver Creek

CARTERET

20a   Roe; Cedar I.

b   Harkers I.

c   Straits

ONSLOW

21a   Grants Creek; Maysville;
        White Oak

b   Harris Creek; Jacksonville

PENDER

22a   Canetuck

b   Riverside; Burgaw

NEW HANOVER

23a   Whiskey Creek; Wilmington;
        Masonboro

b   Myrtle Grove Sound;
        Wilmington; Masonboro
        *Myrtle Grove

cd   Wilmington

BRUNSWICK

N24   Calabash; Shallotte

24a   Freeland; Waccamaw

b   Royal Oak; Supply;
        Lockwoods Folly

SAMPSON

N25   Turkey

25a   Clinton; Mints; McDaniels

b   Turkey

CUMBERLAND

26a   Chasons Store; Cedar Creek

b   Hope Mills; Rockfish

c   Fayetteville; Cross Creek

BLADEN

27a   Bladenboro

b   Elizabethtown

COLUMBUS

28a   Crusoes I.; Old Dock; Lees

b   The Jam, The Corner,
        Macedonia Ch.; Boardman;
        Tatums

c   Whiteville; Welch Creek

NC

ROBESON

29a   Pembroke

b   Barker Ten Mile; Lumberton;
        Howellsville

NORTHAMPTON

30a   Faisons Old Tavern; Conway;
        Wiccacanee

b   Lasker; Roanoke

HALIFAX

31a   Hollister; Essex;
        Brinkleyville

b   Darlington; Halifax;
        Faucett

EDGECOMBE

32a   Rocky Mount

b   Coolmore; Tarboro

WILSON

33a   Black Creek

b   Evansdale; Wilson;
        Stantonsburg

JOHNSTON

34a   Sanders Chapel; Smithfield

b   Smithfield

HARNETT

35a   Manchester; Anderson Creek

b   Erwin; Grove

SCOTLAND

N36   Nashville; Wagram;
        Spring Hill

36a   Gibsons Store; Laurel Hill

b   St. John Ch.; Gibson;
        Williamsons

WARREN

37a   Wise; Smith Creek

b   Marmaduke, Warrenton;
        Fishing Creek, Shocco

FRANKLIN

N38   Moulton; Louisburg;
        Sandy Creek

38ab   Bunn; Dunn

GRANVILLE

39a   Old Watch Curran Home;
        Oxford

b   Abrams Plains; Stovall;
        Sassafras Fork

WAKE

40a   Cary; House Creek

NC (WAKE)

40b   Leesville; Morrisville

41   Raleigh

CHATHAM

42a   Siler City; Staley;
        Matthews

b   Harpers Crossroads,
        Pittsboro; Bear Creek,
        Hickory Mtn. *Center

ORANGE

43a   Hurdle Mills;
        Cedar Grove

b   Orange Grove; Hillsborough;
        Bingham

CASWELL

44   Old Fitch Store;
        Yanceyville; Anderson

ROCKINGHAM

45   Reidsville *Wentworth

GUILFORD

46ab   Guilford College;
        Friendship

c   Greensboro; Gilmer

RANDOLPH

47   Sophia; New Market

DAVIDSON

48   Thomasville

ROWAN

49   Corinth Ch.; Gold Hill;
        Morgan

50a   Milford Hills; Salisbury;
        Franklin

b   Salisbury

MONTGOMERY

51a   Black Ankle; Steeds;
        Little River

b   Rubyatt; Candor;
        Rocky Springs

ANSON

N52   East Rocky Ford; Wadesboro

52a   Forestville Ch.; Pee Dee;
        Lilesville

b   Jones Creek; Morven;
        Gulledge

UNION

53a   New Salem School;
        Marshville; New Salem

b   Wingate, Monroe; Marshville

NC

CABARRUS

54a   Concord

b   Cold Springs Ch.; Concord;
       Baptist Ch.

MECKLENBURG

55   Mint Hill; Matthews;
       Clear Creek

56a   Hopewell; Huntersville;
       Long Creek

b   Charlotte

STOKES

57a   Danbury; Peters Creek

b   Piedmont Springs; Danbury

SURRY

58a   Sage Creek; Mt. Airy;
       Stewarts Creek

b   Ladonia; Mt. Airy;
       Stewarts Creek

YADKIN

59   Boonville

FORSYTH

60   Tobaccoville; Old Richmond

IREDELL

61a   New Hope

b   Trinity Ch.; Statesville;
       New Concord

ASHE

62a   West Jefferson

b   Nathans Creek,
       West Jefferson; Jefferson

WILKES

63a   Chestnut Mtn. Ridge;
       Stony Fork; Elk

b   Wilkesboro, Gilreath;
       Brushy Mtn.

CATAWBA

64a   Banoak; Vale; Bandy

b   Hickory, Love; Newton;
       Caldwell

CALDWELL

65a   Green Valley; Colletsville;
       Johns River

b   Kings Creek, Lenoir

CLEVELAND

66a   Warlick; Lawndale

b   Boiling Springs

NC

MITCHELL

67a   Hughes Settlement,
       Rock Creek; Buladean;
       Harrell

b   Honeycutt; Bakersville;
       Harrell

MCDOWELL

68a   Glenwood; Nealsville

b   Greenlee; Marion; Old Fort

POLK

69a   Mill Springs; White Oak

b   Friendship Ch.; Saluda

MADISON

70a   White Rock; Marshall;
       Shelton Laurel

b   Walnut; Big Laurel

BUNCOMBE

71a   Dillingham; Asheville

b   Lower Hominy; Candler

c   Asheville

TRANSYLVANIA

72a   Wilson St., Brevard;
       Pisgah Forest; Dunns Rock

b   Rock Brook; Brevard;
       Dunns Rock

SWAIN

73a   Stecoah, Dorsey;
       Forneys Creek

b   Wadkins; Bryson City;
       Charleston

MACON

74a   Highlands; Satolah (Ga)

b   Cartoogechaye; Franklin

CHEROKEE

75a   Head of Beaverdam;
       Grandview; Beaverdam

b   Peachtree; Murphy

SOUTH CAROLINA

HORRY

1a   Burgess; Socastee

b   Spring Branch;
       Fair Bluff (NC); Floyd

MARION

2a   Davis neighborhood;
       Centenary; Le Gette

b   Pinderboro; Marion

SC

FLORENCE

3a   Vausetown; Olanta;
       James Cross Roads

b   Sardis; Timmonsville;
       James Cross Roads

c   Pee Dee, Coles Crossroads;
       Florence; Tans Bay

CLARENDON

4abc   Manning

WILLIAMSBURG

5a   Boyd, Spring Gully;
       Andrews; Anderson

bcd   Kingstree; Kings

GEORGETOWN

N6   Georgetown

6a   Hemingway; Carvers Bay

b   Plantersville; Prince
       Frederick, Pee Dee and
       Choppee *Georgetown

c   Waccamaw Neck; Pawleys I.;
       All Saints, Murrells
       Inlet and Waverly Mills

N7-7d   Georgetown

BERKELEY

8a   Macedonia, Hoodtown;
       Bonneau; 2nd St. Stephens

b   Hell Hole; Huger;
       St. Dennis and St. Thomas

c   2nd St. Stephens;
       St. Stephens;
       1st St. Stephens

9a   Pine Ridge School;
       Summerville;
       2nd St. James Goose Creek

b   Cross; Eutaw

c   Moncks Corner;
       St. Johns Berkeley

d   Pinopolis;
       2nd St. Johns Berkeley

CHARLESTON

10a   Awendaw, Charleston;
       St. James Santee

b   McClellanville;
       St. James Santee

c   Mt. Pleasant; Christ Ch.

N11-11e   Charleston

SC (CHARLESTON)

11f	Fishburne Tract, Northwest; Charleston
g	Charleston
2N11	Jasper Court; Charleston
11hij	South of Broad; Charleston

DORCHESTER

12a	Indian Field; Harleyville; Carns
b	Byrd Station; St. George; George

CHARLESTON

13	The Borough; Edisto I.

COLLETON

14a	Hendersonville; Heyward
b	Walterboro; Verdier

BAMBERG

15a	Colston; Bamberg; Buford Bridge
bc	Bamberg

ALLENDALE

N16	Millett
16	Allendale

HAMPTON

17a-d	Hampton; Peeples

BEAUFORT

N18-18ab	Beaufort
c	Port Royal Road; Beaufort
N19	Hilton Head
19a	Okatie, Beaufort
b	Pritchardville, Beaufort; Bluffton
c	Cunninghams Bluff, Blountville, Beaufort
d	Bluffton

MARLBORO

20a	Lower Brownsville; Brownsville
b	Wesley; Clio
c	Blenheim
d	Bennettsville

CHESTERFIELD

21a	Black Creek, Green Hill School; Hartsville; Alligator
b	Chesterfield; Court House

KERSHAW

N22	Camden; De Kalb

SC (KERSHAW)

22a	Boykin; De Kalb
22bc	Camden; De Kalb

DARLINGTON

23a	Dovesville, Doves Depot; Leavenworth
b	Lynches River, New Market, Pond Hollow; Hartsville
c	Palmetto; Darlington
d	Auburn; Hartsville
e	Palmetto; Darlington

SUMTER

N24-24ab	Sumter
c	Loring Mill; Stateburg
d	Sumter

RICHLAND

25a	Lykesland
b	White Rock; Fork
c	Columbia

CALHOUN

26a	Creston, Cameron; Lyons
b	St. Matthews; Pine Grove

ORANGEBURG

27a	Cordova; Zion
b	Livingston; North; Hebron

BARNWELL

28a	Pattersons Mill; Martin; Bennett Springs
b	Meyers Mill; Bennett Springs
c	Hattieville; Meyers Mill; Bennett Springs
d	Barnwell

AIKEN

29a	Oakwood; Montmorenci; Windsor *Aiken
b	Graniteville; Gregg *Ellenton; Silverton
c	Warrenville; Gregg

EDGEFIELD

30a	Philippi Ch.; Johnston
bc	Edgefield; Wise, Pickens

LEXINGTON

31a	Camp Styx; West Columbia; Congaree
b	St. Thomas Ch., Newburgh School; Chapin; Saluda

SC

FAIRFIELD

32a-d	Winnsboro

CHESTER

33a	Armenia; Chester
b	Chester

LANCASTER

34abc	Lancaster; Gills Creek

YORK

35ab	Highland Park Mill; Rock Hill; Catawba
c	Cotton Belt, Beersheba; York *Sharon; Broad River

SPARTANBURG

36a	Holly Springs; Inman; Beech Springs
b	Spartanburg
c	Reidville
d	Spartanburg

UNION

37	Buffalo; Bogansville

NEWBERRY

38a-d	Newberry

LAURENS

39ab	Mountville; Hunter

ABBEVILLE

40a	Abbeville
b	Lebanon; Abbeville

ANDERSON

41a	Eureka Ch.; Anderson
b	Anderson

GREENVILLE

42a	Parsons Mill Road; Greenville; Butler
N42-42e	Greenville

PICKENS

43ab	Pumpkintown; Pickens
c	Dacusville

OCONEE

44a	Flat Shoals School, Tamassee; Walhalla; Keowee
b	Richland; Center, Seneca

GEORGIA

CHATHAM

N1	Savannah
1a	Savannah *Black Ankle
b-h	Savannah

GA

BRYAN

N2	Lanier
2a	Ellabell
b	Lanier

LIBERTY

| 3a | Flemington |
| b | Hinesville |

MCINTOSH

N4	Sapelo I., Crescent
4a	Darien
b	The Ridge; Ridgeville
c	Valona

GLYNN

5a	Frederica, The Beach, St. Simons I.
b	St. Simons
cde	Brunswick

CAMDEN

| 6a | Cherry Point; Kingsland |
| b | St. Marys |

CHARLTON

| 7 | Folkston |

WAYNE

| 8a | Screven |
| b | Jesup |

TATTNALL

| 9a | Reidsville, Cobbtown, Tison, Glennville |
| b | Cobbtown |

EVANS

| 10a | Manassas |
| b | Bellville; Manassas, Hagan |

CANDLER

| N11 | Metter |

BULLOCH

| 12a | Stilson |
| b | Statesboro |

EFFINGHAM

| 13a | Rincon |
| b | Wilson Mill Pond, Oakie; Egypt |

SCREVEN

14a	Sylvania
b	Girard, Sylvania
c	Middleground Road, Red Bluff, Sylvania; Halcyon Dale

GA

BURKE

| 15a | Alexander |
| b | Waynesboro |

RICHMOND

16a	County Home; Augusta
b	Bath; Blythe
cd	Augusta

JEFFERSON

| N17-17 | Louisville |

EMANUEL

| 18a | Adrian |
| b | Twin City, Swainsboro |

MONTGOMERY

| 19a | Kibbee **Tarrytown |
| b | Seward School; Uvalda |

TELFAIR

| 20a | Cobbville; McRae; Milan, Workmore |
| b | McRae |

LAURENS

| 21a | Lollie |
| b | Dublin |

HOUSTON and PEACH

| 22ab | Fort Valley |

BIBB

| 23a | Fort Hawkins, Macon |
| b-f | Macon |

BALDWIN

N24	Milledgeville
24a	Mt. Pleasant Ch.; Milledgeville
b	Carr Station

HANCOCK

| N25 | Sparta |

JASPER

| 26 | Monticello |

GREENE

| 27 | Greensboro |

WILKES

| 28 | Delhi, Washington |

LINCOLN

| 29a | Goshen Highway; Lincolnton |
| b | Lincolnton |

ELBERT

30a	Elberton *Oglesby Quarry
b	Ginntown, Elberton
c	Elberton

GA

HART

| 31 | Sardis; Hartwell |

FRANKLIN

| 32 | Carnesville |

MADISON

| 33ab | Colbert |

CLARKE

N34	Athens
34a	Bogart; Bradberrys
b	Hinton Brown School; Bogart; Bradberrys

WALTON

| N35 | Thompson; Monroe |

ROCKDALE

| N36 | Conyers |

FULTON and DE KALB

N37	Atlanta
37a	Doraville
b	Rock Chapel; Lithonia; Diamond
c	Avondale; Decatur
2N37	Washington Park, Adamsville; Atlanta
37de	Druid Hills; Atlanta
f	Decatur, Atlanta
g	Roswell, Atlanta
hi	Atlanta

HALL

| 38 | Gainesville; Tadmore |

LUMPKIN

| 39 | Dahlonega |

CHEROKEE

| 40 | Ducktown |

GILMER

| 41 | Ellijay; Leaches, Tails Creek |

FANNIN

| 42a | Mt. Liberty, Pierceville; Copper Hill (Tenn); Mobile |
| b | Dial, Blue Ridge; Noontootler |

UNION

| 43 | Lonesome Cove; Blairsville; Owltown |

RABUN

| 44a | Germany; Clayton; Persimmon |

GA (RABUN)   FLA   FLA

   44b   Quartz; Persimmon   DUVAL   VOLUSIA

     c   Persimmon Creek; Clayton;   2a   Mandarin;   4   Spruce Creek, Tomoka Farms;

          Persimmon   South Jacksonville   Daytona Beach

     d   Clayton   bc   Jacksonville   ALACHUA

     e   Flat Creek; Lakemont   ST. JOHNS   5a   Hague, Gainesville

FLORIDA   3ab   St. Augustine   b   Windsor; Gainesville

NASSAU

    1   Fernandina; Amelia I.

INDEX OF COUNTY NAMES TO COMMUNITY NUMBERS

The index consists of county names in alphabetical order followed by the community numbers. It also contains, in italics, the names of several important cities whose names are different from the counties they are in. Where several counties have the same name, they are listed alphabetically by state.

Cayuga NY 48

Cecil Md 1

Centre Pa 32

Charles Md 23, 24

Charles City Va 21

Charleston SC 10, 11, 13

Charleston WVa 39

Charlotte NC 56

Charlton Ga 7

Chautauqua NY 64

Chatham Ga 1

Chatham NC 42

Chemung NY 45

Chenango NY 41

Cherokee Ga 40

Cherokee NC 75

Chester Pa 5

Chester SC 33

Chesterfield SC 21

Chesterfield Va 31

Chowan NC 6

Clarendon SC 4

Clarion Pa 57

Clarke Ga 34

Clay WVa 41

Clearfield Pa 62

Cleveland NC 66

Clinton NY 28

Clinton Pa 29

Colleton SC 14

Columbia NY 16

Columbia Pa 13

Columbia SC 25

Columbiana Ohio 4

Columbus NC 28

Cortland NY 42

Craig Va 63

Craven NC 14

Crawford Pa 66

Cumberland NJ 2

Cumberland NC 26

Cumberland Pa 40

Cumberland Va 43

Currituck NC 1, 2

Dare NC 10

Darlington SC 23

Dauphin Pa 9

Davidson NC 48

De Kalb Ga 37

Delaware NY 40

Delaware Pa 4

Dinwiddie Va 32, 33

District of Columbia DC 1

Doddridge WVa 48

Dorchester Md 6

Dorchester SC 12

Dover Del 3

Duplin NC 18

Dutchess NY 12

Duval Fla 2

Edgecombe NC 32

Edgefield SC 30

Effingham Ga 13

Elbert Ga 30

Elk Pa 63

Emanuel Ga 18

Erie NY 62

Erie Pa 67

Essex NJ 18

Essex NY 27

Essex Va 15

Evans Ga 10

Fairfax Va 2

Fairfield SC 32

Fannin Ga 42

Fauquier Va 5

Fayette Pa 46

Fayette WVa 27

Florence SC 3

Floyd Va 68

Forsyth NC 60

Franklin Ga 32

Franklin NY 29

Franklin NC 38

Franklin Pa 42

Franklin Va 66

Frederick Md 16, 17

Frederick Va 52

Frontenac Ont 3, 4

Fulton Ga 37

Fulton NY 22

Fulton Pa 43

Gallia Ohio 11

Garrett Md 27

Gates NC 4

Genesee NY 59

Georgetown SC 6, 7

Gilmer Ga 41

Glengarry Ont 1

Gloucester NJ 4

Gloucester Va 19

Glynn Ga 5

Goochland Va 41

Grant WVa 6

Granville NC 39

Grayson Va 71

Greenbrier WVa 23

Greene Ga 27

Greene NY 15

Greene NC 16

Greene Pa 47

Greene Va 58

Greenville SC 42

Guernsey Ohio 16

Guilford NC 46

Halifax NC 31

Halifax Va 49

Hall Ga 38

Hamilton NY 26

Hampshire WVa 4

Hampton SC 17

Hancock Ga 25

Hancock WVa 54

Hanover Va 11

Harford Md 10

Harlan Ky 6

Harnett NC 35

Harrisburg Pa 9

Harrison WVa 12

Hart Ga 31

Henrico Va 29, 30

Henry Va 69

Herkimer NY 33, 38

Highland Va 56

Horry SC 1

Houston Ga 22

Howard Md 15

Hudson NJ 19

Hunterdon NJ 13

Huntingdon Pa 34

Hyde NC 11

Indiana Pa 60

Iredell NC 61

Isle of Wight Va 35

Jackson WVa 43

Jacksonville Fla 2

James City Va 22

Jasper Ga 26

Jefferson Ga 17

Jefferson NY 31

Jefferson Ohio 5

Jefferson Pa 59

Jefferson WVa 1

Jersey City NJ 19

Johnson Ky 2

Johnston NC 34

Jones NC 19

Juniata Pa 38

Kanawha WVa 39, 40

Kent Del 3, 4

Kent Md 2

Kershaw SC 22

King and Queen Va 16

King William Va 17

Kings NY 5

Lackawanna Pa 22

Lancaster Pa 7

Lancaster SC 34

Lancaster Va 13

Laurens Ga 21

Laurens SC 39

Lawrence Ohio 12

Lawrence Pa 53

Lebanon Pa 10

Lee Va 75

Leeds Ont 2

Lehigh Pa 17

Lennox and Addington Ont 5

Leslie Ky 4

Letcher Ky 5

Lewis NY 32

Lewis WVa 18

Lexington SC 31

Liberty Ga 3

Lincoln Ga 29

Lincoln Ont 7

Lincoln WVa 34

Livingston NY 57

Logan WVa 33

Loudoun Va 3

Louisa Va 7

Lumpkin Ga 39

Lunenburg Va 47

Luzerne Pa 15

Lycoming Pa 28

Macon Ga 23

Macon NC 74

Madison Ga 33

Madison NY 36

Madison NC 70

Madison Va 6

Mahoning Ohio 3

Manhattan NY 7

Marion SC 2

Marion WVa 11

Marlboro SC 20

Marshall WVa 51

Martin NC 8

Mason WVa 37

Mathews Va 20

McDowell NC 68

McDowell WVa 31

McIntosh Ga 4

McKean Pa 64

Mecklenburg NC 55, 56

Mecklenburg Va 50

Meigs Ohio 10

Mercer NJ 11

Mercer Pa 55

Mercer WVa 29

Middlesex NJ 10

Middlesex Va 18

Mifflin Pa 35

Mineral WVa 5

Mingo WVa 32

Mitchell NC 67

Monmouth NJ 9

Monongalia WVa 10

Monroe NY 58

Monroe Ohio 7

Monroe Pa 19

Monroe WVa 24

Montgomery Ga 19

Montgomery Md 18

Montgomery NY 21

Montgomery NC 51

Montgomery Pa 3

Montour Pa 12

Morgan Ohio 17

Morgan WVa 3

Morris NJ 16

Muskingum Ohio 15

Nansemond Va 37

Nassau Fla 1

Nassau NY 4

Nelson Va 62

Newark NJ 18

Newberry SC 38

New Castle Del 1, 2

New Hanover NC 23

New York NY 7

New York City NY 5, 6, 7, 8

Niagara NY 61

Nicholas WVa 20

Norfolk Va 38, 39

Northampton NC 30

Northampton Pa 18

Northampton Va 23

Northumberland Pa 11

Northumberland Va 14

Ocean NJ 8

Oconee SC 44

Ohio WVa 52

Oneida NY 37

Onondaga NY 35

Onslow NC 21

Ontario NY 51

Orange NY 10

Orange NC 43

Orangeburg SC 27

Orleans NY 60

Oswego NY 34

Otsego NY 39

Owsley Ky 3

Pamlico NC 13

Pasquotank NC 5

Passaic NJ 21

Peach Ga 22

Pender NC 22

Pendleton WVa 7, 8

Perquimans NC 5

Perry Pa 39

Philadelphia Pa 1

Pickens SC 43

Pike Pa 20

Pitt NC 15

Pittsburgh Pa 51

Pittsylvania Va 48

Pleasants WVa 46

Pocahontas WVa 22

Polk NC 69

Portage Ohio 13

Potter Pa 30

Preston WVa 9

Prince Edward Va 45

Prince George Va 34

Prince Georges Md 19

Prince William Va 4

Princess Anne Va 40

Pulaski Va 67

Putnam NY 11

Putnam WVa 38

Queen Annes Md 3

Queens NY 5

Rabun Ga 44

Raleigh NC 41

Raleigh WVa 26

Randolph NC 47

Randolph WVa 16

Rensselaer NY 17

Richland SC 25

Richmond Ga 16

Richmond NY 6

Richmond Va 30

Ritchie WVa 47

Roanoke Va 65

Robeson NC 29

Rochester NY 58

Rockbridge Va 61

Rockdale Ga 36

Rockingham NC 45

Rockingham Va 55

Rowan Ky 1

Rowan NC 49, 50

Russell Va 73

Salem NJ 3

Sampson NC 25

Saratoga NY 23

Savannah Ga 1

Schenectady NY 19

Schoharie NY 20

Schuyler NY 46

Schuylkill Pa 14

Scotland NC 36

Screven Ga 14

Seneca NY 49

Shenandoah Va 53

Snyder Pa 37

Somerset Md 9

Somerset NJ 12

Somerset Pa 45

Southampton Va 36

Spartanburg SC 36

Spotsylvania Va 8

Stafford Va 9

Steuben NY 53, 54

St. Augustine Fla 3

St. Johns Fla 3

St. Lawrence NY 30

St. Marys Md 22

Stokes NC 57

Stormont Ont 1

Suffolk NY 1, 2, 3

Sullivan NY 14

Sullivan Pa 25

Summers WVa 25

Sumter SC 24

Surry NC 58

Susquehanna Pa 23

Sussex Del 5, 6

Sussex NJ 15

Swain NC 73

Talbot Md 5

Tattnall Ga 9

Taylor WVa 13

Telfair Ga 20

Tioga NY 44

Tioga Pa 27

Tompkins NY 47

Toronto Ont 6

Transylvania NC 72

Trenton NJ 11

Trumbull Ohio 2

Tucker WVa 15

Tuscarawas Ohio 14

Tyler WVa 49

Tyrrell NC 9

Ulster NY 13

Union Ga 43

Union NJ 17

Union NC 53

Union Pa 36

Union SC 37

Upshur WVa 17

2. COUNTY NAMES

List 2 gives the pronunciation of the name of the county in which each informant lived. The word *county*, sometimes recorded in phrases of the type *Suffolk County*, is not entered. When the county name is the same as a place name on List 3, e.g., *Baltimore*, all pronunciations are entered on both lists.

The commentary includes other county names relevant to the vitae of informants or their families, where recorded by the field worker. It also includes incidental pronunciations of other county names on List 1. All county names from List 1 entered in the commentary are in italics.

Stresses are marked as indicated by the field workers.

ONTARIO		NY		NY		NY	
1a	ˌgɫɛnˈgɛɐ̶ɫ	3b	---	7ḻ	nu<· ɔ:k	19	skənɛktəd‡ˆ
b	ˈsto<ɐˌmɑnɫ	c	sʌfək	m̲	nu<· ɔ:ᵊk	20a	ˌskoᵛuˈhæᵊr‡ˆ
2a	liᵛidz	d	sʌ<fək	8	brɑnks	b	skəhæˆɐ‡ˆ
b	liᵛidz +	4a	ˈnæˌsɔ·	9a	wɛsttʃɛstɚ	21	mɑntˈgʌmr‡ˆ
	cv li>iˆdz	b	næ·sɔᵛ·ᵊ	b	ˈwɛstˌtʃɛstɚ	22	fʌ>ɫʼtn
3	fɟơnʼtnæk	c	ˈnæˌsɔ:	c	ˈwɛstˌtʃɛstɚ	23a	ˈsæ·ɐɐˌto<·u<g‡ᵛ
4a	ˈfrɑntnˌæˆk	5a	kɪŋz	10a	ɔɐ‡ᵛndʒ	b	ˈsæˆ·ɐɐˌto<·u<gɐ
b	ˈfrɑˆntɐˌnæk	b	---	b̲	ɑrɐ᷆ndʒ	c	ˈsæᷝ·ɐɐˌtoˆ·ugɐ
5	ˌlɪᵛnɐˆks əˆn	c	kwi·nz	11	---	24a	wɑ·ʃ‡ŋtən
	ˈɛˆd‡<ŋtˈn,	def	---	12a	dʌᷝtʃ‡ᵛs	b̲	wɒˆ·ʃ‡ŋtən
	lɛˆn‡ks	g	kɪŋz	b	dʌtʃ‡ᷝs	25a	ˈwɔᷝɐn
6	ɔᵛɐk, ɔᷝˆɐk	h̲	---	c̲	dʌ<tʃɐᷝs	b	ˈwɑ>·ɐ‡<n
7	lɪŋkəˆn	i̲	kwi·nz	13a	ʌɫstɚ	26a	ˈhæmɫtn
8a	wɛlɐˆn +, -ɫ-	6a	rɪtʃmənd	b̲	ʌɫstɐ	b	ˈhæmɫʼtn
b	wɛ>lɐˆn cv wɛ-	b	rɪtʃmənd	14a	ˈsʌ<ɫəvən	c	---
c	ˈwɛ>lɐˆnd	7a	nŭ< ɔ·ᵊk	b	sʌ<ɫɐvn	27a	ˈɛˆs‡<ks
d	wɛˆlɐˆn	b	nu· ɔ:ᵊk	15ab	gri·n	bc	ɛˆs‡<ks
9	ˌwɔᵛtɐˈlɐˆɐ	c	nu<· ɔ·ək	16a	kŏɫʌᷝmb‡ˆɐ	28a	ˈklɪ>nʼtn
10	bræˆ·nt	d	nu<· ɔ:ᵊk	b	kŏɫʌmb‡ˆɐ	b	kɫ‡nˀn
		e	nu<· ɔ·ək	17a	ˌræ·nᵗsəˈlɪɐ,	29a	fr̥᷉æŋkl‡<n
NEW YORK		f	nu<· ɔᵛ·k		ˈ-tslɐ	b	fr̥᷆æŋkl‡<n
1	sʌfək	g	nu<· ɔ:ᵊk	b	ˈrɛntsəlɐ	c	fr̥æˆᵋŋkl‡<n
2a	---	hi	nu<· ɔ·ᵊk	18a	ɒˆ:ɫbən‡ᷝ	30a	ˈseᵛ‡nt ˌlɔᷝnts
b	sʌfək	j̲	nu< ɔ·ᵊk	b	ɒˆ·ɫbən‡ᵗ‡ˆ	b	ˈseᵛ‡nt ˌlɔᷝᵛənts
c	---	k̲	nu· ɔ:ᵊk	c̲	ˈɔ:ᵊɫbən‡	c	ˈseᵛ‡nt ˌlɒ·ɐnts
3a	sʌ<fək						

34

NY		NY		NY		NJ	
30d	---	45a	ʃɨˈmʌ<ŋ	56a	ˈwɜ>ɨˌo<u<mɨŋ	4ab	gɫʊˆ·stɚ
e	se·ɨnt ˈlɚ·ənts	b	ʃɨmʌ<ŋ	b	ˈweˇ·ɨˌo<u<mɨŋ	5a	kæmᵈn
31a	ˈdʒɛˆfəsn	c	ʃɨˈmʌŋ	57a	ˈlɪ>vɨŋstn	b	kæˆ·ᵊmdən
b	ˈdʒɛ>fəsn	d	⁺ʃɨˈmʌˇŋg (?)	b	ˈlɪ>vɨ<ŋstn	6a	ətlænɨk
32a	lu<·ɨs	46a	skɑˆɨlɚ	c	lɪ>vɨ<ŋstn	b	ətˈlænɾɨk
b	lʉ·wɨs	b	ˈskeˇɨˆɫɚ,	58a	meˆnˈro<u<	7a	ˈbɚɫɪŋtn
33a	ˈhɜ>ɚkɨmɚ		ˈskeˇɨɫɚ,		cv ˌmeɘ>nˈro<·ᵁ<	b	bɘlɨŋtən
b	ˈhɜ>ɚkəmɚ		ske<ɨlɚ, skaɨɫɚˆ	b	məˆnˈroʂ·u<	8a	ouʃən
c	ˈhɜ>ɚkəˆmɚ	c	ˈskeɨɫɚ	c	---	b	ɵʐuˆʃən
34a	əˈswiˇigə	c	ˈskɑˆɨlɚ	d	məˆnˈɹo<u<	9a	mʌˇnməθ
	cv əˈsʷɪʐigəᵘ	47ab	⁺ɑmpkɨnz	e	məɘnˈro<u<	b	mʌnməθ
b	---	48a	kjʉˇʉgɨ<	f	məˆnˈɹo<u<	10a	mɪdɫsɛ>ks
c	əzˈwiˇiˌgoʂu<	b	ˌkeˇɨˈɟuʂu<gə	59a	ˈdʒɛˆnəˌsi·ᴶ	b	ˈmɪdɫˌsɛks
d	əˈswiˇigə	c	kəˈɟuʂu<gə	b	ˌdʒɛnɨˈsi·i	c	ˈmɪdɫˌsɛ>ks
	cv əˈsʷiˇigo<u<	d	keˇɨˈɟʉˇʉgə	60ab	ˈɔɚˌliˇinz	d	mɪdɫsɛks
35a	ˌɑnəˈdeɨgə	49a	cv sɪˇnɨ<kə	61a	ˈnɑˆ·ɨˌɛˇgrə	11ab	məsɚ
b	ˌɑ<·nənˈdʊˆ·gə	b	sɛnɨˇkə	b	ˌnɑˆ·ɨˈæ·grə	c	mᵊɘ·sɚ
c	ɑnədʊˆ·gə	c	ˈsɛˆnɨˇkə	62a	i·ɘɪʐ	12a	ˈsʌməsɜ>⁺
36a	mæ·dɨˇsn	d	sɛnəˆkə	b	ˈi·ɘɪʐ	b	sʌməsɨⁱ
b	mædəˆsn	50a	weˆɪʐn	cd	i·ɘɪʐ	13a	hʌn̥tɘtn
37a	əˈneˇɨˆdə	b	weˆ·ɨʐn	63a	ˈkætɘˌɔˇ·gəˆs	b	hʌn̥rɘdən
b	əneˇɨˆdə	51a	ɑnˈt̚ˌeˇɚɪʐə	b	ˈkætɘˌɔˇ·gəˆs	14a	waɾn̥
c	əˈnaʐɨdə	b	enˈt̚ɛɚɨ<ɘʐʉ<	c	kærərʊˆ·gəs	b	wɔɘɘn
38a	hɚkɨˇmɚ	c	ɑ<nˈt̚ɛɚɪʐˌoʂu	d	ˌkætɘˌrʊˆ·gəˆs,	15ab	sʌsɨks
b	hɚkɨmɚ	d	---		ˈkærɘˌɔˇ·-	16ab	mɑɘs
39a	aˆʊtˈsi·go<	e	cv ɑnˈt̚ɛɚɨ<ɵᵁ<	64a	ʃəˈtʊ·kwə	17ab	jʉ>·njən
b	ɑ<tˈsi·gə	52ab	jeˇɨ<ts	b	ʃəˈtʊˆ·kwə	18a	ɛsɘˆks
40a	ˈdɛ>ɫəwɚ	c	jeɨts	c	ʃəˈtʊˇ·ᵊkwəˆ	b	---
b	dɛɫəwɚ	53a	ˌstuˆuˈbɛˆn			cd	ɛsɨks
41	ʃɨˈnæŋgoᵁ	b	stjʉʉˈbɛˆn	**NEW JERSEY**		19a	hʌdsn
42a	koˇətlənᵈ		cv stɨˈbe·n	1a	ˌkɛɨp ˈmeɨˇ	b	hʌʔtsn
b	koˇɚˈtɫənᵈ	54a	ˈstuˇuˌbɛn	b	kɛˆɨp mɛ>·ɨˆ	20a	bɚgən
43abc	bru·m	b	ˌstu<·ˈbɛˆn	2a	kʌʐmbɚlənᵈ	b	bɵɨˆgən
44a	teˇɨˆˈloᵁgə	55a	ˈæləˌgeˇɨnɪʐ	b	kʌˆmbɚlənᵈ	21a	pəseɨk
b	teˇɨˆˈlo·ᵁgə	b	ˈæɫəˌgeˇɨnɪ>i>	3a	sɛˆɨᵊɫəm	b	pəˈseɨk
				b	sæ·ɫəm		

PENNSYLVANIA		PA		PA		PA	
1a	ˌfɪʂɫəˈdɛɫfjə	11b	ˌnɔɚˈθʌmbɚlənd	29ab	kɫɪnˈtn	47b	griˈin
b	fɫədɛɫfjə, ˌ-ˈdɛˡ-	12a	mənˈtu‹•ɚ	30ab	pɑ‹•ɾɚ	48a	wɔᵊʳʃəntən
c	ˌfɪˈɫəˈdɛɫfɫˆə	b	ˌmɑˈnˈtuʂɚ	31a	ǩæˆmrən	b	wɔrʃɫntən
d	ˌfɫɫəˈdɛɫfjə, -dɛˈɫ-	13a	kəˈɫʌmbɫˆ	b	ǩæmrən	c	wɔ•ʃɫntən
e	ˌfɪɫəˈdɛɫfɫˆə, fɪˈ-	b	kəˈɫʌmbɫˆə	32a	sɛʂnɾɚ	49a	ˌwɛstˈmɔrlənd
f	fɪɫədɛɫfjə	14a	skuˈɫkəɫ	b	sɛnˤɚ	b	wɛstmɔrˆɫlənd
g	fɪɫədɛɫfjə, ˌf-ˈd-	b	skuɫkəl	33a	blɛˆᵊr	50a	æɫəˈgɛˆnɫˆ
h	ˌfɪɫəˈdɛɫfɫˆə	15a	ˈlu•zən	b	blɛɚ	b	ˌæɫəˈgɛˇɫˇnɫˆ
2a	bʌks	b	ˌɫu•ˈzən	34a	hʌn̪tɫŋdən	c	æɫəgɛˆnɫ
b	bʌˇks	c	ˌluˈˈzən	b	hʌnt̪ɫŋdən	51a	ˈæɫəˌgɛˆnɫˆ
3a	---	16a	kaˈ•pm	c	ˈhʌntɫŋdən	b	ˌæᵊɫəˈgɛˆnɫˆ
b	məngʌmrɫˆ	b	kɚ‹rbən	35a	mɪʂflən	52a	bɪˆivɚ
c	ˌmɑnˈgʌmrɫ	c	---	b	mɪᵊflən	b	ˈbɪivɚz
4ab	dɛɫəwɚ	17a	ˌliˈ•haɫ	36a	juˈ‹•njən	53a	ɫɔˇrənts
5a-e	tʃɛstɚ	b	liˈ•haˈɫ	b	jʉˈ•njən	b	ɫɔrənts
6a	bɜɫˇks	18a	nɔˆɚθæmptən	37a	snaɫðɚr	54a	bʌˇˈtlɚ, bʌˇˈtlɚ
b	bɜɫks	b	nɔɚθæmptən	b	snaɫðɚ	b	bʷʌˈtlɚ
c	bɜᵊˤks	19a	ˌmʌnˈroˇu	38a	ˌdʒʉ•nɫˆˈæˆ•ɾə	55ab	mɚsɚ
d	---	b	ˌmʌˇnˈroʂu	b	ˌdʒu‹•njəˈæɾə	56a	vɫˈnæŋgo‹u
7ab	læŋkəstɚ	20a	paˈɫk	39a	pɛˈʂɫˆ	b	vəˈnæŋˌgɚˈu
c	læŋkəstər	b	pɑˆɫk	b	pɛʂɫˆ	57a	klaʂrɫˆən
d	læŋkəstɚ	21a	we•n	40a	kʌmbɚlənd	b	klærɫˆən
8a	jɔˆɚk	b	weʂˈɫˇn	b	kʌˇmbɚlənd	58ab	ɑ‹rmstrɔˆ•ŋ
b	jɔɚk	22a	lækəwɒʂ•nə	41a	æᵊdəmz	59ab	dʒɛfɚsn
c	jɔˆᵊrk	b	lækəwɒˆ•nə	b	æ•dəmz	60ab	ˌɪndɫˆˈænə
d	jɔˆɚk	23a	ˌsʌskwəˈhænə	42a	fræŋkɫən	61a	---
9a	d̥ɔ•fən	b	ˌsʌskwɫˈhænə	b	---	b	kæmbrɫˆə
b	dɔ:fən	24a	ˌwaʂɫˈoᵁmɫŋ	43a	fʌˆɫˈtn	62a	kɫɪˆr
c	dɔˇ•ᵊfən	b	waʂɫˈoˇumɫŋ	b	fuˈɫˈtn ɫfʌˆɫ-	b	kɫɪrfiˇ•ᵊɫd
10	jɛp̄ənən	25ab	sʌɫəvən	44ab	bɛdfɚd	63ab	ɛᵊɫk
11a	nɔ‹ɚθʌmbɚɫənᵈ	26ab	brædfɚd	45a	ˈsʌmɚsɛt	64a	mɫˈkijn
		27a	taʂɫ-oˇugə	b	ˈsʌmɚˌsɛt	b	məkijn
		b	ˌtaɫˈoˇugə	46a	feɫᵊɛᵊɫ	65a	wɔɚˇn
		28a	ˌɫaɫɫˈkɑ•mɫŋ	b	ˌfeˇɫɛᵊɫ	b	wɔɚən
		b	ˌɫaɫɫˈkɑmɫŋ	47a	gri•n	66a	krɔˆ•fɚd

PA		WVA		WVA		OHIO	
66b	---	21a	wɛˆbstɚ	42a	ˌkæ·ᵊɫˈhʉ>·n	4a	ˌkɫʌmbɨˆˈæ·nə
67ab	ɪɐɟˆ	b	wɛbstɚ	b	ˌkæɫˈhʉ>·n	b	kəˌɫʌmbɨˆˈænə
WEST VIRGINIA		22a	po·ᵁkəˈhʌnɾəs	43ab	dʒæksn	5a	dʒɛꟳəsn
<u>1</u>	dʒɜfəsn	b	ˌpo<ukɨˆˈhʌ<nɾəs	44a	wəɟ	bc	dʒɛfəsn
2	bɐklɨˇ	23a	gri·nbra>ɛɚ	b	wə·ɟ	6a	ˈbɛɫmənt
3	mɔˆəgən	b	gri·nbrɑɚ	45a	wuᵊd	b	bɛɫmənt
4ab	hæmpʃɚ	24ab	mʌ<nˈro·ᵁ	b	wu<əd	7a	mənˈrŏʂŭ
5	mɪnɐɫ	25ab	sʌ<məz	46a	pɫɛznts	b	mənˈrɐu
6a	græ·ᵊˆnt	26a	rɔˇ·lɨˆ	b	pɫɛ>znts	8a	wɔ·ʃəntən
b	grænt	b	rɔ·lɨ	47ab	rɪtʃɨˆ	b	wɔʃɨ̧ntən
7a	---	27a	ˌfeˇɨˈɛᵊɟ	48a	dɑdrɨdʒ	c	wɔᵊʃɨŋtən
b	pɛndɫtən	b	ˈfɛˆɨɟ	bc	---	d	ˈwɑ>ʃɪŋtən
8a	pɛnɫtən	28ab	bʉ>·n	d	dɑdrɨdʒ	<u>e</u>	wɔˇ·ʃɨŋtən
b	pɛndɫtən	29a	mᵊ>ɚsɚ	49a	ɟa>·ɛ>lɚ	9a	æθənz
9ab	prɛstən	b	mᵊˇɚsɚ	b	ɟaɨˇɫɚ	b	---
10a	ˌmɑngəˈheɨɫɨˆ	30a	ˈwa>ɛoᵁnɨŋ (✓)	50a	hwɛtsɫ	c	æθənz
b	mɑ>ngəˈheˇɨɫ	b	wa>·ɛˈo·ᵁmɪŋ	b	wɛtsɫ	d	---
c	mɑnɑngeˇɨɫjə	31a	məkdaˆ·ʉᵊɫ	51a	mɑ>ɚʃɫ	10a	mɛ·gz
11a	mæ>rɨˆən	b	mækdæˇʉᵊɫ	b	mɔrʃɫ	b	mæˆgz *mɛgz
<u>b</u>	mɛrɨˆən	32a	mɪngo·ᵁ	52a	əha·ɨə	11a	gæˆɫjɨˆ
12a	hɛɚsn	b	ˈmɪŋˌgoᵁ	b	ɐ>uˈha·ɨə	b	gæˆljəˆ
b	hɛɚˇsən	33ab	lo·ᵁgən	<u>c</u>	oˇuˈhaɨə	12ab	lɑ>rənts
13a	teˇɨɫɚ	34ab	lɪŋkən	53a	bruk	cd	---
b	tɛɨɫɚ	35a	wɛɟn	b	---	13a	ˈpɔrɾɪdʒ
14ab	bɑɚbɚ	b	weˇɟn, weˇɟˆn	<u>c</u>	bruk	b	pɔˆɨɟɨˇdʒ, -ɟ-
15ab	ɟʌkɚ	36ab	kæbɫ	54a	ˈhæ·ᵊnˌkʊk	c	---
16a	ræᵊndɑɫf	37ab	meɨsn	b	hæ·ᵊnkʊk	14	ˈtʌˆskeˌrɔ·weˆs
b	rændɑɫf	38a	pʌtnəm	**OHIO**		15a	m̃ɛsˈkɪŋg̃əm
17a	---	b	pʌ<tnəm	1a	ˌæʃtəˈbɨuɫə	b	məskɪŋgəm
b	ʌ<pʃɚ	39a	kəˈcɔːə	b	ˌæʃtəˈbɨuɫɚ	16a	g³ɚnzɨˆ
c	ˈʌ<pˌɪʃɪˆɚ	bc	kəˈnɔˇ·ə	<u>c</u>	ˌæʃtəˈbju<ɫə	b	g³ɚnzɪi
18a	ɫu<·əs	40a	kəˈnɔ·ɨˆ	2a	ɟɹʌmbəɫ	c	g₃>ɚnʂɪˆi
b	ɫʉ>·əs	b	kəˈnɔ·ɨˇ	b	ɟɹʌmbɫ	17	ˈmɔɚ̧n
19ab	brækstn	41a	kle·ɨ̄	3a	məho<unɨŋ	18	vɪnˈtn
20ab	nɪkləs	b	kɫeˇɨ	b	məˈhoˇunɨŋ		

KENTUCKY

1a kɚət̬ɚ, ra^on
b kɚ̆ət̬ɚ
2a ˈdʒɚ<ntsn
b ---
c ˈdʒɚntsn
3a ˈæ·ozlɨ
b ---
c æozlɨ
d ˈbrɛθɨt
e ˈæˇozlɨ
4a ˈlɛ^slɨ^ɨ^
b ˈlɛslə (✓)
c ˈlɛ^slɨ
5ab lɛtʃɚ
6a ˈhɑ>ɚlə^n
b ---
c ˈhɑɚlə^n
7a bɛ^·ɫ
b̲ bɛ^·ᵊɫ

DELAWARE

1a ˈnu^u ˌkæsɫ
b ˈnu˯· ˌkæ·sɫ
c̲ ˈnu<· ˌkæsɫ
2a ˌnu< ˈkæsɫ
b ˈnu^u< ˌkæ·sɫ
3a kɛnt
b kɛ^ᵊnt
c̲ ---
4 kɛnt
5a sʌ˯sɨˇks
b sʌsɨk
6ab sʌsɨks

MARYLAND

1ab sɪsɫ
2a kɛ·nt

MD

2b kɛnt
3a ˌkwiˇin ˈæ>nz
b ˌkwi·n ˈæ·ᵊnz
4a ˈkæ>ɚˌla>ɨˇn
b ˌkæ˯ɚə̆ˈla>·ɛ^n
c ˌkæ^ɚ̩ˈɫeˇɨˇn
5a tɒ^·ɫbɚt
b tɒ^·ɫbət
6a ˈdɒ^·ˌtʃɛstɚ
b ˈdɒ^ɚˌtʃɛstɚ,
ˈdɑtʃɨs-
7a ˌwɑɨˈkɑmɨko^ᵁ
b ˌwɑ>ɨˇˈkɑ>mɨˌkoˇu
c̲ ˌwɑ<ɛ^ˈkɑmɨˌkoˇu
8a wɪ>stɚ
b wᵊɚstɚ
N9 ˈsʌməsɨt
9a sʌmɚsɛt
b ˈsʌ<mɚˌsɛᵊt
10a hɚ<ɚfɚd
b hɒ^ɚfɚd
11 bɔ^·ɫˤə̆mə
12ab bɔ·ɫ†ˇəmɚ
13a bɔ:ɫtə^mə̩
b bɔ·ɫ†ˇəmə
c bɔ·ɫ†ˇəmɚ
d̲ bɔ:ɫ†ˇəmə
e̲ bɔ·ɫ†ˇɨmɔ^ə
f̲ bɔ^:ɫ†ˇəmə
14 kæ^rəɫ
15a hæ˯uə̩d
b hæ·ʉˇə̩d
16 ---
17a frɛdrɨk
b fɛdrɨk

MD

18a məˈgʌ˯mrɨ
b mənˈgʌ^mrɨ
19a ˌprɪnts
ˈdʒɔˇ·dʒɨˇz
b prɪnts dʒɔ·ᵊdʒ,
~ -ɨˇz
20a ˌænɨˈrænɫ
b ænɨrænɫ,
ˌænɨ^ˈræ̃nɫ,
-ˈrʌ^nɫ
c̲ ˌæn ˈrʌndɫ,
~ əˈrʌ̃^ndɫ
21a kɚ^:ɫvət,
kɔˇ·ɫvə̆d
b kɒ̆:lvət, kɔˇ·ɫvət
N22 ---
2N22 se·nt mɛ^rɨz
22a seɨnt mɛᵊrɨˇz
b seɨnt mɛ^ᵊrɨz,
seɨnt mɛ^ərɨz
c̲ seɨnt meᵊrɨz
23ab ---
c tʃɒ:ɫz
24 ---
25 wɒ^ᵊʃɨŋtən
26a wɒ^ɚʃɨŋtən
b ---
27ab gɛɚət

DISTRICT OF COLUMBIA

1ab̲ ---

VIRGINIA

1̲ ɒ·ɒ̆^lɨŋtən
2a fæ^·əfæ^ks
b ˈfæəˌfæ'ks
3a ɫa>udn *ɫa>·uˇdn

VA

3b ɫæ˯ʉdn
N4 prɪnᵗˢ ᵝwɪljəm
5a ˌfɔ·ˈk̆ⁱˇə
b fɔˇ·kiˇə
6a mædəsn
b mæᵊdəsn
7a ˈɉʉ˯·-ɨzə
b ˌlʉ^ʉ˯ˈi·zə,
ˈlʉˇ·ɨˇzə
8a spɚ<tsɫveɨnɟə
b spɑ˯ʼtsɫve·nɟə
c̲ spɑ˯tsɫve·ɨŋɟə
9ab̲ stæ^fəd
10a ˈk̆æ^ʳəˌla>ᵋ>n
b k̆æ^ʳəla·ᵊ<n
11a ˈhæᵊnˈoᵁvə
b ˈhæᵊnˌoᵁvə,
ˈhæ>ᵊnˈ-
N12 ˈwɛsmoˇ·lən, -mə-
12a ˈwɛsˌmo·lən
b̲ ˈwɛsˌmo^·lənᵈ
13a læŋkɨstə
b læ̃ŋkɨstə
14a nɔˇˈθʌ^mᵇələnᵈ
b nəˈθʌmələn
c nɒ<ɒ^θʌ̆mbələnᵈ,
nəˈθʌ̆mələn
N15-15a ---
b ɛsɨks
16a kɪŋ əŋ kwi˯·n
b ---
17ab kɪŋ wɪɫjəm
18 ˈmɪdɫˌsɛ^ks
19a dlɔ̆^:stə
b glɒ̲<ɒ^stə

VA

19c glɔʋ·ᶜstə
20a mæθɨˢ
b   mæθ̣ɹʉᵛẓ
N21 tʃɑ>·ǀz sɪ ᵈ‡
21a ‚tʃɑ>·ᵊɫz ˈsɪɹ‡ᵛ‡
b   tʃɑ·ɫz sɪɹ‡
22   ‚dʒiᵛⁱmz ˈsɪ↑‡ᵛ
23a ɟɔ̢·ᵊk
b   ɟɔ<ᵛɔ̢k
24   wɑ̢ᵊɹ‡k
25   ˈækəˈmæk
26a ---
bc   ˈækəˈmæk
27   ‚ækəˈmæᵊk
28ab ‚nɑ^·ˈθæᵊmptən
29   hɪnərækə
30a ‚hænəˈræ‡ᵛkə
b   ---
cd   hɛnˈre‡kə
30e-31a ---
31b tʃestəfi·ᵊɫ ᵈ
32   ‚dɪ>nˈwɪ>d‡ᵛ
33a ˈdɪᵊn‚wɪd‡
b   dɪᵊnwɪ>d‡ᵛ
34a prɪᵊnts dʒɔ̢·ᶜᵛdʒ
b   prɪ'nts dʒɔ̢·ᵛɔ^dʒ
35a ‚ɑ<ɛ>ǀ ‡ ˈhw̥e‡
     ‚ɑ‡ᵛls ‡ ~
b   ‚ɑ<ᵊᶜɫ ə ˈwe‡t
36a ‚səʊ^fˈhæmptən
b   ‚sə̢ʊθˈæᵊmptən
37   ‚næᵊ̢nts‡ˈmʌᵊn,
     ‚næn†s‡ˈmʌ^ᵊn

VA

38   nɔ<ᵛᵊ^fək
39   nɔ̣<ᵛɔ^fək
40a ‚prɪn'ts‡ᵛs ˈæ·ᵊn
b   prɪn'ts‡z æ·ᵊn
41a gʉ>·dʒlən
b   gʉ̢tʃlən
42a ˈbʌ^·k‡n‚hæᵊm
b   ˈbʌk‡n‚hæᵊm
N43 kæ̢̃mlən
43a kæ̃>mᵇə̃lən ᵈ
b   kæ̢̃mᵇələn ᵈ
44a ‚æpmˈmæᵊɾəks
b   æpəˈmærə'ks
45a prɪn'ts ˈɛ^dəd
b   prɪnts ɛᵊdəd
N46 ---
46a kǽml
b   kæmɫ
47   lu<·nnbɜ>ᵊg
48a pɪ'ts‚łveᵛ‡n‡^
b   ‚pɪ'ts‚łˈve‡nJə
49a hæǀ‡fæks
b   ˈhæᵊǀ‡ᵛˈfæ·ks,
     ˈhæl‡ᵛˈfæᵊks
50a ˈmækl‡n‚bɜ̢ᵊg
b   ˈmɛkl‡ᵛn‚bɜ·ᵊg
51a brʌ^ᵊmz‡k
b   brʌ^ᵊnzw‡k
     ˧ᴺ brʌmz‡k
52a frɛdr‡k
b   frɛdrɪk
c   frɛdr‡k
53a ʃæ·nədo·ɚ
b   ˈʃæ^nədoᵘᵊ
54a wɔ̢ɾ-ən

VA

54b wɔ̢ɾ-ən
55a ˈrɔ̢<ˈkŋ‚hæᵊm
b   rɑ̢k‡ŋhæᵊm
56a ha·‡ᵛlən ᵈ
b   ha>·ɛ>lən ᵈ
57a ᵕ̣ᵊ̢ˈgʌ<ᵊst‡^
b   əgʌᵊstə
58   griᵊ·n
N59 ‚æ^ᵊlbəˈmɑ>·ᵊɫ
59a ‚æɫbə̃ˈmɑ>ɔ<ɫ
b   ‚æɫbəˈmɑ>ɔ<ɫ
60   bæᵊθ *bæθ
61a ˈrɑ̢k‚brɪdʒ
b   ˈrɑ̢kbr‡dʒ
62a nɛ^·ᵊɫsn, nɛ^·ᵊsn
b   nɛᵊlsn
63a krɛ̢‡g
b   ---
64a bɛᵊdfət
b   bɛ·ᵊdfəd
65ab rɔ̢unɔ̢uk
c   ˈrou‚nouk, ˈroᵘᵊ-
66a fræŋkl‡ᵛn
b   frã̃ŋkl‡ᵛn
67a ‚pJʉᵊʔᵊ̢ǀæ̢^ᵊsk̢‡ᵛ‡ ˈhJǀ
b   ‚pJʉ>·ᵊǀæᵊsk‡ᵛ‡^
68a flo·‡ᵛd
b   flɔ̢ǀ^·‡ɾd
69a hɪnr‡ᵛ
b   hɪnr‡
70a blæ·ᵊnd
b   bɫæ·ᵊn ᵈ
71a grɛ‡^sn
b   grɛ>‡sn
72ab ‚bɜkˈhæᵊnən

VA

73   rʌᵊsɫ
74a wɔ^ʃ‡ntən
b   wɔ̢ᵊʃ‡ŋtən
75a ɫɪ^J
b   ɫɪ^iᵛ

NORTH CAROLINA

1   ˈkᵊɚ·‡^‚tʌk
2a   ˈkɵ‡tʌ^k
b   ˈkɵ̢‡‡tʌ^·k
3a   kǽ̢mən ᵈ
b   kǽ̢^ᵊmdən
4ab geᵛ‡ts
5a   pæ‡spətæ‡ᵛŋk (√)
b   pɵ̢^kwɪmənts
6   tʃoᵘǀɑ̢ᵊn
7a   ‚bɜ̢ᵊ‡tiᵛⁱ
b   ‚bɜ̢ᵊ†‡ti̢·ⁱ
N8   mɑ>·ᵊ†n
8a   mɑ̢ɾə†n
b   mɔ̢ɾ̢ə'†n
9ab tɛ̢ɾ̃ɫ
10a ---
b   dæ̢·ɚ
c   dæ·ɚ̣
11a hɑ^‡d
b   hɑ·‡d
12a ˈbʉ̢ᵛ·ᵊ>fəd
     *bu<·fə̢t
b   bɔ̢ufə̢t
13a pʰæ̢ᵊm'pl‡kə̢ᵊu^
b   ˈpæᵊmpl‡kɵ<·u^
N14 kre‡ʋm̨
14a krɛ‡ʋm̨
b   krɛ̢ʋn
c   krɛ̢‡vən

NC		NC		NC		NC	
15a	pʰɪˆʼt	29b	rɑ˛bəsn	48	deˇ‡v‡sn	67b	mɪtʃɫ
b	---	30a	ˌnɔ·θ·ʰæˑəmptən	49	ro·ˈæ·ən	68a	mæ˃kˈdæ·ɵˑˑəɫ
16a	griˑ˛ⁱn	b	ˌnɔ<ˇ·θˈæˑəmptən	50a	roˇᵁˈæ·ə˃n	b	ˌmæ˃kˈdæ·ɵˇˑəɫ
b	gri˛ĩn	31a	ˈhæɫ‡ˌfæks	b	ˌro<ᵁˈæən	69ab	po·ᵁk
17a	wɛˆ‡n	b	hæ˃ɫəfæks, hæ˃ᵊ-	51ab	mənˈgʌ˛mr‡	70a	mæ·əd‡sn
b	wɛ·‡n	32a	ˈɛˆ·dʒ¡koᵁm	N52	æn†sn	b	mæd‡sn
18a	ꭹⁱ˛ɵpl‡n	b	ˈɛdʒ¡ko<um	52a	æntsn	71a	bʌ˛ŋkəm
b	ˈdɵᴴ˛pl‡ˇn (√)	33a	wɪ·əɫ†sn	b	æᵊn†sn	b	bʌ˃ŋkəm
19a	dʒo<uˆnz	b	wɪ˛·əɫsn, wɪ˛əɫsn	53a	ɟɵ·njən	c	bʌ˃ŋkəm
b	dʒɵ˃u˛nz	34a	dʒɵᵊnʼ†sn	b	ɟɵ<ᴴˆnjən	72a	kaˆun'ts‡veˇ‡n‡ˆ
20a	kɑɵtr‡ˇt	b	dʒɑ˛ᵊn'tsn	54a	kəbæˆ·ərəs	b	ˈtræn'tsɫ¡veˇ‡njə
b	kɑ˛ɵ'tɹ‡t	35a	hɑ˃ᵊn‡ˇt	b	---	73a	swɛ˛‡n
c	ˈkɵ˛·ɵtɹ‡ʼt	b	hɑˆən‡ˇt	55	ˈmæklən¡bɵg	b	sʷeᵂ‡n
21a	ɵ˛nzæ̆loᵁ	N36	skɵ˛tlən	56a	ˈmɛklən¡bɵ˛ᵊg,	74ab	meˇ‡kən
b	ɵ˛ᵊnzleˇu˛	36a	skɑˆtlən		ˈmæk-	75a	ˈtʃɛ˛rə¡ki˛ᴶ
22a	pɛᵊndə	b	skɑˆʼtlən	b	mɛkl‡nbɵ·ᵊg	b	¡tʃɛrəˈkiˇᴶ
b	pɛᵊndə̣	37ab	wɑ˛r‡ˇn	57a	sto·ᵁks	**SOUTH CAROLINA**	
23a	¡ŋⁱ˛ɵ¡hænˈoˇuvə˃	N38	fræŋkl‡ˇn	b	sto<uks	1a	¡o<ᵁˈri·
b	¡ŋⁱɵ¡hæˈnoᵁvə	38a	---	58a	sɵ·‡	b	oˇᵁᵁr‡
c	¡nɵ<ᴴˈhæn¡oᵁvə	b	fræŋkl‡ˇn	b	sɵ·ʳ‡	2a	mɛr‡ˆən
d	---	39a	grænv‡ɫ	59	ɟæᵊdk‡n	b	mæᵊr‡ˆən
N24-24a	brʌmz‡k	b	ˈgræˆᵊnv‡ɫ	60	fə̣sa˃·‡ˇθ	3a	flɔ˛ren†s
b	brʌnzw‡k	40a	weˇ‡k	61a	ɑˆ·ᵊdɫ	b	fɫ̣ɵ·rnts
N25	sæᵊmpsn	b	we‡k cv wɛ˛k	b	ɑ˛ɛ˃ədɫ		cv fɫ̣ɵ·nts
25a	sæ̆˛mpsn	41	---	62a	æ‡ˇʃ	c	fɫ̣ɵ·rəˆnts
b	sæmpsn	42a	tʃæᵊɾəm	b	æᵊ˛ʃ	4a	kʼɹæ·r‡<ndə˃n
26a	kʌˆmələnᵈ	b	tʃæ‡ɵm	63a	wɪᵊɫʼks	bc	kʼɹæ·r‡ndn
b	kʌ˃·ᵊmbə̣lənᵈ	43a	ɵ˛ʳ‡ˇndʒ	b	wɪ·əɫks	5a	ˈwɪˆɭjmz¡bɵ˛·‡ˇ
c	kʌmbələnᵈ	b	ɑ˛ʳ‡ˇndʒ	64a	kəˈtoˇ·bə	b	ˈwɪ˛ɭjəˆmz¡bɵ˃ᵊg
27a	ble·dn	44	kæzwəɫ	b	kətɵ˛ᵊbə	c	ˈwɪ˛ɭjəmz¡bɵ˃ˆᵊg
b	ble·‡dn	45	rɵ˛k‡ˇnhæᵊm	65a	¡kɑ˛ɵɫˈwɛ·əɫ	d	ˈwɪˆ‡ɭjɵ̆ˆmz¡bɵ˛·ᵊg
28a	kəˈɫʌmbəs	46a	gɪɫfə̣d	b	¡kɵ<ɫˈweᵊɫ	N6	ˈdʒɔ<·ədʒ¡†ʼɑˆ·un
b	kəɫʌˆᵊmbəs	b	gɪᵊɫfə̣d	66a	kɫiˇ·vlən	6a	dʒɵ·dʒ†a<·ᵁ̃n,
c	kəˈlʌˆmbəs	c	gɪᵊɫfə˃d	b	kɫijvlənᵈ		ˈdʒɵ<rdʒ†a<·ᵁ̃˛n
29a	rɵb‡sn	47	ræᵊndɑ˛ᵊɫf	67a	mɪtʃəɫ		

SC

6b ˈdʒɔˆ‡dʒˌtɑ·on
 cv ˈdʒɔˆ·‡dʒ-
 *ˈdʒɔ‹·ədʒˌtˈɑ·un
 c̲ ˈdʒɔˆ‡dʒˌtɑ·on
N7-7a ˈdʒɔ‹·ədʒˌtˈɑ·un
 b ˈdʒɔ‹·ədʒˌtˈɑˆ·un
 c̲ ˈdʒɔ‹·ᵊdʒˌtˈɑ·un
 d̲ dʒɔ‹ᵊdʒtɑ·un
8abc bȝ‡klǂ‹
9a ˈbȝ‡klǂ‹
 b ˈbȝˈ‡klǂ‹
 c̲ ˈbȝ‡klǂ‹
 d̲ bȝ‡klǂ‹
10a ˈtʃɤ·ᵊlstn
 b̲ ˈtʃɑ‹·əlstn
 c̲ tʃɑ·əlstn
N11 tʃɑ·ᵊlztən
11a tʃɤ·ᵊlstn
 *ˈtʃɑ›·ᵊlztən,
 tʃɑ·l-
 b tʃɑ›·ᵊlstn
 c tʃˈɑ·ᵊlstn
 d ˈtʃɤ·ᵊlstn
 e cv ˈtʃˈɤ·ᵊlstn
 f tʃˈɤ·ᵊlstn
 g tʃˈɤ·ᵊlstn,
 tʃɤ·ᵊl-
2N11 ˈtʃɤ·ᵊlstn
 11h̲ tʃɤ·ᵊlstn,
 tʃˈɤ·l-
 i̲ tʃɑ·ᵊlz̥tən
 j̲ tʃˈɤ·ᵊlstn
12a ˈdɔ‹·ᵊtʃ̣ɪˆstə
 b ˌdɔˆ·ˈtʃɛstə
13 tʃɑ›·əlstn

SC

14a kʊȝⱡǂtən
 b kˈɑleˈtˈn
15a ˈbæ·ᵊmˌbȝ‹·ᵊg
 cv ˈbæᵊmˌbȝ‹·ᵊg
 ⊥ˈbʌ‹ᵊmˌbʌ‹g⊥
 b ˈbæ·ᵊmˌbȝ‹·ᵊg
 c ˈbæ·ᵊmˌbȝ‹᷈g
N16 ˈæⱡ‡ndeˈl
16 ˈæⱡ‡‹nˌdeˈl,
 -ˌdeˈᵊⱡ, ˈæ·lǂn-
17a ˈhæᵊmptˈn, -ⱡn
 b ˈhæᵊmptəˆn
 c ˈhæᵊmptˈn
 d ˈhæᵊmptˈn ⱡ
N18 bɟy›·fəˇⱡ
18a ˈbɟy›·fə‹ⱡ, -fᷔ‹ⱡ
 b ˈbɟy›·fᷔˇⱡ
 c̲ bɟy›·fəˇⱡ *ˈ-fəⱡ,
 bɟy‹·fᷔⱡ
N19 ---
19a ˈbɟy›·fəˇⱡ
 b bᵀᵾᵾˆfəˆⱡ
 c ˈbɟy›·fə›ⱡ *-fəˇⱡ
 d̲ ˈbɟᵾ·fəˆⱡ
20a ˈmɤ·ᷔlbrə
 b ˈmɤ·ᷔlbʌrə
 c ˈmɤ·ᷔlˌbɣˇrə
 d̲ ˈmɤ‹·ᷔˌbɣˇrə
21a ˈtʃɛstəˌfi·ᵊⱡᵈ
 b tʃɛstəfi·ᵊⱡᵈ
N22 ---
22a ˈkˈȝ›·‡ˌʃɔˇ·ᵊ
 b ˈkᷔ‹ʃɔ·
 c̲ ˈkˈȝ›‡ʃ·ᵊ
23a ˈdɑ›·ᵊⱡǂnˈtˈn̥

SC

23b ˈdɑ›·ᷔⱡ‡nˈtˈn
 c ˈdɑ›·ᵊlⱡntˈn
 d ˈdɑ›·ᵊlǂnˈtˈn
 e̲ ---
N24 sʌˆᵊmptə
24a sʌmptə
 bc sʌˆᵊmptə
 d̲ sɣˇᵊmptə
25a ˈrɪtʃlən
 b rɪˆtʃləˈn
 c̲ rɪˆtʃləˆn
26a ˈkælˌhᵾ›n
 b̲ ˈkæᵊlˌhᵾ›·n
27a ɑ›ʳ‡ndʒbȝ›᷈g,
 ˈɑ‹·ɾ‡‹ndʒbȝ›᷈g
 cv ˈɑr‡ndʒˌb᷈g
 b ˈɤr‡ndʒˌbȝ‹·əg
28a ˈbɑ›·ənⱡ
 b ˈbɤ‹·ənwⱡ
 c bɤ‹·ənwⱡ
 d ˈbɤ‹·ᵊnwⱡ
29abc eˆ·kǂ‹n
30a ɛdʒfijᷔⱡ
 b ˈɛˆdʒˌfi·ᵊⱡ
 c̲ ˈɛˆdʒfi·ᵊⱡ
 -ˌfi·ⱼⱡ
31a ˈlɛ‹ᵊksntn
 b ˈlɛˆksntˈn
32a ˈfæˆ·əfi·ⱼl
 b ---
 c ˈfæˆ·ᷔˌfi·l
 d ˈfɛ·əˌfi·ᵊⱡ
33a tʃɛˆᵊstə, tʃɛˆ·ᵊ-
 b tʃˈɛˆ·ᵊstə‹
34a læˆɛŋkǂ‹stə‹,

SC

(34a) -‡stə
 b ˈlæˆɛŋkǂ‹stə‹,
 -ə›
 c læˆɛnkǂ‹stə
35a ʃɔˆ·ɔk
 b ʃɔˆ·ᷔk
 c ʃɔ·ək
36a ˈspɤˈ·ə’tnˌbᷔˆ·g
 cv ˈspɤ›·ə’tnˌbᷔ›g
 b ˈspɤ·ᷔ‹’tnˌbᷔˆ·g
 cv ˈspɤ·ᷔ‹’tnbᷔˇg,
 ˈspɤ·ᷔ‹’tnˌbᷔˆ·g
 c ˈspɤ·ᵊ’tnbȝˆ·g
 cv ˈspɤˈ·ᷔ‹’tnˌbᷔ᷈g
 d̲ ˈspɤ·ᵊ’tnˌbə›·g
 ˈspɤ·’tnˌbə›·ᵊg
 -bȝˆ·g
37 ˈJᵾ·ŋɟəˆn, Jᵾᴴˆn-
38a ˈnɟᵾˌwᵢbɛˈ·ʳ‡‹
N38 ˈnᴶᵾ‹·wᵢbɛˈ·rǂ‹
38b ˈnᴶᵾ‹·w̆ᵢbɛˈ·ř‡‹,
 ˈnɟᵾ·wᵢbɛˈ·ř‡‹
 c̲ ˈnɟᵾ‹·ʷᵢbɛ›·rǂ‹,
 ˈnɟᵾ·bɛ·rǂ‹
 d̲ ˈnɟᵾ·wᵢbɛ·ř‡‹
 *-r-, -bɛ›·-
39a lɤ·rnts
 b̲ ˈlɤ·rnts
40a ˈæˆbvⱡ,
 ˈæˆb‡‹ᵥvɪˆ·ⱡ,
 ˈæˆɛbvɣⱡ
 b ˈæˆb‡ˇvⱡ,
 ˈæˆbvɣ ⱡ, -vⱡ +,
 ˈæˇbəvⱡ,
 ˈæˆbᷔvⱡ +

SC		GA		GA		GA	
41a	æ°ndəsn	(4a)	cv -təʃ	18b	ɨ'mænɹəɬ	37a	dɨʂ 'ḱæ·ᵋb
b	'ɛⱽndəsn	b	'mæⱽk̆ɨnˌtʌⱽ°ʃ	19a	mɣⱽnt'gɣⱽmrɨʂ	b	'di·ɹ ˌk'æ°b
42a	'grii^nvɬ	c	'mæⱽkɨ<ntə^ʃ		**məⱽnt'gɣⱽ°mrɨʂ	c	di· kæ^·°b
N42	'griĩ^ⁿvɣɬ, -vɣ	5abc	glɪ^°n	b	mnt'gɣⱽ°mrɨʂ	2N37	fʌ<ḷtn
	cv grii^n-	d	glɪ^n	20a	'tɛ^lˌfɛ·ɚ	37d	dɨ 'ḱæ·b
	*'gɹ̀i·ɹnvɬ	e	glɪ^°n	b	'tɛ^lˌfæ^·ɚ	e	dɨ 'kæ^·°b
42b	gɹ̀i·ɹnvɬ	6a	'cǽ°mdɨ<n	21a	lɑ>rɨnts	f	---
cd	gri·i^nvɬ	b	'k̆æ·°mdɨ<n	b	lɑrɨnts	g	dɨ 'ḱæ^·°b
e	'grí·nvɯ	7	tʃɑ>·ət'n	22a	p'i·tʃ, ha^ustn	h	fu<ɬtn
43a	cv p'ɪ^kɨ<nz	8a	we^ɨn	b	'haʂ·əstn	i	---
b	p'ɪ^kɪ>nz,	b	we^·ɨn	23a	bɪ^°b	38	hɒⱽ·ɬ
	p'ɪḵɪ>nz̩	9a	t'æ^'tnɬ	bc	bɪb	39	'lʌʂmpkɨ<n
	cv p'i·ḵɪ>nz	b	t'æ'tnɬ	de	bɪ^°b	40	ˌtʃɛrɨ'ki·
c	'p'ɪx̣ɪ^nz,	10a	ɛvɨnz	f	bɪ·°b	41	ǵɪlə̆mɚ, ǵɪlmɚ
	p'ɪ^ḵɪⱽnz̩	b	'ɪ^vɨ<nz	N24	---	42a	'fæ·ɛnɨ<n
44a	ˌo<·u<'koʂ·u<nɨʂ	N11	kæ̃ⁿlə, kæ̃lə	24a	bɔ^:ɬdɨⱽn	b	'fæ·°nɨ<n
b	'o·u<ˌko<·u<ni>iʂ	12a	'bu<ɬə^k	b	---	43	ɹɥ>ʷnɹən
GEORGIA		b	'bʌ^lə^k	N25	'hæŋˌkɚ<k	44a	're^·ɨbə^n
N1	tʃætəm	13a	'ɛfɨŋ,hæ>·°m	26	dʒæspə	b	're>·ɨbə^n
1a	tʃ'æⱽ°tə^m	b	'ɛ^°fn,hæ°m,	27	gri·n	c	're^·ɨbən, -bə̆n
b	tʃæt̪ə^m		'ɛ^fɨ<ŋ,æ^·°m,	28	wɪ>ɬks	d	---
c	---		-,h-	29ab	lɪ^ŋkə^n	e	reɨbən
d	tʃ'ætə>m	14a	skɹ̀ɪvɯ	30a	ɛ^°ɬbə^t *-bəʂt	**FLORIDA**	
e	tʃæⱽt̪ə^m	b	skɹ̀ɪ^və^n	b	ɛ^°lbət *'-ɬbə^t	1	'na^soᵁ
f	tʃæ̥ʂ°təm	c	skɹ̀ɪvɯ, -və^n,	c	ɛlbət	2a	dɥ'vɔ·ᶿɬ
g	tʃæt̪ə^m		-ɨ<vɯ	31	hɑ>ət	b	---
h	tʃæt̪əʂm	15a	bɜ·ᶿ<k	32	fræ^°ŋklɨn	c	dɥ·'vɔ·°l
N2	---	b	bɜ>ɨⱽk	33a	mædɨsn	3a	'se^nt ˌdʒɔ·ᶿn
2a	'bɹɑ<·-ə̆n	16a	rɪ^tʃmn, -mə^n	b	'mædəsn	b	snt 'dʒɔ·°nz
	cv 'bɹɑ·ɹə^n	b	rɪ^tʃmn	N34	k'lɒ<·ək	4	võ'lɥ̈ⱽʃə
b	'bɹɑʂ·-ən	c	rɪtʃmən	34a	klɑ:k	5a	ə'lɒtʃə̪ˌwe^·,
3a	ɹibətɨ	d	rɪ^tʃmn	b	klɒ·ək		ə'lɒtʃə-
b	lɪ^bətɨʂ	N17	dʒɛfə^sn	N35	wɒ^oɬtə^n, wɒ^ɔl-	b	ə'lɒtʃɥ̈ˌwe^·
N4	'ma>k̆ɨntə̪ʃ	17	---	N36	'rɒkˌdeɨɬ		
4a	'mæⱽkɨ<ntəⱽʃ	18a	ɨ'mæ^nɹə	N37	---		

COMMENTARY

The following abbreviations are used in the commentary: b.--born (in); r.--resided (in); F--father; M--mother; P--parents; PGF, etc.--paternal grandfather, etc.

County is to be understood following the place names.

NEW YORK

5d   r. *Bronx* [brɑˆnks] since Oct. 1, 1939

e   r. *Nassau* [næsɔː] since 1927

7g   r. *Kings* [kʰɪnz] since 1905

i   r. *Westchester* [ˈwɛstʃɛstə] since 1916

11   r. *Westchester* [wɛsttʃɛstɚ] since 1921

17a   [ˈr-]: natural

26b   *Warren* cv [wɒˌɚ‡<n]

45d   [ᵗ]: doubtful

46b   r. *Steuben* [ˌstuˇuˈbɛ·n, ˌstuˏᵁ<ˈbɛn cv ˌstuˇᵁᴴbɛᵊn]

51d   *Livingston* cv [ˈlɪɪ>v‡<ŋstn]

58b   b. *Kent* [kˇɛˆnt] (Del)

PENNSYLVANIA

6c   *Berks*: "Dutch" form is [bɑɾ‡ks]

64a   *Potter* [pɑɾɚ]

WEST VIRGINIA

30a   [-n-]: *sic*

OHIO

10b   *: "properly" (*: wife)

OHIO

13b   r. *Geauga* [dʒiˈɒˆgə] 1906–1916

KENTUCKY

2c   M b. *Elliott* [ɛl‡t]

4b   [-ə]: *sic*

7b   formerly *Josh Bell* [ˈdʒɒ‡ʃ ˌbɛˆ·ᵊɫ]

MARYLAND

12a   *Cecil* [sɪsɫ], *Anne Arundel* [ˌæn əˈrʌndɫ], *Calvert* [kælvɚt]

13a   *Cecil* [sɪsɫ], *Anne Arundel* [ˌæn əˈrænɫ], *Calvert* [kæ·ᵊɫvɚt] (St., etc.) **Anne Arundel* [ˌænɫˈrænɫ], *Calvert* [kæᵊɫvɚt]

c   *Cecil* [si·sɫ], *Anne Arundel* [ˌæn əˈrʌndɫ], *Calvert* [kælvɚt] (St.)

d   *Cecil* [sɛsɫ], *Calvert* [kælvɚt] (St. or County), [kɔ·ɫvɚt] (School)

20b   *Cecil* [sɪsɫ], *Calvert* [kɔˇ·ᵊɫvɚt]

c   *Calvert* [kɔˇɫvɚt], *Calvert* [kˇæ·ɫvɚt] (St.)

21a   *Anne Arundel* [ˌæn ‡ˈrʌˌ̃nɫ]

b   *Cecil* [sɪsɫ], *Anne Arundel* [æn ‡rʌndɫ], (correct), [æn ‡rænɫ] (natural)

MD

22b   *Calvert* [kæᵊɫvɚt]

VIRGINIA

7b   [ˈlᴴ·ˇ‡ˇzə]: old-fashioned

11b   [ˈ-ˈ-]: at times

14c   [nəˈθʌmələn]: quick pron.

23a   M b. *Mathews* [mæ·θ‡z]

26a   *Northampton* [nɔˇ·θæmptən]

58   * r. *Albemarle* [æˆlᵇm̃ɑ>·ᵊɫ]

65c   [ˈroᵁə-]: affected

NORTH CAROLINA

5a   [-p-]: *sic*

N14   b. *Carteret* [ˈkɑ<ᵊtˌræt]

18b   [dᴴᴴˡ-]: *sic*

35a   b. *Cumberland* [kʌˆmbələnᵈ]

40b   cv: natural

SOUTH CAROLINA

3b   formerly part of *Darlington* [ˈdɚ·əl‡<ntˈn cv dɒlntˈn]

6a   [ˈdʒɚ<rdʒ-]: modern pron.

8a   *Horry* cv [ˈhɚ·ˌri·] (*sic*)

N16   r. *Barnwell* [ˈbɚ<·ᵊnwl] after c. 1936

16   F's family from *Bamberg* [ˈbæ·mˌbɚˆ·ᵊg, -ˌbɜ>‡g]; *Barnwell* cv [ˈbɑ̃·ˣnw‡l, ˈbɚ<ənwɔ̃l]

24d   *Hampton* cv [ˈhæᵊmptəˆn]

SC

27a MGP from *Lexington*
['lɛksɨŋˌtʻɨˇn, -ɨ̆ŋt̠ɨn]

29a M from Saluda
c̲v̲ [sə'lʉ·də]

b **Edgefield*
c̲v̲ ['ɛ^ᵊdʒˌfi·ᵊl]

40a ['æ^bɨ˷ˌvɪ^ɫ]: "correct"

43c *Calhoun* c̲v̲ [kʻəɫ'hu˷u<n]

GEORGIA

1d b. *Beaufort* [bɹʉ<fə^t] (SC)

GA

N2 * worked in *Evans* ['ɪvɨ<nz]

6a M's family from *McIntosh*
['mæˇkɨ<ntʌ̆<ʃ]

7 b. Pierce c̲v̲ [pɛ^·əs]

N11 formerly part of *Evans*
[ɪvɨ<nz]

12a r. *Chatham* ['tʃʻætə^m]
since 1935

18a M b. Treutlen [tɹʉ·tlən];

GA

(18a) F b. Clay [kleᶧ] (Fla)

b M b. Glascock
[glæᵋskɚ<k]

21b r. *Baldwin* ['bɔˇɔɫɨ<n]
since 1901

22b r. *Bibb* [bɪ^ᵊb]

38 P b. Banks [bæ̃·ŋks]

FLORIDA

5a b. Bradford [bræᵋdvə^d]

3. LOCALITY; POST OFFICE; TOWNSHIP

LANE 2

List 3 gives the pronunciations of those place names on List 1 which the field workers recorded in phonetics, except county names, which are entered on List 2. The arrangement of the entries is the same as for List 1: (1) locality; (2) post office; (3) township.

The commentary includes other place names relevant to the vitae of informants or their families, where recorded by the field worker. It also includes incidental pronunciations of other place names on List 1. (Any such county names are entered in the commentary to List 2.) All place names from List 1 entered in the commentary are in italics.

Stresses are marked as indicated by the field workers.

ONTARIO

1a mɑ<ɚ'tntɑ>un

b 'kɔ^ɚnˌwɒ^·ɫ

2a 'fæ^ɚˌfi·ɫd 'iˇis;
'ɫɨzbəθˌtɑun

b spe^ɨsɚ^z hɪɫ,
əutlɛ^t, 'wɒ̜ɚbɚtə^n;
'lænzˌde·un c̲v̲ -deˇun,
-təŭn, 'læ̃ⁿzde·un

3̲ 'kɪ^ŋᵏstn

4a ˌwuɫf 'ɑ^ɨɫə^nd

b ˌwʌ<ɫf 'eˇɨɫə^n, ~ -nᵗ

ONT

5 'æmɚst ˌe·ɨlə^n,
bæθ; 'ɜ^ɚnɨsˌtɑ·un

6̲ tə'rɑ>nə,
tʻə'rɑ>nt̬o<ᵘ<,
tə'rɑ̃·ntʻo<u,
tʻɚ'rɑ̃·nəˇ

7 seˇᶧnt 'kæ^θrɨˇn

8a ˌɹe·ɨlɪ>iz 'bɹɪ^dʒ;
wɛlə^n +, -ɫ-;
'wĩˇĩ^n̂ˌfɫ̥iˇ·i't
c̲v̲ 'wẽˇᶧŋˌfɫ̥iˇit

ONT

8b 'kweˇɨkɚ ˌɹeᵘ<d;
wɛ>lə^n c̲v̲ wɛ-;
'θɔ̜ɚɫ +

c səŭθ we·ɨ<nfɫ̥iˇit;
'we^ɨnˌ- c̲v̲ 'weˇɨn-,
-n̂ˌfɫ̥-

d ˌpo·ət 'ko<u<ɫbɚn;
hʌ<mbɚstn

9̲ 'rɪ>vɚˌseɨd; gɔ^ɫt;
ˌnɔ̜^ɚθ də^m'friˇiz

ONT

10   'ɛ^kŏ<ŭ< ₁pɟeˇ‡s;
     'bra^nfɚ^d, 'bræ^n-

NEW YORK

1   'ɔᵊr‡^ɛnt; sauθʰoṣułd

2a   iɟst hæmptən

b   ₁sægə'pɑ^nək;
     sɛṣu'θæmptən

c   dʒɔ·dʒ‡ˇkə,
     brɪdʒ'ʰæm'ᵖm;
     iɟst 'hæm'ᵖm

3a   'bruk₁heˇ‡vən vɪł‡dʒ;
     ₁b-'-

b   hʌn̥t‡ŋtən

c   kɔɚəm; brukheˇ‡vən

d   fɔ·ᵊt səlo·ŋgə;
     'nɔ·ᵊθ₁pɔ·ᵊt;
     hʌ<n̥t‡ŋtən

4a   oṣułd 'bruk₁v‡ł;
     ₁głɛ>n 'hɛ>d;
     ɔ‡^stə beˇ‡

b   fɟi·pɔ·ᵊt; hɛmpst‡ˇd

c   ₁i·st 'mɛdoṣu;
     hɛmpstɛd

5a   'flæṣt₁læ^·ᵊnᵈz;
     bruklən

b   ---

c   'oṣu₁zoṣun 'pɑ:ᵊk

def ---

g   'fłæt₁buʃ; bruklən

h   bruklən ha‡ts

i   fłʌʃ‡ŋ

6a   'ɟɐ>·gə₁nʌ<t,
     æ·nədɛ^‡ł;
     stæṣ'tn ɑ^‡łənd

b   tʰɑ·tnvɪᵊł;

(6b) stætn a‡łənᵈ

7a   nŭ< ɟɔ·ᵊk

b   nu· ɟɔ:ᵊk

c   nu<· ɟɔ·ək

d   nu<·· ɟɔ:ᵊk

e   nu<· ɟɔ·ək

f   nu<·· ɟɔˇ·k

g   nu<·· ɟɔ:ᵊk

hi   nu<·· ɟɔ·ᵊk

j   nu< ɟɔ·ᵊk

k   nu· ɟɔ·ᵊk

l   nu<·· ɟɔ:k

m   nu<·· ɟɔ:ᵊk

8   wɛst fɑ>:mz,
     ₁wɛst'tʃɛstə; branks

9a   'tʰæᵊr‡^₁taun

b   mɪdł pætnt; bɛdfɚd;
     'nɔˇɚθ₁kæsł

c   krɔˇ·soṣuvə; bɛdfəd

10a ma^un't seˇ‡əm;
     'ɟu<·njən₁vɪᵊł;
     'gɟi·n₁vɪᵊł

b   gouʃən

11   ---

12a 'pɛks₁vɪᵊł, pɛks slɪp;
     houmz; i·st 'fɪʃ₁kɪᵊł

b   ₁nɔɚθ 'kłoˇuv;
     łə'greˇ‡ndʒ₁vɪ>ᵊł;
     ɟu<·njən veˇ‡ᵊł

c   poṣu'kɪps‡^

13a ma>unt 'mɛr‡^ən;
     'sɔ·gət‡^z

b   hɜəˇ‡‡^

14a 'gre‡əmz₁vɪᵊł;
     'nævɚ₁sɪŋk

14b ₁mɑ^nțə'sɛłə;
     tɑ^·mpsn

15a goᵁʃ‡ˇn stɟi·t;
     dʒu·‡t

b   dʒ‡>ŭ‡ˇt

16a ₁kłʌṣ'mɑ·nt;
     dʒʌṣməntaun

b   błu· stɔ·ɚz; hʌdzən;
     łɪv‡ŋstən

17a 'pi·rə₁bɚ·g

b   saṣuθ skoud‡k

18a fɪłk‡nz hɪł;
     ₁i·st 'bɚ·n

b   'æᵊłṭə₁mɑ<·nt;
     gɪłdɚłənᵈ

c   'ɔ:ᵊłbən‡

19   du<·'e‡nz₁bɚg

20a peˇ‡n groˇuv;
     'mɪdł₁bɚ·g; bru·m

b   ʃæ^ᵊɚən sprɪŋz

21   ₁sɔ·łt 'sprɪŋ₁vɪᵊł;
     foˇɚt płe·‡ˇn;
     'mɪndən

22   'głʌˇvɚ₁vɪᵊł;
     'me·‡₁fi·ᵊłd

23a kŏ'rɪ^nθ

b   'be·ɪ>kə^n ₁hɪ^ł;
     'skɑ^‡łɚvł;
     ₁nɔɚθ'ʌmbɚłn

cv   'nɔˇɚθ₁hʌˇmbɚłn

c   'skɑ·‡łɚ₁vɪ^ł;
     'sæṣ·ɚə₁tɔ^·ugə

24a ha>ɚtfɚd

b   foˇɚt ɛdwɚd

NY

25a   ˈwiˇ·vɚˌtˈɛun;

ˈdʒɑ>nzˌbɝ̥>ɚg

cv ˈdʒɑnz̥ˌbɝ>·ɚg

b   ˈwɑ>ɚnzbɝ̥>ɚg, wɔ̥ˇɚnz-,

ˈwɑ̥>·ɚnzˌ-

26a   ˌleˇɨk ˈpļɛ^znt

b   ˈspɛ^kjʊˇ·ˌleˇtɚ̧;

ˌleˇɨk ˈpļɛ^znt

c   ---

27a   ˈkrɑ̃̇·ũm ˌpɔˇɨnt,

ˈte·ɨkãndɚˌo<u<gə

b   ˈheˇg ˌro<u<d;

ˈte·ɨkãdəˈro<u<gə

c   ˈnɔ̧ɚθ

ˌtɑɨˌkandɚˈo<·u<gə

28a   ˈplæˇtsˌbɝ>ɚg

b   ˌʃeˇ·ɨ‡lzi·, ˈʃeˇ·ɨˌ-

29a   ˈbreˇ·nɚdzˌvɪ>ł;

ˈbɛłˌmɝˇʔ

b   məˈlo<ᵁn

c   məˈlɔ^·un

30a   ˈi·st ˌhɪł;

ˈsɑ·uθ ˌko<u<łˈtn

b   ˌfɔɚt ˈdʒæ^ᵋksn;

ˈhɑ>pɨˌkˈɪnˈtn

c   ˈhɑ>pɨˌkɪⁿˈtn

d   ---

e   ˈhɑpkɨˇnˈtn ˌvɪ^ləˇdʒ;

-ˌkˈɪntə^n

31a   ˈstoɕu<n ˌmɪ·łz;

ˈwɔ·ɚ̧ˌtɛ̧un

cv ˈwɔɚ̧ˌte>un,

ˈwɑ>ɚ̧ˌtæˇun;

ˈɔ^ɚˌliˇinz

b   θɹ̥iˇisɪ> cr θɚ̃ˈɹ̥iˇisə,

NY

(31b)   θɚ̃ɚiˇisə cv θɾiiˆsə,

θɹ̥iiˆsɪ̧

32a   ˌhe·ɨˈmeˇɚkɨ<t

cv ˈ-ˌmɑ̧ɚkə^t;

ˈkʌˇntstəbłˌvɨ<ł

b   ˌnʲu< ˈbɹiˇimə^n;

ˈłe^·uvł

33a   ˌo<uł ˈfoɚ^dʒ; wɛb

b   ˌo<u<łd ˈfɔ̧·ɚdʒ; wɛ^b

c   ˈbɪ>g ˌmuˇ·us,

ˈbɪˇg ˌmuˇus; wɛ^b

34a   ˈfɹ̥u̧ɕu<t ˌvælɨ<;

əˈswiˇigə

cv əˈswɪ̧ɚigə̬ᵘ

b   ---

c   pəˈlæsˌkeˇɨ; ˈɹɪˆtʃlæn

d   əˈswiˇigə

cv əˈswi̧ˇigo<u<

35a   ˈke·ɨ̧ˌkæ·t; ˈɛłˌbrɨdʒ

b   oɚən; mænłɨ^əs; pɑmpɨ^

c   ---

36a   ˌfɛnɚ ˈkɔˇɚnɚz;

ˌkæ·zɨˇˈnoᵁvɨ^

b   ˈpiɾɚˌbɚə; smɪθfi·ᵊłd

37a   łi· sɛnɾɚ

b   me·ɨˇnɚd; mɑ̧ɚ̧əsɨ^

c   ʲu<·ˈɾɨkə

38a   kəˌłʌmbɨ^ ˈsɛ̧ŋtɚ; ɪłjən;

kəˈłʌmbɨ^ *pe·ɨnz hɑłə;

moᵁhɔ^·k

b   ˌɪłɨ^ən ˈgɔˇɚdʒ; ˈɪ-;

łɪtʃfi·ᵊłd

39a   ɛłɨˇt hɪᵊł; wustɚ;

dɨ^keˇɨɚ

b   skeˇɨłɚz łeˇɨk; ɛkstɚ

NY

40a   li· hɑłə;

boᵁvaɚ̧ɨnɨ^ sɛ̧ŋtɚ

b   wɔ^·ł'tn

41   płɪmɚθ

42a   sæ^uθ hɪᵊł;

kɹeɨnz mɪᵊłz; tɹʌˇ·kstən

b   i·st hoˇ·ᵁˇmɚ;

koˇɚ'tłənᵈ

43a   hwɪtnɨz pɔ^·ɨnt;

nænɨ‡^kuk

b   sɛ̧ŋtɚłeˇɨᵊł; łeˇɨᵊł

c   ˈbɪŋəmtən

44a   ˈrɛd ˌbrʌʃ, əˈwi·ˌgoᵁ;

ˈłɑɚunzˌbɛ^ɚ̧ɨ^; nɪkłz

b   hɒ^łtsɨɚ̧ vɛłɨ^; bɑɚ'tn

45a   ˈdʌ<n ˌhɪł; ˈɛ^ł ˌme·ɨɚə;

ˈbɪ>ɪ̧ ˌfɹ̧łæts

b   ˈtɑmpkɨ<nz ˌkɔ̧ˇɚnɚ^z;

ˈhɔ̧ɚshɛ^dz; ˈkæ^tłɨ<n

c   bɪg ˌfłæts

d   ɛłˈme·ɨɚə

46a   ˈmɑ̃ntɚˌɹe·ɨ cv ˌ-tɚˈeˇɨ,

ˈbɑ̧ɚkɚ^z ˌmɪ^ł;

ˈpeˇɨnɨ‡<d ˌpoɕu<st;

ɔˇɚɨ<ndʒ

b   rɛdɨŋ

c   tˈɑunzn; wɑtkɨnz glɛ̃·ᵊn

cv wɑ·tknz glɛˇn

47a   ˌwɪ>ndɪɚ̧ ˈnɑb,

ˈku̧ɕu<pɚ ˌstɹiˇit,

ˈkupɚ ~; ˈnʲu<·ˌfi·ł

b   dɹɨɨ^dn

48a   keˇɨɨɚʊˇ>

NY		NY		NY	

NY

48b mɚɪ›d‡‹ə^n, mɚ'-;
'w‡idz₁po‹·ət;
ǩeˇ‡ʈoʂu‹

c 'bɛ^n'ʈnz ₁koʂɚnɚ^z;
eˇ‡ɚɚ

d 'viˇkʈɹɪ›i›, 'vɪ^kʈɚ‡ɕ;
ǩeˇ‡ʈoʂu‹

49a <u>cv</u> ramɘl‡s

b ---

c ₁wɒ^ʈɚ'ɫuʂu‹

d ₁sɛnɘkɘ 'fɒ·ɫz

50a sɚ›u‹d‡ˇs

b sɚ›u‹dɘ^s

51a we^st 'ɹ‡‹tʃmɚ^n;
lɚ^'voʂu‹ŋɹɚ; rɪtʃmɚ^n

b dʒ‡'niˇivɚ

c neˇ‡pɫz

d ---

<u>e</u> dʒ‡'niˇivɚ

52a ₁we^st 'ɪ'ɫɪɻ
<u>cv</u> ₁wɛ›st 'ɪtlɪɻ;
neˇ‡pɫz

b ₁pɛ^n 'ɹæ·ᵊn;
'me‡₁loʂu, 'bɛ^n'ʈn

c 'bɚɚɪŋtn, 'me‡₁ɫo·ᵁ;
₁pɛ^n 'ɹɛˇᵊn

53a 'ɟu‹wnɹɚ^n₁vɪ·ɫ;
bæ·ᵊθ +

<u>b</u> bæˇ·θ

54a 'kæn‡st‡^o‹ᵁ‹,
-tio‹ᵁ‹, -tiˇ·-o‹ᵁ‹

b 'hɔ^ɚ₁nɛɫ

55a ɹʌ‹ʃfɚ^d

b 'hɚ̥ɚdɪɻz 'koʂɚnɚ^z;
kɟuˇubɚ; 'rʌ‹ʃfɚd

NY

56a ₁ɑɚ'ǩeˇ‡d, 'ǫ̥^ɚ₁-

b 'ǫ̥ɚkeˇ·‡d

57a lɑ·‡'voʂ·ŋɹɚ

b ₁lɚ^'veˇ›u‹ŋɹɚ

<u>c</u> ₁biˇitʃɚ 'ɹoʂu‹d;
lɑ^‡mɚ; l‡'voʂŭ‹ŋɹɚ

58a 'brɚ^‡'tn; 'ɹɑ‹tʃ‡stɚ

b 'pɪ^tsfɚ̃ᵈ

c rɑtʃ‡stɚ <u>cv</u> 'rɑ‹tʃ‡‹stɚ

<u>d</u> 'buʃnɫz 'beˇ‡sn;
'pɪ^tsfɚ'd; 'fɛ̥ˇɚ‡‹ŋtn

<u>e</u> 'rɑ‹tʃ‡‹stɚ
<u>cv</u> 'rɒ‹tʃ‡stɚ

<u>f</u> ɹɑ‹tʃ‡stɚ

59a lɪ›i› 'rɒ·‡; 'bɝ̥›ɚdʒ‡n

b bɛθɚn‡^ sɛnʈɚ; ₁i·st 'b-

60a 'ɹɪ›ndɚ^n₁vɪɫ; ɹeˇ‡ts

<u>b</u> 'æɫbɪɻɚ^n, 'æɫb‡n

61a 'ɔˇɫk‡t; ₁nu‹'feˇ‡n,
'nᴶu‹·₁feˇ‡‹n
<u>cv</u> ₁-'feˇ·‡n

b 'ɒ^ɫ₁kɑt; ₁nu‹·'feˇ·‡n

62a 'kɭ̥æ^ɚnts, 'kl̥ɛˇ-

b i·ᴶdn

c 'dɛlɚwɚɚ ₁pɑ̥ɚk;
'bʌ‹fɚloɻ̥ᵁ‹

<u>d</u> 'oʂɚtʃɚ^d ₁pɑ̥·ɚk

63a wɪlɘbɪ›i›;
ɡɹ̌eˇ‡t vælɪɻ, 'ɡr̃- ₁væ·-

b 'ræ^·ᵋn₁dɔˇɫf

c 'ɛᵊɫk₁de‡ᵊɫ; sæɫɚmænkɚ,
-mæŋk‡^; 'lɪ›ɻɫ væᵊɫ‡^

<u>d</u> ₁sæ^ɫɚ'mæ̃^ᵑkɚ

64a 'wɛɚst₁fi·ɫd, 'wɛ^s₁fi·ɫ

b 'wɛ^s?₁fiˇ·ɫᵈ

NY

64<u>c</u> wɛ^stfi·ɫd

NEW JERSEY

1a g̥oʂuʃɚn

b biˇizɫ‡ɕz pɔ^‡‹nt;
mo̥‹ɚmo^ɚɚ; ʌpɚ

2a 'rɑ›bnz₁tɑ›un;
₁pɔ^t 'nɑ›rɘs; kɚmɚʃɫ

b 'mo̥ɕrɘs₁tæ·u̥^n

3a hɑ›ɚmɚn‡‡^; sɛ^‡ᵊɫɚm;
kwɪnn̥n̥

b hænkɑks brɪdʒ;
lo‹uɚ æᵊɫɚwɛ‡ krɪk

4a ₁ɒ^·ɫmɚ'nɛsɚn; su‹·ɚɫ;
dɛtfɚd

b ₁o‹uk 'gro‹uv,
₁r‡ɕ'pɑ·pɚ; swiᵈzɚbɚ̃;
ɫo‹ugɚ^n

5a 'bru‹klɚn; 'sɪkɫɚ₁vɪᵊɫ;
wɪnzɫɚuᵁ^

b siˇidɚ bruʂk;
'wɪᵊnz₁ɫoʂu

6a pɚɚ't r‡^'pʰʌ‹bɫ‡k

b 'stiᵊɫmɚn₁vɪᵊɫ;
'pɫɛznt₁vɪᵊɫ;
₁ɛg 'hɒ̥‹ɚbɚ

7a ₁sɘʂuθ 'pɑ^ɚk;
'tʃæts₁wɚθ; 'tævɚ₁nɪkɫ

<u>b</u> ₁ræŋ'kɚ›ukɚs; bɚl‡ŋtɚn;
w‡ɫ‡ŋbᵊɚɚ

8a ₁wɑɚn 'grouv;
l‡ɻɫ ɛg hɑɚbɚ

b ₁bɒ̥ɚn‡ɕ'gæt; ɟu‹·nɹɚn

9a ₁ɟuɕu‹nɹɚn 'hɪᵊɫ;
ɪŋɡɫ‡ʃtæ›u̥^n;
mɚ'naɫɚpɘn

NJ

9b   tɛnənt; ˈɪŋglɪʃˌtaˆun;
     mənæləpən

10a ˌpʰɵ^ˌɤθ ˌæ^·ᵊmˈbɔ^·ɤ^

b   prɑ·spɨk płɛɨnz;
     ˈkræmbɛ>rɨ^; mənˈrɵ>u

c   krænbɛ>ɵɨ^

d   haɨłənd pɑɒk;
     nu< brʌnzwɨk

11a fɛdɵəł sɪrɨᶠ^;
     fłɛ>mɨŋtən; hɵ>upwł

b   tᵤɛntən, tᵤɛn'tn

c   ˈrɵ^uˆzˌdɛɨᵊł;
     prɪntstən; łɑ>ᵉnts

12a nɨ^ʃænɨk stɛɨʃən;
     ˈbrænt∫ˌbᵊɵg

b   ˌnu<· ˈsɛntᵤɵ; sʌmɵvɪᵊł;
     hɨłzbᵊɵɵ

13a ˈsna>ɨdɵˌta^un,
     lɪnvɨɨł; ˈrɪŋˌgɵ>·uᵤ;
     ˌi·st ˈæmł

b   kɑ<·pɵ hɪᵊł;
     fłɛ>mɨŋtən; ˈræɵ'tn

14a ju^u<njən brɪk;
     ˈbłɛɵᵤta^·u^n

b   vɨ^ˈ æ·nə; ɪndɨɵpɛndənts

15a ˈstɪłˌwarɵ, ˈstɪᵊł-;
     nɥ>·tn

b   ðə płɛ^ɨ^nz; əgʌˇstɵ;
     fræŋkfɵd̥

16a dʒæksnvł rɵ>ud,
     ˌkɪnɨ^ˈlɔˇ·ᵊn;
     təwaˈkɵ̱ᵤ̆; pɨ^kwanɨk

b   dʒæksnvɪᵊł rɔᵤd;
     təˈwa>·koᵤu; man'tvɪᵊł

17a jɥ>·njən sɛntᵤɵ

NJ

17b əˈłɪzəbəɵ

18a nʌ'tlɨ^

b   nʌtłɨᵤ

c   nu<·ɵk

d   aɵəndʒ

19a dʒɵɵzɨ^ sɪ>rɨ^

b   dʒɵɨzɨ^ sɪ'tɨ^

20a pɑ·rk rɪdʒ

b   ɔ^·ᵊrədɵł

21a wɛɨn

b   łoᵤɵ preᵤknəs;
     pʰæᵤɵsn; weɨ^n

PENNSYLVANIA

1a   ˌfɪᵤłəˈdɛłɉᵊ

b   fɨłədɛłɉə, ˌ-ˈɛ̱ɵ-

c   fræŋkfɵd;
     ˌfɪ>łəˈdɛłfɨ^ə

d   ˌfɨłəˈdɛłɉə, -ˈdɛ>ł-

e   ˌfɪłəˈdɛłfɨ^ə, fɪ>-

f   ˈdʒɵmənˌtæˇ·ɥˇn;
     fɪłədɛłɉə

g   fɪłədɛłɉə, ˌf-ˈd-

h   ˌfɪłəˈdɛłfɨ^ə

2a   ˈlɵɵən; nu<· hɔᵤup;
     ʌpɵ mɛɨkfiˇⁱᵊłd

b   ækwətəŋ; nu< hɵ>up;
     sɔ<ułbɵɵɨ

3a   ˈnɑrəsˌtæˇ·u^n

b   sprɪŋ hæˇus;
     lɔᵤɵ gwɪ>nəd

c   sprɪŋ hæus; lɔᵤɵ gwɪnəd

4a   ˌpɛnɨŋktən haɨts;
     wɪłmɪŋktən; b̥ɛɵł

b   t∫ɛstɵ

5a   ju<·klən

PA

5b   mɵ<ɵʃł'tn;
     ˈwɛst ˌt∫ɛstɵ;
     wɛst ˈbræᵤdfɵd

c   ɪ^gł; ˈjuᵤu<klənᵈ

d   ˈkaɣ̆ənˌvɪᵊł;
     wɛst fałəfɪiˇᵊ̱łᵈ

e   ɛᵊłkvjɥ>·; nɥ>· lʌɵndən

6a   b̥ɛ̆ᵤ̱ɨ

b   rɛdɪŋ

c   hæmˈb̥ɵ̱ɵ̆ᵤ̱k; tɪłᵤən

d   ---

7a   t∫ɛ^ɵɨ^ hɪᵊł;
     piᴶt∫ barəm; fułtən

b   t∫ɛsnət lɛvł; kwɔˇrɨvł;
     ˌᵊɹɥ>·ᵊm^ɵ

c   fɛᵊrma>·u^nt; ɛfrətᵤə;
     ʋɛst ɵrl

d   læŋkəstɵ

8a   ˌsłɛ^ɨt ˈhɪᵊł; dɛᵊłtᵤə;
     piˇᴶt∫ ba>ɵ̃m

b   dɛłtə; ˈpiᴶt∫ ˌbarəm

c   ˌ∫ɵrmənᵤ̱ ˈʋæᵊłɨ;
     ˈhæno^·ʋɵr;
     ʋɛst ˈmæ^nˌha̱ɨm

d   ɉɔ^ɵk

9a   mænədɨ hɪɟ; g̊ræn'tʋɪɟ;
     i·st hæˈno·ʋɵ

b   lɪŋłstaun; hæ>rəsbɵg;
     łoᵁɵ pækstn

c   hærəsbɵ·g

10   haɨɟmənɵ·ɟ; ɟɛp̄ənən;
     nɔ̱ᵊrᵤ̱ɵcn ænʋɟ

11a təbətvɪᵊł; łu:əs

b   ˌtnɨᵤɵcnˈɵ̱ɵcnˈθʌmbɵlənd; pɔɨ^nt

12a waᵤɨt hɵ^:ł; ænᵤ̱ɵcnθənɨ^

PA

12b dæᵊnvł; ˈvæᵊł‡ꞵ

13a griˑnwud væł‡^,
     rɔꞩəzbɒg; ˈɑˌrəndʒɪvɪᵊł;
     griˑnwuᵊd

  b griˑnwud væł‡^,
     rɔꞩəꞩɔꞩ; ɔꞩəndʒvɪᵊł;
     griˑnwuᵊd

14a ˌʋæꞮ‡ ˈʋju‹ˑ; hɪkəns

  b ˈæʃˌlənd

15a ˈmoˇəˌtaꞯun;
     swɪ^it væᵊł‡; rɒ^ˑᵊs

  b mju‹ˑłənbɒg;
     ˌʃɪkˈʃɪn‡^; ju‹ˑnjən

  c kɪŋstən, ˈwɪłks ˌbæꞯ‡^

16a lɪt̩ kæp̄; paˑˌməˇtən;
     loˑəꞩ toˑəmæ^nsɪŋ

  b mɑk tʃʌŋk

  c ˌiˇⁱst ˌmɑk ˈtʃʌ‹ŋk

17a kuˑnꞩʋɪꞁ, tʃæpmənꞩ;
     æꞁəntaꞯˑun;
     ʌpəꞩ məˈkʌntʃ‡^

  b æꞯəntaꞯˑuˇn

18a maˑunt bɛθł

  b piˇəs; iˑstən

19a mɒꞩəꞩ ʃ ł krɪk;
     mɪdł smɪθfiˑᵊłᵈ

  b ˈkrɛꞯsˌkoˇu; bæꞯrət

20a ˌlɔ‹ˑŋ ˈmɛdəꞩ,
     ˌdɪŋmənz ˈfɛꞯ‡;
     mɪᵊłfəꞩ; dɛłəwəꞩ

  b dɪŋmənz fɛꞯ‡; ˈdɛłəwəꞩ

21a skaꞯˑt sɛn̩‡;
     ˌstɑꞩəꞩˈʌkə

  b ˈlɒ^ˑrəłə;
     hoꞯnzdeˑ‡ˇᵊł; ˈbəꞁ‡n

22a fliˇⁱtvɪᵊł; dɒ^ł’tn;
     bɛn’tn

  b hæk, ˈfliˑtˌvɪᵊł;
     dɒ^ˑł’tn; bɛn’tn

23a haꞯəfəꞩ

  b haꞯt leˑk; n‡ŭ‹ mɪłfəꞩ

24a fɑks haꞯloꞯ,
     ˈdʒɛn‡ŋzˌvɪᵊł;
     m‡ˈhupən‡; wɪndəm

  b ˌraꞯːdʒəꞩ ˈhaꞯːlu;
     m‡ˈhɒˇŭpən‡

25a bɛθł, ‡ˈstɛłə;
     ˈfɔꞩksˌvɪᵊł;
     ˈɛꞯᵊkˌlæˑᵊnd

  b ‡ꞩˈstɛꞯłə; ˈfɔꞩksˌvɪᵊł;
     ˈɛłkˌlæᵊnd

26a wɒ^r‡ˇn sɛ^n̩‡; wɒ^r‡ˇn

  b ˈkæmpˌtæˇun;
     waꞩ‡əluˑs‡ŋ; hꞩ‡k

27a ˌtʃɛr‡ ˈflæᵊts,
     ˈhwɪtn‡ˌvꞯł;
     mænzfɪ^iˇᵊłd; kɑˑv‡ntən

  b naꞯ‡z væ l‡ˇ; wɛłzbɒꞩˇ;
     ˈmɪdłˌbꞩꞯ‡

28a ˈhʌnꞯəzˌvɪꞩᵊł;
     ˈjuˑꞩz ˌvɪꞩᵊł; wułf

  b wɪꞮ ꞁəmzpɒꞩt

29a loꞩˑgəntən; griˑn
     *biˇⁱtʃ krɪk

  b mæk‡^vɪᵊł; łəˈmɑꞩ·

30a wɛst bɪŋəm; dʒɛn‡ˇsiˑ

  b fɑ‹ˑks hɪᵊł; juʷłɪs‡ˇs

31a rɪt̩ʃ væᵊł‡^;
     ˌɛmˈpoꞩ‡^əm; ʃɪpən

  b rɪtʃ væł‡^;

(31b) ˌɛmˈpoꞩ‡^əm; ʃɪˇp‡ˇn

32a ˌdʒɒnᵗsnz ˈrʌᵊn,
     ˈma‡łzˌbɒg;
     ˌbɛᵊłˈfɒ^ˑnt; bɒ^ːgz

  b ˈwɪᵊŋˌgꞯ‡; bɔˇːgz

33a ˌblꞱꞯˑˈnɒb; pɔ^rꞁ‡dʒ;
     ˈgriˇɪnˌfiˑᵊłd

  b bɒˑfmən sɛ‡łmənt;
     ˌta‡ˈrɒꞩun; sna‡dəꞩ

34a nɒ^ˑsvɪᵊł; błɛꞩz mɪᵊłz;
     t‡ᵊł

  b kæˑsvɪᵊł; kæˑs

  c ˈhʌnt‡ŋdən

35a ˈɑ‹ꞩ‡ʃ ta·un; mærəwonə;
     brætn

  b ˌfꞩgəsn ˈvæᵊł‡ꞩ;
     m‡kveˇ‡taun; ɒꞩłəvəꞩ

36a ˈæłənˌwuᵊd; grɛꞯg

  b weꞩ‡t diˇꞩ væꞯᵊł‡^;
     æᵊłənwuᵊd; grɛꞩg

37a trɑ^kslʋɪꞱꞁ; ædəmꞩ

  b ˌɪnd‡^ˈpɛn’tnꞩ;
     pɔꞩt trꞯvꞩtn; tʃæpmən

38a spruˑs hɪᵊł;
     ˌpɔ‹t‡ ˈrꞯ^əł

  b łɔˇˑsᵗ krɪk væꞯᵊł‡^;
     ˈmɪfłənˌtaun; fəˈmænə

39a ˈɛʃˌkɒ^ˑł, ˈɪkəsˌbɒg;
     mɪłꞩztaun; səˈvɪᵊł

  b nuꞯ błuˑmfiˑᵊłd; sɛnꞩəꞩ

40a ˈnuꞯˑˌbɒg; ˈho‹ꞯpˌwɛᵊł

  b ˌmaˑꞯʋnt ˈhꞩˑup;
     ˈnuꞩˑˌvɪᵊł;
     ʌˇpəꞩ mɪꞩflən

PA

41a ˈhʌ‹nʇəsˌ̲taun;
     ˈgɛʇəsˌbɚg; stɚˈbæᵊn

  b fɛˇɚfi·ᵊɫd;
     ˌhæmɫʼtnˈbæ·ᵊn

42a o‹uk gro‹uv;
     tʃeɾmbɚzbɚg; ɫɛɾəkɛnɫ

  b ---

43a ˌbʌˆk ˈvæ›ᵊɫɫˆ;
     ˈhænˌkɒ‹k; ɟ̊ʉ›·njɐn

  b pɪdʒən koʂuv;
     wɔˇ·fɚdzbɚg; bɛθə›ɫ

44a ˈkɫɪɚˌvɪᵊɫ; mənˈro‹u

  b ˌklɪɚ ˈrɪdʒ; ɛvɚɚt;
     wɛst prɚ‹vədənts

45a hʌmbɚt; ˈkɒnˌfɫu‹·ənts;
     ɫoˇᵁɚ tɚ̆rkɫˆfut

  b bu‹·n, ˈʃæŋksˌvɪᵊɫ;
     friˇidnz; sto‹unɫ krɪk

46a ˈgriˇⁱnˌbraɛr,
     əˈhaɛəˌpaɛᵊɫ;
     ˈdʌnˌbɒ‹r; stu‹ɚd

  b braˆ·uˇnzvɪᵊɫ, do̲ˆ·sn;
     ˌlʉ›·ˈzɚn,
     ˌlouɚˌtaɛˆˈrɐuˆn

47a ˌnʉ›· ˈfri›ɪˌpo·ʇt

  b weɪnzbɚ̆rg; hwaɫtɫˆ

48a bɚ̆rnzvɪᵊɫ; wɛst fɪnɫɫˆⁱ

  b ˈbʌfɚˌlɚ›u;
     ˈhɚ›upˌwɛˆᵊɫ

  c ʃugɚ rʌ‹ᵊn; ˌɛɫɫˆˈfɔr;
     ˈnɒɫŋˌhæ·ᵊm

49a krɪᵊsp; rɛktɚ; ku‹k

  b mænzvɪᵊɫ, stɔˇ·ɫztaun;
     ɫɪgəniˆr̩; kuk

50a əˈɫɪzəbəθ

PA

50b mɫˈki·zˌpɔˆrt;
     əˈɫɪzəbəθ

  c ɫ̥ˈlɪzəbəθ; fɔrwərd

51a wɪɫkənzbɚ̆rg

  b griˇintri·, -triˇi;
     ˈpɪtsˌbɚ̆rg

52a kæᵊnɫtən; dɒrɫɪŋ̊n

  b dɒrɫɫtən

53a prɪntstən;
     ˈnuˆu ˌkæᵊsɫ; sɫɪpə rɒk

  b wægɫtaun; nuˆu‹ kæᵊsɫ;
     ˈsɫɪpə rɒᵊk

54a nɪksn; bʌ̆ʼtlɚ, bʌ̆ˇʼtlɚ;
     pɛˆᵊn

  b ˈbraunzˌdɛɫᵊɫ; bʷʌʼtlɚ;
     pɛˆᵊn

55a ɫɪ›izbɚ̆rg; ˌvo‹uˈɫæᵊnt;
     sprɪŋfiɪld

  b mɚ̆rsɚ; fɪnɫɫɫˆ

56a ˈhænəˌvɪɫ; kɒhɾ̥əntən

  cv ˈkɒhrəntən; kənæᵊɫ

  b ˈnɪkɫˌvɪᵊɫ; ɛmɫəntən;
     ˈrɪtʃˌɫæ·ᵊnd

57a kɪsɪŋ maɫˆnz;
     ˈraɫˆmɚzˌbɚg; mæ›dəsn

  b iˇⁱst brɛɫdɫˆ; mædəsən

58a ˌbrɪkˈtʃɚrtʃ;
     kɛɫɫɫˆstɛɫʃən; bɚ̥ɚɫ

  b brɪktʃɚrtʃ; fɔˆrd sɪɾɫˆ;
     bɚ̥əɫ

59a əˈnaɫɚ; məkæᵊɫmənt

  b maunt pɫɛznt;
     ˈsʌmɚˌvɪᵊɫ; bi·vɚ

60a kriˇit; ˌɪndɫˆˈænə;
     sɪnɾɚ

PA

60b ˈdʒæksnvɫᵊɫ; bɫɚrzvɪᵊɫ;
     ˈbɫækɫɫk

61a sʌ‹məhɪᵊɫ, sauθ fɔrk;
     sɫdmən; kroʂɫ

  b nɔrθ ɛ›bənzbɚ̆rg;
     kæmbrɫˆə

62a ˈfɛɾˌvju‹·; mɔrəsdeˇɫˇɫ;
     ˈgreˇɫʰham

  b seˇɫɫəm; wɛst dɫˆkeˇɫɾɚ;
     bɒˆ·ᵊgz

63a wɪnzlo·ᵁ hɪᵊɫ; bɛnəzɛt

  b kɚ̣·zɫˆ; fɒks

64a ˌdʒændɚ ˈrʌn,
     ʃɪŋɫhaʐus;
     ˌlɪɾɫ ˌdʒɛnɫˇ'siʲ;
     sɪˆɚɫz

  b wɛst ɛɫdɹɚˇd

65a ˈfæˆɚˌvɫu, ˌjæŋkɫˆ ˈbuʃ;
     wɔɛɫˇn; ʃugɚ groᵁv

  b ˌtɪdɫˆˈu‹t krɪk roˇud;
     tɹɚpiˇidɚ; ˈtɹaɫʌmp

66a kɒnɫˆət ɫɛˆɫk;
     ˌlɪist ˈfɒɫɚˌfɪˆɪɫd

  b kɒnɫˆət sɛnɾɚ;
     ˈɫaʐɫnzvɫɫ

67a ˈɑ‹ɚˌbʌkɫ; wɑ·tsbɚg;
     vɫˈnæŋgou (✓)

  b wɑtsbɚg; æmɚɫɫˆ

WEST VIRGINIA

1 ʃɛpədztaˆ·un

2 maɚtnzbɚg; hɛdʒɚzvɪᵊɫ

3 ˌrɑk ˈgæᵊp; ʌˆmps

4a əˈgʌstɫˆ; hænən rɒ‹·k;
    ʃɚ·mən

  b rɑˆmnɫˆ

WVA · WVA · WVA

5	bɛlɨŋtən; wɛɫ'tn	16a	waɨmɚ; ˈdraɨˇ fɔɐk	27b	hɔˇ·vɚ; ˈha·ɛˌkoʂ·u;
6a	dʒɵdnz rʌˆᵊn	b	bɛˏv̆ɵɫɨˆ		ˈnʌˏɾ¡ɔˇ·ɫ
b	piˇⁱɾɵzbɵg	17a	---	28a	gɔɵdn; kruk
7a	ma·ˏɛˆləm	b	frɛntʃ krɪk; miˇid	b	ˈloˏu ¡gæp; wɔ·ʃøntən
b	ˈbrændɨˆ¡waˏɛn; bɛθɫ	c	blæk lɪk rʌˏᵊn, æbɵt;	29a	¡krɪstʃønz ˈrɪdʒ;
8a	kɵɐ skuˏ·ɫhaˆŭs;		¡bʌˏkˈhænən; miˇid		ˈɛˆᵊɫ¡guᵊd; ˈi·st ¡rɨvɚ
	maˆŭθ əv sɪnɨˆkə;	18a	bæbɫøn; dʌˏfɨˆ; kɵˏɫønz	b	bɛnt mæʉntn, æθønz;
	ɟʉ·njøn	b	wɛstøn; kɵɵthæˇ·ʉˇs		prɪntstøn; plɪmøθ
b	ˈsᵊɵkɫ¡vɪ·ᵊɫ	19a	kraɨˇts mæʉntn;	30a	baˏɵ hoˏᵁɫ fɔɐk;
9a	fɛløzvɪᵊɫ; nuˏ·bᵊɵg;		lɪɾɫ bᵊɵtʃ; hɵlɨˆ		pa·ˏɛˏnvɪ·ᵊɫ; sɛntɵ
	riˇinoʂu	b	mɑˏɾøsn ˈtʃɵtʃ; sʌtn;	b	¡o·sɨˆˈæ̃nə
b	kʌˏzɵt; pɫɛznt		hɑlɨ	31a	trɛɨs fɔɐk; pænt̪ɵɵ
10a	foʂuɫɨˆ rʌˏᵊn;	20a	krɛˆgzvɪˆ·ᵊɫ; bi·vɚ		†peˇɨntɵ; sændɨˆ rɪ·ᵊvɚ
	ˈbɫæks¡vɪᵊɫ; kɫeˇɨˆ	b	mʌdɫt̪ɨˆ; ˈsʌmɵz¡vɪᵊɫ;	b	¡krɛɨn ˈrɨdʒ; bræ·dʃɔˏ·;
b	dɔˇ·ɫtøn;		hæmɫtøn		sæ·ndɨ rɪ·vɚ
	ˈmɔˇ·ɵgøn¡tæˇ·ʉˇn;	21a	gɔɔˆlɨˆ rɪvɚ,	32a	ˈnɔ·gɨˆ¡tʌˏk; ˈhɵˏɵ¡di·
	kɫɪn'tn		¡boˆ·ᵁˈlɛɵ;	b	ˈnɔ·gɨˆ¡tʌˏ·k; ¡hɵˏɵˈdi·
c	mɔɵgøntæˇ·ʉn; mɔɵgøn		ˈdʒɵ̃ɾ̥ɨˆz¡vɪˆ·ᵊɫ;	33a	krɔ·lɨˆz kriˏⁱk;
11a	dɛnts rʌˏ·ᵊn; mæ̃nɨŋn̥		fɔɐk lɪˆk		†ʃæpmønzvɪ·ᵊɫ
b	¡deɨvøs ˈrɪdʒ;	b	bræʉnz mæʉntn;	b	mɪtʃɫ haɨˇts;
	fɑ·rmɨŋtøn; lɪŋkøn		¡ri·ˈpli·t; hækøz vælɨ		ˈhɛˆn¡lɔˇ·sn; lo·ᵁgøn
12a	aɨzɨks krɪk; wɪɫtsnbɵg;	22a	ɛᵊk; ˈmɑɵlɨŋtøn; ˈɛdrɨˆ	34a	hæmløn; wɛst ~; kæˆɵɵ̆ɫ
	sɑɵdøs	b	hɪɫzbᵊɵɵ; ɫɪˏɾɫ ɫɛvɫz	b	hæᵊmløn; kæˆɵɵɫ
b	ɫoˆ·st krɪ·k; grænt	23a	smʉˏ·t	35a	meɨnød bræntʃ;
13a	bɛɫdʒøm; græ·ᵊˏˆftøn;	b	rɛˏnɨk; foˆɫɨŋ spri·ŋz		ˈka·ɵɵz¡vɪᵊɫ; grænt
	buˏ·ðz krɪk	24a	dʌˏtʃ kɔˇɵnɵ; ˈkɑɫ¡weᵊɫ;	b	weˇɨn, weˇɨˆn; ɟʉ·njøn
b	ˈmi·d¡læ·ᵊnd;		sɛkŋ kri·k	36a	mɛɵɵts kriˇik;
	fɫɛˏmɨŋtøn; bʉˏ·ðz krɪk	b	sɪŋks groˇ·ᵁˇv;		sɔˇ·ɫt raˏ·k; møkɑˏmøs
14a	mɛdøvɪᵊɫ; biˇ·ɫɨŋtøn;		sɛkønᵈ kri·k	b	†ɔˇ·mz kriˇik;
	gɫɛˆɨd	25a	bɑɵgɚ sprɪŋz; †ɑɫkøt;		ˈbɑɵbøz¡vɪ·ᵊɫ;
b	fɑks hɵˆ·ɫ; fɪɫøpɨˆ;		ˈgri·n¡brɑɵ rɪvɚ		møˈkɑˏ·møs
	pɫɛznt	b	loᵁøɫ; tɑɫkøt	37a	†ʉɪbɫ; ɟʉ·njøn
15a	seˇɨn dʒɔˇɵdʒ	26a	to·nɨˆz fɔɐk; klᵊɵ kri·k	b	hɛndɵsn; aɵbʌˏkɫ
b	ˈhɔɵ¡ʃʉˏ·; pɑɵsnz;	b	søveɨɵ (√); træp hɪˆ·ᵊɫ	38a	lænøm; poˇukɨˆ
	seɨn ˈdʒɔɵdʒ	27a	ˈrʌˏsɫ¡vɪ·ᵊɫ; ˈnʌˏt̪¡ɔ·ɫ	b	ha·ˏɛzɵ; poukɨˆ

WVA	WVA	OHIO

WVA

39a saˆ·ʉθ tʃɑ·ˏɫztən

b tʃɑˏəɫztən

c̠ tʃɑ·ˢɫztən

40a ˈɡreŧpˌvaˑˏ·ɛn;
     sɪsnvɪˢɫ; po·ᵁkŧˆ

b pɪntʃ; ɛˢɫk

41a ˈbɪkˌmoˑɚ; plɛˆ·ˢzənt

b mæʉntn hoˏum; kɫeˇŧ;
   hɛnrŧˆ

42a keŧɾŧˆz rʌ<·ˢn;
     ænəməɾaŧˇɚ; ʃˢɵədən

b ˈsɪkəˌmoɚ; mɪˢɫstoˇʉn;
   ʃəmən

43a sændŧˆvɪˢɫ

b pɑɵtʃmənt væˢɫŧˆ;
   rɪplŧˆ

44a lɪ·ˢn kæ·mp;
     ˈpæˏɫəˌstiˑn; tʌˏkɚ

b ri·dŧˆ krɪk;
   pɑˏɫəstɑˏ·ŧn;
   ŧˆˈɫɪzəbəθ

45a ˌkrʌˢm ˈhɪˢɫ; bɛˢɫvɪˢɫ;
   hɛɵɵs

b ˈmæfŧˆˌtaˆ·ʉn,
   lɵˇuməs ri·dʒ;
   ˈpɑˆᵩkɵzbɚɡ; kɫeˇŧ

46a ˌkɫeŧ ˈpɔ·ŧnt;
     seŧnt meˏɾŧ; Jʉ·njən

b ʃuɫts; sɛˆŧnt mˢɵŧˆz;
   dʒɛfɚsn

47a reˇŧsŧˆ; pŧˆtroˇuɫjəm;
     ɡræ·ˢnt

b hˢɵʃɵz rʌ<·ˢn;
   pɛnzbɵˇ-ɵˇ; kɫɛˏ·ŧ

48a ˈbʌ<kˌaˏ·ŧ; seˇŧɫəm;

WVA

(48a) ɡræˏnt

bc ---

d ʃʉɡɚ kæmp; bɫæˢndvɪˢɫ;
   nʉˏ· mɪɫtn

49a pɵslŧ; sŧstɵzvɪˢɫ

b taŧˇɫɚ; ˈmækɫˌrɔŧ

50a dʒæksnzbɵˇrɡ; ɡrænt

b dʒæksənbˢɵɡ; ɡræ·nt

51a kæmrən rɪdʒ; ɫɪbɚɾŧˆ

b bɪɡ rʌ<ˢn; kæmən (√);
   ɫɪbɚŧˆ

52a pəˈtoᵩumŧk;
     wɛst ɛɫəɡzændɚ; ɫɪbɚŧˆ

b wɑdɫz rʌ̆ˢn;
   ʃɔɵt ˈkriˇik; rɪtʃlənd

c̠ ˌlɛˏðɵwuˏd ˈlɛˏ·ŧn,
   wudzdɛˏ·ŧɫ; hwiˏɫŧŋ;
   ˌtraŧɵˈdɛɫfŧˆɵ

53a ˈdʒɛnˌtiˏɫ rɪdʒ;
     wɛˢɫzbɵɡ; bʌfɫoᵩu

b ---

c̠ tɛnt kəmjʉˏ·nɵŧˆ;
   koˆɫjɚz; krɒˆ·ˢs krɪk

54a hɑˏrdnz rʌ<·ˢn;
     nʉ· kʌ<mbɵlənd; kɫeˇŧ

b læŋfɵts rʌˇn;
   ˌnʉ ˈkʌ<mbɵlənd; kɫɛˆŧ

OHIO

1a ˈiˑɡɫˌvɪˢɫ; dʒɛfɚsn;
    ɒˆ·stŧˇnbɚɡ

b dʒŧni·vɚ; haˏɵpɵzfiˇ·ˢɫd

c̠ dʒɛvɚsn

2a ˈwɪɫˌdɛɚ; koˇɵtlənd;
    tʃæmpŧˆˢn

b tʃæmpŧˆˢn haᵩŧts; wɔˆɵən

OHIO

3a iˑst ɡouʃən tʃɵtʃ;
    bŧˆˆˈɫɔŧˆt; ɡo<uʃən

b ˈɛˢɫzˌwɵɵ; ˌbɵɫən ˈsɛntɚ

4a ˈwɛˢɫzˌvɪˢɫ; mæˏdəsn

b ɫɪˢzbən; sɛntɚ

5a seᴵləm

b iˑst sprɪŋfiˑɫd;
   ˈbɫuˏ·mŧŋdeŧˢɫ; seˇŧɫəm

c ˌrɛd ˈrɪdʒ; smɪθfiˑˢɫd

6a ˈɑɵmˌstrɔ·nz ˈmɪˢɫz;
    wɔ·ʃŧŋtəvʉ

b seŧnt klɛɵzvɪˢɫ;
   rɪtʃlæˢnd

7a streŧ fɔɵk;
    ˈɡreŧzˌvɪˢɫ; wɔˇ·ʃɵntən

b ˈɡreŧzˌvɪˢɫ; wɔɵʃɵntən

8a ˌpaŧn ˈrɪdʒ; fɫɛˏɵmŧŋ;
    ˈwɑˏɾɵˌtaun

b məsˈkɪŋɡəm, -ˈkɪŋəm

c bɑɵɫɵ, -lŏᵩᵁ, vɪntsnt;
   ˌmɛɵŧˆˈɛɾɵ

d ---

e̠ ˌmærŧˆˈɛtɵ

9a bruks; ˈɔˇ·ɫbənŧˆ;
    ɛɫŧɡzændɵ

b ʃeid

c ˌhwaŧtˈhɒˆ·ɫ; æθənz

d ---

10a ˈstaŧvɵzˌvɪˢɫ;
     poɵtlənd; lɛvmŋən

b sʌtn tʃɵtʃ;
   ˌreˇŧˈsiˑn; sʌ<tn

11a θɪvɵnɵ; nɔrθɵp; hærɵsn

b bɪdˌweˢɫ; ˌrækˈkʉˏ·n

12a ˈskɑttaˆʉn; wɪnzɚ

OHIO		KY		MD	
12b	əˈreˇ‡b‡ˆə ⊥reˇ‡b‡ˆ; wɪɫgəs; me‡sn	4a	ˈsɪmən ˌfɔ·ək ˈskʉᴴˆl; ˌbɪ·g ˈrɑk	2a	skɪnɵz nɛˆ‡ˇ⟨k; ˌrɑk ˈɦɔˇ·ɫ
cd	---	b	haꝫ·ᵊdn	b	mɪɫ‡ŋtən
13a	ˈhaɪrəm	c	ˈʤaꝫ·ᵊˌhɪ·ᵊɫ	3a	dəˈmɪnjən, kɛnt ˈɑ·ɛˆɫənᵗ; ʧɛstə
b	rəˈvɛnə	5a	ˌlaꝫ·‡nˈfɔ⟨ək		
c	---	b	ˌǩɪŋdəˆm ˈkʌꝫ·m; ˌɵ⟨skəˈlʉ·s‡	b	praꝫ‡səz stɛˆ‡ʃən; ˌtʃᵊɵʧ ˈhɪᵊɫ
14	ˌnʉᴴˆ f‡ˇləˈdɛɫf‡ꝫ; goᵁˈˇ⟨ʃn	cv	ˌɑ⟩skəˈlʉᴴˆs‡	4a	wɪɫ‡stən; dɛntən
15a	ˈkɔɵnˌkɔ⟩d (√)	6a	kɹʌꝫm‡z	b	ˈbɵˇzˌvɪᵊɫ; dɛnⁿn
b	nuˈˇ ˈkɑnˌkɔɵd	b	---	c	prɛᵊstən
16a	ˈɵˇuˇ⟨ɫ ˌkʋˆ·nkoꝫɵd, ˈkʋnˌkɔꝫɵd; ˈsɛnək‡‡ˆ ˌvɪ·ᵊɫ; ˈrɪtʃˌlæ·ᵊn	c	ˈke·‡ˌwɵꝫ·d	5a	tɪᵊɫmənz a⟩‡ˇlənt
		7a	ɪ·ŋgrəˆm	b	iˇɪstən
b	griˇˈinwŭˇ⟨d; sɛn‡kəvɪ·ᵊɫ; rɪtʃləˆnd	b	ˈmɪdlzbɜˆr‡	6a	wɪŋ‡ˇt
c	loˇ⟨ɵ sɪt‡‡ˆˇ; rɪtʃləˆn			b	sɛˆe⟩ɫəm
17	ˈhoˇ⟨uˇ⟨pˌwɛˆᵊɫ; mɔ·ᵊɫd‡ꝫ; pɛˆ·ᵊn		**DELAWARE**	7a	wuˇ⟨lɵdz
		1ab	wɪɫm‡ŋtən	b	ˌʌˇ⟨pɵ ˈfɛ⟩ɵ‡; ˈsɔʋˆ·ɫzˌbɛ⟩ɵ‡
18	məˈkɑɵθɵ; ɛɫk	c	ˈwɪɫmɪŋtən		
		2a	ˌrɛd ˈlɑ‡ˇn; ˌnuˇ ˈkæsɫ	c	ˈsɔʋˆ·ɫzˌbɛ⟩ᵊ‡
KENTUCKY		b	ˌhɵuˆˈkɛsən, maꝫɵʃɫtən; mɪᵊɫ krɪk	8a	iˇidn
1a	ˈheˇ‡z ˌbrɛˆntʃ; mɔˇ⟨ɵhɛˆ·ᵊd			b	ˌsnoˇ⟨u ˈhɪᵊɫ
b	gřɛˇ‡sn	3a	ˌwɪ⟩ɫəˈgroˇ⟨ᵁv; ˌwɑ‡ˇˈoᵁm‡ŋ; ˈmɵ·d‡kɫ	N9	ˌprɪnts‡ˇs ˈᵊn
2a	ˈbʉ·ᴴˆnz ˌǩæ·ᵊmp	b	ˌbɛˌθɛzdə ˈ‡ʃɵtʃ; hɵˇ⟨ɵtl‡; wɛst doˇ⟨uvɵ	9a	diˇ·ᵊlz ɑ⟩·ɛlənᵗ
b	---	c	doꝫuvɵ	b	we⟩ɫ‡ŋtən; ˌprɪnts‡ˇs ˈᵊ·ᵊn; dʌˇ⟨bl‡ˇn
c	ˌɔɵɫ ˈsprɪŋz	4	mɪɫfəd nɛˆk		
3a	ˈoˇ⟨ᵁˇ⟨ɫ ˌstiˇ·ɫ ˈgre·‡vjɑ⟩ɵd; ˈbʉ⟩·nvɫ, bʉ⟩·ʉꝫn-	5a	ʤɔˇ⟨ɵʤꝫtɛꝫun	10a	hɪkr‡; fɵ⟨rəsᵗ hɪᵊɫ
		b	ˈbrɪʤˌvɪᵊɫ; nænˌ‡koˇ⟨uk	b	bɛnsn
b	skoˇ⟨ᵁˇ⟨vɫ, -vəɫ	6a	ˈnʉ·ˌfæˇ·und; fræŋkfɵd; ˈgʌmbɵꝫˌɵ	11	ˈblʉ· ˌmæˇ·ʉnt; ˈmʌˆŋktən
c	ləˈroˇ⟨ᵁˇ⟨z			12a	boˇ·ɵ‡ŋ
d	ˈæθəl cv ˈɛˇθəɫ	b	ˌsænd‡ ˈlænd‡ŋ; dæ·gzbɵ·ɵ; bʋˆ·ɫʇɵmɵ	b	wɑˆ‡thaus; ʌˆpɵkoˇ⟨uˆ
e	ˈkæ·o ˌkri·ˇɪˆk; ˈɛˆvɵˌsoˇ⟨ᵁˇ⟨ɫ +		**MARYLAND**	13a	bɔːɫtəˆme̦
		1a	bæˌⁿɫ swɔˇ·mp; ˌpɔˆɵꝫ‡ˆˈpɑ⟩zət	b	bɔ·ɫⁱˇɵmɵ
		b	raꝫꝫ‡ŋ sʌn	c	goꝫuvɵnz; bɔ·ɫⁱˇɵmɵ
				d	bɔːɫⁱˇɵmɵ

MD

13e　bɔ·ɫɥ†ɨmɔ^ə

　ƒ　bɔ^:ɫɥ†əmə

14　sɪɫvɚ rʌ̨ᵊn;

　　ᶥwɛs₁mɪnstɚ; mɑɛɐzəˆz

15a　flɔ‹ᴿənts; wudba›·ɛ›n

　b　flɔ‹rənts; wudba›·ɛ›n

16　---

17a　frɛdrɨk

　b　ɟɛ›lə sprɪŋz; fɛdrɨk;

　　tʌˆskərɔ^·ɚ

18a　le·ⁱhɪᵊɫ; sɪɫvə sprɪŋz

　b　nɔᵛ·ᵊwuᵊd,

　　₁sænd‡ ᶥsprɪŋ;

　　ᶥrɔ‹₁kvɪᵊɫ

19a　rɪtʃ‡ᵛ; bɛn‡ᵛnz

　b　ᶥkwɔ‹s₁ko‹ᵁ

20a　ʃe·ⁱd‡ sa›·‡ᵛd

　b　tɹesⁱz lænd‡ᵛn;

　　nʌ̨twəɫ, nɛtwɐ̌ɫ

　c　əᶥnæpl‡ᵛs

21a　prɪnts frɛd‡k

　b　bɔ:ɒsto·ᵁ

N22　---

2N22　ᶥfi ₁nɑ›tʃ ro^·d,

　　rɪˆdʒ; ₁sɪn ᶥtɪn‡gəz

22a　₁mæ†əpɜ̌ɚᶥnɑ›·‡;

　　pɟɪ̨ǫsnz; pətʌˆᵊksn

　b　ᵢrɪ›və ᶥsprɪŋ;

　　ᶥæ·v‡ₙʲɥ

　c　lɛ̂ˆnǫdtæᵛun

23a　ᶥnændʒ‡mɔ^·‡

　b　ᶥnændʒ‡ᶥmɔ‡

　c　pɑ›mfr‡ᵛt

24　₁gælən† ᶥgri·n;

　　ᶥwɔ·ɫ₁dɔ·f

MD

25　ᶥki·d‡ʂz₁vɪᵊɫ

26a　₁sa›·ɛˆdl‡ŋ ᶥhɪᵊɫ;

　　ᶥhæᵊn₁kɑ›k

　b　heᵛ‡gɐstaun

27a　draɛ rʌᵊn; swɔ̃ŋ̩n

　b　₁dɪ^ɚ ᶥpɑ›ɚk

DISTRICT OF COLUMBIA

1a　wɔ‹ʃ‡ntən

b　waɑʃ‡ŋtən

VIRGINIA

1　₁æ^ɟ‡ᵛgᶥzæ^·‡ᵛndr‡^ə

2a　hʒɐndən; ᶥdre‡nz₁vɪᵊɫ

　b　ᶥkð̃vᵁɫ₁tʃɛstə;

　　ᶥwuʌᵊd₁brɪdʒ;

　　₁mæʂunt ᶥvɚ̊ᵊ^nən

3a　ᶥɫʌvə’ts₁vɪᵊɫ

　b　gu‹s krɪk; lɪŋkən;

　　mæʂun‡ gɪˆɟəd

N4　he·‡ᵛmɔ‹:ḱ‡t

5a　kɔ‹:†əz rʌˆᵊn væɟ‡ᵛ;

　　du·d‡; mɔ‹:ᵊʃəɫ

　b　wɔᵛr‡ᵛn̩tə

6a　nɛ·ᵊðǫz

　b　mæᵊdəsn; rɑʂb‡sn

7a　₁bɛˆɫz ₁krɔ:sᶥro:dz;

　　ᶥɟ̨‹·̨‡zə

　b　mo·lən; ₁lɐᵁ̨ʂi·zə,

　　ᶥlɐᵛ·‡ᵛzə; mɪnrɛɫ

8a　ɔ:ɫsəp; lɪv‡nstən

　b　poᵊst o·k

　c　frɛdr‡’ksbǫʂ·g

9a　rɛ^’kt‡ɨ; əkwaɛ‹ᵊɚ

　b　əᶥkwɑ‹·‹ᵋᵊ‹ə tʃɚ^·tʃ;

　　stæ^fəd

10a　₁no·ᵁᶥlæ·kə

VA

10b　ᶥmʌɫ₁bɛᴿ‡ ᶥple‡s;

　　di̥ʐ·ᶥdʒɑ›ɔn‡t;

　　₁boᵁɫ‡ᵛn ᶥgri·n

11a　₁ko·ᵁᵛɫ ᶥhɔ^·ᵊbə

　b　ᶥhæ›ᵊn₁oᵁvə, ᶥhæᵊnᶥ-

N12　oᵛ·ᵊɫdənz

12a　₁smɪ›θ ᶥmæunt;

　　hɔ̨nəz mɪᵊɫ; wɔ̨ʃ‡ŋtən

b　bɟɛˆnəm; o^·ķ ᶥgro^·v;

　　wɑ̨ʃ‡ntən

13a　₁kɐɚˆᶥtoᵁmən; hwiᵊmz

　b　ᶥmou₁lʌᵊsk;

　　ᶥwe‡t ₁tʃæᵊpɫ

14a　ᶥhɑɛ›ᵊsɪn†θ

　b　riᵛ·moʂu; ₁wɑ‹ɛ›ᶥkɑ^m‡kə

　c　₁waɛᶥkɑ^ᵊm‡kə tʃǫ̨·tʃ,

　　wəᶥkɑ^məkə ~

N15　₁ræᵛpəᶥhæᵛnək

15a　bre·‡z

　b　wæᵊ^ᵊz wɔ̠·ɔ^f;

　　ᶥdʌ›ᵊnzvɫ, dǫ‹nzvɫ;

　　₁ræᵊpəᶥhæᵊnək

16a　kɪŋ ən kwiʂ·n;

　　sti·vm̩zvɪᵊɫ

　b　₁weᵊs ᶥpɔ·‡nt;

　　bɟɥənə vɪᵊstə

17a　₁sɛntrəɫ gəᶥrɔ̨ᵊdʒ;

　　vɛn†ə; ð̃kwɪn̩n

　b　ᶥbɟɥ·lə₁vɪᵊɫ;

　　₁mæ›ŋəᶥhɪk

18　səᶥlu‹·də

19a　gɪn‡; sɛ·ᵊvən; æᵊbnə

　b　₁ɛʂ‡ˆḱ‡lɪ^ʲz

　c　zəᶥnoᵛun‡ᵛ; wæᵊ^ə

VA

20a ʋɪnˠə hɑːbə;

  ˌniˑˈloᵁmən,

  oᵁˇˈniˌiˆmoᵁˇ

 b iˑst rɪ‹və;

  poət heɹˇwəd

N21 ˈhoˑɟˌˌkrɑɹᵊf;

  ˌˌtʃɪkəˈhɑɹmnɨ

21a gɪləmz;

  ˈprɑɹᵛɨˇˌdɛᵊn† ˈfoˑədʒ

 b rɥᵛᵘθvɪᵊɫ; tɑ‹ˑᵊ‹lə

22 dɑ‹ᵋ‹ᵊskən;

  ˌpæ̆‹ʋəˈtæˑᵊn

23a mɛsɨˇk

 b græˑftən

24 ɔˑɨˇstə pɔˑɨnt; dɛᵊnbɨˇ

25 tæᵊnˈdʒᵊɚˑ

  *ˌtæ‹ᵊnˌdʒɪᵊɚ ˈɑ‹ˑɛ‹lən†;

  –ˈdʒɪˆᵊɚ

26a ˈkrædəkvɨɫ

 b lɪˆiˇ mɒɹˑᵊn†;

  ˈdʒʌstɨsvɪᵊɫ

 c ˈækəˌmæk

27 ˌdʒɪŋkɨɨˆˈtɪᵊg ɑˑɛ‹lən†,

  ˌdʒɪŋkəˈtɪg ɑ‹ɨˇlən†

  ↱ˈʃɪŋkətɪg

28a dɒˆˑɫbɨᶻₒ;

  keˇɨp tʃɒ‹ˑɫz;

  keˇɨpʋɪᵊɫ

 b brɪdʒtæˆʋɹn

29 diˇⁱp rʌˆᵊn; tʌˆkɨˆhoᵁˇ

30a rɪtʃmənd

 b ---

 c rɪˇtʃmənd

 d rɪtʃmənd

 e ---

VA

31a biˇˑⁱtʃ; məˈtoᵁəkə

 b ˌmɪdˈloˇˑᵁˇθɨən

32 pɪɹ̪təzbəˑᵊˠg

33a ˈdiˇˑwɪᵊt

 b drᵊnwɪ‹dɨˇ;

  roˑᵁᵂɒ‹ˑᵊnˡə

34a prɪᵊnts dʒɒɹˑᵓˇdʒ;

  blæɨˇnd

 b nᴵˆɥˑvɫ; ˌdɪspɨˈtænˡə

35a ˌmɪlz ˈswɜ̃ˑmp;

  ˈsmɪfˌfiˑᵊɫ; hɑˑˑdɨz

 b wɨ̃ˑnzə

36a bɔˑɨkɨnz; keɨprən

 b koᵊtlənd; dʒɪˈrɥɹˑzələm

37 hɑɹlən

38 diˇɹp kriˇɹk

39 nᴜ‹ɒˆfək

40a ˌbæk ˈbeˆɨ

 b ˌbæ‹ˑk ˈbeˇɨˆ

41a heˑɨdnzvɪᵊɫ

 b ˈtæᵊb̥ˌskɑˆᵊt;

  kɛnˈts stoᵁˇ; bəˑᵊd

42a ˌwɪᵊnˈdʒɑˑ‹nə;

  dʒiˇˑmz rɪ‹ᵊvə

 b mæ‹ɥnt teɨbə; skɑˈtsvɪᵊɫ

N43 ˈkʌɹmlən ˈkoˑᵊtəˇʋˆs

43a sæᵊrə; gɪnɨ mɪᵊɫz;

  mæᵊdɨsn

 b gɪnɨ mɪᵊɫz; mæᵊdɨsn

44a wɛslɨ tʃæˑpɫ;

  ˌæpmˈmæᵊɹəks;

  səʋ‹θsɑ‹ᵋ‹d

 b ˈɛˑᵊvəˌgriˇˑⁱn;

  ˈsəˇu‹θˌsɑˑᵊ‹d

45a θɹɑɹk; hæmˈpm

VA

45b reˆɨs; lɑɹkɨt

N46 ---

46a lɪntʃɨɹz steˑʃən;

  ɑ‹ˑtə rɪ‹və

 b ˈlɪntʃˌbəˆᵊg

47 kiˑzvɫ; plɛznt groˆˑv

48a ˈklɑ‹ˑɛ‹mæˑks; tʃæᵊrəm;

  pɪg rɪˑᵊvə

 b ˈkɒɹᵊnˌkɒˇɒd; tʃæˆᵊrəm

49a skɑɹᵊtsbɔɹˑᵊg; roᵁnoᵁk

 b ɹʌɹᵊŋᵍə; ˈhæᵊlɨˇfæˑks,

  ˈhælɨˇfæᵊks; miɟdvɫ,

  ˈmiˑɟdzvɫ

50a rɪksɨz mɪᵊɫ (✓);

  ˌtʃeˇᵋɹs ˈsɪdɨˇ

 b bɔˑɨˇt̪ən

51a ɛˑᵊbənɨˇ

 b ˈgɒɹᵁɫsnˌvɪᵊɫ; mɨhɛrɨn

52a tʃɛsnət grɜ‹ʋ;

  ˈg̊eɨnzˌbəˑə

 b brɥˑstæˑɥˇn

 c ˌoˇuˈpʰɛ‹kən; ˌʃɔˇˑˈniˑ

53a stoˑunɨˆ kriˑk; beˇɨsɨˆ;

  ˈæ‹ʃb̥ɨˆ

 b mæunt dʒæksən; æɨˆʃbɨˆ

54a bræˆˑɥntæˆˑɥn

 b ˌrɑɹkˈlæˑᵊnd; səkˈsɛᵊs;

  siˇˑdəvɪᵊɫ

55a hæɹəsnbəˇˆəg

 b hɛəˆsnbəˇg

56a ˌkræbˈbɑɹɹəm;

  bluˇᵂ græˆɨˇs

 b pɪᵊzgə; hɑ‹ˑɛ‹ tɑˆˑũn;

  bluˑ græᵊs

VA

57a ʃəˈræᵊndə;
   ˈɪɪᵊnᵈˌhɝᵊs†;
   seuθ rɪᵊvə̨

b stʃʉˏᵊˈts dræ·ᵗˇf†;
   se^u^θ rɪᵊvə

58 ʃɪflᵗˇt haȥlə;
   mɪʃən hum; ˈmʌ^nˌro·

N59 be^tsv‡l

59a ˈsɪᵊzˌmaȥᵊnt;
   ˌra>ɛ>ˈvæᵊnə

b ˌdʌnˈloᵊrə;
   ˈʃaσ‹łətsˌvɪᵊł

60 bɝ·nzvɪᵊł *dra‡ˇ rʌᵊn;
   bɝnzvɪᵊł; wɪljəmzvɪᵊł

61a həʉ^s mæˇunⁿoⁿn,
   hwɪsł kriˇˇk;
   kaᵊrz kriˇˇk *karz
   kriȥk s̲ †k̲ᶜʲɑȥrz ~

b lɛˈks‡ŋtən

62a ˌdʌȥ·ᵊtʃ ˈkri·k;
   æᵊłmə; ˈroȥkˌfɪ·ʃ
   *soˇ·ᵊndəz

b nɛl‡sfo·ᵁd; roȥkfɪ·ʃ

63a kreȥ‡gz kri·k;
   ba^ᵊbɝz kri·k;
   ˈŋⁱʉˌkæᵊsł

b pʰɛ>ɹnt bæ·ᵊ^ŋk

64a bæˈtɹ‡ kriˈᴶk;
   ˌbɪ^·g ˈa>·ᵊ‹lən†;
   ˈtʃɑ‹·l‡mæunt

b rɛ·ᵊd læᵊnᵈz,
   pɪʲks roȥud; bɛ·ᵊdfəd

65a k̆ɛ^‡v sprɪŋ

b ˌʌ^pɝ ˌbæk ˈkrik;
   sɛ^‡ləm

VA

65c̲ ˈrouˌnouk, ˈroᵁə-

66a ʃʉ>ˈtn kri·k;
   ɛ^ᵊnd‡kaȥᵊt

b ˈsɪdnəzˌvɪᵊł;
   raȥk‡ mæʉnt

67a mæˈks kriˇ·k;
   ˌhσ‹·ɛ>ˈwσȥᵊsᵗ‡^

b dɹɛ^‡^pə

68a i·sᵗvʲʉ^ᵂ; floˇ·‡ˇd
   æ·ᵊłəm rɪ·ᵊd3; sa^·ᵁəȥz

69a speᵊnsə; hoˇᵓs pɑ<:stə

b ˈrɪd3ˌwe‡^

70a blæ·ᵊnd

b błæ·ᵊnᵈ; sɛ·ᵊdn

71a ɪ·ᵊnᵈᵊpɛᵊnᵈən'ts

b ˌɪ·ᵊnᵈᵊ^ˈpɛᵊndənts

72a stou^n kou^ł bræ‡ntʃ;
   steˇ‡sᵗ‡^; grɜ·ᵊndᵗ‡^

b łoˇ·g‡^ baȥᵊrəm
   bræ·‡ˇntʃ;
   ˈhwa·ᵊ‹tˌwʉ^ˇ·ᵊd;
   gaȥɝ·dn

73 doˇɝ'tn; ˌkæᵊsłˈwʉ>·ᵊdz;
   kaȥpɝ kriˇⁱk

74a ˌmɛᵊdəˈvʲʉ‹ᵁ^

b̲ ˈæ·ᵊb‡ndən

75a d3oˇᵁ^nzvł

b ˈd3oˇᵁ^nzˌvɪᵊł

NORTH CAROLINA

1 naȥ·ᵊts σ‹·ɛȥłən†

2a poᵗ‡^nt ˈhɑ>rbɝ;
   pσplɝ bræ‡ntʃ

b mo‹uʲa^ᵊk

3a ˌoȥuł ˈtɹæᵖp

b ˌbɛ^·ᵊłˈkro·ᵊs

NC

4a ˌfoeᵊt ˈɑ>·ɛ>lən†;
   ɹʉȥᵂᵊᵊ, ʲoeᵊ; hoˇʔch

b tɹσȥᵊtʉəł

5a ø̲uˈkɪᵊsˌkøu^;
   ˈɪɪzɞ̆bəθ sɪᵊᵗ‡

b ˈwɪᵊnˌfoˇ·ł

6̲ iᴶdntən

7a tɹæp; koułre‡n

b ˈæ·ᵊsk̆ⁱʉvł; wĩˇ·ᵊ̃nzə̨

N8 o^ᵁˇk sɪ‡ᵗ^; ˈhaȥᵊbˌguᵊd

8a wɪljəmstən; grɪfn

b hɑ^ł‡ sprɪᵊŋz;
   wɪljəmstən

9a k̆ə̆ˈlʌ^·ᵊmb‡; ˌæl‡ˈgeˇ‡ᶠȥ

b kəˈlʌ^·mb‡^ə̨;
   ˌæl‡ˈgɛ^‡^tə̨^,
   ˌæ>·l‡ˈgɛ^‡tə̨

10a ---

b ˌɹøuˈdæᵊn'tθ‡^

c mæ̃n‡‡^øu^

11a ˈɛŋᵍəłˌhσȥəd;
   mɪˇ·dłtən;
   łɛȥ‡k łæᵊnd‡ŋ

b ˌtʰɑ·‡n‡ ˈøuk;
   ˌswσᵊn ˈkwoˇ·ᵊɝ̨

12a ˈbɹɪˇvɝ ˌdæ·ᵊm;
   waȥᵊʃ‡ntən; ˌlaȥᵊŋ ɛ^‡kɝ
   *ˌblʌnts ˈkri·k

b wɑ^ᵊʃ‡ntən

13a ˈhσɝʔnzˌwɪᵊł (√)

b mɛ^·ᵊr‡t

N14 kəˈhu^k‡^; ˈhæʉ‡ˌlɑȥk

14a ˈə̨ᵊ^nł

b ˈvæntsˌbɝrə

c̲ ˈŋⁱȥʉ> bən

NC

15a ˈʃɛᵊɫməˌdɑ‹·ɛɹn;
    griɹĩnvɫ; ˈtʃi·ˌkɒɹᵊd

b w˨˯ⁿʃ̬ᵊvɫ

16a ˈɡ‹·ᵊbə̰; ˌsneᵛuˆ ˈhɪ·ᵊɫ

b ˌsnɐ̲ɹu̲ɹ ˈhɪ·ᵊɫ; huḵətən

17a ɛˆmɤ̄ˆ-əs; dʌˆ·ᵊdlɤ̄

b mæunṭ ɔɹᵊlɤ̄v

18a ˈtʃɪŋkɤ̄ɹˌpɪ·ᵊn;
    sɑɹɤ̄prəs kriˆ·k

b ˈfrɛˆnˌʃ ɹ ᵊp;
    ˈwɔ̰ˆɔᵛˌsɔ̰ˆɔᵛ; fe·snz

19a ˌplɛznt ˈhɪ·ᵊɫ;
    ˈkʰɹᵊnˈʔstən;
    ˈtʰʌˆḵɤ̄ˌho‹ᵁˆ

b tɹɛṇtən; bi·və kri·k

20a rɐu; siᵛidɐ ɑ›·ɤ̄ɫənᵗ

b ˌhɑɹɵkɵz ˈɑɹɤ̄ᵛlənᵗ

c stɹɛɹ·ɤ̄ʔts

21a grænᵗs̲ ˈkri·k;
    ˈme·zˌvɪᵊɫ; hwɑˆɤ̄ʔ o·k

b hɛrɤ̄s kr˨ˆĩk;
    ˈdʒæ̇ˈksnˌvɪᵊɫ

22a ˈḵeˆɤ̄ˌntʌˆk

b ˈbɵ·ˌgɔ·

23a hwɪskɤ̄ kriᴶk;
    wɤ̄lmɤ̄ntən;
    meᵛɤ̄snbɵ̰rə

b mɵ·ṭɫ grɵɹuv sæˆuˆnd;
    wɪlmɪŋtən

c wɪlmɪŋtən

d ---

N24 ˈkæḻɤ̄ˈbæʃ; ˌʃɛᵊˈloˆ·t

24a friˈlən; wɔᵛ·kəmɔᵛ·

b rɔɤ̄ɫ o‹ᵁk; səˈplɑ‹·ɤ̄ᵛ;
    ˌlɑɹˈkwudz ˈfɔɹᵊlɤ̄

N25 tɵ·kɤ̄

25a mɪᵊnts; mæ̰ɹkdæɹnɫz

b tɵ·ḵɤ̄

26a tʃeᵛɤ̄snz sto·ᵊ;
    sijdə̰ kri›ᴶk

b ho‹up mɪ·ᵊɫz;
    ˈrɔɹ·kˌfɪʃ

c fɛˆ-ətvɫ, fɛˆᵊdvɫ;
    krɔᵛɔs kri›ᴶk

27a ble·dnbə̰ᵛrə

b əlɪzəbəθtaˆũn

28a ˌkrʉ›·so‹ᵁz ˈɑ›·ɛ›lənᵗ;
    o‹ᵁɫ dɑɹk

b mæsɤ̄doᵁnɤ̄; boˆ·ᵊdmən

c hwɑ·ɛ›tvɫ;
    wɛɫtʃɤ̄z kri›·k

29a ˈpʰɛᵊmˌbruᵊk

b bɑᵊ̃kɵ ˈtɛˆᵊn mɑ›·ɛ›ɫ;
    ɫʌɹmɵtən; haˆ·ᵁᵊzvɫ

30a feᵛɤ̄snz ə›uɫᵈ tæᵊvən;
    ˈkɑɹˌnᵂeᵛɤ̄;
    wɪɹⁱkɤ̄keᵛɤ̄nɤ̄

b læ·ᵊɹskə; ˈrɐ·uˌnɐuk

31a ˈhɔɹɫɤ̄ᵛstɤ̄; ˈɛ·sɤ̄ks;
    ˈbrɪŋksvɪᵊɫ

b ˈdɑ›·lɤ̄ntən; hæ›ɫəfæks,
    hæ›ᵊ-; fɔᵛɔsɤ̄ᵛt

32a rɑɹḵɤ̄ mæᵛuˆnt

b ˈkʉ›ᵊ̃ɫˌmoɵ; tɵᵛ‹·ᵊbrɵ

33a blæɹˈk kriɹik

b ɛˆ·vɤ̄nzdeᵛɤ̄ᵊɫ; wɪɹ·ᵊɫsn,
    wɪɹᵊɫsn; stænᵛnzbɵ·g

34a sæ·ɤ̄ˆndɵz tʃæpɫ;
    smɪffi·ᵊɫᵈ

b smɪffiᵛiᵊɫᵈ

NC

35a ˈmæᵊntʃɛᵊstə;
    ˈændəsnz krik

b ɵ·ʊ̰n, ɵ·vin; grɵᵛuɹv

N36 wɛˆgrəm

36a lɑ‹rɵ̆ɫ hɪ·ᵊɫ

b ɡ̰ɹ ᵊpsn

37a wa›·ˆɛ›z

b wɑɹrɤ̄ntən;
    fɪʃɤ̄ᵛn krɪˆik, ʃaˆkə

N38 moᵛ·ᵊɫtən; ˈlʉɹ-ɤ̄sˌbɜ̰ᵊg;
    sæᵊndɤ̄ kri·k

38a ---

b bʌˆ·ᵊn; dʌˆ·ᵊnz

39a ɔɹˈksfəd

b ˈsto‹uˌvɔᵛɔɫ

40a keɤ̄rɤ̄; haˆusɤ̄ᵛz kri·k

b liᴶvɫ; mɵɹrɤ̄ᵛsvɫ

41 ˈrɔˆ·ɔᵛlɤ̄

42a ste·lɤ̄; mæθesɤ̄ᵛz

b pɪˈtsbɵ̰ʳə;
    hɪkrɤ̄ mauˆnʔtn

43a hɵᵊ̰ɹɹdɫ mɪ·ᵊɫz

b ɑɹʳɤ̄ᵛndʒ groᵛuv;
    hɪ·ᵊɫzbɵʳə

44 ʝæᵊntsvɫ (✓)

45 riɹᴶdzvɫ

46a gɪɫfəd kɔɹlɤ̄dʒ;
    frɛˆ·ndʃɪp

b gɪᵊɫfəd kɑɹlɤ̄dʒ;
    frɛᵊnʃɪp

c ˈgriᵛᴶnzˌbʌrə

47 soᵁfɤ̄ᵊˆ; ˌnⁱʉ ˈmaɵḵɤ̄ᵛt

48 ˈtɔᵛɔmesˌvɪᵊɫ

49 kɔɹɹɪnɤ̰θ; goˑɫᵈ hɪᵊ›ɫ;
    mɵɵgən

NC

50a ˈsɔˇ·ɫzˌbɛ>ˉɟ

 b ˈsɔˇɔɫzˌbɛ^ˉɟ

51a ˌblæ>k ˈæ·ŋkɫ; stiˀ·dz;

 lɪ>·ʈɫ rɪ·ᵊvɚ

 b ˌrʉᵁ>bɟ^ˈæ·ᵊt; kændə

N52 we·dzbɜ>rə

52a fɑˣˉɟˇsvɫ;

 ˌpiˀɟ ˈdiˀɟ; la>·ɛ>ɫvɫ

 b dʒoˇᵁnz krɪ>ɟk;

 mɔˇɔvɟˇcˇn; gʌˣ·lɟˇdʒ

53a mɑ·ə̣ʃvɪᵊɫ;

 ŋɟʉ· se·ɟ̌ləm

 b wɪngɟ̌t, ˈmᵊ̃ˣnˌroˇᵁ

54a ˈkɑ>ᵊˌnˌkɔɚd

 b kᵊ̃^nkɔɚd

55 mɪnt hɪᵊɫ

56a ˈhoˇᵁᵛpˌwɛᵊɫ;

 hᵊ̃^nᶠ ̣əzvɫ;

 loˇ·ɔˇŋ krɪˀᴶk

 b ʃɑ·ᵊ>lət

57a dænbɛˉɟ

 b dæᵊnbɛˣˉɟ

58a seˇɟdʒ krɪˀᴶk;

 mæʉ̣t æˀɚ-ɟ;

 sʈ̣ʉ·ədz krɪˀik

 b ləˈdoˇʉnɟ^ə;

 sʈ̣ʉ^·əts kriˇᴶk

59 bu<·nvɫ

60 təˈbækəˌvɪᵊɫ

61a nᴵu<· hoˇᵁᵛp

 b steˇɟtsvɫ

62a weᵊst dʒɛᵊvɚsn

 b neˇɟθənz kriᴶk,

 ˌweᵊst ˈdʒɛᵊvɚsn

63a stoˇ·ᵁnɟ fɔɚk; ɛ^·ᵊɫk

NC

63b ˈgɪᵊɫˌriˀɟθ;

 brʌˣʃɟ mæʉnˀn

64a bænoᵁˇk; ve·ᵊɫ

 b hɪkrɟ^; ŋ̣ᴵʉ^tn;

 ˌkɔ̣ˣɫˈwe·ᵊɫ

65a kɔ̣ˣᵊlɟ·ˈtsvɪ·ᵊɫ;

 dʒɑ̣ˣᵊnz rɪ·ᵊvɚ

 b kᵊ̃ŋz kriᴶk, ɫəˈṇo·ᵊ̌ɚ

66a wọ̣^·ᵊɫɟk; ˈlɔ̣ˣᵊnˌdeˇɟᵊɫ

 b bɔ·ɟɫŋ sprɪŋz

67a hᴵˀu<·z sɛʈ̣ɫmɪ̃·ᵊ̃nt,

 rɔˣk krɪˀik;

 ˌbju<·ləˈdi·n; hæˣᵊ̃ɫᵈ

 b hʌˣ·ᵊnɟkʌ^·ᵊt; hæˉɚɫᵈ

68a glɛˣᵊnwu<ᵊd;

 nɪiˇɫzvɪ·ᵊɫ

 b ˈgrɪiˇnˌɫɪ^iˇ;

 mæˀɟ̣̌^ən; oˇuɫᵈ fo·ɚt

69a mɪᵊɫ sprɪ̃ᵊ>ŋz;

 hwa>·ɛ>ʈ o·ᵁᵛk

 b səˈlʉ·dɟ^

70a hwa<·ɛ>t ḥ̌ɟ̣ᵊ̌ɔˣk;

 ʃɛɫ'ʈn laˣɾ̣əɫ

 b wɔˇɔɫnət ʈ̣wɔɛnɟt

71a ˈdrɪɫɟˇnˌhæᵊn; æᵊ̃ˣʃvɫ

 b loᵁ̣ɚ haˣmɟnɟ^; kæᵊnlɚ

 c ˈæᵊʃvɫ

72a brɟvaˣɚd;

 ˌpɪɚzdɟ^ ˈfɔˇɚst;

 dʌ^·ᵊnz rɔˣk

 b brɟvaˇ^ɚd

73a stiᴶkɔ^·ɟ, ˈ-ˌkɔ^·ɟ^;

 dɔˇɚsɟ; fɔˀɚnɟz kriˇᴶk

 b waˣdkrɪᵊnz;

 ˌbrɑ<·ᵊ̌ˣ>sn ˈsɪʈ̣ɟ;

NC

(73b) ʈʃɑˣɚɫztn

74a ˈha>ɟˌlæᵊnᵈz; səˈto·ᵁɫə

 b ˌkɑ̣ˣˌtuˀskɟ^ˈdʒɛˇɟ;

 fræŋklɟˇn

75a ˌgræᵊnˈvʄᵊʉᵃˣ; biᴶvɚdæᵊ̃m

 b pɪ̣ʈʃɟˀiᴶ; mɚ·fɟ^

SOUTH CAROLINA

 1a bɜˇ·dʒɪsɟˇz

 b ˌfɛ·ę̣ ˈblʌˣᵊf; flɔ·ɟd

 2a de·ɟˇv̤s; sɛ̣ņ̣tņ̣ᵊ̃^ˉrɟ;

 ˈli· ˌgeᵊt

 b pɪndəbʒˉɚ; mæᵊ̃rɟ^ən

 3a ˈdʒᵊ̃·mzɟˇz ˌkrɔ·s

 ˈro^·dz

 b sɚ·ədɟ<s; ˈʈ·ɪˣ^mənzvɯ;

 ˈdʒe·ᵊmzˌ k‘ᴶ̣ɔ̣>ᵊˇs

 ˌɟə>·ᵊdz cv dʒe·mzɟ<z

 ˈk‘ᴶ̣ɔ̣ˇc·ᵊs ˌɟo·ᵊdz

 ⊥N ˈdzi·ᴶmzɟ<z ～ ～

 c ˈp‘i·ᴶ ˌdi·ᴶ,

 ˈk‘o·ᵊlz

 ˈk‘ᴶ̣ɔ̣>ᵊsˌɟo·ᵊdz;

 fˌɟọ·rəˣnts;

 ˈʈ‘æ·ᵊnz ˌbe·ɟ

 4ab mæ·ᵊnɟ<ŋ

 c mæᵊnɟ<ŋ

 5a boˇ·ɟd,

 ˈsprɪ̣̃^ŋ ˌgyˇlɟˣ;

 ˈa^ᵊndʉɟz; ˈa^ᵊndəsn

 b ˈk‘ɪ^ᵊ̌ŋˌsʈ̣ᴶi·

 c ˈk‘ɪ^ŋsʈ̣ᴶi·

 d ˈkrɪ^ɟŋˌsʈ̣ᴶi·

N6 ˈdʒɔ<·ədʒˌʈ‘a^·un

 6a ˈhɛmɪŋweˣ·

SC

6b ˈpḷaᵊntəˆzˌvɪˆᵊl;
ˌprɪnts ˈfr̥ɛˆdrɪ<ks
*dʒɔ<·ədʒˌtˈa·un

c ˈwɔ·ᵊkəˌmɔˆᵊ ˈnɛˆᵊk;
ˈpɔ·əlɪ<z ˌɔ<ɪləˆn;
ˈɔᵛᵊl ˌseˆᵊnts

cv ˈmʌ̰·ə̣lz ˈɪˆnlɛˆt,
ˈwe·ᵊvəlɪ̰ ˌmɪlz, weˆᵊ-

N7-7a ˈdʒɔ<·ədʒˌtˈa·un

b ˈdʒɔ<·ədʒˌtˈaˆ·un

c ˈdʒɔ<·ᵊdʒˌtˈa·un

d dʒɔ<ᵊdʒtɑ·un

8a ˈmæ·ᵊsɪ̰ˌdo·ᵊnɪ̰,
hʉ̰ᵊd; ˈbʌ̰nˌoˆ·ᵊz

cv ˈbɔ̞ˆˌnoˆ·z̰, bə'-;
sɪnt ˈsti·vmz

b ˈhɛˆᵊl ˌhoˆ·ᵊl;
ˈhjʉ·ˌdʒi·

c ˈsɛˆkə̃ˆᵗ ˌsɪnt
ˈsti·vəˆnz; ˈsə̃ˆ·ə̃ ˌ~;
ˈfɜ̰ɪ̰s sɪ ˈ~

9a ˈpˈa̰·ɪn ˌrɪˆᵊdʒ
ˌskʉ·l; ˈsʌˆᵊməˌvɪˆᵊl;
ˈsɛˆᵊkəˆnt ˌsɪ<nt
ˈdʒeˆ·ᵊmz

b ˈki̯ɔ<·ᵊs; ˈjʉ·ˌtɔ<·

c ˈmʌˆŋks kˈɔ<·ənə;
snt ˈdʒɔ̰·ᵊnz

d sɪnt ˈdʒɔ̰ᵊnz

10a ˈo·-ɪnˌdɔ̞ˆ·, ˈtʃσ·ᵊlstn

b məˈklɛləˆnˌvɪˆᵊl;
snt ˈdʒeˆ·ᵊmz ˈsæᵊnˌti·

c ˌmʌ<unt ˈpḷɛˆznt;
ˈkr̥əɪs ˌtʃɜ>ɪtʃ

N11 tʃɑ·ᵊlztən

SC

11a tʃσ·ᵊlstn *tʃa>·ᵊlztən,
tʃa·l-

b ˈtʃa>·ᵊlstn

c tʃˈσ·ᵊlstn

d ˈtʃσ·ᵊlstn

e cv ˈtʃˈσ·ᵊlstn

f ˈfɪ>ʃəˆn ˌtˈæk̰t,
ˈnɔ<·ᵊθˌwɛˆst;
tʃˈσ·ᵊlstn

g tʃˈσ·ᵊlstn, tʃσ·ᵊl-

2N11 ˈdʒæᵛspə ˌkˈoo̰·ᵊt;
ˈtʃσ·ᵊlstn

11h ˈsʌ<uθ əᵛv bɹɔᵛ·ᵊd;
tʃσ·ᵊlstn, tʃˈσ·l-

i tʃa·ᵊlz̰tən

j ˈsʌᵛuθ əᵛv ˌbɹɔ̰·ᵊd;
tʃˈσ·ᵊlstn

12a ˈi·ᵊndʒən ˌfi·ᵊwz,
ˈɪˆᵊndʒɪn ˌfi·ᵊl;
ˈhσ·lɪ̰ˌvɪˆᵊl; ĉˈσ·ənz

b bə̰ˆᵊd steˆʃən;
ˌsə>nt ˈdʒɔ̰ˆ·ᵊdʒ

13 ðə ˈbʌ̰·rə;
ˈɛˆdɪ<stɔ< ˌa·ɪləˆn,
ɛˆdɪstɔ<· ~

14a ˈhɛ>ᵊndəsnˌvɪl

b ˈwɔ·ᵊltəˌbɜˆ·rə;
ˈvɜˆ·ᵊˌdeᵛ·ə cv və'-
kˈoˆ·ᵊlsn; ˈbæ·ᵊmˌbɜ̰·ᵊg

15a cv ˈbæ·ᵊmˌbɜ̰·ᵊg
⊥ˈbʌ̰ˆᵊmˌbʌ̰g;
ˈbjʉ>·fəˆdz ˌbɹɪˆᵊdʒ

b ˈbæ·ᵊmˌbɜ̰·ᵊg

c ˈbæ·ᵊmˌbɜ̰·ᵊg

N16 məˈlɛˆᵊts

SC

16 ˈæḷɪ<nˌde·l, -ˌde·ᵊḷ
ˈæ·lɪn-

17a ˈhæᵊmptˈn, -tn;
ˈpˈi·plzɪ<z

b ˈhæᵊmptəˆn; pˈi·plzɪ<z

c ˈhæᵊmptˈn; ˈpˈi·plz

d ˈhæᵊmptˈn ɪ; ˈpi·plz

N18 bjy>·fəᵛt

18a ˈbjy>·fəɪ̰t, -fə̃ɪ̰t

b ˈbjy>·fə̃ᵛt

c ˈpˈo̰·ɪt ˌrɔ<ɪˆəl ˈro̰·ᵊd;
bjy>·fəᵛt *ˈ-fət,
ˈbjy̰·fə̰t

N19 ˈhɪḷtəᵛn ˈhɛᵛd

19a ˈo̰kətɪ̰, ˈbjy>·fəᵛt

b ˈprɪtʃə̃dvɪ·l, bˈɪʉ̯ˆfəˆt

c ˈk̰ˈʌ̰nɪ>nəᵛmz blʌ̰f,
bɹʌntvɪ·l, ˈbjy>·fə>t
*-fəᵛt

d blʌ̰ftn

20a lo<u<ə ˈbra·o<nzvl;
bra·unzvl

b wɛˆslɪ̰; ˈkḷa̰·-o<u<

c ˈblɛˆnɪ<m cv ˈblɪᵛnəˆm

d ˈbɪᵛnɪ<tsˌvɪˆᵊl, -vɯ

21a ˈha>ətsvł

b tʃestəfi·ᵊɪ̰ᵈ

N22 ---

22a ˈboᵛɪk̰ɪnz; ˈdi ˌk̰ˈæᵛ·ᵊb

b ---

c ĉˈæᵊmdɪ<n; dɪ ˈĉˈæᵊlb

23a ˈdɣᵛᵊvzvl cv -ˌvɪᵊl,
ˈdɣᵛᵊvz ˌdi·ʲˌpa>ᵊt (√);
ˈlɛˆᵊbmzwɜ̰·ᵊθ

SC

23b ˈlɪɪ^ᵊntʃɨ<z ˌlɪ^ᵊvɚ᷃,
     ˈnjʉ·ˌmɑ̣>·ɵ̌k̆ɨ<t;
     hɑ>·ɵtsvl

c   ˈp‘æ̣^ᵊˌmɛ^țə;
     ˈdɑ>·^ᵊlɨnt‘n

d   ˈɔˇ·^ᵊbə^n; ˈhɑ>·^ᵊtsvl

e   p‘æ̣^ᵊlmɛ^ᵊțə

N24 sʌ^^ᵊmptə

24a sʌmptə

b   sʌ^^ᵊmptə

c   ˈlo<·r̆ɨ<ŋ ˌmɪ^ᵊl;
     ste·^ᵊtsbɜ᷃·^ᵊg
     cv –bɜ>ɨg

d   sɣˇ^ᵊmptə

25a lɑ·ɨ̆ˇks</lən

b   ˈhwa>ɨt ˌrɑ>^ᵊk; fɔ̣·ɵk

c   k‘ɵ̆ˈlɣˇ^ᵊmbjə

26a kr̆ɛ^^ᵊstn, kr̥̆ɛˇ^ᵊstə^n,
     ˈkæ^^ᵊm̥ᵣn̩; lɑ>·ɨnz,
     lɑ᷃·ənz

b   snt ˈmæ^ᵊθjʉ·z

27a kɑ̣ɝˈdo·u<və
     cv kəˈdo^ᵊvə

b   ˈlɪɪ^vɨŋstn; nɔ^ð̆θ;
     hi·brn̩

28a ˈp‘æṭəsnz ˈmɪ^^ᵊɫ;
     ˈmɑ>·ˈtn;
     ˈbɪ^ˇnɨ<t ˌsprɪ^^ᵊŋ

b   ˈmɑ᷃·ɨ̆əz ˌmɪ^^ᵊl

c   ˈhæ̣^ᵊțɨ᷃ˌvɪ^^ᵊɫ;
     ˈmɑ>·jəz ˌmɪ^^ᵊɫ;
     ˈbɪnət ˌspr̥^^ᵊŋz

d   ˈbɵ<·^ᵊnwɫ

29a ˈo<·kˌwu<^ᵊd;
     ˈmæ̃^ð^ⁿˀməˈrɪ^ᵊntsɨ᷃;

SC

(29a) ˈwɨnzɵ *e^·kɨ<n

b   gr̆æ·^ᵊnɨtvɫ
    cv ˈgr̆æ^nɨˀˌvɫ;
    gr̆ɛ·^ᵊg

c   ˈwʊ<·–ɨ<nˌvɪ^^ᵊl,
    ˈwʊ·r̆n̩–; grɛ^ɨg

30a ˈfɪlɨpɑ·ᵋ> ˈtʃɜ̆^·tʃ;
     dʒɑ>^ᵊnsn

b   ˈɛ^dʒˌfi·^ᵊɫ; wa᷃·^ᵊz,
    p‘ɪ^kɨ<nz

c   ˈɛ^dʒfi·^ᵊɫ, –ˌfi·jɫ;
    wa᷃·^ᵊz, ˈp‘ɪ^kɨ<nz

31a ˈk‘æ^ᵊmp ˌstɪ^^ᵊks;
     ˈwɛ^^ᵊs kəˈlɣˇ^ᵊmbɨ᷃;
     ˈkɔŋgəˌr̆i

b   snt ˈtɔ̣^·mə^s,
    ˈnjʉˌbɵ>ɨg ˌskʉ·ɫ;
    ˈtʃ‘e^·pɨ<n;
    səˈlu<·^ᵁ<dɨ᷃

32a ˈwɪ^^ᵊnzˌbʌrə

b   – – –

c   ˈwɪ^^ᵊnzˌbʌ᷃·rə

d   ˈwɪ^^ᵊnzˌbɣˇ·rə

33a ɑ>·^ᵊˈmijnɨ; tʃɛ^^ᵊstə,
    tʃɛ^·^ᵊ–

b   tʃ‘ɛ^^ᵊstə᷃

34a ˈæ^ɛŋkɨ<stə᷃, –ɨstə;
    ˈğɪ^lz ˌk̆jiˇk

b   ˈæ^ɛŋkɨ<stə̣᷃, –ə̣>;
    ˈğɪ^^ᵊɫz ˌk‘jˇ·jk

c   ˈæ^ɛnk<stə

35a k‘ə̣țɔ^ɔbə

b   ˈha>·^ᵊlə^n ˌp‘ɵ<·ə̣k
    mɪ^^ᵊɫ; ˌrɵ·^ᵊk ˈhɪ^^ᵊɫ;
    k‘ə̣ˈtɵ^ᵊbə

SC

35c kɑ>·ˈtn bɛɫt, biˈɜ·ʃɪbɨ;
     jɔ·ɵk

36a ˈhɵlɨ᷃ ˌsp̥ɪ^ŋz̆ᶻ;
     ˈɪ^nmə>n, ˈ–mæ̃^n;
     ˈbi·jtʃ ˌspjɪ^ŋz

b   ˈspɵ̣·ɵ᷃ˈtnˌbɵ̣^·g
    cv ˈspɵ̣·ɵ᷃ˈtnbɵ̆g

c   ˈri·ʲdvɫ, ˈri·jdvɫ

d   ˈspɵ̣·^ᵊˈtnˌbɵ᷃·g,
    ˈspɵ̣·ˈtnˌbɵ᷃·^ᵊg,
    –bɜ^·g

37   bʌfəloᵁ

38a ˈnjʉ·wˌbɛ·ʳɨ᷃

N38 ˈnʲʉ·wˌbɛ·rɨ᷃

38b ˈnʲʉ<·w̆ˌbɛrɨ᷃,
     ˈnjʉ·wˌbɛ·r̆ɨ᷃

c   ˈnjʉ<·ʷˌbɛ>·rɨ᷃,
    ˈnjʉ·bɛ·rɨ᷃

d   ˈnjʉ·wˌbɛ·r̆ɨ᷃ *–r–,
    –bɛ>·–

39a ˈma᷃·ə>nˀvɫ, ma>o<ntvɫ;
     hɣˇɣ̆ə>

b   mɑ<·untvɫ, ˈmæˇ·untvɫ;
    ˈhɣˇ·ɣ̆ə^

40a ˈæ^bvɫ, ˈæ^bɨ᷃ˌvɪ^ɫ,
     ˈæ^ɛbvɣˡ

b   ˈlɛ^bənn; ˈæ^bɨˇvɫ,
    ˈæ^bvɣˡ, –vɫ +,
    ˈæˇbəvɫ, ˈæ^b̆vɫ +

41a ʲˡʉrijkə; æ^ⁿdə̣sn

b   ˈɛˇndəsn

42a p‘ɵsɨ^nz̆ mɪ᷃·ɣˡ rɵ᷃·ᵁd;
     ˈgrii^nvɫ; ˈbɣˇțlə

N42 ˈgriĩ^ⁿvɣˡ, –vɣ
     cv grii^n– *ˈğji·jnvɫ

SC

42b　gᵘ̯i·ɟnvɫ

  cd　gri·i^nvɫ

  e　'gr̯i·nvɯ

43a　cv pʌ̧ŋkɨ<nta^un;

    cv p'ɪ^kɨ<nz

  b　'p'ɣ̌ŋkɪ>n,taɤ·on,

    -kŋ-, p'ɣ̌ŋkɪ>-,

    -ɪ>ⁿ,tã̧·ðⁿ (?);

    p'ɪ^kɪ>nz, p'ɪ̧kɪ>nz̥

    cv p'i·ɦɪ>nz

  c　'de·kẽsvɪɤ·ɣ̧ɫ, -ᵥɪ̧>·ɫ

44a　'flɛ̌t ˌʃo<·u<ɫ̧z

    'skɐ>uɤɫ,

    cv t'ə'mʊ^õsɨɤ;

    'wʊɤɫ,hʊ<lɚ

    cv ˌwa>ɫ'ha>·lɛɤ;

    'k̃'ii^,wii^

  b　'rɪɤtʃ,læ̃·ɛ̆; sɛ̃^ntə,

    'sɛ̃^nəkəˇ

GEORGIA

N1　sə'væ^ənə

  1a　sə'væˇ·ᵊnəɤ

  b　səvænə, sə'væ^ᵊnə

  c　---

  d　sə'væ·ᵊnə

  e　cv sə'væ·ᵊnə

  f　sə'væɤᵊnə

  g　sə'væˇ·ᵊnəˇ

  h　səˇ'væˇnəˇ, -væɤ·-

N2　---

  2a　'ɛlə,bɛ^ɫ

  b　lə'ne·ə

  3a　fɭɛɤmɨntən

  b　'ha>·ɨnz,vɪ^ᵊl

N4　'sa>pəɟo^, krɛ^ᵊsənᵗ

GA

4a　de^·rɨɤn

  b　ðə 'rɪ^ᵊdʒ; rɪ^ᵊdʒvl

  c　və'lo·nə

5a　'frɛɤdˌri·kə,

    ðə bi·tʃ,

    snt 'sa·ɨmə^nz a·ɨlə^n

  b　snt 'sa<·ɨmə^nz

  c　brʌˇnzɨ<k

  d　'brʌ̧nzɨ<k

  e　brʌˇᵊnzɨ<k

6a　'tʃɛ·rɨ ˌpoˇɨnt;

    ḱɪ^ᵊŋzləˇn

  b　snt 'me·r̂ɤz

7　'fo<·ᵁ<kstn

8a　skr̂ɨ<vm̩

  b　'dʒɛ^sɨˇp

9a　'riⁱ^dzvɪ>ɫ, -vɫ,

    ka>bstn, k'a>btn,

    t'aɤ·ᵊsn, glɛnvl, -vɫ,

    'glɛ^n-

  b　'kɒbtɛun

10a　mənæ^ᵊsɨˇs

  b　'bɛ^lvl; mə'næ^ᵊsə^s,

    he^·gɨ<n

N11　mɛ̧tə

12a　'stɪ^ɫsn

  b　'stеɨ̆ts,bʌ̧̆r̆ə

13a　rɪ̌ˇŋkən

  b　'wɪlsn 'mɨɫ ,pa>ᵊn,

    o·ḱɨɤ; i·dʒə^p cv -ɨˇp

14a　sɪɤɫ've^·ɨ̧ŋjə>

  b　sɨɫ've·ɨ̧ŋjə>

  c　'mɪ^dɫ,gᵘ̯aɤ<n 'ro<·u<d,

    cv 'rɛ^ᵊd ,bɭʌ^f,

    sɨ̧ɫ've·ɨ̧ŋjə;

GA

(14c)　'hæɫsn ,de·ɨɫ

15a　,ɛlɨg'zæᵊndə

  b　'we^·nz,bɣɤ·rə

16a　'k'a^onɨɤ ,ho·ᵊm;

    ə'gɣˇᵊstə

  b　cv bæᵊθ; blе<ɨθ

  c　ə'gʌɤstə

  d　ə'gɣˇᵊstə

N17　'lɐˇɨsvɫ

17　lɐ^^ɨ<svɪ·ᵊɫ

18a　e·ɨ̧dɹ ɨə^n

  b　'twɪn sɪ̧ɨ,

    'swеɨnts,bɜ>ᵊ̃ə

19a　'ḱɪ^ᵊbɨɤ

    **'tæ^·rɨ̧,tæ^·ən

  b　'sɐˇ·əd ,skɐ·ɫ, sɐ·əd;

    ,ɟɐ·'væ·ᵊldə

20a　'ka>ᵊbvɪ^ᵊl; 'mæk,re·ɨ;

    maɤ·ᵊlə^n, 'w3>·ᵊrk,mo<·ᵊ>

  b　'mæᵊk,re·ɨ

21a　la>lɨ^, -ɨɨ^

  b　'dɣˇblɨn

22a　,foət 'væ^ɭɨɤ

  b　---

23a　,fo<ət 'hɔˇᵊkɨ<nz,

    me·ɨ̧kə^n (?)

  bc　me·kən

  d　'me^·kə^n

  e　me·ɨ̧kə^n

  f　me·kən

N24　---

24a　mæʉnt plɛzn'ᵗ tʃ3ɨtʃ;

    mɪɭɨdʒvɪᵊɫ

  b　'k'ʊ·ə ,ste·ɨʃn, -z ~

N25　spa>ᵊdɨ̧

GA

26   ˌmɒ‹ntɨˈsɛlə

27   griˑnzbʌˠə

28   ˈdɛlˌhaʑˑə

29a   ˈgo‹ˑᵁ‹ʃɨ‹n ˈhɑˆɨˌweˆˑ;
      ˈlɪˆŋkəˆntn

b   ˈlɪˆŋkəˆntn

30a   ɛˆᵉlbətʻn *ˈ-ɫ-,
      ˈo‹ˑu‹gɫzbɨʑ kʻw̥ɒ‹ˑrɨʑ

b   ˈɛˆᵉlbətʻn *ˈɛˆᵉɫbəˆtʻn

c   ɛlbətn

31   ˈhɑ›ətwɫ

32   kʻɑ›ˑe̥nzvɫ

33a   kɑ›ɫbət

b   ˈkɒˑɫbət

N34   ˈæˆθɨ‹nz

34a   boˆˑᵁgɑˑᵉt; ˈbrædˌbɛˠɨ

b   ˈhɪˆnʼtn ˌbræon skʉˑwl;
      ˈbo‹ˑu‹ˌgɑ›ˑe̥t;
      ˈbræˑᵋbˌb̥ɜˆˑrɨʑz

N35   tʻɒmpsn; ˌmʌnʑnˈrou

N36   ---

N37   ɛtɬæ‹ntə

37a   ˈdo‹ˑu‹rəˌvɪˆᵉɫ
      cv ˈdoʑˑurəˌvɪˆᵉɫ

GA

37b   ˈrɒk ˌtʃæᵋpɫ;
      ˌlaʑˑᵉθo‹ˑu‹ŋɹə;
      ˈdaʑˑᵉməˆnz

c   ævəndeɨɫ; diˈkeɨ̥tə

2N37   ædəˆmzvɪˑᵉɫ;
       əˆtlæˑntə
       cv ətˈlæˆᵉn̥tə

37d   ˈdɹʉɨd ˌhɪˑɫz; ətlæntə

e   ---

f   ætˈlæˑᵉn̥tə

g   æᵋtˈlæᵋntə

h   ətˈlæᵋn̥tə

i   ətˈlæˑntə

38   geˇɨnzvɫ; tædmoᵁɚ

39   dɨˈlɒnɨˇgə

40   ˈdʌˆkˌtꝫʊ

41   ˌɛˆɬɨˈdꝫeˑɨ, ˈ-ˌ-;
     liˆˑiˆtʃɨz, tʻeɨ̥ɫz kriˆˆˆk

42a   cv ˈpɹɜˆˑəsˌvɪˆᵉɫ;
      ˈkɒp̥ɚˆ ˌhɪˆɫ;
      ˈmo‹ˑu‹ˌbiˑɫ

b   daʑˑᵉɫ, ˈblʉˑʷ ˌrɪˆᵉdꝫ;
     ˌnʉwnˈtʻʉˑwtlɚ

43   ˌloˑn̥təm ˈkoˑv;

GA

(43)   ˈblæɵzvɫ; æˑʉɫtæʉn

44a   ˈdꝫɜʑɨmənɨʑ; pɚˈsɪˆməˆn

b   kʻw̥ɒˇˑɵts;
     pʻɵˆˈsɪˆməˆn

c   pʻɵˆˈsɪˆməˆn ˌkr̥ɨˑᴶk

d   kʻˈɬeɨ‹ʼtn

e   ˌflæt ˈkriˑᵎˆk;
     leɨkmɑ›nt

FLORIDA

1   ˈfɜʑˑᵉˆnə›nˌdiˑnə,
    ˈfɜˆɨnn-

2a   ˈmæˑᵋndərɨn;
     ˈsæˇoθ ˌdꝫæᵋksnˌvɪˆᵉɫ

b   ---

c   ˈdꝫæᵋksnˌvɪˆᵉɫ

3a   ˌseˆnt ˈɔˑᵉgəˆstin

b   seˆnt ɔgəˆstin

4   sprʉʑʉ›s kriˇᵎˆk
    cv ˈsprʉˑs ˌkriˑᵎˆk,
    təˈmoˇukə ˌfɵɵmz,
    ~ fɑ›ɵm;
    ˈdɛˆɨˌtɔ̃nɵ̆ ˌbiˑtʃ

5a   heˆɨg, geˑɨnzvi

b   wɪnzɵ; geɨnzvi

COMMENTARY

The following abbreviations are used in the commentary: b.--born (in); r.--resided (in); F--father; M--mother; P--parents; PGF, etc.--paternal grandfather, etc.; Twp.--township; P. O.--post office

ONTARIO

1a   b. Lancaster [ˈɫænˌkæstɚ];

ONT

(1a)   r. *Cornwall* [ˈkɔ‹ɵnwɵˆɫ]
       and Alberta [æɫˈbɵtə]
       1919-27; M b. Vankleek Hill
       [vænklɪk hɪˑᵉɫ]

b   b. Moulinette
     [ˈmoˑᵁɫˌnɛˆt]; r. briefly

ONT

(1b)   in Morrisburg [ˈmɒˆɵɨsbɵg]

2b   b. Long Point [ˈlɔˇŋ
     ˌpoʑɨnt]

4a   r. Saskatchewan
     [sɨˈskætʃɨwɒʑn]; visited
     Syracuse [ˈsɛɵɵˌkɨ̵ʉᵁˆz],

ONT

(4a) *Rochester* [ˈrɑtʃɛstɚ](NY);

M b. Bothwell [bouθwɫ]

b 1 yr. at Peterborough
[piˑⁱ^t̬ɘbɜ>ɵəz] Teachers
College; visited *Oswego*
[ˌɒsˈwiˑgoᵁ] (NY)

6 [t̬ˈɵˈrɑ̃ˑnəˇ]: natural

7 r. Port Dalhousie [ˌpoɵt
dəˈɫu̞ṣu<zꞏ^,
ˌpoɵt̬əˈlu̞ʉ>z‡ˑ^],
Waterloo [wɔˇ·t̬ɵˌɫu̞ṣu<],
Jordan [dʒɔɵdn], Picton
[pˈɪkt̬ən], Beamsville
[biˑⁱ^nzvɫ]

NEW YORK

5e r. Rockville Centre
[ˈrɑ̣ḳˌv‡ɫ sɛ>n̩t̬ə],
in *Hempstead* [hɛmpst̬əd]
Twp. since 1927

h r. Morningside Heights
[ˈmɔ·n‡ŋˌsa‡d ˈha‡ts]
since 1902

7f r. summers at Shandaken
[ˌʃænˈdeˇ‡kən]

g r. *Brooklyn* [bɾ̆ṵuklən]
since 1905

i r. on Old Mamaroneck Road
[oṣuɫᵈ məˈmærənɛk roṣud],
White Plains [hw̥a‡t
pɫeˇ‡nz] since 1916

9a b. Ossining [ɑsən‡ŋ]

11 r. Shrub Oak [ʃrʌb oṣuk],
Mohegan Lake [moṣuhiˑgən
leˇ‡k] P. O., in Yorktown
[jɔɵkt̬aun] Twp. since 1921

NY

12a b. Beekman [biᴶkmən] Twp.

23b b. Brownville
[ˈbrɑ·uˆn̩ˌv‡^ɫ]

c b. Victory Mills
[ˈv‡^kt̬ɹ‡< ˌm‡^ɫz]

25a *Weverton* formerly called
The Factory [ð‡^ ˈfækt̬ɹ‡ʐ]

b r. 7 yrs. in Stony Creek
[st̬ɵ>un‡ʐ kr‡^k]

26b b. West Hill [ˈwɛ^st
ˌh‡>ɫ]

27a school in Cubtown
[ˈkʌb̩ˌt̬ˈeˑˑun]

28a b. Schuyler Falls
[ˈskɑ‡lɵ ˌfɔˇ·ɫz];
school in Saranac
[ˌsæ>ɵəˈnæˑk]

29a b. Rodman [ˈrɑdmn̩]

c b. Churubusco
[ˈⁱtʃɛɵəˌbʌsko<ᵁ]

30e M b. Bangor [ˈbæn̩ˌgʐɵ]

31a *Oswego* cv [əˈswiˇgoṣu<]

b b. West *Theresa* [ˌwɛ^s
ˈθr̥̊iˑs‡<]; *Watertown*
cv [ˈwɒrɵˌt̬ɛ>un]

33b *Utica* cv †[ju̞ˇu̞t̬‡ʐk̊ˈiˇi]

c *Old Forge* cv [ˌⁱo<u<ɫ
ˈfɔɵdʒ]

34a *Pulaski* cv [pəˈɫæsˌkɑ^·‡]

b *East Hampton* cv [ˈiˇist
ˌhæᵐpt̬n̩]

c *Syracuse*
cv [ˈsɛ^ɵɵˌkjuṣu<s]

35b b. near De Ruyter
[d‡^ reˇ‡ɾɵ]

NY

36a r. in Canastota
[ˌkæ·nəˈstout̬‡^] since
1936

37a b. Western [ˈwɛstən] Twp.

38b high school in Chittenango
[ˌⁱtʃ‡t‡ˈnæŋgə]

42b b. *Truxton* [trʌkstən]

44b b. Hagadorn Hill
[ˈhægəˌdɵn ˌh‡ᵊɫ]

45c *Catlin* cv [ˈk̊æ^t̩ln]

46b b. between Tyrone
[t̬ˈero<u<n,
ˈt̬eˇ‡ˌro̞ˇun, -ro·un]
and Bradford [ˈbrædfɵ̣d,
ˈbrædfɵd] on Old
Knickerbocker Farm [o<ᵁɫ
ˈn‡kɵˌbækɵ ˈfɑ^ɵm]
([-æ-]: *sic*); r. Bath
[bæ^ᵊθ, bæθ cv bæ^·θ];

F b. Switzer Hill
[ˈsweˇ‡ts̬ɵ ˈh‡·ᵊɫ];
Rochester
cv [ˈrɑ<‡tʃɛstɵ],
Horseheads
cv [ˈhɔ<ɵsˌhɛ·ᵊdz],
Orange [ɔˇɵ‡ndʒ] Twp.

47a school in *Lounsberry* Hill
[ˈlɑ<unzˌbɵɵ‡ʐ h‡ɫ
cv ˈle<unzˌbɵ̣ɵ‡ʐ ˈh‡^ɫ]
and Trumbulls Corner
[ˈt̬ɹʌˇmbɫz ˌkɔɵnɵ^z];
Binghamton cv [ˈb‡^m‡<ŋtn],
Elmira cv [ɛ˓ɫˈmeˑ‡ɵ‡ʐ],
Jersey City cv [ˌdʒʐ>ɵz‡ʐ
ˈs‡^t̬‡ʐ] (NJ)

NY

48a r. *Ira* [ˈe̞ʒ̰ɪ̈ʚɪ̈‹];

Seneca Lake <u>cv</u> [ˈsɛˆn̴ɪ̈‹kə

ˌleˇɪ̈‹k]

d high school in Wolcott

[wʊɫkəˆt]

49a b. *Varick* <u>cv</u> [væʚɪ̈‹k] Twp.;

Geneva <u>cv</u> [dʒɪˈniˇivɪ̈‹]

d F b. Montezuma

[ˌmɑˑnt̴ɪ̈ˈzuˑmə];

MGM b. Interlaken

[ˈɪn̨t̴ʚˌleˑ ̴ ̡kəˆn]

50a b. *Joy* [dʒɔˆɪ̈]

b b. Marion Village

<u>cv</u> [ˈmɛ̞ʚɪ̈‹əˆn ˌvɪlɪ̈dʒ]

51a P. O. formerly Richmond Mills

[ˈrɪtʃmə̃ˆn ˌmɪɫz]

b r. 7 yrs. in Gorham

[ge̞ˋʚəˆm]; school in

Billsboro [ˈbɪˋlʒ̰ˌbʒˋʚ

<u>cv</u> -ɫz-]; *Seneca Falls*

<u>cv</u> [ˌsɪˋnəkə ˈfɔˑɫz]

52a school in *Italy* Valley

<u>cv</u> [ˈɪˈt̨lɪ̰ ˌvælɪ̰]

b b. Jerusalem

[dʒʚˈuʂu‹sələˆm] Twp.

c graduated from *Penn Yan* and

Dundee [ˈdʌ‹nˌdiˇi] High

School

54a r. *Adrian* [eˈɟɹɪ̈ˆən],

Hornell [ˈhɔˇʚ̴ˌnɛˑɫ],

Corning [kˈɔˇʚnɪ̈‹ŋ],

Bridgehampton

[ˈbrɪˋdʒˌhæmpt̴n]

b b. Greenwood [ˈgriˑnˌwu‹d];

r. *Canisteo*

NY

(54b) [ˈkænɪ̈sˌti ˑoˍ ᵁ‹]; M, MGP

b. Rexville [ˈrɛksvɫ]

55a b. Houghton [ˈhoʂˑuˋ‹ˈtn]

b *Rushford* Lake

<u>cv</u> [ˌrʌ‹ʃfʚˆd ˈleˇɪ̈‹k]

56a F b. Eagle [hiˑᴶgɫ] Twp.;

Buffalo <u>cv</u> [ˈbʌ‹ffˌl̥oʂuˋ‹]

Syracuse

<u>cv</u> [ˌsɪ̰ˇʚəˈkjuʂ ᵁ‹z]

58a *Penn Yan* <u>cv</u> [ˈpɛˆn

ˌɟæˆˑˑˆn], *Syracuse*

<u>cv</u> [ˈsɪ̈ʚəˌkjuˋˑs]

b b. *Murderkill* Hundred

[mɜ̞ˋˑʚdəkɪ̆ɫ ˈhʌ‹ndʚˆd

<u>cv</u> ˈmɜ̞ˋʚdʚˌk̆ɪɫ

ˈhʌˇndɑ̨ əˆd] (Del);

Rochester <u>cv</u> [ɹɑ‹tʃʚˆstʚ

d [fɛˇʚɪ̈‹ŋtn]: *sic* (Ed.);

b. *Rochester* [ɹɑ‹tʃɪ̈‹stʚ

59a b. Byron [be̞ˆɪ̈ʚəˆn]

60a b. Somerset

[ˈsʌ‹mʚˌsɛˆt] Twp.

b b. Eagle Harbor [ˈiˇigɫ

ˌhɑ̨ʚbʚ]; *Rochester*

<u>cv</u> [ˈɹɑ‹tʃɪ̈stʚ]

61a [-ɫ-]: strongly velarized;

r. Wilson [wɪ̈ɫsn]

62a b. Newstead [ˈnʉˑstəˆd]

Twp.; *Buffalo*

<u>cv</u> [bʌ‹fələ̨]

b school in North Collins

[ˈnɔ̨ˆʚθ ˌkɑ‹lɪ̨nz]

63b *Little Valley*

<u>cv</u> [ˈlɪ̨t̨ɫ ˌvæˇɟɪ̨ʚᶦ‹]

c [sæɫəmæŋkɪ̈ˆ]: old-

NY

(63b) fashioned

64b b. West Portland

[wɛst pɔ̨ʚtləˆn]

NEW JERSEY

10b b. South *Brunswick* [sæʉθ

brʌnzɪ̈k] Twp.

c b. Monroe[mənrɑ̨ˋᵙ] Twp.

13a b. Pleasant Valley

[pɫɛˋzənt væˋᵊɫɪ̈ʂ]

14a b. Frelinghuysen

[friˇɫɪ̈ŋhɑ̨ˆɪ̈zən] Twp.

b b. Cummins [kʌmənz]

16a b. near Pompton Plains

[pɑmptən pɫɛɪ̈nz]

20a formerly Washington

[wɑˋʃɪ̈ŋtən] Twp.

b formerly Palisade

[pælɪ̈ˇseɪ̈d] Twp.

PENNSYLVANIA

5a b. Charlestown

[tʃɑˋʚləstɑˆ ˑun]

([-əs-]: *sic*) Twp.

b b. Pocopson [pəkɑpsn] Twp.

6c *Hamburg*: "Dutch" form is

[hɔ̨ʂmbɑ̨ɾ̆ɪ̈k]

14a b. Klingerstown

[k̲lɪŋəɾstaun]

23a b. Brooklyn [bruklɪ̈ˇn],

near Dimock [dɪmək]

27a M b. Charleston

[tʃɑˋʚɫztən] Twp.

45a interviewed near Ursina

[ˌʚˋɾˈzaɛnə]

51a b. Allegheny City

[ˈæɫəˌgɛˆnɪ̈ sɪɾɪ̈ˆ]

PA

(51a) (now part of the North Side

of *Pittsburgh*

['pɪts͵bɚg])

57b b. West Monterey [wɛst

'mɒnɾəɾɛˆ‡]

65a *Fairview*: old-fashioned

67a [-ng-]: *sic*

WEST VIRGINIA

16a b. Alpena [͵æᵊɫ'pi·nə]

26b [sə-]: *sic*

30a b. *Oceana* [͵oᵁs‡ˆ'æn‡ˆ]

District

51b [-ɚn]: *sic*

OHIO

9a b. *Lodi* [ɫoʂudaǂ] Twp.

12b ⊥: uneducated; b. Waterloo

[͵waɾəˈlʉ>·]; r. Symmes

[sɪᵊmz] Twp.

15a *sic*; *Senecaville*

<u>cv</u> ['sɛnəˆkɪ͵vɪ>·ɫ]

16a M b. Sarahsville

[sɛɾəzvɪ·ᵊɫ]

b b. Millfield

['mɪ·ɫ͵fiˇɪɫd]

c b. Whigville [hwɪgvɪ·ᵊɫ]

17 M b. on Big Wolf Creek

['bɪˆg ͵wu<ɫf 'kr̆ɪˆk]

KENTUCKY

1a b. Bet [bɛˆt]

4a *Hyden* [haʐᵊdn]

5b F b. on Smoot Creek

['smʉᵁˆt ͵kri·iˆk]

DELAWARE

6a b. near Selbyville

[sɛᵊɫb‡vɪᵊɫ]; F b. Head

DEL

(6a) of Sound [hɛˆ‡ˇd ‡ˆ

sæ·ʊnd]; PGF b. Sinepuxent

[͵sɪn‡ˆ'pʌksn] (Md)

MARYLAND

6a b. Bloodsworth I.

[bɫʌ<dzəθ ɑʂ‡lənt]

20b [nɛtwə̌ɫ]: old-fashioned

21b b., educated Bowensville

[boᵁ‡ˇnzv‡ɫ]

VIRGINIA

7b ['lʉˇ·‡ˇzə]: old-

fashioned

8a *Fredericksburg*

<u>cv</u> ['frɛdr‡ksbʌʐ·ᵊg]

11b ['-'-]: at times

13a b. Irvington [əəv‡nt̪ən]

14c [wə'kaˆməkə]: quick pron.

15b [-ɔ<-]: allophone of /ʌ/

19a *Guinea*: nickname

22 b. Norge [nɒˆ·ᵊdʒ]

23a F b. *Messick* Point

[pɑˆɛnt]

b MGF b. Poquoson [pəkoəsn]

([-oə-]: *sic*)

27 * b. Assateague

[͵æsə'tɪg] I.

28b b. near Seaview [si·vjʉ]

42b b. near Diana Mills

[da>ᵋ>æᵊnə mɪᵊɫz]

50a [-s‡z]: *sic*

56b b. Monterey ['maʐnɾə͵ɾeǂ]

58 * r. *Doylesville*

['dɔˆ·‡ˇlzv‡l]

62b b. Avon ['eǂ͵vaʐᵊn]

64b school in Moneta

VA

(64b) [͵moᵁ'niˇ͜ɾə]

65<u>c</u> ['roᵁə-]: affected

69b b. Irisburg

[a>ᵋ>ʳ‡ˇsbʌʐ·g]

NORTH CAROLINA

3a b. South Mills

[͵saˆʊθ 'mɪᵊɫz]

7b b. *Colerain*

['keʐuˆɫ͵rɛˆ‡ˆn]

10b b. Salvo ['sæᵊɫ͵vɵʊ]

13a *sic*; b. on the Sound at

Spring Creek [sprɪŋz

kri·k] and Bay River

[bɛ‡ rɪ·vɚ]

14b b. Neuse River Landing

[njʉ>·s rɪᵊvə læᵊnd‡ˇn]

26<u>c</u> [fɛˆᵊdvɫ]: old, natural

30a *Lasker* <u>cv</u> [lɑ<·skə]

33a b. on Contentnea Creek

[kən'tɛn'tn‡ˆ kri·k]

34a b. near Benson [bɛᵊn'tsn]

35b [ɚ·vɪn]: old-fashioned

44 *sic*

66b b. Belwood [bɛˆ·ᵊɫwuᵊd]

67a F b. on Toe River

[toˇo< rɪ·vɚ]

71a [-n]: *sic* (Ed.)

73a M b. on Kirklands Creek

[k̆jɚklənz kriˇjk,

k̆i̯ʐɚk- ~]

74a F b. on Tuckasegee River

[tʌˆk‡sɪjdʒ rɪᵊvɚ]

SOUTH CAROLINA

1a b. on other side of

Chinners [t̆ʃɪnəs‡z]

SC

(1a) Swamp; grew up at Pawleys
       Swamp [pɔˇ·lɨz swɔˇ·mp]

3b   b. Vausetown
       [ˈvɔ·ᵊsɪtˈæˇ·o‹n], on
       Lynches River [ˈlɪ^ᵊntʃɨz
       ˌɹɪ^ᵊvɚ]; *Georgetown*
       c̲v̲ [ˈdʒɔ‹·ᵊdʒᵢtˈæˇ·on]

4a   b. Santee [ˈsæᵊn?ˌtˈi]
       Twp.

b   b. Summerton [sʌ^ᵊmətˈn]

c   b. Juneville [dʒʉ·wnvɨˉl],
       on border of Santee
       [ˈsæ̃ᵊnˌtˈiᴶ] Twp.

5a   b. Central [sɛ^n?tɹl]
       neighborhood

b   b. Gourdins Depot
       [gɨ^ˈdɑ·ɨnz ˈdi·po·
       c̲v̲ gɜ›ˈdɑ·ɪnz ˈdi·ˌpˈoᵷ],
       in Suttons [ˈsʌ'tnz, sʌ^-]
       Twp.

6b   r. Snow Mill [sno· ˈmɪ^ᵊl]
       1883-9

N7   b. Windsor [wɪ^nzə]

7b   b. Mindaville
       [ˈmɪ^ᵊndəvɪᶎᵊl], on
       Waccamaw [ˈwɔᶎᵊkəˌmɔ‹·ᵊ]
       Neck

8a   [hʉᶎᵊd]: *sic* (Ed.)

c   b. Russellville
       [ˈrʌ^ᵊsɯɪvɪ^ᵊl];
       Georgetown
       c̲v̲ [dʒɔ^·ᵻdʒᵢtɑᶎ·on],
       Columbia c̲v̲ [kəˈlʌᶎᵊmbɨᶎ],
       Florence c̲v̲ [ˈfɹɔ·rəˆnts]

9a   *Columbia* c̲v̲ [kˈəˈlʌ^ᵊmbɨᶎ]

SC

9b   b. Millpond [ˈmɪ^ˌpɒᶎᵊn];
       r. 6 mos. Jedburg
       [ˈdʒɛ^ᵊtˌbɜᶎ·ᵊg]

11a   r. *Florence* [flʊrᵢnts]
       1880-2

12a   b. beside Four Hole Swamp
       [ˈfo‹· ˌhoˇ·ᵊl
       ˈsw̥ɔ^·ᵊmp]; *St. George*
       c̲v̲ [snt ˈdʒɔ·ᵊ^dʒ‹z],
       George c̲v̲ [dʒɔ^·ᵊdʒɨ‹z]

13   F, PGP r. Wadmalaw
       [ˈwɑ›dməˌlɔ·ᵊ, -məlɒ·]

15a   Colston: "I always spell it
       Colson"; *Macon*
       [ˈme^·c̥ɨ‹n] (Ga)

c   b. Fishpond
       c̲v̲ [ˈfɪ^ᵊʃˌpɒ^n] Twp.

N16   r. *Hattieville*
       [ˈhætɨᶎˌvɪ^ᵊl], in
       Bennett Springs [ˈbɪnɨ‹t
       ˌspᶈɪ^ᵊŋz] Twp. since 1936

17a   b. Pond Town
       [ˈpˈɔ^ᵛᵊn ˌtˈæᶎon];
       Columbia [kˈǒˈlᵧˇᵊmbɪ›ⁱ›]

b   b. Nixville Crossroads
       [ˈnɪ^ksˌvɪ^l
       ˈkᴶɔ^ᵛᵊsˌro·ᵊd];
       r. Estill [ˈɛ^ᵊsˌtɛ^ᵊl]

N18   b. Ladies I. [ˈle·dɨᶎ
       ˌɑ·ᵊlə›n]; worked in
       Savannah [sə›ˈvɑ^nə] (Ga)
       1896-7

18b   *Port Royal* c̲v̲ [ˌpˈoᶎ·ᵊt
       ˈrɔᶎ·ᵻl, ˌpˈoᶎ
       ˈrɔᶎ·ᵻ̌›l],

SC

(18b) *Georgetown*
        [ˈdʒɔᶎ·ᵊdʒᵢtˈɑ^·un]

c   GGM of * from Connecticut
        [kəˈnɛtᶎᶎkut]

19b   *Charlotte* [ˈʃɑ›·ᵊlə^t]
        (NC), *Pittsburgh*
        [ˈpɪtsbɜ›ᶴg] (Pa)

c   summer home on Huspah
        [hʌ‹spə›] River

d   *Georgetown*
        c̲v̲ [ˈdʒɔ·ᵊ^dʒᵢtæ·on]

20a   *Marion* c̲v̲ [ˈmæ·rɨn],
        Columbia [kəˈlᵧˇᵊmbᶡə
        c̲v̲ kəˈlᵧˇᵊmbɪ›i›],
        Charlotte [ˈʃɑ·ələ^t]
        (NC), *Wilmington*
        [wɪ^ᵊlmɨ‹ntn] (NC)

b   formerly Red Bluff [ˈrɛ^ᵊd
        ˌblᵧˇᵊf] Twp.; *Georgetown*
        c̲v̲ [ˈdʒɔᶎ·ədʒᵢtɑ·on]

c   b. *Brownsville*
        [ˈbrɑᶎonzvɪ];
        Columbia [kəˈlᵧˇᵊmbᶎᶴ]

d   b. *Blenheim* [blɪ^nə^m],
        in Red Hill [ˈrɛ^ᵻd
        ˌhɪ^ᵊl] Twp.; *Beaufort*
        [bᴶʉ·fə^t]

22a   merchant in *Camden*
        [kˈǎᵊmdᶎ‹n]; *Georgetown*
        [ˈdʒɔˇ·ᵊdʒᵢtˈæˇo‹n],
        Beaufort [ˈbᴶʉ‹·fə^t]

23a   [ˌdi·ᴶˌpɑ›ᵊt]: *sic*;
        Columbia [kˈəˈlʌ^ᵊmbᶎᶴ]

b   b. Bethune
        [bəˈθʉ·ʷn]

SC

N24 railway brakeman on Denmark
['dæ·ᵊn₁mɑ>·ək] ([-æ-]:
sic)-Lane Division

24b b. Shiloh ['ʃɑ·ɨ₁lo<]
Twp.; r. Lynchburg
['lɪ^ᵊntʃ₁bɜ^·ɨg] Twp.;
school at Pleasant Grove
['p‘ɹ̥ɪᵛᵊznt ₁gɹ̝o<·ᵊv]

d b. *Stateburg*
['ste^·ᵊt₁bɜ>·ɨg];
Camden cv [c̝‘æᵛᵊmdɨ<n]

27a b. Pine Hill ['p‘ɑ>ᵊn
₁hɪ·ᵊl]; school at Middle
Willow ['mɪdl ₁wɪ>lə];
P b. Wesley Grove ['wɛslɨ<
₁gro·ᵊβə̆x] ([-βə̆x]:*sic*);
Raleigh ['rɔlɨ] (NC)

b school at Beaver Creek
cv ['bi·və ₁kr̝̍o̝i·k]

28c b. *Ellenton* ['ɛ^lɨ<nt‘n];
r. Greenland ['gr̝i·nlə>n]
section 1933-6

d b. near Elko ['ɛ^l₁ko<·]

29a b. Tabernacle [tæᵊbənɪ^kl]
Twp.; attended Edisto
['ɛ^ᵊd₁ɨsto<] School;
Darien cv ['de^·rɨx̝n,
de^·rɨx̝æ·ᵊn] (Ga); * b.
Monetta [mə'nɛ^ᵊt̝ə]

b *Warrenville*
cv ['wɒ·rɨnvł]

c b. Talatha [tə'le·ᵗθə]

30b b. Antioch
['æ·ᵊnt̝ɨx̝o<·k], in
Colliers ['k‘ɒɭɹ̥ə^z] Twp.;

SC

(30b) r. *Augusta* [ə'gɣᵛstə] (Ga)
1916-17; *Aiken* cv [e^·kɪ>n],
Columbia cv [k‘ɹ̥ɣᵛmbɹ̥ə^]

31a *Columbia* cv [kə̆'lɣᵛᵊmbɨx̝]

32a b. Horeb ['ho<·u<rə^b]
neighborhood

35c *Greenville* cv [gri·nvl],
Spartanburg
cv ['spɑ>·ᵊˀtn₁bɜ>·ᵊg,
spɒ<tə^nbɜ>·ᵊk], *Charlotte*
cv ['ʃɑ>ᵊlət] (NC)

Columbia
cv [k‘ə'ɹ̥ɣᵛmbɹ̥ə̝x]

36a * b. Wellford ['wɛ^łfə^d]

b b. Glenn Springs ['gɹ̝ɛ^n
₁spɹ̥ɨ<ŋz] Twp.

c F b. Fergersons Creek
['fə̝x·gə̆snz ₁k‘ɹ̥̍o̝ijk];
Rock Hill cv [₁rɒk 'hɪ·ł] GA

38a F b. Maybinton [me·ɪbə^nn̩
cv '-bmt‘n̩] Twp.; *Columbia*
cv [k‘ə̆'ɹ̥ɣx̝mbɨx̝]
([-bɨx̝]: *sic*)

b b. Mendenhall
['mɛ^nd̝ɨ<nhʊ^oł] Twp.

c b. Dutch Fork ['dɣᵛtʃ
₁fɒ^ɔk, ~ fɔ̝x̝·ə̝rk] section

39a b. Cross Hill ['k‘ɹ̝o̝ᵛɔ^s
₁hɪ·ᵊł] Twp.; *Columbia*
[k‘ə'ɹ̥ɣᵛmbᴶɨᵛ], *Brevard*
[bɹ̝ɨ<·ᵛvə̝<·ᵊd] (NC)

b b. near Beaver Dam Ch.
['bi·ᴶvə ₁dæ^·m
tʃ‘ə^ɨtʃ]; F, PGF b.
Old *Mountville* ['o<·u<ł

SC

(39b) ₁ma^untvł, 'o<·uł
₁mɑ<·untvł]; relatives at
Duncan Creek [dɣᵛŋkɪ>nz
k‘ɹ̥̍o̝i·ᴶk]

40a ['æ^bɨx̝₁vɪ^ł]: "correct"
pron.

b b. Cedar Springs ['sii^də
₁spr̝̥ɪ^ŋ] Twp.

41b b. Garvin [gɑ>·vn] Twp.
N42 *Spartanburg*
cv ['spɒ<·ˀtn₁bȩ·g]

42b b. Hilly Home ['hɪ^łx̝
₁ho<·ᵁm], in Cleveland
[k‘ɹ̥̍o̝i·ᴶvln̩] Twp.

43b [-ⁿ]: doubtful

44b b. Tugaloo
['t‘ɥ>ugə₁lo<·u] or
Center ['sɛ^ⁿtə] Twp.

N1 *Aiken* [e·kɨ<n] (SC),
Raleigh [rɔᵛ·lɨ] (NC)

1b 2 yrs. at Tocoa [tə'koə]
Bible College; trained in
hospital in *Brunswick*
[brʌ<nzwɨx̝k, -zᵂɨ<k];
M b. Bainbridge
[be·nbrɨd̝ʒ], reared in
Macon [me·kən]; *Ellabell*
['ɛlə₁bɛᵊł], *Lanier*
[lə'neᵛə]

c *Jacksonville*
cv ['dʒæᵋksnvɨ<ᵊł] (Fla),
Buffalo ['bʌfɭo<] (NY)

e *Columbia* [k‘ɹ̥̍'ɹ̥ʌ^mbᴶə^]
(SC)

GA

3b   r. on Canoochee River
[kə'nʉ·t∫ɨ̧ ˌrɪ^və̧^]
and Taylors Creek
['te^·ᵊlə^z ˌkŗi·k]

4a   *Columbia* [kə̆'le^mbɨ̧] (SC)

c   b. Manchester
['mæˇᵊnt∫ɛ^ᵊstə]; 1 yr.
boarding school in *Darien*
['de^·r₮n̩]

6b   *Charlotte* ['∫ɒ·ᵊlə̧t] (NC)

7   *Jesup* [dʒɛ^ᵊsə^p]

9a   r. Hopewell ['hoᵁpˌwɛ^ł,
'houpwł], Lanes Bridge
['le₮nz ˌbrɪdʒ], *Brunswick*
[brʌ̧nz₮<k]

N11 r. Tremont ['tJ̥imaunt]

12a r. Coffee Bluff
['kʻɔ<·ᵊf₮̧ ˌbJɣˇf]
since 1935

13b prep. school in *Dahlonega*
[də'lɒn₮<gə]; *Newark*
cv [nJʉ·ək] (NJ)

14b r. Hilltonia
['hɪ^łˌtʻo<·u<nJə] 1895–
1905; *Columbia*
[kʻə'lʌ^mbɨ̧] (SC)

c   relatives at Big Branch Ch.
['bɪ^ᵊg ˌbJæə^<nt∫
't∫ɜ^₮t∫]

15b b. Sardis ['sɒ<·əd₮<s]

16a school in *Blythe* [bla̧₮θ]

18a F b. Green Cove Springs
['gri·n ˌkoᵁʊ sprɪŋz] (Fla)

19a r. Kite [ka̧·ə^t];
* attended Old Mt. Pisgah

GA

(19a) ['o<·u<l ˌmæˇont
'pɪ^ᵊzgə] School

20a b. China Hill ['t∫a̧·ᵊnə
ˌhɪ^ᵊl]; *Macon*
cv [me·₮k₮n]

21b r. *Milledgeville*
['mɪ^l₮<dʒˌvɪ^ᵊł] since
c. 1942

22b r. Rutland District
['rɣˇtlə^n ˌdɪ^ᵊstJ₮<k],
Walden ['wɒ^ɔld₮n] P. O.

23a [-₮-]: doubtful; *Brunswick*
cv [brɣˇᵊnz₮<k]

c   M b. Painesville [pe·nzvl]
(Ohio); F b. *Madison*
[mædəsn] (Ohio)

f   contacts in Millen
[mɪl₮<n], Tylersville
['t'a̧·ᵊləˇzˌvɪ·ᵊl],
Fort Valley ['foət
ˌvæɟ₮, ˌ~ '~]

N24 *Macon* s ['me·kən]

29a *Columbia*
cv [kə'lɣˇmb₮̧] (SC)

b   *Columbia*
[kə̆'lɣˇᵊmbJə^] (SC)

31   b. Lowndesville
[la^unzvł] (SC)

34b *Athens* cv [æᴱθ₮<nz]

N37 b. *Dublin* [dʌblɪn̩]; *Macon*
['me·₮kə^n], *Columbia*
[kə'lʌ̧mb₮^ə] (SC)

37c b. Chamblee [∫æ^·mbl₮];
F b. Harlem [hɑ·ələ^m];
M b. Thomson [t'ɑ>mpsn];

GA

(37c) *Macon* [me₮kən], *Greenville*
[gri^nvə^ł] (SC)

e   r. Avondale [ævənde₮ł],
Columbia [kə'lʌ^mbJə]
(SC), Pensacola
[pɛnsə'koˇᵁˇlə] (Fla);
M b. Prosperity
[prə'spɛr₮t₮] (SC)

i   *Greenville* [gri·nvł] (SC)

40   *Macon* [me₮kə^n]

42a church at Frytown
['fŗɑ^₮ˌt'æˇon]

44a b. Burton Lake
['b3>·ʊ'tn̩ ˌle·k]

b   r. 1 yr. in Colorado
[kɒlə're·₮<do<·ʊ]

e   contacts in Chattanooga
[ˌt∫æɟə'nʉˇᵘgə,
-'nʉ̧ʉ>gə] (Tenn)

FLORIDA

1   *Wilmington* ['wɪ^lm₮<ntn̩]
(NC), *Greenville*
['gŗi·nvɪ^ᵊl] (SC)

2c   *St. Augustine*
cv [snt 'ɔ·ᵊgəˌsti·n],
Brunswick
cv [brʌ^ᵊnz₮<k] (Ga)

3a   r. Tocoi ['t'o·ˌkoˇ·₮]
till age 15

4   r. Port Orange ['poˇə̧t
ˌɑ>ʳ₮ndʒ] 1920–6; *Columbia*
[kə'lʌ̧mbJə] (SC), *Macon*
[meˇ₮kə^n] (Ga)

5b   *Jacksonville*
['dʒæ^ᵊksnvŭ̃]

GEOGRAPHICAL NAMES

In this section Lowman and McDavid differed sharply in their field procedures. Lowman, closely following the order of the work sheets, relied on interrogation and usually secured a full quota of responses. McDavid, especially in his earlier records, was reluctant to press the unlettered and untravelled for these names, but recorded <u>cv</u> responses wherever possible; as a result there are often omissions in SC-Fla, less often elsewhere.

4. NEW ENGLAND

WS 86.1

LANE 4

The states from Maine to Connecticut were usually identified as *New England* or (*the*) *New England States*. The predominant stress pattern in *New England*, ~ ˈ~ or ˌ~ ˈ~, is unmarked; in (*the*) *New England States*, stress is marked as indicated by the field workers.

(*The*) *Eastern States*, a synonym found mainly in New York State, is entered separately on List 4a. Incidental examples of *England* and *English* are entered on List 4b. All other terms appear in the commentary.

ONTARIO

1a	nu̢$^{u<}$ ɪŋ^{g}ɫən
b	n^{ɪ}ʉ ɪŋglə^n,
	~ ~ ste^{ɪ}ts
2a	---
b	ˌnʉ̢ʉ˃ ˈɪ̆^ŋglə^n ˌsteᵛ^{ɪ}ts
<u>3</u>	<u>cv</u> nju̢u< ɪ^ŋglə^n
4a	---
b	nʉᵛ^{ʉ} ˈɪŋglə^n ˌste^{ɪ}ts
5-<u>6</u>	---
7	ˌnʉ$^{ʉ^}$ ˈɪŋgɫə^n ˌste^{ɪ}ts
8a	---
b	ˌn^{j}ʉᵛʉ ˈiᵛŋgləᵛn
	ˌsteᵛ·^{ɪ}ts
c	<u>cv</u> nju̢u< ɪ^ŋlə^n,
	~ ɪ^ŋg-, ŋ̊u̢u< ~
d	nu̢u< iᵛŋlə^n,
	~ ~ ste·^{ɪ}ts <u>cv</u> ˌnju̢u<
	ˈɪ˃ŋlə^n ˌ~
<u>9</u>-10	---

NEW YORK

1	nɨ˃w ɪŋgɫənd
2a	---
b	nɨ^u^ ɪ̆ŋglənd
c	---
3a	nɨu< ɪ˃ŋglənd
b	nɨu< ɪŋglən^{d}
c	nu<· ɪŋglənd
d	nɨu< ɪ˃ŋglən^{d}
4a	nu<· ɪŋglənd
b	nɨu< ɪŋglən^{d}
c	nu· ɪŋglən$^{d̥}$
5a	nu<· ɪ^ŋglən^{d}
b	nu<· ɪŋglən^{d}
c	nu· ɪŋglənd
d	nu<· ɪŋglən^{d}
e	nŭ̢ ɪŋglən^{d}
f	nŭ^ŭ ɪŋ̆glən^{d}
g	nu̢$^{u<}$ ɪŋglən^{d}
<u>h</u>	nu<· ɪŋglən^{d}

NY

5<u>i</u>	n^{j}u< ɪ˃ŋgɫənd
6ab	nu<· ɪŋglənd
7a	nu^{w} ɪŋglən^{d}
b	nu· ɪŋglənd
c	nu<· ɪŋglən^{d}
d	nu<· ɪŋgɫənd
e	nu<· ɪŋ^{g}lən^{d}
f	nʉ˃· ɪŋglən^{d}
g	nʉ˃· ɪŋglən$^{d̥}$
hi	nu<· ɪŋglənd
<u>j</u>	nu<· ɪŋglən^{d}
<u>k</u>	nju· ɪŋglənd
<u>lm</u>	nu<· ɪŋglənd
8	nu· ɪŋglənd
9abc	nu<· ɪŋglənd
10a	nu<· ɪŋgɫənd
<u>b</u>	nu<· ɪŋglənd
11	nu<· ɪŋglən^{d}

NY

12a	nɨuˇ< ɪŋglənᵈ
b	nuˇ<· ɪŋglənd
<u>c</u>	nᴶuˇ< ɪŋglənd
13a	nuˇ<· ɪŋglənd
13<u>b</u>-14b	nuˇ<· ɪŋglənᵈ
15a	nɨuˇ< ɪŋglənd
b	nɨu ɪŋᵍɫənᵈ
16ab	nuˇ· ɪŋglənd
17a	nɨuˇ< ɪŋglənᵈ
b	nuˇ· ɪŋglənd
18a	nɨu ɪŋglənd
b	nuˇ<· ɪŋglənᵈ
<u>c</u>	nju· ɪŋglənd (√)
19	nuˇ· ɪŋglənᵈ
20a	nɨuˇ< ɪŋɫənd
b	nŭˇ< ɪŋglənd
21	nuˇ· ɪŋɫənd
22	nuˇ· ɪŋglənd
23a	---
b	nuˇ ɪˆŋləˆn
c	<u>cv</u> nɨ·w ɪˆŋləˇ>n, nuʂ -ləˆn
24a	nɨuˇ< ɪŋglənᵈ
<u>b</u>	nuˇ· ɪŋglənᵈ
25a	ˌnuˆu ˈɪˆŋglɪˇn ˌsteˇ‡ts
b	njuˆˇ· ɪˆŋləˆn
26a	---
b	ðɪ nɨuˇʷ ˈɪˆŋglə^n ˌsteˇ·ˆ‡ts
c	---
27a	njuˇ<u ˈɪˆŋləˆn ˌsteˇ‡ts
b	---
c	ˌnju ˈwɪˆŋləˆn ˌsteˇ‡<ts

NY

28a	ˌnɨˇ·ʷ ˈɪˆŋgləˆn ˌsteˇ‡ts
b	---
29a	nuˇ< ɪŋgləˆnd
b	nuˇ ˈwɪˆŋgləˆn ˌsteˇ·‡ts
c	njuˇ ɪˆŋləˆn
30a	---
b	ˈnjuˇ< ˌɪ>ŋgləˆn ˈsteˇˇ‡t
cd	---
e	ˌnjuˇ· ˈɪˆŋgləˆn ˌsteˇ·‡ts
	<u>cv</u> ˈnjuˇ ˌɪˆŋgɫəˆn, ˈnuˇ ~
31a	---
b	ˌnuʂuˇ< ˈɪˆŋgləˆn ˈsteˇ‡ts
	<u>cv</u> nɨɨ ˈɪˆŋgləˆn ˌsteˇ·‡<ts, ˈnᴶuˇu ˌɪˆŋgləˆn, nuˇu ɪˆŋgləˆn
32a	---
b	ðəʐ ˈnuˇu ˌɪˆŋgləˆn ˈsteˇ‡ts
33a	---
b	nuˇ ˈɪˆŋgləˆn ˌsteˇ‡<ts
c	nuˇˇ· ɪˆŋgləˆn
34a	nɨɨˇ> ɪˆŋgləˆn
bc	---
<u>d</u>	<u>cv</u> nuˇu ɪˆŋgləˆn, njuʂuˇ< ~, ~ ɛˆŋgləˆn
35a	nɨu ɪŋgɫənᵈ
b	nɨu ɪŋglənd
<u>c</u>	---
36a	nɨu ɪŋglənᵈ
b	nɨuˇ< ɪŋglənd steˇts
37a	nɨˆu ɪŋglənd
b<u>c</u>	nuˇ<· ɪŋgɫənd
38a	nɨuˇ< ɪŋgɫənd

NY

38b	nɨ>u ɪŋglənd
39a	nɨu ɪŋgɫənd
b	nɨ>u ɪŋgɫənd
40a	nɨ>u ɪŋgɫənd
b	nuˇ· ɪŋglənd
41	nu ɪŋgɫənd
42a	nɨuˇ< ɪŋgɫənd
b	nuˇ< ɪŋglənᵈ
43a	nɨuˇ< ɪŋglənd
b	nuˇ< ɪŋglənd
<u>c</u>	nuˇ<ʷ ɪŋglənd
44a	nɨuˇ< ɪŋglənᵈ
b	nuˇ· ɪŋgɫənd
45abc	---
<u>d</u>	nuˇu ˈɪˆŋgləˆn ˌsteˇ‡ts
46a	nɨˇ ˈwiˆŋgləˆn ˌsteˇ‡ts
b	*nᴵuˇ< ˈɪŋglən steˇ‡ts
c	ˌnuˇ· ˈɪŋglən ˌsteˇ‡ts
47a	nuʷ ˈɪˆŋgləˆn ˌsteˇ‡<ts
b	nuʷ ɪŋglənd
48a	nᴶɨ>ʷ ˈiˇŋgləˆn ˌsteˇ‡<ts
b	---
c	<u>cv</u> ˈnuʂuˇ< ˌɪˆŋgləˆn, ˈnɨɨ ~
d	nuʂw iˇŋgləˆn, ðə ˈnuʂuˇ< ˌɪˆŋgləˆn ˈstɛˇˆ‡ts
49ab	---
c	nuʂuˇ< ˈɪŋgɫəˆn ˌsteˇ·‡ts
d	nuʂuˇ< ɪŋgləˆn <u>cv</u> nuʂʷ ɪŋgɫəˆn
50a	---
b	<u>cv</u> njuʂuˇ< ɪˆŋgləˆn, nᴶuˇ<uˇ< ~ ˌsteˇ‡<ts
51a	njuʂuˇ< ˈɪˆŋgləˆn ˌsteˇ‡ts

NY

51bcd ---

  e   c͟v nʉˇʉ ɪ^ŋləˆn

52a-53a ---

53b c͟v njuʂu‹ ɪ^ŋləˆn

54a *nu‹ 'ɪŋləˆn ˌsteⁱts

  b nŭʂ^W 'ɪŋləˆn ˌsteⁱts

55a nju·^W 'ɪˆŋləˆn ˌste·ⁱts

    c͟v nʉʉˆ ɪ^ŋləˆn, nʉ

    'wɪˆŋləˆn steˇⁱts

  b c͟v ˌnʉ·w 'ɪˆŋləˆn

    ˌsteˇ·ⁱts

56a ˌnⁱʉ 'ɪˆŋləˆn ˌsteˇts

  b 'nⁱʉ ɪ›ŋləˆn 'steˇⁱts

57ab ---

  c njuˇu ɪ^ŋglə̆ˆnd

    c͟v ~ ɪ^ŋləˆn

58a nuˇu ɤ^ᵑgləˆn

    c͟v ~ ɪ^ŋləˆn

  b njuʂu‹ 'ɤ^ᵑgləˆn

    ˌsteˇ·ⁱts

  c ---

  d nʉˇʉ ɪ^ŋgləˆn

    c͟v nuˇw ɪ^ŋləˆn

  e ðə ˌnuˇu 'ɪ̝ŋləˆn

    ˌsteˇⁱts c͟v nʉˇʉ

    ɪ^ŋləˆn

  f ---

59a c͟v ˌnjuˇu 'ɪ^ŋləˆn

    ˌsteˇⁱts

  b nɪ›u‹ ɪŋglənᵈ

60a ---

  b c͟v ˌnuˇ· 'wɪ^ŋləˆnᵈ

61a 'nu‹ ˌɪˆŋləˆn 'steˇ·ⁱts

  b nʉ 'ɪ^ŋglə̆ˆn ˌsteˇ·ⁱts

62abc ---

NY

62d c͟v nuˇu ɪ^ŋləˆn, ~

    'ɪ^ŋg- ˌsteˇⁱts

63a njʉˇ 'wɪˆŋləˆn ˌstɛ^ⁱts

  b c͟v 'nʉ· ɪ̝ᵑləˆn

    steˇⁱts (?)

  c nⁱu ɪŋglənd

  d nʉ›w ɪ^ŋləˆn

64a ˌnjʉ 'ɪ^ŋləˆn ˌste·ⁱts

  b ˌnʉ·^W 'ɪ^ŋləˆn ˌste·ⁱts

  c c͟v nᴶʉ ɪ^ŋləˆn,

    ~ ~ ˌste·ⁱts

NEW JERSEY

1a nu‹· ɪŋᵍlənᵈ

  b nuʂ· ɪŋglənd

2a nu‹· ɪŋglənᵈ

  b nu‹· ɪŋlənᵈ

3a nu‹· ɪŋᵍlənᵈ

  b nʉ›· ɪŋᵍlənᵈ

4a nu‹ ɪŋglənd

  b nu‹· ɪŋlənᵈ

5a nu‹· ɪŋgłənᵈ

  b nu‹· ɪŋglənᵈ

6a nʉ›· ɪŋglənd

  b nuʂ ɪŋᵍłənᵈ

7a nu· ɪŋgłənᵈ

  b nʉ›· ɪŋglənᵈ

8ab nu‹· ɪŋglənd

9a nuu‹ ɪŋᵍlənᵈ

  b nʉ›· ɪŋglənᵈ

10a nu‹· ɪŋglənd

  b nʉ›· ɪŋglənᵈ

  c nʉ›· ɪŋglənd

  d nu‹ ɪ›ŋglənd

11a nʉ›· ɪŋglənᵈ

NJ

11b nu‹ ɪŋglənᵈ

  c nu‹· ɪŋglənᵈ

12a nʉ›· ɪŋglənᵈ

  b nu‹· ɪŋglənᵈ

13a nʉ›· ɪŋglənd

  b nʉ›· ɪŋgłənd

14a nuʂu‹ ɪŋłənᵈ

  b nu‹· ɪŋglənd

15a nu‹· ɪˇŋglənᵈ

  b nuʂ ɪŋglənᵈ

16a nu‹· ɪŋglənᵈ

  b nuʂ^u ɪŋglənᵈ

17a nu‹ ɪŋglənᵈ

  b nʉ›· ɪŋglənᵈ

18a nu‹· ɪŋglənᵈ

  bc nu‹· ɪŋglənd

  d nu^W ɪŋglənd

19a nu‹· ɪŋglənd

  b nu· ɪŋglənd

20a nu‹· ɪŋglənd

  b nu· ɪŋglənd

21a nu‹· ɪŋglənᵈ

  b nu‹· ɪŋglənd

PENNSYLVANIA

1a nu· ɪŋglənd

  b nu· ɪŋlənᵈ

  c nuʂ ɪŋglənᵈ

  d nu‹· ɪŋglənd

  e nu· ɪŋglənd

  f nu‹· ɪŋglənᵈ

  gh nu‹· ɪŋglənᵈ

2a nu‹· ɪŋglənᵈ

  b nu‹· ɪŋglənd

3a nu‹· ɪŋglənᵈ

  b nŭ^ŭ‹ ɪŋglənᵈ

PA

3c	nuᐸ ɪŋglənd
4a	nu· ɪŋglənd
b	nuᐸ· ɪŋlənd
5ab	nuᐸ· ɪŋlənᵈ
c	nuuᐸ ɪŋᵍlənd
d	nʉᐳ· ɪŋlənᵈ
e	nuᐸ· ɪŋlənᵈ
6a	nu· ɪŋlæˆnɫ
b	nu· ɪŋglənd
c	nu· ɪŋg̊lənɫ
d	nuᐸ· ɪŋglənd
7ab	nuᐸ· ɪŋglənᵈ
c	nu· ɪŋlənd̥
d	nuᐸ· ɪŋlənᵈ
8a	nʉᐳ· ɪŋglənᵈ
b	nʉᐳ ɪŋglənᵈ
c	nuᐸ· ɪŋglən̲ɫ
d	nuʂ ɪŋglənd
9a	nu· ɪŋlənd̥
b	nu· ɪŋglənᵈ
c	nʉᐸ ɪŋglənd
10	nŭˆŭᐸ ɪŋlən̲ɫ
11a	nu· ɪŋglənᵈ
b	nuᐸ ɪŋglənd
12a	nuᐸ ɪŋglən
b	nu ɪŋglənᵈ
13ab	nuᐸ· ɪŋglənᵈ
14a	nuᐸ· ɪˆŋlæˆn̲ɫ
14b-15b	nu· ɪŋglənᵈ
15c	nu· ɪŋglənd
16a	nu· ɪŋlæˆnɫ
b	nu· ɪŋlənᵈ
c	---
17a	nu· ɪŋlənɫ
b	nu· ɪŋlənd̥ᵈ

18a	nu· ɪŋglənᵈ
b	nuᐸ· ɪŋlənᵈ
19a	nʉᐳ· ɪŋglənᵈ
b	nu· ɪŋglənᵈ
20a	nuᐸ· ɪŋglənᵈ
b	nuᐸ· ɪŋlənd
21a	nɪu ɪŋglənᵈ
b	nu· ɪŋglənᵈ
22a	nɟuᐸ ɪŋglənᵈ
b	nu· ɪŋglənᵈ
23a	nɟu ɪŋglənᵈ
b	nɟuᐸ ɪŋlənᵈ
24a	nu· ɪŋglənᵈ
b	nu ɪŋglənᵈ
25a	nɟŭᐸ ɪŋᵍlənᵈ
b	nu ɪŋglənᵈ
26a	nɟᐸuᐸ ɪŋglənᵈ
b	nuʷ ɪŋglənᵈ
27a	*nɟuᐸ ɪŋglənᵈ
b	nɟuᐸ ɪŋglənᵈ
28a	nu· ɪŋɫənd
b	nuᐸ· ɪŋɫənd
29a	nuᐸ· ɪŋglənᵈ
b	nu· ɪŋɫənd
30a	nɟuᐸ ɪŋglənᵈ
b	nɟuᐸ ɪŋlənɫ
31a	nuᐸ· ɪŋlənd
b	nu· ɪŋglənd
32a	nu· ɪŋɫənᵈ
b	nuᐸ· ɪŋɫənᵈ
33a	nuᐸ· ɪŋglənd
b	nuᐸ ɪŋglənd
34a	nuᐸ ɪŋglənᵈ
b	nuᐸ· ɪŋglənd
c	*nuᐸ ɪŋglənd

35ab	nuᐸ· ɪŋglənᵈ
36a	nuᐸ· ɪŋᵍɫən
b	nuʂ ɪŋglənᵈ
37a	nuᐸ· ɪŋlənɫ
b	nuᐸ ɪŋlənɫ
38a	nʉ? ɪŋglənᵈ
b	nuᐸ· ɪŋglənᵈ
39a	ᐳnuᐸ ɪŋglənᵈ
b	nuᐸ ɪŋlənᵈ
40a	nuᐸ· ɪŋglənᵈ
b	nuʂ ɪŋglənᵈ
41a	nuᐸ· ɪŋglənᵈ
b	nʉ· ɪŋglənᵈ
42a	nuᐸ ɪŋglənᵈ
b	nuᐸ· ɪŋglənd
43a	nuᐸ ɪŋᵍlənᵈ
b	nuᐸ· ɪŋglənd
44a	nuᐸ ɪŋglənᵈ
b	nʉᐳ· ɪŋglənd
45a	nuᐸ ɪŋglənd
b	nuᐸ· ɪŋglənd
46a	nʉ· ɪŋɫənd
b	nʉ· ɪŋglənd
47a	nʉᐳ· ɪŋglənᵈ
b	nʉᐳ· ɤˇŋglənd
48a	nʉᐳ· ɪŋɫənd
b	nʉ· ɪŋɫənd
c	nʉ ɪŋglənd
49a	nʉᐳ· ɪŋglənd
b	nʉᐳ· ɪŋɫənd
50a	---
b	nʉᐳ· ɪŋglənd
c	nʉ· ɪŋɫənd
51ab	nʉᐳ· ɪŋglənd
52a	nuᐸ· ɪŋɫənd

PA

52b nʉ>· ɪŋɫənd

53a nuu< ɪŋɫənd

b nu^u< ɪŋlənd

54a nu< ɪŋlənd

b nʉ· ɪŋlənd

55a nu ɪŋlənd

b nu<·· ɪŋlənd

56a nu< ɪŋlənᵈ

b nʉ>· ɪŋlənd

57a nʉ· ɪŋlənd

b nʉ>· ɪŋlənd

58a nu<·· ɪŋlənᵈ

b nʉ>· ɪŋlənd

59a nu<·· ɪŋlənᵈ

b nu< ɪŋlənd

60ab nʉ· ɪŋlənd

61a nu<·· ɪŋlən

b nʉ· ɪŋlənd

62a nu< ɪŋlənd

b nu<·· ɪŋlənt

63a nu<·· ɪŋlənd

b nu< ɪŋlənd

64a nɨw ɪŋlənd

b nɨu< ɪŋlənd

65a nɨu ɪŋlənᵈ

b nu< ɪŋlənd

66a nu· ɪŋlənᵈ

b nɨu ɪŋɫənd

67ab nɨu< ɪŋlənd

WEST VIRGINIA

1 nᴵ^u< ɪŋlənᵈ

2 nᴵ^ʉ> ɪŋlənᵈ

3 nu< ɪŋlənᵈ (√)

4a nᴵ^u< ɪŋlənt

b ŋ̍ⁱˇ ʉ ɪŋlən

WVA

5 nʉ> ɪŋlənᵈ

6a nu<·· ɪŋlənᵈ

b nŭ̦ŭ ɪŋlənᵈ

7a nu> ɪŋlənᵈ

b nᴵʉ ɪŋlənd

8a nʉ ɪŋlənᵈ

b ŋ̍jʉ·· ɪŋlənᵈ

9a nu<·· ɪŋlənᵈ

b nu<·· ɪŋlənd

10a nᴶʉ> ɪŋlənd

b nu< ɪŋlənᵈ

10c-11a nʉ ɪŋlənᵈ

11b nʉ· ɪŋlənd

12a nu< ɪŋɫənd

b nu<·· ɪŋlənᵈ

13a nu<·· ɪŋlənd

b nu<·· ɪŋɫənᵈ

14a nu<·· ɪŋlənᵈ

b nu< ɪŋlənᵈ

15a nu<·· ɪŋlənᵈ

b nu< ɪŋlənd

16a nⁱʉ ɪŋɫənᵈ

b nu<·· ɪŋlənᵈ

17a ---

b nu< ɪŋlənd

c nu<·· ɪŋɫənd

18a njʉ· ɪŋɫənd

b nu<·· ɪŋlənᵈ

19a njʉ> ɪŋlənd

b nⁱʉ< ɪŋlənᵈ

20a nⁱʉ ɪŋlənd

b ŋ̍ⁱʉ ɪŋlənd

21a ŋ̍ⁱʉ ɪŋlənᵈ

b nʉ ɪŋlənᵈ

22a nᴶʉ ɪŋlənd

WVA

22b nⁱʉ ɪŋlənᵈ

23a ŋ̍jʉ ɪŋlənᵈ

b nᴶʉ ɪŋlənd

24a ŋ̍jʉ ɪŋlənᵈ

b ŋ̍jʉ· ɪŋlənᵈ

25a ŋ̍jʉ ɪŋlənᵈ

b ŋ̍ᴶʉ ɪŋlən

26a ŋ̍jʉ ɪŋlənᵈ

26b-27a ŋ̍jʉ· ɪŋlənᵈ

27b-28a ŋ̍jʉ ɪŋlənᵈ

28b njʉ ɪ̃ŋlənᵈ

29a ŋ̍jʉ ɪŋlənᵈ

b ŋ̍jʉ· ɪŋlənᵈ

30a ŋ̍ⁱʉ ɪŋlənᵈ

b ŋ̍jʉ>· ɪŋlənᵈ

31a ŋ̍jʉ ɪ̃ŋlənᵈ

b ŋ̍ⁱʉ ɪ̃ˇŋlənᵈ

32ab njʉ ɪŋlənᵈ

33a njʉ ɪŋlənd

b ŋ̍ᴵ^ʉ ɪŋlənᵈ

34a njʉ ɪŋlənᵈ

b nu<· ɪŋlənd

35a njʉ ɪŋlənd

b njʉ ɪŋlənᵈ

36a nu<·· ɪŋlənᵈ

b nᴶʉ> ɪ̃ŋlənᵈ

37a nu<·· ɪŋlɨŋ

b nʉ> ɪŋlənd

38a nu<·· ɪŋlənᵈ

b nʉ>· ɪŋlənd

39a nᴶʉ> ɪŋlənd

b nu<·· ɛŋlənᵈ

c nu< ɪŋlənd

40a nⁱʉ ɪŋlənᵈ

b nⁱˇʉ ɪŋlənt

WVA

41ab nⁱɐ ɪŋglənᵈ

42a nɐ ɪŋɫənᵈ

  b nu<· ɪŋɫənd

43a nu< ɪŋglənᵈ

  b nɐ> ɪŋglənᵈ

44a-45a nu<· ɪŋglənd

45b nɐ>· ɪŋglənᵈ

46a nɐ>· ɪŋglənd

  b nɐ> ɪŋglənᵈ

47a nu<· ɪŋɫənd

  b nɐ>· ɪŋglənᵈ

48a nɐ>· ɪŋglənd

  bc - - -

  d nɐ>· ɪŋɫənd

49a nɐ>· ɪŋglənd

  b nɐ>· ɪŋɫənᵈ

50ab nu< ɪŋglənd

51a nu<· ɪŋglənᵈ

  b nu̲< ɪŋglənᵈ

52a nɐ>· ɪŋglənᵈ

  b nu< ɪŋglənd

  c̲ nuʂ ɪŋglənᵈ

53a nu<· ɪŋglənᵗ

  b - - -

  c̲ nu< ɪŋglənd

54a nɐ· ɪŋglənd

  b nɐ ɪˆŋɫənd

OHIO

1a nɨu ɪŋglənᵈ

  b nɨuʂ ɪŋglənᵈ

  c̲ nu< ɪŋɫənd

2a nu< ɪŋglənᵈ

  b nu< ɪŋglənd

3a nu<· ɪŋɫənd

  b nuʂ ɪŋglənd

OHIO

4ab nu<· ɪŋɫənd

5a - - -

  b nu<· ɪŋɫənd

  c nu< ɪŋglənᵈ

6a nu<· ɪŋglənᵈ

  b nu<· ɪŋglənd

7a nu<· ɪŋglənᵈ

  b nu< ɪŋglənᵈ

8a nu· ɪŋglənᵈ

  b - - -

  c nɐ>· ɪŋglənd

  d - - -

  e̲ nᴶu< ɪŋglənd

9a nu< ɪŋɫənᵈ

  b - - -

  c nuʂ ɪŋglənd

  d - - -

10a nɐ> ɪŋglənᵈ

  b nu<· ɪŋglənd

11a nu< ɪŋglənd

  b nu<· ɪŋglənd

12a ŋⁱɐ> ɪŋglən

  b nɐʐ ɪŋglənᵈ

  cd - - -

13a nɪ>ᵘ ɪŋᵍlənd

  bc - - -

14 c̲v̲ nɐᵘˆ ɪˆŋɫləˆnd

15ab - - -

16a c̲v̲ 'nɐᵛɐ ɪŋɫləˆn 'stɛˆɨts

16b-18 - - -

KENTUCKY

1a-7b̲ - - -

DELAWARE

1a-c̲ nuˆu< ɪŋglənᵈ

2a nu< ɪŋlənᵈ

DEL

2b nuˆu< ɪŋglənᵈ

3a nuˆu< ɪŋglənᵗ

  b nu< ɪŋlənᵗ

  c̲ nu<· ɪŋglənᵈ

4 nu<· ɪŋglənᵗ

5a nɐʐ· ɪŋlən

  b nuʂ ɪŋglənᵈ

6a nɐ<ɐ ɪŋlənᵗ

  b nuʂ· ɪŋglənᵗ

MARYLAND

1a nɐ>· ɪŋglənᵈ

  b nu< ɪŋglənᵈ

2a nⁱɐ ɪŋglənᵈ

  b nɐ>· ɪŋɫən

3a nuˆu< ɪŋglənᵈ

  b nⁱɐ ɪŋlənᵈ

4a nᴶɐ> ɪŋglənᵈ

  b nuu< ɪŋglənᵈ

  c niʐ>ɐ ɪŋlənᵗ

5a nⁱʐɐ ɪ̃ŋᵍlənᵈ

  b nɪɐ> ɪŋlənᵈ

6a nⁱɐ> ɪŋᵍlənᵈ

  b ŋⁱʐɐ ɪŋlən

7a nⁱɐ ɪŋlənᵗ

  b nuˆu< ɪŋglənᵈ

  c̲ nɐˆu< ɪŋᵍlənᵈ

8a nⁱɐ ɪŋlənᵗ

  b nɐˆu< ɪŋlənᵈ

N9 nⁱɐ ɪŋlənᵈ

9a nⁱɐ ɪŋglənᵈ

  b nuˆu< ɪŋlənᵈ

10a nⁱˆ ɪŋlənᵈ

  b nɐˆɐ ɪŋᵍlənᵈ

11 nɐ>u< ɪŋlən

12a nɐ>· ɪŋglənd

MD

12b   nɐᵛɐ ɪŋlənd

13a   nuşŭ ɪŋᵍlənᵈ

b   nᴵɐ ɪŋlənᵈ

c   nuş ɪŋglənᵈ

d̲   nⁱ˅ɐ> ɪŋglənᵈ

e̲   nᵻ^ɐ> ɪŋlənᵈ

f̲   ŋɉɐ ɪŋᵍlənᵈ

14   nɐ>u< ɪŋlənᵈ

15a   nuş· ɪŋlənᵈ

b   nɐşɐ ɪŋlənᵈ

16   nuş ɪŋlənᵈ

17a   nɐɐ> ɪŋlənᵈ

b   nuşʷ ɪŋlənᵈ

18a   nᴵ^ɐ ɪŋlənᵈ

b   nɐᵛɐ ɪŋlənᵈ

19a   nᴵ^ɐ> ɪŋlənᵈ

b   nᴵɐ ɪŋlənᵈ

20a   nⁱɐ ɪ̃ŋlənᵈ

b   nᵻ˅ɐ> ɪŋlənᵈ

c̲   nᴵ^ɐ ɪŋᵍlənᵈ

21a   nᴵ^ɐ ɪŋlən

b   nɐᵛɐ> ɪŋlənᵈ

N22   ---

2N22   nɉu> ɪŋlən

22a   nⁱu< ɪŋlən

b   ŋᴵ^ɐ ɪŋlənᵈ

c̲   nɉɐ ɪŋlənᵈ

23a   ŋᴵ^ɐ ɪŋlənᵈ

b   ---

c   ŋɉɐ ɪŋlən

24   nɉu<· ɪŋlən

25   nɐᵛɐ> ɪŋlənᵈ

26a   nᴵ^ɐ ɪŋlənᵈ

b   ---

27a   nᴵu< ɪŋlənᵈ

MD

27b   nu< ɪ̃ᵛŋglənd

DISTRICT OF COLUMBIA

1a   nuş ɪŋlənᵈ (√)

b̲   nⁱ˨ɐ ɪŋglənᵈ

VIRGINIA

1̲   ŋⁱ˨ɐ ɪŋlənᵈ

2a   nᴵ^u< ɪŋᵍlənᵈ

b   ŋⁱ˨ɐ ɪŋlənᵗ

3a   nɉu< ɪŋlən

b   ŋⁱ˨ɐ> ɪŋᵍlənᵈ

N4   ŋɉɐ˨ ɪŋlən

5a   ŋɉɐ> ɪŋlənᵈ

b   ŋⁱɐ ɪŋlənᵈ

6a   ŋⁱɐ>· ɪ̃ŋlən

b   ŋɉɐ> ɪŋlən

7a   ŋⁱɐ> ɪŋlən

b   ŋⁱɐ ɪŋlən

8a   nⁱ˅ɐ> ɪŋᵍlənᵈ

b   ŋⁱɐ> ɪŋlənᵈ

c̲   ŋⁱɐ ɪŋlənᵈ

9a–10a   ŋⁱɐ ɪŋlən

10b   ŋⁱɐ ɪŋlənᵈ

11a   ŋⁱɐ ɪŋlən

b   ŋⁱ˨ɐ ɪŋlən

N12   ŋɉɐ ɪ̃ŋlən

12a   ---

b̲   ŋⁱɐ ɪ̃ŋlənᵈ

13a   ŋⁱɐ ɪŋlənᵗ

b   ŋⁱɐ˨ ɪŋlənᵈ

14a   nⁱɐ ɪ˙ŋlən

b   ŋɉɐ ɪŋlənᵈ

c   ŋⁱɐ ɪŋlənᵈ

N15   ---

15a   ŋⁱ˨u< ɪ̃ŋlənᵈ

b   ŋᴵ^ɐ> ɪŋlənᵈ

VA

16a   ŋⁱ˅ɐ ɪŋlənᵈ

b   ŋⁱɐ ɪŋlən

17a   ŋⁱɐ ɪŋlən

b   ŋⁱ˨ɐ ɪ̃ŋlənᵈ

18   ŋⁱ˅ɐ> ɪŋlənᵈ

19a   ŋⁱɐ ɪŋlənᵗ

b   ŋⁱɐ ɪŋlən

c̲   ŋⁱɐᵛ ɪ̃ŋlən

20a   ŋⁱɐ ɪŋlənᵗ

b   ŋⁱɐ ɪŋlənᵈ

N21   nŭ<ŭ ɪŋlən

21a   ŋⁱ˨ɐ ɪŋlənᵈ

b   ŋⁱ˨ɐ· ɪŋlənᵈ

22   ŋⁱɐ< ɪŋlən

23a   ŋⁱɐ ɪŋlən

b   nɉɐ> ɪŋᵍlənᵈ

24   ŋⁱɐ ɪŋlənᵈ

25   ŋⁱɐ ɪŋlənᵗ

26a   ---

b   ŋⁱɐ ɪŋlənᵗ

c   ŋⁱ˨ɐ ɪŋlənᵈ

27   nuş ɪŋᵍlənᵗ

28a   ŋⁱɐ ɪŋlənᵗ

b   ŋⁱɐ ɪŋlənᵈ

29   ŋⁱ˅ɐ ɪŋlən

30a   ŋⁱ˨ɐ ɪŋlən

b̲   ---

c̲   nⁱ˅ɐᵛ ɪŋᵍlənᵈ

de̲   ŋⁱɐ ɪ̃ŋlənᵈ

31a   *ŋⁱ˨ɐ ɪŋlənᵈ

b   ŋⁱ˨ɐ> ɪŋlənᵈ

32̲   nᴵɐ> ɪŋlənᵈ

33a   nɪ^ɐᵛ ɪŋlən

b   nⁱɐ< ɪŋlən

34a   ŋⁱɐ> ɪŋɫən

VA

34b–35a	ŋⁱʉ ɪŋlən
35b	ŋᴵ^ʉ ɪŋɫən
36a	ŋⁱʉ ɪ̈ŋlən
b	ŋⁱʉ< ɪ̈ŋlən
37	ŋⁱʉ ɪŋᵍlən⁺
38	nⁱʉˑ ɪŋlənᵈ
39	ŋⁱ̈ʉ ɪ̈ŋlən
40a	ŋⁱʉᵝ ɪŋlən
b	ŋⁱʉ< ɪ̈ŋlənᵈ
41a	ŋᴵ^ʉ ɪŋlən
b	ŋⁱʉ ɪ̈ŋlənᵈ
42a	ŋⁱ̈ʉ ɪŋlən
b	ŋⁱʉ> ɪŋlənᵈ
N43	ɲuˑ ɪŋlən
43a	ŋⁱ̈ʉ ɪŋlən
b	ŋⁱʉ ɪŋlənᵈ
44a	ŋⁱ̈ʉ ɪŋɫən
b	ŋⁱʉ> ɪŋlənᵈ
45a	nⁱʉ ɪ^ᵊŋlən
b	ŋⁱʉ ɪŋlən
N46	---
46a	nɟʉ<ᵘ< ɪ̈ŋlən
b	ŋᴵ^ʉ ɪŋlən
47	ŋⁱˑʉ ɪŋlənᵈ
48a	ŋⁱʉ ɪŋlən
b	ŋⁱʉ ɪŋlənᵈ
49a	ŋⁱʉ< ɪŋlən
b	ŋᴵ^ʉˑ ɪŋlən
50ab	ŋⁱʉ ɪŋlən
51a	ŋᴵ^ʉ ɪ̈ŋlən
b	ŋⁱ̈ʉ ɪŋlən
52a	nuˑ ɪŋlənᵈ
b	nᴵʉ ɪŋlənᵈ
c	nⁱʉ> ɪŋɫənᵈ
53a	nuˑ ɪŋlən

VA

53b	ŋⁱʉ ɪ^ŋlənᵈ
54a	ŋᴶʉ> ɪŋlən
b	ŋᴵ^ʉ̠> ɪ̈ŋlən
55a	ŋⁱ̈ʉ> ɪŋlənᵈ
b	nⁱʉ<ˇ ɪŋlənᵈ
56a	ŋⁱʉ< ɪŋᵍlənᵈ
b	ŋɟu<ˑˑ ɪŋᵍlənᵈ
57a	nu<ˑˑ ɪŋlən
b	ŋⁱʉ>ˇ ɪŋlən
58	---
N59	nɟʉ<w ɪ̈ŋlənᵈ
59ab	ŋⁱʉ ɪŋlənᵈ
60	ŋɟʉ> ɪŋᵍlənᵈ
61a	*nɟʉ ᵂ ɪŋᵍlənᵈ
b	ŋⁱˇ̈ʉ ɪŋlənᵈ
62a	ŋⁱʉ ɪˀᵊŋlən
b	ŋⁱ̈ʉ> ɪŋlən
63a	ŋⁱ̈ʉ ɪŋlən
b	ŋⁱʉ ɪˀŋlən
64a	ŋⁱ̈ʉ< ɪŋlən
b	ŋⁱˀ̈ʉ ɪ̈ŋlən
65a	nɟʉ ᵘ< ɛŋᵍlənᵈ
b	nɟʉ<ʉ> ɪŋɫlənᵈ
c	ŋⁱʉˇ ɪŋᵍlənᵈ
66a	ŋⁱˀ̈ʉ> ɪŋlən
b	ŋⁱˀ̈ʉ ɪŋlən
67a	ŋⁱˀ̈ʉ> ɪˀᵊ>ŋɫən
b	nᴵˀ̈ʉ ɪ̈ŋlən
68a	ŋⁱ̈ʉ ɪŋlən
b	ŋⁱ̈ʉ< ɪŋlən
69a	ŋⁱʉ ɪŋlən
b	ŋⁱʉ ɪ̈ŋlən
70a	nɟʉˀᵘ> ɪŋᵍlənᵈ
b	nⁱʉ ɪŋᵍlənᵈ
71a	ŋⁱˀ̈ʉ ɪ̈ŋlən

VA

71b	ŋⁱʉ ɪŋlən
72a	ŋⁱ̈ʉ ɪŋlən
b	ŋⁱ̈ʉ ɪ̈ŋlən
73	ŋⁱʉ ɪŋlən
74a	ŋⁱ̈ʉ ɪŋᵍlənᵈ
b	ŋⁱ̈ʉ ɪŋɫən
75a	ŋⁱˀ̈ʉ ɪŋlən
b	nᴵˀ̈ʉ> ɪŋᵍlənᵈ

NORTH CAROLINA

1	ŋⁱʉ ɪŋlən
2a	nⁱˀʉ ɪŋlən
2b–3a	ŋⁱʉ ɪŋlən
3b	ŋⁱ̈ʉ ɪŋlənᵈ
4a	ŋⁱʉ< ɪŋlənᵈ
b	ŋⁱʉ< ɪŋlən
5a	ŋⁱ̈ʉ ɪŋlən
b	ŋⁱʉ< ɪ̈ŋlən
6	ŋⁱ̈ʉ< ɪŋlənᵈ
7a	ŋⁱ̈ʉ ɪŋlən
b	ŋⁱ̈ʉ ɪ̈ŋlən
N8	ŋⁱ̈ʉ> ɪŋᵍlən
8a	ŋⁱʉ ɪŋlənᵈ
b	ŋⁱ̈ʉ ɪŋlənᵈ
9ab	ŋⁱ̈ʉ< ɪŋlən
10a	---
b	ŋⁱ̈ʉ ɪŋlən
c	ŋᴵ^ʉ ɪŋlənᵈ
11a	ŋⁱʉ ɪˀᵛŋᵍlənᵈ
b	ŋⁱʉ ɪŋᵍlənᵈ
12a	ŋⁱˀ̈ʉ ɪŋlən⁺
b	ŋᴶʉ< ɪˀᵛŋlənᵈ
13a	ŋⁱʉ ɪ̈ŋlən
b	ŋᴶʉˀ̈ʉ< ɪŋlənᵈ
N14	nuˀ ɪŋlən
14a	ŋⁱʉ ɪŋlən⁺

NC

14b nɟʉ·ˠɪ̃ᵍŋᵍlənᵈ

c ŋ̟ⁱˢ̌ʉ> ɪŋglənᵈ

15a ŋ̟ⁱʉ ɪŋlən

b ŋ̟ⁱʉ< ɪ̈ŋlənᵈ

16a ŋ̟ⁱʉ ɪŋᵍlənᵈ

b ŋ̟ⁱʉ< ɪ̈ŋlənᵈ

17a ŋ̟ⁱʉ ɪŋlənᵈ

b ŋ̟ⁱˇ̌ʉ ɪŋlən⁺

18a ŋ̟ⁱʉ ɪŋlənᵈ

b ŋ̟ⁱʉ ɪˇŋlənᵈ

19a ŋ̟⌣ʉ ɪ̈ŋɫənᵈ

b ŋ̟ⁱʉ ɪŋlənᵈ

20a nɟʉ ɪŋɫən

b ŋ̟ⁱˇ̌ʉ ɪˆ·ŋlən⁺

c ŋ̟ⁱʉ ɪˇŋlənᵈ

21a ŋ̟ⁱʉ ɪŋlənd

b ŋ̟ⁱˇ̌ʉ ɪ̈ŋlənᵈ

22a nɟʉ ɛˆŋlənᵈ

b ŋ̟ⁱʉ ɪŋlənᵈ

23a ŋ̟ᴵˢ̌ʉ> ɪŋᵍlən⁺

b ŋ̟ⁱˇ̌ʉ ɪŋᵍlənᵈ

c nʉ ɪŋᵍlənᵈ

d ---

N24 ɲu< ɪ̈ˇŋlən

24ab ŋ̟ⁱʉ ɪŋlənᵈ

N25 ŋ̟ɟʉ> ɛ̃ŋələn

25a ŋ̟ⁱʉ ɪŋᵍlən

b ŋ̟ᴶʉˇ ɪŋᵍlənᵈ

26a ŋ̟ⁱˇ̌ʉ ɪŋlənᵈ

b ŋ̟ⁱˇʉ ɛˆŋɫənᵈ

c ŋ̟ᴵˆʉ> ɪŋᵍlənᵈ

27a ŋ̟ⁱʉ ɪŋlən

b ŋ̟ⁱʉ ɪ̈ŋᵍlənᵈ

28a ŋ̟ⁱʉ> ɪ̈ŋlən

bc ŋ̟ⁱʉ ɪŋlənᵈ

NC

29a nɟʉ ɪ̈ŋᵍlənᵈ

b ŋ̟ⁱʉ< ɪŋlənᵈ

30a ŋ̟ⁱʉ ɪŋlən

30b-31a ŋ̟ⁱˇ̌ʉ ɪŋlən

31b ŋ̟ⁱʉ ɪ̈ŋlənᵈ

32a nɟʉ· ɪ̈ŋlən

b ŋ̟ⁱˇ̌ʉ ɪŋlənᵈ

33a ŋ̟ⁱʉ< ɪ̈ˇŋlən

b ŋ̟ⁱʉ< ɪŋlənᵈ

34a ŋ̟ⁱʉ ɪŋlən

b ŋ̟ⁱˇ̌ʉ ɪŋᵍlən

35a ---

b ŋ̟ⁱˇ̌ʉ< ɪ̈ˇŋlənᵈ

N36 ŋ̟ⁱˇ̌ʉ> ɪŋlən

36a ŋ̟ⁱʉ ɪŋlən

b ŋ̟ⁱʉ ɪŋlənᵈ

37a ŋ̟ⁱʉ ɪŋlən

b ŋ̟ⁱʉ ɪ̈ŋlənᵈ

N38 ŋ̟ⁱʉ> ɪŋlən

38a ŋ̟ⁱʉ ɪŋᵍlənᵈ

b ŋ̟ⁱʉ ɪ̈ŋᵍlənᵈ

39a ŋ̟ⁱʉ ɪŋlən

b ŋ̟ⁱʉ ɪŋlənᵈ

40a nɟʉ ɪ̈ŋlən⁺

b ŋ̟ⁱˇ̌ʉ ɪŋlənᵈ

41 ŋ̟ᴵʉ ɪŋlənᵈ

42a ŋ̟ⁱˇ̌ʉ ɪŋᵍlənᵈ

b ŋ̟ⁱˇʉ ɪˇŋᵍlənᵈ

43a ŋ̟ⁱʉ ɪŋɫ̈ˇn

b ŋ̟ⁱˇ̌ʉ ɪŋlən

44 ŋ̟ᴵˢ̌ʉ ɪŋlən

45 ŋ̟ⁱʉ ɪŋlən

46a ŋ̟ᴵˢ̌ʉ> ɪŋlən

b ŋ̟ⁱˇ̌ʉ ɪˇŋlənᵈ

c ŋ̟ᴵˢ̌u< ɪŋᵍlənᵈ

NC

47 nⁱʉ ɪŋŋlən

48 ŋ̟ⁱˇ̌ʉ ɪŋlənᵈ

49 nⁱˇʉ ɪŋlənᵈ

50a ŋ̟ⁱʉ ɪŋᵍlənᵈ

b ŋ̟ⁱˇ̌ʉ ɪŋlənᵈ

51a ŋ̟ⁱˇ̌ʉ ɪŋlən⁺

b ŋ̟ⁱʉ ɪˇŋᵍlənᵈ

N52 ɲʉ> ɪ̈ŋlən

52a ŋ̟ⁱˇ̌ʉ ɪˇ̈ŋᵍlən⁺

b ŋ̟ⁱʉ ɪŋlənᵈ

53a ŋ̟ⁱʉ ɪŋlən⁺

b ŋ̟ⁱʉ ɪŋlənᵈ

54a nⁱʉ ɪŋlən

b ŋ̟ⁱʉ ɪŋᵍlənᵈ

55 ŋ̟ᴵˆʉ ɪŋlən

56a ŋ̟ᴵʉ ɪŋlənᵈ

b ŋ̟ᴵʉ ɪŋlənᵈ

57ab ŋ̟ᴵˆʉ> ɪŋlən

58ab ŋ̟ⁱʉ ɪ̈ŋlən

59 ---

60 ŋ̟ⁱˇʉ ɪŋlənᵈ

61a nᴵu< ɪŋlənᵈ

b ŋ̟ᴵˢ̌ʉ ɪŋlən

62a ŋ̟ⁱʉ> ɪŋlən⁺

b ŋ̟ⁱˇ̌ʉ ɪŋlənᵈ

63a ŋ̟ⁱˇ̌ʉ ɪŋlən

b ŋ̟ⁱˇ̌ʉ ɪ̈ŋlənᵈ

64a ŋ̟ⁱʉ· ɪŋᵍlən

b nᴵˢ̌ʉˆ ɪŋlən

65a ŋ̟ⁱʉ ɪŋlən

b nⁱʉ ɪŋlənᵈ

66a ŋ̟ⁱʉ ɪˇŋlən

b ŋ̟ⁱʉ ɪ̈ŋlən

67a ŋ̟ⁱˇ̌u< ɪ̈ŋlən⁺

b nⁱʉ ɪŋlənᵈ

NC

68a	ŋ ᶦ ʉ ɪŋlən
b	ŋ ᶦ ˇ ʉ ɪŋlən
69a	ŋ ᶦ ʉ ɪŋlən†
b	n ᶦ ˇ ʉ ɪŋlən ᵈ
70a	ŋ ᶦ ʉ › ɪŋlən
b	ŋ ᶦ ʉ ɪŋlən ᵈ
71a	ŋ ᶦ ʉ ɪŋlən
b	ŋ ᶦ ˇ ʉ › ɪŋlən
c	nʉ ˇ u ‹ ɪŋlən ᵈ
72a	s̲ ŋ ᶦ ʉ › ɪŋlən
b	ŋ ᶦ ˇ ʉ ɪŋlən
73a	ŋ ᶦ ʉ ɪŋlən
b	n ᶦ ʉ ɪŋ ᵍlən
74a	ŋ ᶦ ˇ ʉ › ɪŋlən
b	ŋ ᶦ ˇ ʉ › ɪŋlən†
75a	ŋ ᶦ ʉ ɪŋlən
b	ŋ ᶦ ʉ ɪŋ ᵍlən

SOUTH CAROLINA

1a	ŋ ᶦ ʉ › ɪŋlən ᵈ
1b-2b	ŋ ᶦ ʉ ɪŋlən ᵈ
3a	ŋ ᴶ ᶦ ʉ ɪŋlənd
b	---
c̲	nʲʉ · ɪ ^ ə ŋlə^n
4a	---
b	nʲʉ · ɪ ^ ‡ ŋlə^n, ~ ɪ ^ ‡ ŋg-
c	nʲʉ ɛ^ŋlə^n
5a	*nʉ ‹ · ʉ ɛ^ŋlə^n
bc	---
d̲	nʲʉ ɪ ^ ‡ ŋlə^n, ˈ~ ɪ~ ˈste · ᵊts
N6	---
6a	nʲʉ › · ɪŋɬən
b	---
c̲	nʲʉ · ɪ^ŋglə^n

SC

N7-7a	---
7b	c̲v̲ nʉ ɪŋglə^nd, nᴶ ʉ ɪ^ŋlə^n
c̲	---
d̲	ˌnʲʉ ˈi ˇ ŋlɪn ste^ᵊts
8ab	---
c	c̲v̲ nʲʉ · ɪ ^ ə ŋglə^n
9a	ˈnʲʉ · ˌɪ ^ ə ŋlə^n
b	---
c̲	nʲʉ · ɪ ^ ə ŋlə^n
d̲	c̲v̲ nʲʉ ɪ ^ ə ŋlə^n, ˈnʲʉ · ˌɪ ^ ə ŋglə^nd
10a	---
b̲	c̲v̲ nu ‹ · ɪ^ŋlə^n
c̲	nʲʉ · ɪ^ŋlə^n c̲v̲ nʉ · ~
N11	nʲʉ ɪŋlən stěĕts
11a	nʲʉ · ʉ^ ɪŋlə^n
b	n ᶦ u ‹ ɪŋlən, n ‡ u ~ ste · ᵊts
c	ˈnᴶ ʉ ‹ ˌɪ ^ · ŋlə^n ste^ · ts, ˈnʲʉ · ˌɪ ^ ŋ ᵍlə^n ~ (?)
d	nʲʉ › · ɪ^ŋglə^n
e	---
f	c̲v̲ nʲu ɪ^ŋglə^n
g̲	nʉ ɪ ˇ ŋlə^n
2N11	nʲʉ › ɪ ˇ ŋlə^n
11h̲	nʲʉ ɪŋlə^n
i̲	nʲu ‹ · ɪ ˇ ŋ ᵍlən ᵈ
j̲	nʲʉ ‹ ɪ^ŋglə ɣ n ᵈ c̲v̲ ~ -lə › n, nʲy › · ~
12a	---
b	nʲʉ ɪŋlən
13	---
14a	nʲu ‹ ɪŋlən ᵈ

SC

14b	c̲v̲ nʲʉ ɪ ^ ə ŋlə^n
15a	ˌnʲʉ ‹ · ˈɪ ^ ŋlə^n ˌste · ᵊts
	c̲v̲ nʲʉ · ɪ ^ ə ŋlə^n
b	nʲʉ i ˇ ŋlə^n
15c-17c	---
17d	nʲʉ · ˈɪ ^ ŋlɪn ˌste · ᵊts
N18	n ‡ ʉ ‹ ɪ ^ ŋlə › nd
18a	nʲy › ʔɪ ^ ŋlə ɣ n
b	nᴶ y › ɪ › ŋlə › n ste^ · ts
c̲	ˌnʲy › ˈɪ ^ ŋlə › n ˌste^ · ts c̲v̲ ˈnʲy › · ˌ-lə › n ᵈ
N19	---
19a	nʲy › ˈʔɛ ^ ŋlə › n ˌste^ · ᵊts
b	n ᴵ ʉ › ɪŋlən
c	nʲy › · ˈɪ ^ ŋglə › n ste^ · ts
d̲	---
20a	nʲʉ · ɪ ^ ŋlə^n
b	nʲʉ ‹ · ɪ ^ ŋlə^n
c	nʲʉ · ɪ ^ ŋlə^n
d̲	c̲v̲ nʲʉ · ɪ ^ ŋlə^n, ˈ~ ˌ~
21a	ŋ ᶦ ʉ ɪ ˇ ŋlən
b	ŋ ᶦ ʉ ɪ ˇ ŋ ᵍlən ᵈ
N22	---
22a	c̲v̲ nʲʉ ɪ ^ ə ŋlə^n
b	---
c̲	c̲v̲ nᴶ ʉ ‹ · ɪ ^ ə ŋlə^n (?)
23a	nʲʉ i ˇ · ə ŋlə^n
b	ˈnʲʉ · ˌɪ ^ ə ŋlə^n ˈste^ · ts
c	nʲʉ · ɪ ^ ə ŋlə^n
23d-24c	---
24d̲	c̲v̲ nʲʉ ‹ · ʷ ɪ ^ ə ŋglə^nd,

SC		SC		GA	
(24d)	ˈnjʉ ˌiˇŋləˆn	36d	cv njʉ· ɪˆŋgləˆn	1e	nʉ· ɪˆŋləˆn
25a	njʉ ɤˇə̃ɫən	37	ˈnᴵʉ ˌɪŋlən ˈste·ᵗts (?)	f	njuˇ· ɪˇŋᵍlənᵈ
bc	njʉ ɪˇŋləˆn	38a	ˈnjʉ·ʷ ˌɪˆŋləˆn	g	---
26a	ˈnjʉ· ˌiˇŋgləˆn	N38	ˈnjʉ· ˌɪˆŋgləˆn ˈste·ᵗt	h	cv nɨˆʉ ɪʒŋgləˇnᵈ
b	---	38b	ˈnjʉ·ʷ? ˌɪˆŋgləˆn ˈste·ts	N2–2b	---
27a	nᴵʉ ˈɪŋlən ˌste·ts			3a	njuˇ· ɪŋlən
b	ˈnjʉ· ˌɪˆəŋləˆn	c	cv njʉˇ·ʷ ɪˆŋgləˆn	b	---
28a	njʉ· ɪˆŋləˆn	d	njʏˇ·ʷ iŋləˆn	N4	ɲuˇ· ɪ̃ŋlən
b	---		cv ˈnjʉˇ·ʷ ˌɪˆŋgləˆn	4a	ˈnjʉ ˌɪˆəŋləˆnd
c	njʉ ɪˆŋləˆn	39a	ˌnjʉ ˈɪˆŋgləˆn ˌste·ˆts	b	---
d	ˈnjʉ ˌɪˆŋgləˆn	b	ˈnjʉ ˌɪˆŋgləˆn ste·ˆ·ᵗts	c	nɨʒ·ʉ ɪˆəŋgləˆn
29a	njʉ· ɪˆŋgləˆn		cv ˌnjʉˇ·ʷ ˈ~	5a	nɨˇ<u ˈɪˆəŋgləˆn
b	---	40a	njʏˇ·ʉ ɪˆŋlə̃ⁿ,		ˌste·ˆəts
c	njʉ· iˇŋgləˆn		ˈnjʏˇ·ʉˆ ˈɪˆŋlə̃n		cv nʉ· ɪˆəŋgləˆn
30a	nᶦʉ ɪŋlən	b	njʏˇ·ʉˆ ɪˆŋlə̃n	b	---
b	njʉ· ɪˆŋgləˆn	41a	nᶦʉ< ɪ̃ŋlənᵈ	c	cv nu· ɪˆŋgləˆn
c	ˌnjʉ ˈɪˆŋgləˆn ˌste·əts	b	njʉ ɛŋlə̃n	d	---
31a	njʉ·r ɪˆŋgləˆn, ˈnjʉ· ˌ~	42a	nju<ʷ ɛˆŋlə̃n	e	nʉ>· ɪˆəŋgləˆn
b	njʉ· iˇŋgləˆn	N42	ˈnjʏˇ·ʉˆ ˈɪˆŋgˈlə̃ˆn (?),	6a	---
32a	ˌnjʉ·ʷ ˈɪˆəŋgləˆnd		~ ˈɪˆŋglə̃n	b	ˌnjʉ ˈɛˆəŋgləˆn
	ˌste·ts	42b	njʉ ɪˆŋglə>n		ˌste·ˆts
bc	---		cv njɨˆʉ ɛˆŋgləˇn,	7–8a	---
d	njʉ ɪˆəŋgləˆn		nˀᴶʉ<ʷ ɪ>ŋglə>n	8b	njʉ· ɪˆəŋgləˇn
33a	nᶦˇʉ ɪŋglənᵈ	c	njʉˆʉ>ᴵʷ ɪˇŋlə̃n,	9a	ˈnᴵʉ ˌɪŋgləˆn ˈste‡ts
33b–34a	---		njʉˇʉʒʷ ~	b	---
34b	ˌnjʉʷ ˈiˇŋgləˆn ˌste·‡ts	d	---	10a	njʉ· ɤˇŋlənᵈ
c	cv njʉʷ ɪˆəŋgləˆnd	e	ŋᴵʉˆ ɪˆ·ŋgləˆn	b	---
35ab	---	43a	---	N11	nʉ ɪ·ŋgləˆn, ~ ɛˆŋlən
c	nᴵ ɛˆ‡ŋgləˆn, ~ e·‡ŋ-,	b	njʉ<w ɪˆŋglə̃n	12a	---
	~ ɪŋgləˆn	c	njʏʷ ɪˆŋglə̃n, njʏu> ~	b	nᴵʉ ɪŋgləˆn
36a	---	44a	ˈnjʏ>ʉˆ ˈɪˆŋglə̃n	13a	njuʒ ɪˇŋᵍlənᵈ
b	? ˌnjʉ·ʷ ˈɪˆŋgləˇn	b	cv njʏ>w ɪˆŋglə̃n	b	njʉ iˇŋgləˆn
	ˌste·‡ts	**GEORGIA**		14a	---
c	cv njʉˇ<·ʷ ɪˆŋgləʒn,	N1	ˌɲu< ˈɪŋlən ˌste·ts	b	njʉ< ɪˆŋgləˆn
	njʉ· ˈɪˆŋgləˇn ˌste·ᴵts	1a–d	---	c	---

GA

15a   nⁱ ʉ ɪŋlən

b   ---

16a   ˈnʉːʉ ˌɪˆŋləˆn

b   nᵘ˂ʉ ɪˆʉləˆn

c   ---

d   njʉˑ ɪˆŋglɛ̆ˆn

N17   nᴵ ʉ ɪŋlən

17   nᴵ ʉ ɪŋlən

18a   ŋⁱ ʉ ɪŋləˆn

b   ˌnⁱ ʉ ˈɪˆŋlən ˌsteɟts

19a   **ˈnjʉˑ ˌɤˆə̃nˆŋləˆn

b   ˈnjʉˑ ˌɪˆᵊŋləˆn

20a   njʉˑ ɪˆŋləˆn

b   ---

21a   nᴵ ʉ ɪŋləˆn

b   ---

22a   ˌnjʉ ˈɪˆŋlən ˌsteˑɟts

b   njʉˑ ɛˆᵊŋləˆn

23a   ---

b   ˌnⁱ ʉ ˈɪŋlɟn ˈsteˑts

c   ˌnⁱ ʉ ˈɪŋləˆn ˌsteˑts

d   cv njʉˑ ɪˆᵊŋləˆn

e   nᴵ ʉˑ ɪŋlən,
       ˌnᴵ ʉˆ ˈɪˆŋləˆn
       ˌsteɟts

GA

23f   ˌnⁱ ʉ ˈɪŋlɛ̆n ˌsteˑts

N24   ---

24a   nⁱ ʉ ɪŋlən

b   njʉ ɪˆŋləˆn

N25   ---

26   ˈnᴵ ʉ ˌɛˆŋlən steɟts

27   nᴶ ʉ ɪŋlən steᵛˑɟts

28   nᴵ ʉ ɛŋləˆnd

29a   njʉˑ ɪˆŋləˆn

b   njʉˑ ˈɪˆŋləˆn ˌsteˆˑts

30ab   ---

c   nᴵ ʉ ɪŋləˆnd,
       nᴵ ʉᵂ ɛˆŋləˆn,
       nᴵ ʉ ʉˆ ɪŋ-

31   nᴵ ʉ ɪŋlən

32   nᴵ ʉ ɪŋləˆn, ～ ɪŋ̆-

33a   ˌnⁱ ʉ ˈɪŋləˆn ˌsteɟts

b   nⁱ ʉ ɪŋləˆn, ～ ɪŋg-

N34   ---

34a   ŋⁱ ʉ ɤŋlən

b   njʉˑ ɪˆŋləˆn

N35   nᴵ ʉ ʉˆ ɛˆŋləˆn

N36-37a   ---

37b   ˌnjʉ ˈɛˆɟŋləˆn ˌsteˆˑts

c   ---

GA

2N37   ˌnⁱ ʉ ˈɪŋləˆn ˌsteɟts

37d   ˌnⁱ ʉ ˈɪŋləˆn ˌsteˑɟts

ef   ---

g   ˌnjʉˑ ˈiᵛŋləˆn ˌsteˑɟts

h   cv njʉˑ ɪˆŋləˆn, nʉ˂ˑw ～

i   nʉˑʉˆ ɪŋləˆnd

38   ---

39   ˈnⁱ ʉ ˌɪŋlən ˈsteɟts

40-41   ---

42a   njʉˑ ɪˆŋləˆnt

b   ---

43   nⁱ ʉ ɪŋlən

44ab   ---

c   njʉˑ ɛˆŋləˆn

de   ---

FLORIDA

1   ˈnjʉˑ ˌɪˆŋgləˆn

2a   ˈnʉˑ ˌɪˆŋgləˆn ˈsteˑᵊts

b   ---

c   ˈnjʉ ˌɪˆŋgləˆn ˈsteˆˑts

3a   njʉ iᵛŋləˆn, ～ ɪˆŋg-

b   nʉ ɪˑŋləˆn

4   nⁱ ʉ ɪŋgləˆn

5a   ---

b   njʉˑ ɪˆŋlən

4a. EASTERN STATES

The regular stress pattern, (～) ˈ～ ˌ～,
is not marked.

NY

5a   iˑstən steɟts

7j   s̲ iˑstən steɟts

9b   s̲ iˑstən steɟts

12c   s̲ iˑstən̩ steɟts

NY

13a   s̲ ð̆ɟˆ iˑstən steˑɟts

14a   ð̆ɟˆ iˑstən steɟts

16b   ð̆ɟˆ iˑstən̩ steɟts

18a   ð̆ɟˆ iˑstən steɟts

b   ð̆ɟˆ iˑstən steɟts

NY

20ab   ð̆ɟˆ iˑstən steɟts

22   ð̆ɟˆ iˑstən steˑɟts

24a   ð̆ɟˆ iˑstən steɟts

26a   iˑsteˆn steᵛɟ˂ts

b   ð̆ɪᶻ iˑsteˆn steᵛˑɟts

28b   ð̆ɪᶻ iˑstən steᵛˑɟts (?)

NY

29b	ðɪ﹥ i·stən ste·ᵗ ts
30a	i·stɐˆn ste·ᵗ ts
31a	ðɪ᷉ iˇistən steˇ·ts
32a	iˇistɐˆn ste·ᵗ ts
35a	ð‡᷉ i·stən steᵗ ts
b	ð‡ˆ i·stən ste·ᵗ ts
36a	ð‡ˆ i·stən steᵗ ts
37a	ð‡ˆ i·stən steᵗ ts
43c	ði· i·stən steˇ‡ts

NY

44a	ðɪˆ i·stən ste‡ts
48d	ð‡ iˇistɐˆn steˇ‡<ts
50a	ðə ‡istɐˆn ste·‡ts
51b	‡istɐˆn steˆ‡ts
52a	iˇistɘn steˇ‡ts
c	ð‡ iⁱˆstən ste‡ts
53a	iˇistən ste·ts
57a	ðɪ᷉ iˇistɐˆn steˇts
60a	ðɪ᷉ iJstɐˆn steˇ‡ts

NY

62b	i·stɐˆn steˇ·ᵗts
c	i·stən ste·ᵗ ts

NEW JERSEY

8b	ð‡᷉ i·stən ste‡ts
20b	s ð‡ˆ i·stən ste‡ts

GEORGIA

2a	cv i·ᴶstə᷉n steˆ·ts
23b	i·stən ste·ts
37i	i·stɐˆn steᵗ ts

4b. ENGLAND, ENGLISH

Primary stress on the first syllable
is unmarked.

ONT

5	cv ɪˆŋlɘˆn
7	cv ɪŋɫ‡ʃ
8b	cv ɪˆŋlɘˆn

NEW YORK

28b	cv ɪˆŋgl‡ʃ
31a	ɪˆŋlɘˆn
32a	cv ɪˇŋglɘˆn
33b	cv ɪˆŋl‡<ʃ
48d	cv ɪŋɫɘˆn
49d	ɪŋɫɘˆn
63d	cv ɪˆŋglɘˆn, -l‡ʃ

KENTUCKY

7a	cv ɪŋlɘˆn, ɪŋl‡ʃ

SOUTH CAROLINA

5a	εˆ‡ŋlɘˆn
7b	cv εˆ·ŋlɘˆnd
11b	ɪŋlən
d	cv εˆŋgl‡<ʃ
h	cv ð‡᷉ ɪˆŋgl‡<ʃ
17c	cv ɪˆŋ̩lɘˆn
18b	ɪˆŋglɪˆʃ
c	*cv εˆŋgl‡᷉ʃ
20c	ɪˆŋlɘˆn
22c	cv ɪˆ◌ᵊŋl‡<ʃ
23a	cv iˇŋlɘˆn
26b	cv ɪˆŋl‡<ʃ
27b	cv ɪˆŋlɘˆn
30b	cv ɪˆŋlɘˆn
32d	cv iˇᵊŋlɘˆn

SC

36b	cv εˆŋglɘˆn
38a	ɪˆŋlɘˆn
N42	cv ɪˆŋglɘ᷉n

GEORGIA

1c	cv ɪˆŋɫn̩
d	cv ɪˆŋglɘ﹥n, ɪˆŋlɘˆn
2a	ɪŋɫn̩ cv εˆ·‡ŋglɪˆʃ
5a	cv ɪˆŋlɘˆn
c	ɪˆᵊŋlɐ̆n
e	cv iˇŋlɘˇn
8b	cv ɪˆᵊŋlɘˇn
20a	e·‡ŋlɘˆn
22a	cv ɪŋlɘˆn
b	cv ɪˆŋglɘˆn
26	cv ɪŋl‡ʃ

COMMENTARY

ONTARIO

4a   ˌæt'łæˇntɨk ˌste·ts

NEW YORK

18c   [nju·]: *sic*

28b   [ɨ]: doubtful

29b   ˌdɑ·un 'i·st

31b   'nɔɵθ ətˌlãnɨk 'steˇɨts

33b   dɑ·un 'iˇist

34c   cv nʉˇʉ ɪˆŋgləˆndɚ

49d   cv ðə koust, iⁱˆstɚn 'si·bo·ɚd

50a   ['ɔˇł ˌłɔ·ŋ] *the Eastern States*

51c   ˌdɑ·un 'iˇistɚnɚ

52c   [noˇɵθ]: includes New York State; 'iⁱˆstɚn 'si·bo<ɚd

54b   'iⁱˆstɚn ˌpɑ<ɚt

63a   cv [ðə 'iˇist] = *New England*

b   [ŋ]: doubtful

NEW JERSEY

20b   s̲: rare

WEST VIRGINIA

3   [nu<]: *sic*

KENTUCKY

7a   *England* people
cv ['~ ˌpi·ⁱˆpəˆł];
English sparrow
cv [ˌ~ 'spɑ>rəˆ]

DISTRICT OF COLUMBIA

1a   [nuş]: *sic*

VIRGINIA

N59   [ˌdaˆun 'i·st] = tidewater Virginia

SOUTH CAROLINA

7d   ˌdʌşun 'i·st

11c   [ᵍ]: doubtful

g   noˆ·ᶿθ

h   • ðə i·ɨst

19a   noˆ·ᶿðəˇn steˆ·ts

22c   [ᴶ]: doubtful

23a   Yankee country ['ɹæˆᵉŋkɨş ˌkˈʌşᶿn'ɟɹɨş]; don't specially like 'em yet [ˌdo·ᵉnt 'spɛˆᶿʃłɨş lɑ<ɨk əˆm 'ɹɛˆᶿt]

24a   noˆ·ðən steɪts

25b   nɔ·əθ'i·stɚn ˌsteˆ·ts

SC

32a   i·ᴶst

34b   noˆɔθ'i·ɹstəˆn ˌste·ɨts

35c   'nɔ·əθəˆn ˌste·ɨts

37   [ɨ]: doubtful

N38   ðə noˆoθ

39a   ['nɔş·əθəˆn ˌsteˆ·ts]; blue bellied yankee ['bɹy· ˌbɛlɨşd 'ɹæᵋŋkɨş]

40b   noˆəθ

N42   [ˈ]: doubtful

42c   ɹæˆᵋŋkɨ<

GEORGIA

1a   *'ɹæᵋŋkɪ> ˌtˈɑ<·un

N11   ðɨ θecn ɨ

21a   'nɔ·əðən ˌsteɨts

N35   ðɨ 'noˇɔðən ˌpɑ>ət

2N37   ˌætlæn'tɨk ˌko<ˇˢ 'steɨts

37i   nɔθeˈi·stəˆn ˌsteɨts

FLORIDA

2c   ˌdɑ·un 'i·st

4   'nɔɵθən ˌsteɨts

5. MASSACHUSETTS

WS 86.1   LANE 8

There is considerable variety in the pronunciation of *Massachusetts*. In addition to the predominant 4-syllable forms of the type [mæsəˈtʃusəts], there are also 3-syllable forms of the type [mæsˈtʃ-]. The penultimate syllable, in addition to the prevailing [-tʃu-], may have [-tju-], [-tu-], [- țˈu-], [-dʒ-], etc. The

final syllable is usually of the type [-səts], but may have such forms as [-səs], [-sət], [-zəts], [-zət], [-ɾɨt], [-ʃəs], [-ʃən], [-ʃɨ], or [-sɨ], etc.

The predominant stress pattern, [-ˈtʃ-] or [ˌ-ˈtʃ-], is not marked.

ONTARIO		NY		NY		NY	
1a	mæsətʃʉsɨts	5e	mæsətʃu‹·zəts	13a	mæsətʃu‹·səts	26c	---
b	mæsɪtʃu‹sɨts	f	mæsətʃŭˆŭsəts	b	mæsŏtʃu‹·səts	27a	mæˇstʃuˆ·usɨts
2a	---	g	mæstʃuşᵘsəts	14ab	mæsətʃu‹·səts	b	---
b	mæsətʃʉ¿ʉ›sɨts	hi	mæsətʃu‹·səts	15a	mæsətʃɨuşzɨts	c	cv ˈmæᵋsəˌ tʃʉˇu‹sɨts
3	mæsətʃʉˇʉsɨts	6a	mæ¿sətʃu·səts	b	mæsətʃɨ›u·şɨts	28a	cv ˈmæsəˌtʃʉˇsɨts
4a	mæsətʃʉʉˆsɨts	6b-7a	mæsətʃu‹·səts	16a	mæsətʃu·səts	b	mæs̥ətʃuˇ·sɨts
b	mæsətʃuşᵘ‹sɨts	7b	mæsətʃuʷsəts	b	mæˆ·sətʃu·səts	29a	---
5-8a	---	c	mæ·sətʃu‹·səts	17a	mæsətʃɨu‹sɨts	b	mæsətʃʉˇu‹sɨts
8b	mæsətʃʉˇʉˆsɨts	def	mæsətʃʉ›·səts	b	mæsətʃu‹·səts	c	mæ·sətjʉ·sɨts
c	mæsətʃuşu‹sɨts	g	mæ›sətʃʉ›·səts	18a	mæsətʃɨu‹·səts	30a	mæˇstʃu‹·sɨ‹ts
d	mæsətʃʉˆ·sɨts	h	mæsətʃʉˆ·səts	b	mæ·sətʃu‹·səts	b	mæˇsğ̥tʃuş·sɨ‹ts
9-10	---	i	mæsətʃu‹·səts	c	mæsətʃu·səts	cd	---
NEW YORK		j	ˈmæ›səˌtʃu‹·səts	19	mæsətʃu‹·səts	e	ˈmæ›sətʃʉ›·sɨts
1	mæstʃuwzɨts,	k	mæsətʃu‹·səts	20a	mæsədʒɨu‹sɨts	31a	mæstʃuşu‹sɨts
	mæsə-	l	mæsəţju‹·səts	b	mæ·stʃu‹·səts	b	mæ̆¿sŏtʃʉ·ʉˆsɨts
2a	---	m	mæsətʃu‹·səts	21	mæˆ·sətʃu‹səts		cv mæsğ̥tʃʉ¿ʉ›-,
b	mæstʃuᶜʷzɨˇts	8	mæsətʃu·səts	22	mæˆ·sətʃu‹·zəts		mæsətʃʉˇʉ-,
c	---	9a	mæsətʃuşsəts	23a	---		mæstʃuşu‹-
3a	mæsŏdʒu‹zəts	b	mæsətʃu‹·səˆts	b	mæˆ·ᵊstʃuş·sɨ‹ts	32a	mæsğ̥tʃu‹·sɨts (?)
b	mæsətʃu‹ţəts	c	mæsətʃʉ›·səts	c	cv mæstʃʉ¿usɨts,		cv mæsətʃuˇu-
c	mæsətʃu‹·zəts	10a	mæ·stʃu‹·səts		mæ·ss-, mæsə-	b	ˈmæsəˌtʃu·sɨts
d	mæsətʃu‹·səˆts	b	mæsətʃu‹·səts	24a	mæsətʃusɨts	33a	---
4a	mæsətʃʉ›·səts	11	mæ¿sətʃu‹·zəts	b	mæsətʃu·sɨts	b	mæsətjʉ¿·usɨts
b	mæstʃu‹·sɨˇts	12a	mæsətʃɨŭşsɨts	25a	mæˇstʃʉ¿·u‹sɨts	c	mæsŏtʃuˇusɨ‹ts
c	mæˇsətʃu‹·səts	b	mæsətʃu‹·səts	b	mæsətʃuˇ·usɨts	34a	cv mɛˇsətʃu‹u‹sɨts
5abc	mæsətʃu‹·səts	c	mæsətʃu‹·zəts	26a	mæstʃuˇ·sɨ‹ts	b	---
d	mæ›sətʃu‹·səts			b	mæşətʃuˇşɨts	c	cv mæsətɨʉsɨ‹ts

NY

34d mæsətʃuʂu<ʂ‡ts
35a mæsətʃu<·s‡ts
  b mæsədʒ‡us‡ts
  c ---
36a mæsdʒ‡us‡ts
  b mæsətʃ‡uz‡ˇts
37a mæsətʃ>us‡ˇts
  b mæsətʃŭˆŭs‡ˇts
  c mæstʃu<·s‡ˇts
38a mæsətʃ‡u<s‡ˇts
  b mæsətʃ‡>u<s‡ˇts
39a mæsətʃu<·s‡ˇts
  b mæstʃ‡>us‡ˇts
40a mæ·sdʒ‡>u<·z‡ˇts
  b mæsədʒu<·s‡ˇts
41 mæsətʃu<s‡ˇts
42a mæsətʃ‡u<z‡ts
  b mæstʃu<s‡ts
43a mæstʃ‡u<s‡ˇts
  b mæsətʃu<s‡ts
  c mæsətʃu<·s‡ˇts
44a mæsətʃ‡u<s‡ts
  b mæsətʃu<·z‡ˇts
45abc ---
  d mæstʃuˇus‡ts
46a mæsətᴶʉˇʉs‡ts
  b mæzətʃuz‡ts,
     mæsətʃu<z‡ts
  c mæˇsətʃuˇᵁs‡ts,
     -tʃʉᵁˆ-
47a mæstʃuʂu<z‡ts
  b mæsətʃuʂ‡ˇts
48a mæstᴶu<u<s‡ts
  b ---
  c mæsətᴶuʂu<s‡ts

NY

(48c) cv -tʃʉʑʉ>-
48d mæsətᴶuʂu<s‡ts
49ab ---
  c mæstʃuʂu<s‡ts
  d mæsətʃuʂu<s‡ts
     cv -z‡ts
50a mæstʃuʂu<s‡ts
     cv -u<u<ʂ‡ts
  b mæstʃu<u<s‡ts
51a mæsətʃʉˇʉs‡ts
  b mæzətʃʉʉˆẓ‡ts
cde ---
52a mæstʃu·s‡ts
  b ---
  c mæstᴶu<s‡ts
53a mæstʃuʂu<s‡ts
  b mæsətʃʉˇʉs‡ts
54a mæsətʃu·s‡ts,
     '-ˌtʃ-
  b 'mæsəˌtʃuʂu<s‡ts
55a mæsətʃuʂu<ʂ‡ts
  b 'mæsəˌtʃʉʉs‡ts
56a mæstʃʉʑʉ>s‡ts
     cv mæsətʃuˇus‡ts
  b mæsətʃʉʉs‡ts
57a mæsətᴶuʂus‡ts
  b ---
  c mᴇˇˇsətʃʉ·ʉˆs‡ts
58a mæsətʃuˇus‡ts
  b 'mæsətʃʉs‡ts
  c ---
  d mæsətʃʉˇus‡ts
     cv -s‡<ts
  e mæsətʃuˇus‡<ts
     cv mæstʃuˇus‡ts

NY

58f ---
59a mæsᴇˇtʃuˇuʂ‡ts
  b mæstʃ‡u<·s‡ts
60a mæsᴇˇtʃuʂu<s‡ts
  b mæsᴇˇtʃuˇus‡ts
61a mæsətʃu<s‡<ts
  b mæsətʃʉ<s‡<ts
62a ---
  b mæsətʃu<·s‡<ts
  c 'mæsəˆˌtʃʉ·s‡ts
  d mæsᴇˇtʃu<s‡ts
63a mæsətʃuʂus‡<ts
     cv -tᴶʉˇʉ-,
     -tʃʉˇ·ʉs‡ts
  b cv mæsətʃʉ·s‡<ts
  c mæsətʃ‡uˇ<z‡ˇts
  d mæsətʃʉ>·ʉʑs‡<ts
64a mæsətʃʉˇs‡ts
  b mæsətʃʉ>·s‡ts
  c ---

NEW JERSEY

1a mæsətʃʉ>·səts
  b mæʑ·sətʃʉ>·səts
2a mæsətʃu<·səts
  b mæsətʃʉ>·səts
3a mæsəstʃʉsəs
  b mæsətʃʉ>·səts
4a mæsətʃʉ>·zəts
  b mæsətʃʉ>·səts
5a mæsətʃʉ>·zət
  b mæsətʃuˆu<zəts
6a mæsətʃʉ>·səts
  b mæsətʃʉ>·sət
7a mæ·sətʃʉ>·ʃəs
  b mæsətʃʉ>zəts

NJ

8ab mæsətʃu<·səts
9a mæsətʃu<·səs
  b mæsətʃʉ>·səts
10a mæsətʃu<·zəts
  b mæsətʃʉʉ>·səts
  c mæsətʃʉ·səts
  d mæsətʃu<·səts
11ab mæsətʃʉ>·səts
  c mæsətʃʉʉ>·səts
12a mæsətʃʉ·zəts
  b mæsətʃʉ>·səts
13a mæsətʃʉ>·səs
  b mæsətʃʉ>·səts
14a mæsətʃu<·səts
  b mæsətʃʉ>·səs
15a mæsəstʃʉrəts
  b mæsətʃʉ>·səs
16a mæsətʃu<·zət
  b mæsətʃʉ>·səts
17a mæsətʃʉ>səts
  b mæsətʃʉ>·səts
18a mæsətʃu<·səts
  b mæsətʃʉ>·səts
  c mæ>sətʃu<·səts
18d-19a mæsətʃu<·səts
19b mæʑsətʃu<·səts
20a mæsətʃu<·səts
  b mæsətʃu<·səts
21ab mæsətʃu<·səts

PENNSYLVANIA

1a mæsətʃu·səts
  b mæsətʃu<·səts
  c mæsətʃuʂ·səts
  d mæsətʃu<·səts
  e mæsətʃu·səts

PA		PA		PA		PA	
1f	mæsətʃʉ>·səts	15a	mæsətʃu·sɨts	33a	mæsətʃu<rəs	50b	mæsətʃʉ>·rəs
g	mæsətʃu<səts	b	mæ>sətʃu·səts	b	mæsətʃu<·rəs	c	mæsətʃʉ·zəts
h	mæsətʃu·səts	c	mæsətʃu<·zɨˇts	34a	mæsətʃʉ>·rəs	51a	mæsətʃʉ·rəs
2a	mæ·sətʃu<·səts	16a	mæsətʃu·təs	b	mæsətʃu<·səts	b	mæsətʃʉ>·səts
2b-3a	mæsətʃu<·səts	b	mæsətʃu·səts	c	*mæsətʃu<səts	52a	mæsətʃu<rəs
3b	mæsətʃu<·sət	c	---	35a	mæsətʃu<·rəs	b	mæsətʃʉ>·səts
c	mæsətʃu<·səts	17a	mæsətʃusəts	b	mæsətʃu<·zəts	53a	mæsətʃuusəts
4a	mæsətʃʉu<səs	b	mæsətʃu·səts	36a	mæsətʃu<rəs	b	mæsətʃʉ>·səts
4b-5b	mæsətʃu<·səts	18a	mæsətʃu<·zəts	b	mæstʃu<·rəs	54a	mæsətʃu<·rəs
5c	mæsətʃʉ^u<səts	b	mæsətʃu<·səts	37a	mæsətʃu<·səts	b	mæsətʃʉ·səts
d	mæ>sətʃʉ·səs	19a	mæsətʃʉ>·zəs	b	mæsətʃʉ>səts	55a	mæsətʃu<·səts
e	mæ·stʃʉ>·rəs	b	mæsətʃu<·səs	38a	mæsətʃu<·səts	b	mæsətʃʉsəts
6a	mæsətʃu·səts	20a	mæsətʃu<·təs	b	mæsətʃu<·rəs	56a	mæsətʃʉ>·səts
b	mæsətʃu<·səts	b	mæsətʃʉ>·sɨts	39a	mosætʃu<səts	b	mæsətʃʉ·səts
c	mæsətʃuʐəts	21a	mæstʃɨu<səs	b	mæsətʃu<səts	57a	mæsətʃʉ>·rəs
d	mæsətʃu<·zəts	b	mæsətʃu<·sɨˇts	40a	mæ>sətʃʉ>·rəs	b	mæsətʃʉ>·səts
7a	mæsətʃɪsəts	22a	mæsətʃɨu<zɨˇts	b	mæsətʃu<səts	58a	mæsətʃu<·səts
b	mæsətʃʉ>·səts	b	mæsətʃu·sɨˇts	41a	mæsətu·təs	b	mæsətʃʉ·səts
c	mæsətʃu·səts	23a	mæsətʃɨu<sɨˇt	b	mæsətʃʉ>·səts	59a	mæsətʃu<·zɨˇts
d	mæsətʃu<·səts	b	mæstʃɨu<zɨˇts	42a	mæsətʃu<rəs	b	mæsətʃʉ>·səts
8a	mæsətʃʉ>·ʃəs	24ab	mæsətʃu·sɨˇts	b	mæsətʃʉ>u<zəts	60a	mæsətʃʉ·səts
b	mæsətʃʉ·səts	25a	mæsətʃɨŭ<zɨˇts	43a	mæsətu<·təs	b	mæsətʃʉ·zəts
c	mæθətʃu<·səts	b	mæsstʃu·sɨʐts	b	mæsətʃu<·səts	61a	mæsətu<·səts
d	mæsətʃʉ>·səts	26a	mæsətʃu·sɨˇts	44ab	mæsətʃʉ>·səts	b	mæsətʃʉ·səts
9a	mæsətʃu<sə	b	mæsətʃŭʷsɨˇts	45a	mæsətʃu<·səts	62a	mæsətʃu<·rəs
b	mæsətʃu<·səs	27a	*mæsətʃɨu<·sɨˇts	45b-46b	mæsətʃʉ·səts	b	mæsətʃʉ>·səts
9c-10	mæsətʃu<·səts	b	mæsŏtʃu·sɨˇts	47a	mæsŏtʃʉ·rəs	63a	mæsətʃu<·zəts
11a	mæsətʃu·səts	28a	mæsətʃu·səts	b	mæsətʃʉ<·ʉzəts	b	mæsətʃʉ>·se^ts
b	mæsətʃu<·səts	28b-29a	mæsətʃu<·səts	48a	mæsətʃʉ>·rəs	64a	mæsətʃɨwsɨˇts
12a	mæsətʃu<·zəts	29b	mæsətʃu·səts	b	mæsətʃʉ·səts	b	mæsətʃŭ̧sɨˇts
b	mæsətʃu<·səts	30a	mæstʃɨu<sɨts	c	mæsətʃʉ·rəs	65a	mæsətʃu·zɨˇts
13a	mæsətʃu·rəs	b	mæsətʃɨu<sɨˇts	49a	mæsətʃʉ>·səts	b	mæsətʃu<·zɨˇts
b	mæsətʃu<·səts	31a	mæsətʃu<·sɨˇts	b	mæsətʃʉ·səts	66a	mæsətʃŭŭsəts
14a	mæsətʃu<·sət	b	mæstʃu<·sɨˇts	50a	---	b	mæsd͡ʒŭ<sɨts
b	mæsətʃu<·səts	32ab	mæsətʃu<·səts			67a	mæsətʃɨu̧sɨˇts

PA		WVA		WVA		WVA	
67b	mæsetʃu·sɉˇts	18b	mæsetʃʉʃes	36a	mæsetʃʉ>·zets	52c	mæsetʃʉ>·sats
WEST VIRGINIA		19a	ˈmæseɪtʃʉɫt	b	mæsetʃu<·res	53a	mæsestʃu<·res
1	mæsetʃʉ>·sets	b	mæsetᴵʉres	37a	mæsetʉ·sets	b	---
2	mæsetuˆu<ʃes	20a	mæsɉˆtᴵˇʉʃes	b	mæsetʃʉ>sets	c	mæsetʃʉ>·sats
3	mæsetʃu<·sets	b	mæsetʃʉres	38a	mæsetu<·sets	54a	mæsetʃʉ·sets
4a	mæsetʃu<·ses	21a	mæsˌ·setʃʉ·res	b	mæsestʃʉ>·res (✓)	b	mæsetʃʉ·res
b	mæsetʃʉseˆs	b	mæsetʃʉ·res	39a	mæsetʃʉ·ses	**OHIO**	
5	mæsetʃʉ>·res	22a	mæsetʃʉ>·res	b	mæsetʃʉ>·sets	1a	mæsetʃɉu·sɉts
6a	mæsetʃʉ>·ʃes	b	mæsetʃʉres	c	mæsetʃʉ·sets	b	mæsetʃɉuˤsɉˇts
b	mæsetʃʉsets	23a	mæsetʃʉ>·ss	40a	mæsetʃʉ>·ses	c	mæsetʃu<·sɉˇts
7a	mæsetᴵˆu<res	b	mæsetʃʉ>·res	b	mæsetʃʉ·res	2a	mæsetʃʉ>·res
b	mæsetʃʉ·sets	24a	mæsetʃʉsets	41a	mæsetʃʉ>·zets	b	mæsetʃu<·ses
8a	mæsestʃʉ·ses	b	mæsetʃʉ·ses	b	mæsetᴵʉʃez	3a	mæsetʃu<·sets
b	mæsetʃʉ>·sets	25a	mæseţᴵʉsets	42ab	mæsetʃʉ>·res	b	mæsetʃʉ>·sets
9a	mæɾetu<ʃɉˆz	b	mæseţᴵʉses	43a	mæsetu<·ʃes	4a	mæsetʃusets (✓)
b	mæsetʃʉ·res	26a	mæţestᴵʉʃen	b	mæsetʃʉ·res	b	mæsetʃu<·sets
10a	mæsetʃʉ>·ses	b	mæsetʃʉ·sets	44a	mæsetu<·ses	5a	---
b	mæsetu<ʃɉˆ	27a	mæstʃʉ·res	b	mæsetʃʉ>·res	bc	mæsetʃʉ>·sets
c	mæsetʃʉ·sets	b	mæsetʃʉ·sets	45a	mæ·setʃʉ>·res	6a	mæsetu<·ses
11a	mæsetʃʉ·ses	28a	mæseţɾʉres	b	mæstʃʉ>·ses	b	mæsetʃʉ·sets
b	mæsetʃʉ·sets	b	mæsetʃʉ·sets	46a	mæstʃʉ·ses	7a	mæsetʃu<ɾets
12a	mæsetu<·ʃets	29a	mæsetʃʉ·res	b	mæsetʃʉ·res	b	mæ·setʃʉ>·res
b	mæsetʃʉɾets	b	mæsetʃʉ·zets	47a	mæsetʃuˤ·sets	8a	mæsetʃusets
13a	mæsetʃʉ>·sets	30a	mæsetᴵʉres	b	mæstʃʉ·ses	b	---
b	mæsetʃʉ·zet (✓)	b	mæsetᴵʉses	48a	mæsetʃʉ·sets	c	mæsetʃʉ>·ɾets
14a	mæsetʃʉ>·sets	31a	mæseţᴵʉsets	bc	---	d	---
b	mæsetʃʉsets	b	mæ·setᴵʉʃen	d	mæsestʃʉ>·res	e	mæsetʃu·sɉˇts
15a	mæsetʃʉ>res	32a	mæsetᴵʉţet	49a	mæsetʃʉ·res	cv	-dʒu·-
b	mæsetʃʉ·res	b	mæsestᴵʉʃes	b	mæ·stʃʉres	9a	mæsetʃu<·set
16a	mæɾetʃʉ·ses	33a	mæseţᴵʉsets	50a	mæsetʃʉ·sets	b	---
b	mæsetu<·res	b	mæsetᴵˀʉsets	b	mæsetʃʉ>·ses	c	mæsetʃuˤ·sets
17a	---	34a	mæsetʃʉses	51a	mæsetʃʉ>·sets	d	---
b	mæsetʃʉ>·res	b	mæsetʃʉ>·ses	b	mæsetʃʉ·res	10a	mæsetʃʉ>·zes
c	mæsetʃʉ>·zets	35a	mæsestʃʉ>·sɉˆ	52a	mæsetʃʉ>·res	10b-11a	mæsetʃʉ>·sets
18a	mæsetʃʉ·res	b	mæsetʃʉ·sets	b	mæsetʃʉ>·zets	11b	mæsetʃʉ·sets

OHIO

12a mæsətu‹·t∫əs

 b mæsət∫ʉ·səts

 cd ---

13a mæsɤ̆t∫ɪ›ᵁzɨts

13b-18 ---

KENTUCKY

1a-7b ---

DELAWARE

 1a mæsət∫ʉ›·səts

 b mæ·sət∫ʉ›·səts

 c mæsət∫ʉ›·səts

 2a mæsət∫ʉ̆ŭzəts

 b mæsət∫ʉ·səts

 3a mæ·sət∫ʉ·sɨ›ts

 b mæsət∫ʉ·sɨ›ts

 c mæsətuʒu‹səts

 4 mæsətu‹·∫ɨ^

 5a mæst∫ʉzɨts

 b mæsət∫ʉɾəs

 6a mæsəstu‹·ɾɨ^z

 b mæsət∫ʉ·sɨts

MARYLAND

 1a mæsət∫ʉ·zəts

 b mæsɤ̆t∫ʉ›·ɾəs

 2a mæsɤ̆t∫ʉ·sɨts

 b mæsətʉˇ∫ət

 3a mæsəst∫ʉ›·∫ɨ

 b mæsət∫ʉ·səts

 4a mæsət∫u‹·zɨˇts

 b mæsət∫ʉzɨˇts

 c mæst∫i›ʉsɨts

 5a mæsət∫ʉsɨˇts

 b mæsətᴵʉsɨdʒ

 6a mæsɤ̆tuusɨˇ

 b mæsət∫ʉ›·sɨtš

MD

 7a mæsətu‹·sɨˇt

 b mæsət∫ʉzɨts

 c mæst∫ʉsɨˇts

 8a mæsəstᴵʉ∫əs

 b mæsət∫ʉ·sɨˇts

N9 mæsətᴵʉzɨⁿts

 9a mæsətᴵʉsɨˇts

 b mæst∫ʉ·sɨts

 10a mæsət∫ʉ·zɨˇts

 b ˈmæsət_t∫ʉ·sɨˇts

 11 mæsət∫ʉsɨts

 12a mæsət∫ʉ›sə^ts

 b mæsət∫ʉ›·sə^ts

 13a mæsət∫ʉ·ɾəs

 b mæsətᴵʉsɨdz

 c mæsət∫ʉ›·zəts

 d mæsət∫ʉ·sə^ts, -tᴵʉ̆-

 e mæsət∫ʉ›sɨˇts

 f mæsət∫ʉʉʒsə^ts

 14 mæsət∫ʉ›·zəⁿts

 15a mæsətᴵʉ∫ən

 b mæsət∫ʉ·səts

 16 mæsət∫ʉʒsə^ts

 17a mæsət∫ʉ·səts

 b mæsət∫ʉ›·səts

 18a mæsᵗɨˢtᴵʉ∫əs

 b mæsət∫ʉsɨˇts

 19a mæst∫ʉzɨts

 b mæsət∫ʉʉʒsɨˇts

 20a mæsət∫ʉsɨˇts

 b mæsət∫ʉ·sɨts

 c mæsət∫ʉ›·sɨts

 21a mæsət∫ʉsɨts

 b mæstʉˇʉʉzɨts

N22 ---

MD

2N22 mæsəstu‹∫ɨˇs

 22a mæsətᴵʉ›sɨˇs

 b mæsət∫ʉ·sɨts

 c mæsətᴶʉ›sɨts

 23a mæsətᴵ^ʉsɨˇts

 b ---

 c mæsət∫ʉ·sɨts

 24 mæsəst∫ʉ›sɨt

 25-26a mæsət∫ʉ·səts

 26b ---

 27a mæsət∫ʉ›·səs

 b mæsət∫ʉ›·səts

DISTRICT OF COLUMBIA

 1a mæsətᴵʉusə^ts (✓)

 b mæsət∫ʉ·sɨˇts

VIRGINIA

 1 mæsət∫ʉsɨˇts

 2a mæ·sətᴵu‹sɨˇts

 b mæ·sətᴵʉsɨts

 3a mæsət∫ʉ›·sə^s

 b mæsətᴵu‹·sə^ts

N4 ---

 5a mæsətᴵu‹·sɨ’ts

 b mæsətᴵu‹·sɨˇts

 6a mæsətᴵu‹·sɨˇt

 b mæ·sətᴵʉsɨts

 7a mæsɤ̆tᴵʉsɨt

 b mæsɤ̆tᴵʉ∫əs

 8a mæstᴵʉsɨˇt

 b mæsətᴵʉsɨt

 c mæsətᴵʉsɨts

 9a mæsətᴵʉɾəs

 b mæ^sət∫ʉ·sɨts

 10a mæsətᴵʉsɨˇ

 b mæ^sətᴵʉsɨts

VA

 11a mæsətᴵʉ∫ən

 b mæsətᴵʉsɨˇts

N12-12a ---

 12b mæsɤ̆t∫ʉ›·sɨts

 13a mæstə̨ʒəs

 b mæstᴵʉsɨˇs

 14a mæsɤ̆t∫ᴵʉsɨts

 b mæsəst∫ʉsɨts

 c mæsət∫ʉzɨˇts

N15 ---

 15a mæstᴵʉ∫ɨ

 b mæ·st∫ʉ·sɨts

 16a mæsətᴵʉsɨts

 b mæsət∫ʉ›·sɨˇts

 17a mæ·stᴵʉtəs

 b mæsətᴵ^ʉsɨts

 18 mæsət∫ʉ·zɨts

 19a mæsᵗətᴵʉ∫ɨ

 b mæsɤ̆tᴵʉ∫ɨz

 c mæsɤ̆tᴵʉzɨts

 20a mæsətᴵʉˇɨⁿts

 b mæsətᴵʉsɨts

N21 mæstʉʒ·∫ə

 21a mæsətᴵʉ∫əs

 b mæ·sətᴵ^ʉ·sɨˇts

 22 mæsətᴵʉˇu‹∫ɨˇ

 23a mæ·stᴵʉ∫ə

 b mæst∫ᴵʉ›sɨˇs

 24 mæsətᴵʉ‹sɨˇts

 25 mæsət∫ʉ·sɨts

 26a ---

 b mæsətᴵʉsɨts

 c mæsɤ̆tᴵʉsɨts

 27 mæsətᴵʉ∫ɨt

 28a mæsɤ̆stᴵʉˇɨts

VA		VA		VA		NC	
28b	mæ·sət̖ⁱ ʉsɨts	46a	mæsətɹʉᵘ˂zɨɟt	64b	mæsə̆tʃʉ˂ʉsɨts	7b	mæ·sətʃʉ˂ᴴsɨts
29	mæsət̖ⁱ ʉsɨᵛts	b	mæsətʃʉ·sɨts	65a	mæsətɹʉsəᶺts	N8	mæsət̖ʉ ʃɨt
30a	mæsət̖ⁱ ʉsɨts	47	mæ·st̖ⁱ ˀʉzɨt	b	mæsətiʉ˂səts	8a	mæsət̖ⁱ ʉʃən
b	---	48a	s̱ mæsət̖ⁱ ʉsɨᵛts	c	mæ·sət̖ⁱ ʉsɨts	b	mæsət̖ ʉsɨts
c	mæsətʃʉᵛsɨᵛts	b	mæsət̖ⁱ ˀʉʃəs	66a	mæsət̖ⁱ ʉɹɨ	9a	mæsət̖ⁱ ʉsɨt
d	mæsətʃʉsɨᵛts	49a	mæsət̖ⁱ ʉ˂sɨts	b	mæsət̖ ʉsɨts	b	mæsət̖ⁱ ʉsɨts
e	mæ·sət̖ⁱ ʉsɨts	b	mæsət̖ⁱ ʉsɨts	67a	mæsə̆t̖ⁱ ˀʉᵛəs	10a	---
31a	*mæsət̖ⁱ ˀʉsɨᵛts	50a	mæsə̆t̖ⁱ ʉsɨts	b	mæsətʃʉ·səts	b	ˌmæsətʃʉ˂ᴵzɨˀks
b	mæᵊsə̆tʃʉ·sɨᵛts	b	mæsət̖ⁱ ʉsəs	68a	mæsət̖ⁱ ˀʉsɨ	c	ˌmæ·st̖ⁱ ʉˈsɨts
32	mæ·sətʃʉᵛᴴsɨts	51a	mæsə̆t̖ⁱ ʉ˂ʃɨt	b	mæsət̖ⁱ ʉ˂sɨt	11a	mæsət̖ⁱ ˀʉsɨts
33a	mæstʃʉ·sɨᵛts	b	mæ˃sə̆t̖ⁱ ʉsɨts	69a	mæsət̖ⁱ ʉsɨts	b	mæsət̖ⁱ ᵛʉ˂sɨts
b	mæsə̆t̖ⁱ ˀʉ˂sɨts	52a	mæsətʃʉ˂·səts	b	mæsə̆t̖ⁱ ᵛʉsɨts	12a	mæsət̖ⁱ ʉsɨ
34a	mæɨstʃʉˢᴴsɨᵛts	b	mæsət̖ⁱ ʉʃəs	70a	mæsətɹʉ˂ᴴ˃səts	b	mæ·st̖ⁱᵛ ʉ˃ᵞʌsɨts
b	mæᵊstᴵᶺʉsɨts	c	mæsətʃʉᴴ˃ʃəʃ	b	mæsəᶺtʃʉ·səᶺts	13a	mæsəˢt̖ⁱ ʉ˂sɨts
35a	mæsətʃʉᶺsɨts	53a	mæsətʃʉ·t̖ɨᶺ	71a	mæsətʃʉ·səps	b	mæsət̖ⁱ ʉsɨts
b	mæsətᴵᶺʉsɨts	b	mæsətʃʉ˂səᶺts	b	mæsə̆tʃʉ·səts	N14	mæstʃʉ˃səs
36a	mæsə̆tʃʉ˂t̖ɨ	54a	mæsət̖ⁱ ʉsɨᵛt	72a	mæsət̖ⁱ ʉʃəs	14a	mæsət̖ⁱ ʉsɨˀts
b	mæ·sət̖ⁱ ʉsɨts	b	mæsə̆tʃʉ˃·sɨts	b	mæsətʃʉ˂ᴴzəts	b	mæˀsətʃʉsɨts
37	mæsət̖ⁱ ʉt̖əs	55a	mæsətʃʉzəᶺts	73	mæsə̆t̖ⁱ ʉt̖əs	c	mæst̖ⁱ ʉ˃sɨts
38	mæsətʃʉˀsɨts	b	mæsətʃʉ˂·səᶺts	74a	mæsət̖ⁱ ʉt̖əts	15a	mæsət̖ⁱ ʉprɨ
39	mæᵊsət̖ⁱ ʉsɨᵛts	56a	mæsətʃʉ˃·səᶺts	b	mæsə̆t̖ⁱ ʉsəts	b	mæsət̖ⁱ ᵞʉ˃ᴴsɨˀts
40a	mæsət̖ⁱ ʉsɨ	b	mæsətʃʉ˂·səᶺts	75a	mæsəᶺt̖ⁱ ʉ·səᶺt	16a	mæsət̖ⁱ ʉʃɨ
b	mæsət̖ⁱ ʉ˂sɨts	57a	mæsət̖ⁱ ʉsəs	b	mæᵊsətʃʉ·səts	b	mæsət̖ⁱ ʉ˂·sɨˀts
41a	mæsət̖ⁱ ʉsɨᵛts	b	mæsətʃʉ˂·ʃəs			17a	mæsət̖ⁱ ʉ˂sɨts
b	mæsət̖ⁱ ʉsɨᵛts	58	---	**NORTH CAROLINA**		b	mæsə̆tʃʉ·sɨts
42a	mæst̖ⁱ ʉʃən	N59	mæᶺsətu˂ʃəs	1	mæ·sət̖ⁱ ʉᵛsɨk	18a	mæsət̖ⁱ ʉsɨᵛt
b	mæst̖ⁱ ʉʃəs	59ab	mæsətʃʉ·sɨts	2a	mæst̖ⁱ ʉ˃sɨts	b	mæsət̖ⁱ ʉsɨts
N43	mæsə̆t̖ⁱ ʉʃən	60	mæstɹʉ˃t̖əs	b	mæsət̖ⁱ ʉsɨts	19a	mæsət̖ⁱˢ ʉsɨts
43a	mæsət̖ⁱ ʉsɨᵛts	61a	*mæsə̆tʃʉᵛsəts	3a	mæsət̖ⁱ ʉʃəs	b	mæsət̖ⁱ ʉsɨts
b	mæᶺ·səst̖ⁱ ʉ˂sɨts	b	mæsətʃʉ˂səᶺts	b	mæsət̖ⁱ ʉsɨts	20a	mæstʃʉsɨs
44a	mæ·sət̖ⁱ ʉsɨ	62a	mæsətʃʉ·sɨts	4a	mæst̖ⁱ ʉ˂ʃɨ	b	mæsət̖ⁱ ᵛʉsɨts
b	mæsət̖ᴵᶺ ʉsɨts	b	mæsət̖ⁱ ʉzɨts	b	mæsə̆t̖ⁱ ʉ˂sɨts	c	mæsətʃʉ˂ᵘ˂sɨˀts
45a	mæst̖ⁱᵛ ʉᵛzɨt	63a	mæsə̆t̖ⁱ ʉt̖əs	5a	mæsət̖ⁱ ʉ˂t̖əs	21a	mæstʃʉ˃·sɨᵛts
b	mæsət̖ⁱ ʉsɨts	b	mæsəᶺt̖ⁱ ʉt̖əs	b	mæsət̖ⁱ ʉsɨᵛt	b	mæst̖ⁱ ʉsɨts
N46	---	64a	mæsəst̖ⁱ ʉ˂ʃɨ	6	mæsət̖ⁱ ʉsɨˀts	22a	mæst̖ʉʃəs
				7a	mæstɨt̖ⁱ ʉsɨᵛs		

NC

22b	mæsɤ̆tʃɥᵘˤsɪts
23a	mæsəʈⁱˤɥʃəs
b	mæ·stʃɥˤᵘˁsɪts
c	mæsəʈɥsɪts
d	---
N24	mæsəʈⁱɥˤʃɪ
24a	mæsəʈɥ·sɪts
b	mæsəʈⁱɥsɪts
N25	mæsəʈʃuˤsɪt
25a	mæsəʈⁱɥsɪts
b	mæsəʈʃɥsɪˤts
26a	mæsəʈⁱɥsɪts
b	mæ·sɤ̆tʃɥ ᵘˀsɪˤts
c	mæsətʃɥ ᵘˀsɪˤts
27a	mæsɪstⁱɥʈɪdʒ
b	mæsəʈⁱɥsɪts
28a	mæsəʈⁱɥʃən
b	mæsɪʈⁱɥsɪts
c	mæsətʃɥ·sɪts
29a	mæssətⁱˀɥ̆sɪks
b	mæsəʈⁱˀɥˤsɪts
30a	mæsəʈⁱɥsɪt
b	mæsəʈᴵɥˤsɪts
31a	mæsətⁱˤɥʃə
b	mæsəʈⁱɥˤsɪts
32a	mæsətⁱɥsɪt
b	mæsətʃɥ ᵘˀsɪts
33a	mæsəʈɥˤsɪ'ts
b	mæsɤ̆tʃɥ ᵘˀsɪts
34a	mæsəʈⁱɥʃən
b	mæsəʈⁱɥsɪts
35a	mæsʈⁱɥsɪt
b	mæsəʈⁱˤɣˤsɪˤts
N36	mæsətʃɥ>sɪts
36a	mæsəʈⁱɥʈəs

NC

36b	mæsəʈⁱɥsɪts
37a	mæsəʈⁱɥˤʃən
b	mæsɤ̆tʃɥˤɥ ᵘˀsɪts
N38	mæsəʈⁱɥʃəs
38a	mæsəʈⁱɥʃən
b	mæsəʈⁱᵛɥsɪts
39a	mæsəʈⁱɥʃɪt
b	mæsɤ̆tʃɥ·sɪts
40a	mæᵊsəstʃɥʈəks
b	mæsəʈⁱˤɥ>zɪᵛts
41	mæsətɥ ᵘˀsɪᵛts
42a	mæsəʈⁱɥsɪts
b	mæsətʃɥ ᵘˀsɪᵛts
43a	---
b	mæsəʈⁱɥsəs
44	mæsətʃɥ ᵘˀsɪts
45	mæsəstⁱɥ̇ˤɪᵛ
46ab	mæsətʃɥ ᵘˀsɪᵛts
c	mæsətʃɥ>ᵘˀsɪᵛts
47	mæsətʃᴵɥʃən
48	mæsəʈⁱɥʃəs
49	mæsətɥ ᵘˀsɪts
50a	mæsətʃɥ ᵘˀsɪᵛts
b	mæsəʈⁱɥsəs
51a	mæsəʈⁱɥʃɪ
b	mæsətʃɥ ᵘˀsəs
N52	mæsəʈⁱɥ
52a	mæsɤ̆tʃɥ ᵘˀɪɣˤᵛts
52b–53a	mæsəʈⁱɥsɪts
53b	ˌmæ·səʈⁱɥ'sɪts
54a	mæsəʈᴵ̥ɥʃɪ
b	mæsəʈⁱɥʈəs
55	mæsəʈᴵˀɥsəs
56a	mæ·sətʃɥˤᵛˀsəʃsɪts
b	mæ·səʈᴵˀɥsɪts

NC

57a	mæsəʈᴵˀɥ>sɪᵛt
b	mæsəʈᴵˀɥ>sɪts
58a	mæsəʈⁱɥsɪ'ts
b	mæsətⁱɥʈəs
59	---
60	mæsəʈⁱɥsɪᵛts
61a	---
b	mæ>səʈⁱɥsɪts
62a	mæsəʈⁱɥsɪt
b	mæsətʃɥ ᵘˀsɪts
63a	mæsəʈⁱɥsɪ
b	mæsəʈⁱɥsɪs
64a	mæθətʃɥ ᵘˀsɪt
b	mæsəʈⁱˤɥ>·sə^s
65a	mæᵊsətʃɥ ᵘˀsɪts
b	mæsəʈⁱɥsɪᵛts
66a	mæsəʈⁱɥsɪᵛt
b	mæstʃɥ ᵘˀsɪts
67a	mæsətʃuˤsəs
b	mæsətʃᴵɥsɪts
68a	mæsətⁱɥʈəs
b	mæsəʈⁱˤɥ·səs
69a	mæsəʈⁱɥsɪt
b	mæsəʈⁱɥsɪts
70a	mæsəʈⁱɥsɪs
b	mæsətʃɥ ᵘˀsɪts
71a	mæsəʈⁱɥʃəs
bc	mæsətʃɥ ᵘˀsɪᵛts
72a	---
b	mæsətʃɥ ᵘˀsɪts
73a	mæsɪʈⁱɥsɪts
b	mæsətᴵɥsɪt
74a	mæsəʈⁱˤɥsɪt
b	mæsətʃɥ ᵘˀsɪts
75a	mæsətʃⁱɥ>sɪts

NC

75b	mæsəʈⁱɥsɪts

SOUTH CAROLINA

1a	mæ>·sɪ^ʈⁱɥʈəs
b	mæsəʈⁱɥsɪts
2a	mæsəkⁱˀɥ̇ɪ^
b	mæsɤ̆tʃɥᵘˤsɪts
3a	mæsətʃɪˤ^uˁsɪt
b	---
c	ˈmæᵊsɪˤˌtʃɥ·sɪˤts
4ab	---
c	mæᵊsət'ɥ·ᵂsɪˤts
5a	*mæᵛᵊsətɥ·ˀɥsɪts
bc	---
d	mæᵊsɪˤʈⁱˀɥ·sɪˤts
N6	---
6a	mæsɪtɥ>sɪˤ
b	---
c	mæᵛᵊsətʃɥ·ᵘˀsɪˤt
N7–7a	---
7b	cv mæᵊsɪˤˌt'ɥ·sɪˤts
c	---
d	ˈmæᵊsɪˤˌtʃɥ·ˀwsɪˤts
8abc	---
9a	cv mæᵛᵊsət'ʲɥ·wsɪˤts, ˈ-sɪˌt'̥ʲɥ·–
b	---
c	mæᵊsətʲɥ·sɪˤts
9d–10b	---
10c	cv ˈmæᵛᵊsɪˤˌtʃɥ·sɪˤts
N11	mæsɪtʃɥ>·sɪs
11a	ˈmæᵛsəˌtʃɥ·ˀsɪˤsts
cv	ˀɪˌt'̥ʲy>ɥˤ–
b	mæᵛsɤ̆tʲɥ>sɪs
c	ˈmæsɪˌtʃɥˀsɪˤts
d	ˈmæ^·sɪˤtʲɥ>sɪˤts

SC		SC		SC		SC	
11e	cv mæˇsət∫ʉ<·s‡<ts	21b	mæsət∫ʉᵘ^s‡ts	33b	ˈmæ^ᵊsɘ͵t∫ʉ·ws‡ts	44b	*ˈmæ^s‡tɹy>ʉ^s‡ts
f	---	N22	---	34a	---		GEORGIA
g	mæsŏt∫y·ˇ·s‡ts	22a	ˈmæ·ᵊsɘ͵t∫'ʉ·ʉs‡ts	b	ˈmæ^ᵊsŏ͵t∫ʉ·ws‡<ts	N1	mæsətu<s‡s
2N11	ˈmæs‡ɽ͵t∫ʉ<·s‡<ts	b	---	c	cv mæ^ᵊsət∫'ʉ·ws‡<ts	1a	cv ˈmæs‡ɽ͵t∫ʉ<·ᵂs‡ts
11h	ˈmæˇsət'j̥ʉ<·ᵂs‡ts	c	ˈmæᵊs‡͵t∫'ʉ<·s‡ts	35ab	---		*ˈmæsŏ͵t'ʉ·-
	cv ͵-ˈt∫ʉ<s‡<ts	23a	mæᵊsət'j̥ʉ<·z‡<tˢ	c	mæsətᴵʉž‡tš (?)	bcd	---
i	mæsət∫ʉ>s‡ts	b	---	36a	---	e	mæsətɹʉ<·ws‡ts,
j	mæˇsət∫ʉ<·s‡ɕts	c	mæˇᵊsət'j̥ʉ<·s‡<ts	b	mæ^sŏt'j̥ʉ<·ws‡<ts		mæˇsət∫ʉ<·ws‡ts
12a	---	23d-24c	---	c	cv mæ^s‡ɕt∫'ʉ·ws‡<ts	f	mæˇsət∫uɕ·s‡ts
b	mæsət∫ʉs‡s	24d	cv mæᵊsət∫'ʉ·ws‡<ts,	d	cv mæ·sət∫ʉ<·s‡ɕts	g	---
13	---		ˈmæˇᵊsɘ͵t∫'ʉ<·ᵂ-	37	mæs‡t∫ʉᵘ^s‡ts	h	mæ^sət'j̥˚‡^ʉ^s‡ɕts
14a	mæsətɹʉ>z‡ts	25a	mæsətɹʉs‡ˇs	38a	mæsətɹy·ws‡ts	N2	---
b	ˈmæᵊs‡ɕt∫ʲʉ·ws‡<ts	b	ˈmæˇsət∫ʉ·s‡ts	N38	mæ^s‡tɹʉ·ᵂs‡<ts,	2a	mæs‡t∫ʉ<ɕ‡ts (?)
15a	ˈmæᵊsɘ͵t∫ʲʉ·s‡ts	c	mæᵋsə^t∫ʉ·s‡<ts		mæ^sət∫ʉ·ᵂs‡ts	b	---
	cv mæ·s‡<t∫ʉ·-	26a	ˈmæ·ᵊsɘ͵t∫ʉ·ɕ‡<ts	38b	ˈmæ^sət∫y>·ᵂs‡ts	3a	mɑɕ·sət∫uɕ·s‡ˇts
b	ˈmæᵊs‡ɕ͵tɹʉ<·s‡<ts	b	---	c	cv mæsət∫y>·ᵂs‡<ts	b	---
15c-17c	---	27a	mæsətᴵʉs‡ts	d	mæ^s‡t∫y>·ws‡ts	N4	mɑst∫uɕ·ţe^ə
17d	mæsət∫ʉ<s‡ts	b	ˈmæᵊsət'j̥ʉ·s‡ts	39a	mæs‡t'j̥ʉ·ws‡<ts	4a	ˈmæˇs‡t∫ʉ·s‡ts
N18	ˈmæˇsət∫ʉ<·s‡ts (?)	28a	mæᵊsət'j̥ʉ·s‡ts	b	ˈmæsŏ͵t∫ʉ>·ws‡<ts	b	---
18a	mæˇsət∫y>s‡<ts	b	---	40a	mæ^st∫y>ʉs‡ɕts	c	ˈmæᵊsɘ͵tʉ·s‡<ts
	cv mɑ^sət̥j̥y>sᶒts	c	ˈmæᵊsɘ͵t'j̥ʉ·s‡ts	b	ˈmæ·s‡͵t'j̥y>ʉ^s‡tˢ	5a	mæᵊsətʉ>·s‡<ts (√)
b	mæˇsəˇt∫y>·s‡<ts	d	mæ·ᵊsə^t̥j̥ʉ·s‡<ts	41a	mæsətᴵʉs‡ts		cv mæsŏt∫ʉ>·s‡ts
c	ˈmæˇs‡ˇ͵t∫y>·s‡<ts	29a	mæᵊsət∫ʉs‡<ts	b	ˈmæ^s‡͵t∫ʉ<ʉɕs‡<ts	bcd	---
	*cv -s‡ɕ͵-	b	---	42a	ˈmæˇss͵t∫ʉ>uɕs‡ɕts	e	ˈmæᵊsŏ^͵t∫ʉ·s‡ts
N19	---	c	mæᵊsŏt∫ʉ·s‡ts	N42	s ˈmæ^sət∫y>s‡ɕts,	6a	---
19a	mæ·sɘt∫yɕs‡<ts	30a	mæsətᴵʉs‡ˇts		-∫‡ɕt	b	ˈmæˇs‡͵tɹʉ·s‡ts
b	mæsz̨tᴵʉs‡ts	b	cv mæs‡ɕt∫'ʉ<·ws‡<ts	42b	mæ^s‡t'j̥y>·ws‡<ts	7-8a	---
c	mæs‡<tɹy>·s‡<ts	c	ˈmæs‡͵t∫'y>·s‡<ts,	c	ˈmɛˇsə^͵t∫ʉ·ʉ>s‡ɕts	8b	mæᵊs‡ɕt∫ʉs‡ts
d	---		-sɘ͵t'j̥ʉ·w-	d	---	9a	mæsətᴵʉᵘ^s‡ts
20a	mæ·s‡t∫ʉ·s‡ts	31a	mæᵊsət'‡ʉ·s‡<ts	e	mæsətȷʉᵘ^s‡ts	b	---
b	---	b	mæ·ᵋsət∫ʉ·z‡<ts	43a	---	10a	mæsət∫ʉ>·s‡ts
c	mæᵊsətɹʉws‡<ts,	32a	ˈmæ^ᵊsɘ͵t'j̥ʉ<·ws‡<ts	b	ˈmɛˇs‡ˇ͵t∫y>ʉɕs‡ɕtˢ	b	---
	-t∫ʉ-	bc	---	c	mɛˇsət̥j̥y>ʉ^s‡ɕts,	N11	mæs‡t∫ʉ·ʉ^s‡ts
d	---	d	mæᵋs‡t∫ʉ·ws‡ts		-t∫y>ʉ^s‡ts	12a	---
21a	mæsəţᴵʉʃən	33a	mæsətᴵʉʃ‡n	44a	ˈmæˇsŏ͵t∫ʉ·ᵘɕs‡ts	b	mæsət∫ʉs‡ts

GA		GA		GA		GA	
13a	mæˇsətʃuʂsɪ̧ɪ̧ts	21b	---	30c	mæ^sɪtʃʉ·sɪts	38	---
b	mæᵊsɪtʃʉ>·sɪts,	22a	mæsətʃʉˇʉsɪ̵ts	31	mæsətᴵʉᴴ^sɪts	39	mæsə̆tʉ·sɪts
	mæᵊsɪ<tʃʉ·sɪ<ts	b	mæᵊstʃʉ·sɪts	32	ˈmæsɪˇ₁tᴵʉᴴ^sɪts	40	---
14a	---	23a	---	33a	mæsətʲ̧ʉᴴ^sɪs	41	cv mæsətʃʉ·sɪts
b	ˈmæᵊsə₁tʃʉ<ᵂsɪts	b	mæsɪtᴵʉᴴ^sɪts	b	mæsətʉsɪts,	42a	mæ·sətʻʲʉʂɪ̧ts
c	---	c	mæsɪtʲʉsɪts		-tʃʉsɪ̵ts	b	---
15a	mæsətᴵˇʉʃəs	d	---	N34	ˈmæᵋsə₁tʉ·sɪ<ts	43	mæsətᴵʉsəs
b	---	e	mæsətᴵʉ·sɪts,	34a	mæsətʃᴵʉsɪts	44ab	---
16a	ˈmæᵊsətʃʉ·sɪ<ts		-tʃʉ·sɪ̵ˇts	b	ˈmæᵋsə₁tʻʲʉ·wsɪ<ts	c	mæᵋsɪtʻʲ̥ʉ·ᵂsɪ<ts
b	cv mæᵊsətʲʉ·sɪ<ts	f	mæsətʲʉ·ᴴ^sɪˇts	N35	mæ^sətᴵʉ·sɪts	de	---
c	---	N24	---	N36-37a	---	**FLORIDA**	
d	ˈmæᵊsŏ̧₁tʃʉ·sɪ̵ts	24a	mæsətʃᴵʉsɪs	37b	ˈmæ·ᵋsə₁tʲʉ·wsɪ<ts	1	ˈmæᵊsə₁tʃʉ·sɪ<ts
N17	---	b	ˈmæᵋsə₁tʲ̧ʉ·ᵂsɪ<ts	c	---	2a	ˈmæᵊsɪ₁tʃʉ·sɪts
17	mæsətʉsəs	N25	---	2N37	mæsətᴵʉᴴ^sɪts	b	---
18a	mæsətʲ̧ʉᴴ^sɪts	26	mæsətᴵʉᴴ^sɪ̵ts	37d	mæsɪˇtʃʉ·sɪts	c	ˈmæᵊsə₁tʃʉ>sɪ<ts
b	mæsɪtʲ̧ʉ·sɪts	27	ˈmæ·ᵊsŏ̆₁tʉsɪts		cv -tʃʉᴴ^-	3a	mæᵊsətʃʉ·sɪ<ts
19a	**ˈmæᵊsə₁tʻʲʉ·sɪts	28	mæsətᴵʉsɪts	ef	---	b	---
b	mæᵊsətʲʉ·sɪ<ts	29a	mæᵋsə^tʻʲʉ·ᵂsɪ<ts	g	ˈmæᵊsə₁tʃʉ·ᵂsɪ<ts	4	mæsətʃʉ<ʉ^sɪts
20a	mæˇᵊstʲʉsɪ<ts	b	mæᵊsɪtʻʲʉ·sɪ<ts	h	cv mæᵊsɪtʃʉ·sɪ<ts	5a	---
b	---	30ab	---	i	ˈmæsɪ₁tᴵʉ·ᴴ^sɪ̵ts	b	ˈmæᵊsɪ₁tʃʉ>·sɪ̵ts
21a	mæsətʃʉ·sɪts						

COMMENTARY

NEW YORK		WVA		MD		SOUTH CAROLINA	
32a	[ŏ̆]: doubtful	38b	[stʃ]: *sic*	(13d)	correct; [tᴵˇʉ]:	N18	[ɪ]: doubtful
PENNSYLVANIA		**OHIO**			old-fashioned,	35c	[š]: doubtful
65b	field record: [-z]	4a	[ʊ]: *sic*		natural	**GEORGIA**	
WEST VIRGINIA		**MARYLAND**		**DISTRICT OF COLUMBIA**		2a	[ɪ]: doubtful
13b	[-t]: *sic*	13d	[tʃʉ·]: modern,	1a	[tᴵˇʊ]: *sic*	5a	[tʉ>·]: *sic*
						13b	[tʲʉ·]: "I say"

6. NEW YORK

New York was usually elicited as the name of the state, but sometimes as the name of the city. The latter are marked with a superior [2] unless *city* was also recorded in phonetics.

In addition to *New York*, other forms recorded were (*the*) *State of New York*, *New York State*, and *York State*.

York State was generally characterized as old-fashioned or as heard from others.

The prevailing stress pattern in *New York*, ˌ~ ˈ~ or ~ ˈ~, is unmarked; otherwise, stress is marked as indicated by the field workers.

ONTARIO		NY		NY		NY	
1a	nʉˇʉ ɹɔˇɚk	3c	nu<·· ɹɔɛk	8	nu· ɹɔ·ᵊk	23b	nuˇ· ɹɔˇɚk, ˌnŭˇ
b	nᴵʉ ɹoˇɚk	d	nᵼu< ɹɔ·ᵊk	9ab	nu<·· ɹɔɛk		ˈɹɔˆɚk ˌsteˇɪ>t
2a	---	4a	nu<·· ɹɔɛ̣k	c	nu< ɹɔ·ɛ̣k	cv	nŭ< ɹɔˇɚk
b	ˈnusu< ˌɹɔɛ̣k	b	nᵼ>ŭ< ɹɔˇ·k	10a	ɹɔɛk steᵼt	c	ˈnju< ˌɹɔˇɚk
	ˈsteˇᵼ<t cv nə	c	nu<·· ɹɔ:k	10b-11	nu<·· ɹɔɛk		ˈsteˇɪˆt
	ɹɔ<ɚᵏ, ðə ˈsteˇᵼt	5a	nu<·· ɹɔˆ·ᵊk	12a	nᵼŭ< ɹɔɛk	24a	nᵼu< ɹɔɛk
	ə ˌnᴶusu< ˈɹɔˆɚk	b	nu·· ɹɔ·ək	b	nu< ɹɔɛk	b	nu· ɹɔˇk
3	nʉˇʉ> ɹɔɛ̣ɚk	c	nu<·· ɹɔ·ᵊk	c	nu< ɹɔ·ᵊk	25a	ˈnʉ· ˌɹɔˇɚk,
4a	cv nᵼu< ɹɔɛk,	d	nu<·· ɹɔ:ᵊk	13a	ɹɔˆrk steᵼt		ˈɹɛ̣ɚk ˌsteˇ·ᵼ<t
	ˌŋᴵʉ> ˈɹɔɛk ˌsteᵼt	e	nu< ɹɔ:ᵊk	b	nu<·· ɹɔ·ᵊk	cv	ˈnʉ>u ˌɹᴶɔˇɚᵼk
b	ˈŋᴵuꜱu< ˌɹɔˆɚk	f	nŭꜱŭ ɹɔ·ᵊk	14a	nu· ɹɔɛk	b	ˌnᴶu ˈɹɔɛ̣k
5	---	g	nu< ɹɔ·ᵊk	b	nu<·· ɹɔˇɚk		ˌsteˇᵼt
6	nʉˇʉ ɹɔɛ̣k (√)	h	nu< ɹɔˇ·ᵊk	15a	ɹɔˆɚk steᵼt	26a	steˇɪt ə ˌnʉˇ
7	ˈnuꜱu< ˌɹɔ<ɚk	i	nᴶu< ɹɔɛk	b	nᵼu ɹɔɛk		ˈɹɔɛk, ˈnuˇ ˌɹɔˇɚ<ɚk
	ˈsteᵼt, nʉˇʉ ɹɔɛk[2]	6a	nu<·· ɹɔ·ᵊk	16a	nu· ɹɔ·ᵊk	b	nuˇ ɹɔˇɚk
8a	---	b	nu<·· ɹɔˇ·ᵊk	b	nu· ɹɔ·ək	cv	ˈnᴶʉˇ· ˌ~[2]
b	nuꜱu< ˈɹɔɛ̣k ˌsteˇᵼt	7a	nŭ< ɹɔ·ᵊk	17a	ˈɹɔˆɚk ˌsteᵼt,	c	---
c	nᴶuꜱu< ɹɔɛk	b	nu· ɹɔ:ᵊk		steᵼt̬ ə ˌnᵼu< ~	27a	ˈɹɔꜱ·ɚk ˌsteˇᵼt,
	ꜱᴵˈɹɔ<ɚk ˌste·ᵼ<t	c	nu<·· ɹɔ·ək	b	nu· ɹɔɛk		nə̬ ~ ~,
d	nŭꜱŭ< ɹɔˆɚk	d	nu<·· ɹɔ:ᵊk	18a	nᵼu< ɹɔˇɚk		nᴶuˇ·u ɹɔɛk
9	nʉˆʉ ɹɔˇɚk	e	nu<·· ɹɔ·ək	b	nu<·· ɹɔɛk	b	cv nᴶuˆu ɹɔɛk
10	nŭꜱŭ< ɹɔ̣ɛk	f	nu<·· ɹɔˇ·k	c	nu· ɹɔ·ᵊk (√)	c	nuˆu ɹɔ<ɚk
NEW YORK		g	nu<·· ɹɔ:ᵊk	19	nuꜱ· ɹɔˇ·k		cv ˈnʉˇu ˌɹɔɛk
1	nu<w ɹɔ·ᵊˆk	hi	nu<·· ɹɔ·ᵊk	20a	nᵼu ɹɔˇrk		ˈsɪˆt̬ɪꜱ
2a	---	j	nu< ɹɔ·ᵊk	b	nu< ɹɔɛk	28a	nʉˇ ˈɹɔˆ·ɚk
b	nᵼˆŭ ɹɔ·k	k	nu· ɹɔ·ᵊk	21	nu· ɹɔɛk		ˈsɪˆt̬ɪꜱ
c	---	l	nu<·· ɹɔ:k	22	nu· ɹɔˇɚk	b	nᴶuˇ· ɹɔˇ·ɚk,
3ab	nᵼu< ɹɔɛk	m	nu<·· ɹɔ:ᵊk	23a	---		nᴶuˇ·u ɹɔˇɚk,

NY

(28b) nɐ>u ʃɔ^ɚk

   cv nᴶɐ> ~²

   s̲ ꜚᴵʃɔˇʃ ˌsteˇ·ꞇ

29a cv ˈnu·· ˌʃɔ^ɚk

   ˈsteˇꞇ

b nᴶɐ> ʃɵˇɚk

   cv ˌnuˇ ˈʃɔ̧ɚk

   ˌsteˇꞇ<ꞇ

c nɐ ʃɔ̧<ɚk

30a ŋɐ> ʃɔ̧<ɚk

   cv ˈnɐˇ·ɐ ˌ~

b cv nɐ ʃɔɚk,

   ~ ˌsteˇꞇ

cd ---

e ˈnɐ>·· ˌʃɔɚk

   ˈste·ꞇˇ·ꞇ ꜚˈʃ- ~

31a nᴶuṣu< ʃɔ^ɚk

   cv nuṣu< ʃɔ̧ɚk,

   ˈsteˇꞇ ɵ ˌ~

   ˈʃɔ̧·ɚk

b nɐ̆ˇɐ̆ ʃɔ̧ɚk

   ꜚ~ ˌsteˇꞇ

   cv ˈnᴶuṣ ˌ~ ˈ~,

   ˈ~ ˌsteˇꞇ<ꞇ

32a ˈnu·· ˌʃɔ̧ɚk

   ˈste·ꞇ, ˈʃɔ̧ˇ̧ɚk ~

b ˈnɐɐ ˌʃɔ̧^ɚk,

   ˈʃɔ^ɚk ˌsteˇꞇ

   cv ˈnɐˇu ˌʃɔ̧ɚk

   ˈsɪꞇɪ̧

33a ---

b cv nuˇu ʃɔɚk,

   ~ ʃɔ̧<ɚk, ˈ~

   ˌʃɔˇɚk, ˌnuˇ·

   ˈʃɔ^ɚk ˌsteˇ·ꞇ

33c nuˇu ʃɔɚk

34a nɐɐ ʃɔˇɑ^ɚk

   cv ˈnɐˇu ˌʃɵˇɚk

   s̲ ꜚᴵʃɔˇc<ɚk ˌsteˇꞇ<ꞇ

b ---

c cv ˈnᴶuṣu< ˌʃɵ>ɚk²

d ˈʃɔ<·ɚk steˇꞇ,

   nᴶɵ ~ ~

35a nꞇu< ʃ̧ɚk

b nꞇu ʃɔˇɚk

c ---

36a nꞇu ʃɔˇɚk

b nꞇu ʃɔ̧ɚk

37a nꞇu ʃɔˇɚk

b nu·· ʃɔˇɚk

c nuṣ· ʃɔˇɚk

38a nꞇu< ʃɔˇɚk

b nꞇ>u< ʃɔ̧ɚk

39a nꞇu ʃɔˇɚk

b nꞇu ʃɔ̧ɚk

40a nꞇ>u ʃɔɚk

b nu· ʃɔ̧ɚk

41 nu< ʃɔˇɚk

42a nꞇu< ʃɔ^ɚk

b nu< ʃɔɚk

43a ˈʃɔˇc<ʃ ˌsteꞇ

b nu< ʃɔɚk

c nu<ᵂ ʃɔɚk

44a nꞇu< ʃɔɚk

b nu· ʃɔɚk

45a cv ˌnɐ ˈʃɔɚk

   ˌsteˇꞇ<ꞇ

bc ---

d cv ˈnuṣ·u< ˌʃɔɚk,

   ~ ~ ˈsteˇꞇ<ꞇ,

(45d) ˌnuṣu< ˈ~ ˌsteˇꞇ

46a nɐɐ ˈʃɵ̧ɚk

   ˈste·ꞇ cv ˈnᴶɐ̧u>

   ˌʃɔ<ɚk ˈsɪꞇꞇ<

   s̲ ꜚᴵʃɔɚk ˌste·ꞇ

b nᴵɐ̆ṣ ʃɔṣɚk,

   ~ ~ steꞇ

c nɪu< ʃɔ^ɚk,

   nɐ>ɐ ˌʃɔˇɚk

47a ˈnuṣu ˌʃɵ̧ɚk,

   ˈʃɔ̧ɚk ˌsteˇꞇ<ꞇ

   cv ˈnuṣu< ʃɔṣɚk

b nuᵂ ʃɔṣɚk

48a ˌnuṣu< ˈʃɔṣɚk

   ˌsteˇꞇ<ꞇ

b cv ˈsteˇꞇ ɵ

   ˌnɐˇɐ ˈʃɔ·ɚk

c ˈnᴶuṣu< ˌʃɔ<ɚk

   ˈsteˇꞇ<ꞇ

d ˈʃɔ<ɚk ˌsteˇꞇ,

   ˌnᴶuṣu< ~ ~

49ab ---

c nuṣu< ʃɔṣɚk

   *ˈnu< ˌʃɔṣɚk

d ˈnɐ> ˌʃɔ^ɑ^ɚk ꞇ,

   nuṣ^u< ʃɔɚ^k

50a ˈnuṣu< ˌʃɔ̧ɚk,

   ˈʃɔ<·ɵ̧ɚk ˌsteˇꞇ<ꞇ

b cv ˈnᴶuṣu< ˌʃɔ̧ɚk

   ˈsteˇꞇ<ꞇ, nuṣu<

   ʃɔ̧ɚk²

51a ˈʃɵ̧ɚk ˌsteˇꞇ

   cv nᴶu< ˈʃɔ<ɚk ~,

   ˈnᴶɐ ˌʃɔ̧ɚk ~

b nɐ̧ɐ> ʃɔ̧ɚk

(51b) cv ˈnᴶu< ˌʃɔ^ɚk

   ˈsteˇꞇ<ꞇ; ˌnɐˇɐ

   ˈʃɔ̧ɚk ˌ~, nᴶu<u<

   ʃɔ<ɚk² s̲ ꜚˈʃɵ̧ɚk

   ˈsteˇꞇ

51c cv ˈnuˇu ˌʃɵ̧·ɚk

   ˈsteˇꞇ

d ---

e cv nɐˇɐ ʃɔ·ɚk

52a nuṣu< ʃɔɚk,

   ˈ~ ˌʃɔ̧ɚk

   cv ˈnᴶuṣu< ˌʃɔ̧ɚk

b ---

c nu< ʃɔˇɚk,

   nꞇ̆ɐ ʃɔṣɚk

53a ˈnuṣu< ˌʃɔ̧ɚk,

   ~ ˌʃɔ·ɚk cv ~

   ˌʃɔṣɚk ˈste·ꞇ<ꞇ

b ˌnᴶu< ˈʃɔ·ɚ̆k

   ˌsteˇ·ꞇ cv nɵ

   ˈʃɔ̧ɚk ˌsteˇꞇ<ꞇ

54a ˈnu< ˌʃɔˇɚk,

   ˈnɐˇ^u ˌʃɔ^ɑ^ɚk,

   ˈnᴵu< ~, ~ ~

   steꞇ, ~ ~ ˈsɪꞇꞇ

b nu< ʃɔ^ɚk,

   ˈnuṣu< ˌ~

   cv ˈnɐ ˌʃɔ̧ɚk

55a ˈnuˇu ˌʃɔ̧ɚk,

   nu·ˇ· ʃɔ^ɚk,

   ~ ˌsteˇ·ꞇ

b ˌnɐ· ˈʃɵˇɚk

   ˌsteˇꞇ ꜚˈʃɔ·ɚk ~

56a ˈʃɔ^ɚk ˌsteˇ·ꞇ

NY		NY		NJ		PA	
56b	nɹɹ ʃɔˇçɹk, ˈnuˇu ˌʃɔˇɹk ˈsteˇɹt	(62b)	ˈʃɔˆ·ɹk ˌste·ɹt	7a	nu· ʃɔʂɹk	1g	nu< ʃɔɹk
	c̲v̲ ˌ~ ʃɔɹk²	62c	nɹ› ˈʃɔ̧çɹk ˌsteˇɹt	b	nɹɹ·‹ ʃɔk	h	nu< ʃɔʂ·ᵊɹk
			c̲v̲ nu·‹ ʃɔˆɹk	8a	nu·‹ ʃɔˆɹk	2ab	nu·‹ ʃɔˆɹk
57a	nuˇu ʃɔ̧çɹk	d	ˌnu< ˈʃɔ‹ɹk	b	nu·‹ ʃɔk	3a	nu·‹ ʃɔɹk
	⊥~ ˌsteˇɹ‹ɹt		ˌste·ɹt ⊥ˈʃɔˇçɹk ~	9a	nuʂu ʃɔk	b	nŭˆŭ‹ ʃɔk
	c̲v̲ ~ ˌste·ɹt, nuʂu‹ ʃɔˆɹk	63a	ˈnu·‹ ˌʃɔ̧çɹk ˈsteˇɹt	b	nɹ› ʃɔk	c	nu·‹ ʃɔk
b	---		⊥ˈʃɔˇɹk ˌsteˇɹt	10a	nu·‹ ʃɔˆ·ɹk	4a	nu· ʃɔˆɹk
c̲	njuʂu‹ ʃɔ‹ɹk	b	nɹ·ɹ ʃɔ‹ɹk	b	nɹ›·‹ ʃɔk	4b-5b	nu·‹ ʃɔˆɹk
58a	ˈnɹ›ɹ ˌʃɔɹk ˈsteˇɪ›t		⊥ˈʃɔˆçɹk ˌsteˇɹt	c	nɹ›·‹ ʃɔ‹ᵊɹk	5c	nuu‹ ʃɔˆɹk
	c̲v̲ ˌ~ ˈʃɔˆɹk ˌsteˇɹt, nu‹ ʃɔɹk		c̲v̲ ˈnɹ ˌʃɵ›ɹk	d	nu·‹ ʃɔ‹ᵊk	d	nɹ›·‹ ʃɔˇɹk
b	nuˇu ʃɔ‹ɹk, ˈʃɔʂçɹk ˌsteˇɹ·t	c	nɹu ʃɔk	11a-12a	nɹ›·‹ ʃɔk	e	nu·‹ ʃɔk
c	---	d	c̲v̲ nu‹ ʃɔɹk, ˈnɹ·ɹ ˌ~, ˌnɹ ˈʃɔ‹ɹk ˌsteˇɹt	12b	nu·‹ ʃɔk	6a	nu· ʃɔᵊʳk
d̲	nuˇu ˈʃɔɹk ˌsteˇɹt			13ab	nɹ›·‹ ʃɔk	b	nu· ʃɔ·ʳk
e̲	nuˇŭ ʃɔɹk	64a	ŋɹˇ ʃɒɹk	14a-15a	nu·‹ ʃɔk	c	nu· ʃɔrk
	c̲v̲ nɹ ~², nu‹ ʃɔʂɹk		c̲v̲ ˈnjuˇ‹ ˌ~, ˈʃɔˆçɹk ˌsteˇɹt, ˈʃɔɹk ˌsteˇ·ɹt	15b	nŭ‹ ʃɔʂɹk	d	nu·‹ ʃɔk
f̲	---	b	nɹ· ʃɔˇ‹ɹk, ~ ~ ˈste·ɹt	16a	nu·‹ ʃɔk	7ab	nu·‹ ʃɔˆɹk
59a	ˌnjuˇu ˈʃɔˇɹk ˌsteˇɹt	c	c̲v̲ ˈnjuˇ·‹ ˌʃɒɹk	b	nuʂ· ʃɔk	c	nu· ʃɔᵊʳk
b	nɹu‹ ʃɔˇɹk		**NEW JERSEY**	17a	nɹ›·‹ ʃɔˇ·ᵊk (✓)	d̲	nu·‹ ʃɔk
60a	nʲuʂu‹ ʃɵˇɹk	1a	nu·‹ ʃɔˆɹk	b	nɹ›·‹ ʃɔk	8ab	nɹ›·‹ ʃɔˇɹk
b̲	c̲v̲ nuˇu ʃɔ‹ɹk, ˈnjuˇ·‹ ˌʃɵˇɹk	b	nuʂ ʃɔʂɹk	18ab	nu·‹ ʃɔ·ᵊk	c	nu·‹ ʃɔᵊʳk
61a	steˇɹ‹t ə nu‹ ˈʃɔˇɹk, ~ ʃɔɹk, ˈ~ ˌsteˇɹt, nɹ‹ ʃɔˇɹk	2a	nu·‹ ʃɔˆɹk	c̲	nu·‹ ʃɔk	d̲	nu‹ ʃɔk
		b	nu·‹ ʃɔʂɹk	d̲	nu ʃɔk	9ab	nu·‹ ʃɔk
b	ˈʃɔʂɹk ˌsteˇɹt, ˌnu‹ ~ ~	3a	nu·‹ ʃɔˆɹk	19a	nu·‹ ʃɔ·ɹk	c̲	nɹ›·‹ ʃɔk
62a	ˈnu·‹ ˌʃɒ̧ɹk	b	nɹ›·‹ ʃɔʂɹk	b̲	nu·ʃɔ·ᵊk	10	nu‹ ʃɔrk
b	nu‹ ʃɔˆ·ɹk,	4a	nu· ʃɔˆɹk	20a	nu·‹ ʃɔᵊʳk	11a	nu· ʃɔk
		b	nu·‹ ʃɔˆɹk	b	nu· ʃɔ·ᵊk	b	nu·‹ ʃɔˆɹk
		5a	nu·‹ ʃɔʂɹk	21a	nu·‹ ʃɔk	12a	nu·‹ ʃɔʂɹk
		b	nu· ʃɔ‹ɹk	b	nu·‹ ʃɔʂɹk	b	nu ʃɔʂɹk
		6a	nɹ›·‹ ʃɔk		**PENNSYLVANIA**	13ab	nu·‹ ʃɔʂɹk
		b	nuʂ· ʃɔˇ‹ɹk	1a	nu·‹ ʃɔʳk	14a	nu·‹ ʃɔᵊʳk
				b	nu· ʃɔˆɹk	b	nu·‹ ʃɔˆrk
				c	nuʂ· ʃɔˆɹk	15abc	nu· ʃɔk
				d	nu·‹ ʃɔk	16a	nu· ʃɔᵊʳk
				e̲	nu·‹ ʃɔk	b	nu· ʃɔk
				f̲	nɹ›·‹ ʃɔk	c	---

PA		PA		PA		WVA	
17a	nu· ɔork	34c	*nu< ɔɐk	53b	nu^u< ɔ^rk	7b	nᴵʉ ɔ<ɐk
b	nu· ɔəᴿk	35a	nu<· ɔ^ɐk	54a	nu<· ɔork	8a	nʉ ɔɐk
18a	nu· ɔ^ɐk	b	nu<· ɔɔ̧ɐk	b	nʉ· ɔork	b	ŋjʉ· ɔ^ɐk
b	nu· ɔ̌ɐk	36a	nu<· ɔɐk	55a	nu· ɔ^rk	9a	nu< ɔɐk
19a	nʉ>· ɔɔ̧ɐk	b	nu< ɔɔ<ɐk	b	nʉ>>· ɔ^ə̌rk	b	nu<· ɔork
b	nu<· ɔɐk	37a	nu< ɔork	56a	nu<· ɔ^ɽk	10a	ŋᴶʉ· ɔɐk
20a	nu<· ɔ^ɐk	b	nu< ɔɐk	56b–57a	nʉ>· ɔork	b	nu< ɔ̌rk
b	nu<· ɔɔ̧ɐk	38a	nʉ̧ ɔɐk	57b	nʉ>· ɔ^rk	c	nʉ ɔɐk
21a	nɪu< ɔ̌ɐk	b	nu<· ɔɔ̧ɐk	58a	nɪu< ɔork	11ab	nʉ· ɔɐk
b	nu· ɔɔ̌k	39a	nu<· ɔ^ɐk	b	nʉ>· ɔork	12a–13b	nu<· ɔɐk
22a	nɨu< ɔ̨^ɐk	39b–40a	nu< ɔ^ɐk	59a	nu<· ɔ^ɽk	14a–15b	nu< ɔɐk
b	nu· ɔɔ̧ɐk	40b	nu< ɔɐk	b	nu< ɔ^ɽk	16a	nⁱʉ ɔ̌ɐk
23a	nɨu ɔ̌ɐk	41a	nu< ɔ^ɐk	60ab	nʉ· ɔork	b	nu<· ɔɐk
b	nɨu< ɔɐk	b	nʉ>· ɔ^ɐk	61a	nu<· ɔ^rk	17a	---
24a	nu· ɔ̨^ɐk	42a–43b	nu<· ɔ^ɐk	b	nʉ· ɔ^rk	bc	nu<· ɔɐk
b	nu· ɔɔ<ɐk	44ab	nu<· ɔɐk	62ab	nu< ɔork	18a	njʉ ɔɐk
25a	nɨŭ< ɔɔ̧ɐk	45a	nu<· ɔ^ɽk	63a	nu<· ɔork	b	nu<· ɔɐk
b	nu· ɔɐk	b	nu< ɔ^rk	b	nu<· ɔɐk	19a	njʉ>· ɔɐk
26a	nɨ<u< ɔɔ̧ɐk	46a	nʉ ɔ̌rk	64a	nɨw ɔ̨^ɐk	b	ŋⁱʉ ɔ^ɐk
b	nuᵂ ɔ̌ɐk	b	nʉ ɔ^rk	b	nɨu ɔ̨^ɐk	20a	nⁱʉ ɔ·rk
27a	*nɨu< ɔɔ̧ɐk	47a	nʉ>· ɔ^rk	65a	nɨu ɔ̌ɐk	b	nʉ ɔork
b	nɨu< ɔɔ̌k	b	nʉ· ɔ^rk	b	nu<· ɔ^ɐk	21a	ŋⁱʉ ɔɐk
28a	nu ɔɔ̧ɐk	48a	nu<· ɔork	66a	nu· ɔork	b	nʉ ɔɐk
b	nu<· ɔɐk	b	nʉ· ɔ^ɐk	b	nɨu< ɔ̌rk	22a	njʉ ɔ̌ɐk
29a	nu< ɔɐk	c	nʉ· ɔork	67ab	nɨu< ɔ̌ɐk	b	ŋⁱʉ ɔɐk
b	nu· ɔɐk	49a	nʉ>· ɔork	**WEST VIRGINIA**		23a	ŋjʉ ɔɐk
30ab	nɨu·u< ɔ̨^ɐk	b	nʉ>· ɔ^ɽk	1	nᴵ^ ʉ> ɔ̌ɔk	b	njʉ ɔɐk
31a	nu<· ɔ̌ɐk	50a	---	2	nᴵ^ ʉ> ɔɐk	24ab	ŋjʉ ɔɐk
b	ɔɐk steɨt,	b	nʉ>· ɔ^rk	33	nᴵ^ u· ɔɐk (√)	25a	ŋjʉ· ɔɐk
	nu· ~ ~	c	nʉ· ɔork	4a	nᴵ^ u< ɔ^ɐk	25b–26a	ŋjʉ ɔɐk
32a	nu· ɔ^ɐk	51a	nʉ>· ɔ<rk	b	ŋⁱ̧ʉ ɔɐk	26b–27a	ŋjʉ· ɔɐk
b	nu<· ɔɔ̧ɐk	b	nʉ>· ɔork	5	nʉ>· ɔ^ɐk	27b	ŋjʉ ɔ·ɐk
33a	nu< ɔ^ɽk	52a	nu<· ɔork	6a	nu<· ɔɐk	28a	ŋjʉ· ɔɐk
b	nu<· ɔ^ɐk	b	nʉ ɔork	b	nuɔ̧· ɔɐk	b	ŋjʉ ɔɐk
34ab	nu<· ɔɐk	53a	nuu< ɔɔ̧rk	7a	nu< ɔɐk	29ab	ŋjʉ· ɔɐk

WVA		WVA		OHIO		KY	
30a	ŋⁱʉ ꞁɔæk	48bc	---	9a	nu‹· ꞁɔrk	4b	ˈŋᵻʉ· ˌꞁɔˆ·ək
b	ŋJʉ ꞁɔæk	d	nʉ› ꞁɔæk	b	nu ꞁɑ›ək	c	ˈŋᵻʉ·ʉˆ ˌꞁɔæk
31a	ŋJʉ ꞁɔ·ək	49a	nʉ›· ꞁɔˆək	c	nu‹· ꞁɔˆək	5a	ˈŋᴵʉ·ʉˆ· ˌꞁɔ‹·ək
b	ŋⁱʉ ꞁɔæk	b	nʉ› ꞁɔˆək	d	nu ꞁɑ‹ək	b	ŋᵻʉ· ꞁɔ‹·ək
32ab	nJʉ ꞁɔæk	50a	nu‹ ꞁɔrk	10a	nʉ›· ꞁɔæk	6a	ˈŋᵻʉ ˌꞁɔᵛ·ək
33a	nJʉ ꞁɔrk	b	nu‹· ꞁɔˆək	b	nu‹· ꞁɔæk	b	---
b	ŋⁱʉ ꞁɔæk	51a	nu‹· ꞁɔæk	11a	nu‹· ꞁɔ·ək	c	ˈnᵻʉ ˌꞁɔ·ək
34a	nJʉ ꞁɔᵛək	b	nu‹· ꞁɔᵛrk	b	nu‹· ꞁɔæk	7a	ŋᵻʉʉˆ ꞁɔ·ək
b	nu‹· ꞁɔæk	52a	nʉ›· ꞁɔˆək	12a	ŋⁱʉ ꞁɔᵛrk	b	ŋᵻʉ ꞁɔ·ək
35a	nJʉ ꞁɔᵛək	b	nu‹· ꞁɔæk	b	nʉₛ ꞁɔæk		
b	nJʉ ꞁɔæk	c	nuₛ ꞁɔæk	cd	---	**DELAWARE**	
36a	nu‹ ꞁɔæk	53a	nu‹· ꞁɔæk	13a	nɪ›ᵁ ꞁɔˆrk	1a	nuˆu‹ ꞁɔᵛək
b	nJʉ ꞁɔæk	b	---	b	nʉ› ꞁɔæk	bc	nuˆu‹ ꞁɔæk
37a	nu‹ ꞁɔrk	c	nu‹· ꞁɔæk	c	nu ꞁɑæk	2a	nu‹ ꞁɔₛək
b	nʉ› ꞁɔæk	54a	nʉ· ꞁɔrk	14	nʉʉˆ ꞁɔæk,	b	nuˆu‹ ꞁɔˆək
38a	nu‹· ꞁɔᵛək	b	nʉ· ꞁɔˆrk		nJʉʉˆ ꞁɔᵛək,	3a	nᵁu‹ ꞁɔₛək
b	nʉ›· ꞁɔᵛək				nʉʉˆ ꞁ~ ˈsteᵛᵻt	b	nʉ› ꞁɔᵛək
39a	nJʉ ꞁɔæk	**OHIO**		15a	---	c	nu‹ ꞁɔᵛək
b	nu‹ ꞁɔæk	1a	nᵻu ꞁɔæk	b	nʉ ꞁɔæk	4	nu‹· ꞁɔᵛək
c	nu‹ ꞁɔᵛək	b	nᵻu‹ ꞁɔᵛək	16a	nʉˆʉ ꞁɔₛək	5a	nʉₛ ꞁɔₛək
40a	nⁱʉ ꞁɔæk	c	nu‹· ꞁɔæk	b	nʉᵛʉ ꞁᵊᵛək	b	nuₛ· ꞁɔᵛək
b	ŋⁱʉ ꞁɔæk	2a	nu‹ ꞁɔᵛək	c	nʉᵛʉ· ꞁɔₛək	6a	nʉ‹ʉ ꞁɔæk (√)
41a	nⁱʉ ꞁɔ·ək	b	nu‹· ꞁɔæk	17	nʉʉˆ ꞁɔˆək	b	nuₛ· ꞁɔₛək
b	nⁱʉ ꞁɔæk	3a	nu‹· ꞁɔˆək	18	nJʉ ꞁɔₛək		
42a	nʉ· ꞁɔˆək	b	nu‹ ꞁɔæk	**KENTUCKY**		**MARYLAND**	
42b-43a	nu‹· ꞁɔæk	4a	nu‹ ꞁɔrk	1a	nJʉ ꞁɔæk	1a	nʉ›· ꞁɔˆək
43b	nʉ›· ꞁɔæk	b	nu‹· ꞁɔæk	b	nʉʉˆ ꞁɔæk,	b	nu‹· ꞁɔˆək
44a	nu‹ ꞁɔæk	5a	nu ꞁɔᵊk		nJʉ· ꞁɔæk	2a	nᴵʉ ꞁɔæk
44b-45a	nu‹· ꞁɔæk	bc	nu‹· ꞁɔæk	2a	ˈŋᴵʉ ˌꞁɔ‹ək	b	nʉ› ꞁɔ·ᵊk
45b	nʉ› ꞁɔæk	6a	nuₛ ꞁɔæk	b	---	3a	nuˆᵁu‹ ꞁɔˆ·ᵊk
46a	nʉ›· ꞁɔˆrk	6b-7b	nu‹· ꞁɔæk	c	nᴵʉ ꞁɔ‹·ək	b	nᴵʉ ꞁɔæk
b	nʉ› ꞁɔæk	8a	nu· ꞁɔæk	3a	ŋᵻʉ ꞁɔₛək	4a	nJʉ› ꞁɔₛək
47a	nu‹· ꞁɔæk	b	nu ꞁɔrk	bcd	---	b	nuu‹ ꞁɔₛək
b	nʉ› ꞁɔæk	c	nu‹· ꞁɔæk	e	nᵻu· ꞁɔˆ·ək	c	nⁱ›ʉ ꞁɔₛᵊk
48a	nʉ ꞁɔæk	d	nu ꞁɑːæk	4a	ˈŋᵻʉ ˌꞁɔ·ᵊk	5a	nⁱʉ ꞁɔₛək
		e	nJu‹ ꞁɔæk			b	nɪʉ› ꞁɔˆək
						6a	nᴵʉ ꞁɔₛək

MD

6b   ŋⁱˇ ɐ ˌɔʂɵk

7a   nᴵ ɐ ˌɵɑk

b   nuˆu‹ ˌɔʂɵk

c̲   nuʂuˢ‹ ˌɔʂɵk

8a   nᴵ ɐ ˌɔˆɵk

b   nɐˆuˢ‹ ˌɑˆɵk

N9   nⁱˇ ɐ ˌɔˇ·k

9a   nᴵ ɐ ˌɔʂɵk

b   nuˆuˢ‹ ˌɑˆɵk

10a   nᴵˆ ɐ ˌɵɑk

b   nɐˆ ɐ ˌɔˆɵk

11   nɐ›uˢ‹ ˌɔːᵉk

12a   nɐ›· ˌɔ‹ɵk

b   nɐ ɐ ˌɔˆɵk

13a   nuʂŭ ˌɔːᵉk

b   nᴵ ɐ ˌɔˆɵk

c   nu‹ ˌɔˆɵk

d̲   nⁱʂuˢ‹ ˌɔːᵉk

e̲   nᴵˆ ɐ ˌɵɑk

f̲   ŋᴶ ɐ ˌɔˆːk

14   nɐ›uˢ‹ ˌɔˆɵk

15a   nuʂ· ˌɔˆ·ᵉk

b   nɐʂɐ ˌɔˇ·ᵉk

16   nuʂ ˌɔˆɵk

17a   nɐɐ› ‹ˌɔ‹ɵk

b   nuʂ ʷ ˌɔˆɵk

18a   nᴵˆ ɐ ˌɔːk

b   nɐˇɐ› ˌɔ·ᵉk

19a   nᴵˆ ɐ ˌɔːk

b   nᴵ ɐ ˌɔːk

20a   nⁱˇ ɐ ˌɔˇᵉk

b   nᴵʂɐ ˌɔ·ᵉk

c̲   nᴵˆ ɐ ˌɔːk

21a   nᴵˆ ɐ ˌɔˆːk

b   nɐˇɐ› ˌɔːk

MD

N22   ---

2N22   nɟu‹ ˌɔːk

22a   nⁱ ɐ› ˌɔˆ·ᵉk

b   ŋᴵˆ ɐ ˌɔːk

c̲   nᴶ ɐ ˌɔːk

23a   ŋᴵˆ ɐ ˌɔːk

b   ---

c   nɟɐ ˌɔˇk

24   nᴶu·· ˌɔ·k

25   nɐˇɐ› ˌɔɵk

26a   nᴵˆ ɐ ˌɔˇɵk

b   ---

27a   nᴵu‹ ˌɔˆɵk

b   nu‹ ˌɔˆɵk

DISTRICT OF COLUMBIA

1a   nuʂ ˌɔ·ᵉk

b̲   nⁱˇ ɐ ˌɔːᵉk

VIRGINIA

1̲   ŋⁱˇ ɐ ˌɔɑˆk

2a   nᴵˆu‹ ˌɔˇᵉk

b   ŋⁱ ɐ ˌɔʂ·ᵉk

3a   nɟu‹ ˌɵɑk

b   ŋⁱˇu ˌɵɑk

N4   ŋɟuʂ ˌɔˇ·k

5a   ŋɟɐ› ˌɔːk

b   ŋⁱ ɐ ˌɔʂ·k

6a   ŋⁱ ɐ› ˌɔˇ·k

b   ŋɟ ɐ ˌɔɵk

7a   ŋⁱ ɐ› ˌɔˇ·ᵓk

b   ŋⁱ ɐ ˌɔˇ·ᵓk

8a   nⁱˇ ɐ› ˌɔ·k

b   ŋⁱˇ ɐ ˌɔˇᵓk

c̲   ŋⁱˇ ɐ ˌɔ·k

9a   ŋⁱˇ ɐ ˌɔˇᵓk

b̲   ŋⁱˇ ɐ ˌɔˇ·ᵓk

VA

10a   ŋⁱˇ ɐ ˌɔˇ·ᵉk

b   ŋⁱ ɐ ˌɔˇᵓk

11a   ŋⁱ ɐ‹ ˌɔʂ·ᵉk

b   ŋⁱˇ ɐ ˌɔ‹ɑʂk

N12   ŋⁱˇ ɐ› ˌɔ·k

12a   ---

b̲   ŋⁱ ɐ ˌɔˇ·k

13a   ŋⁱ ɐ› ˌɔ‹ɑˆk

b   ŋⁱˇ ɐ ˌɔˇ·k

14a   nⁱ ɐ ˌɔˇ·k

b   ŋᴶ ɐ ˌɔ‹ɑˆk,

   nɐˆɐ› ~

c   ŋⁱ ɐ ˌɔ‹ɑˆk

N15   ---

15a   ŋⁱˇu‹ ˌɔˇ·k

b   ŋᴵˆ ɐ› ˌɔˇ·k

16a   ŋⁱˇ ɐ ˌɔˇ·ᵉk

b   ŋⁱ ɐ ˌɔˇᵓk

17a   ŋⁱˇ ɐ ˌɔʂ·ᵉk

b   ŋⁱˇ ɐ ˌɔˇᵓk

18   ŋⁱˇ ɐ› ˌɔˇ·k

19a   ŋⁱ ɐ ˌɔˆːk

b   ŋⁱ ɐ ˌɔɑˆ‹ɑˆk

c̲   ŋⁱ ɐ ˌɔˇᵓk

20a   ŋⁱ ɐ ˌɔ·k

b   ŋⁱ ɐ ˌɔˇ·k

N21   nŭ‹ɐ ˌɔ·k

21a   ŋⁱʂ ɐ ˌɔˇᵓk

b   ŋⁱˇ ɐ› ˌɔˇᵉk

22   ŋⁱˇ ɐ‹ ˌɔʂɑˆk

23a   ŋⁱ ɐ ˌɔʂɔˇk

b   nᴶ ɐ› ˌɔʂ·ᵉk

24   ŋⁱ ɐ ˌɔˇᵓk

25   ŋⁱ ɐ› ˌɔ‹ɵk

26a   ---

VA

26b   ŋⁱ ɐ› ˌɵɑk

c   ŋⁱˇ ɐ ˌɔʂ·ᵉk

27   nuʂ ˌɔˆɵk

28a   ŋⁱˆ ɐ ˌɔˆ·k

b   ŋⁱ ɐ ˌɔʂ·ᵉk

29   ŋⁱˇ ɐ ˌɔˇᵓˆk

30a   ŋⁱˇ ɐ ˌɔˇ·k

b̲   ---

c̲   nⁱ ɐˇ ˌɔʂ·ᵉk

de̲   ŋⁱ ɐ ˌɔˇᵓˆk

31a   *ŋⁱˇ ɐ ˌɔˇ·k

b   ŋⁱˇ ɐ ˌɔˇ·k

32   nŭˆ ˌɔʂᵓˆk

33a   nᴵˆ ɐˇ ˌɔʂᵓˆk

b   ŋⁱ ɐ ˌɔʂᵓˆk

34a   ŋⁱ ɐ› ˌɔʂᵓˇk

b   ŋⁱˇ ɐ ˌɔʂᵓˆk

35a   ŋⁱ ɐ ˌɔ·k

b   nᴵ ɐ ˌɔʂᵓˇk

36a   ŋⁱ ɐ‹ ˌɔˇᵓk

b   ŋⁱ ɐ‹ ˌɔʂᵓˇk

37   ŋⁱ ɐ ˌɔʂɵk

38   nⁱ ɐʂ ˌɔ‹ɑʂk

39   ŋⁱ ɐ ˌɔ‹ɑˆk

40a   ŋⁱˇ ɐ ˌɔ‹ɵk

b   ŋⁱ ɐ̆ ˌɔ‹ɵk

41a   nᴵˆ ɐ ˌɔˇᵓˆk

b   ŋⁱ ɐ ˌɔʂ·ᵉk

42a   ŋⁱ ɐ ˌɔˇ·ᵓk

b   ŋⁱ ɐ ˌɔˇᵓk

N43   ꭐuʂ ˌɔ·k

43a   ŋⁱ ɐ ˌɔˇ·ᵉk

b   ŋⁱ ɐ ˌɔ·k

44a   ŋⁱ ɐ ˌɔˇɔk

b   ŋⁱˆu‹ ˌɔʂᵓˇk

VA

45a   n ⁱ ʉ ɹɔ˅·ᵓk
  b   ŋ ⁱ ʉ ɹɔ˅·k
N46   ---
46a   nɟʉ ᵘ˂ ɹɔ·k
  b   ŋ ᴵ^ ʉ ɹɔ˅ᵓk
47   ŋ ⁱ˅ ʉ ɹɔ˅:k
48a   ŋ ⁱ ʉ ɹɔ^ᵓ˅ɑɹ k
  b   ŋ ⁱ ʉ ɹɔ˅ᵓk
49a   ŋ ⁱ˅ ʉ ɹɔ˅ᵓk
  b   ŋ ᴵ^ ʉ ɹɔ˅ᵓk
50a   ŋ ⁱ ʉ ɹɔ˅·k
  b   ⁱnⁱ ʉ ⁱɹɔ^ᵓ˅k
51a   ŋ ᴵ^ ʉ ɹɔ˅·k
  b   ŋ ⁱ ʉ ɹɔ˅·ᵊk
52a   nu˂· ɹɔæk
  b   nᴵ˅˂ ɹɔ˅ɵk
  c   nⁱ˅˃ ɹɔ˅·ᵊk
53a   nuᶾ· ɹɔᶾᵊk (✓)
  b   nʉ˃· ɹɔ˂ᵊk (✓)
54a   ŋɟʉ˃ ɹɔ^ᵊk
  b   ŋ ᴵ^ ʉ˃ ɹɔᶾᵊk
55a   nⁱ˅ᶾʉ˃ ɹɔæk
  b   nᴵ^ ʉ˂ ɹɔ˂ᵊk
56a   ŋ ⁱ u˂ ɹɔæk
  b   ŋ ⁱ u˂ ɹɔ˂ᵊk
57a   nu˂· ɹɔᶾᵊk
  b   nⁱ˅ᶾu˂ ɹɔᶾᵊk
58   ---
N59   nɟʉ˂ʷ ɹɔ^·k
59a   ŋ ⁱ ʉ ɹɔ˅·k
  b   ŋ ⁱ ʉ ɹɔ˅·ᵓk
60   ŋɟʉ˃ ɹɔ˂ᵊk
61a   *nɟʉ ɹɔᶾɹk
  b   ŋ ᴵ^ ʉ˂ ɹɔ˂ᵊk
62a   ŋ ⁱ ʉ ɹɔ˅ᵓk

VA

62b   ŋ ⁱ ʉ ɹɔ˅·k
63a   ŋ ⁱ ʉ ɹɔæ·k
  b   ŋ ⁱ ʉ ɹɔæk
64a   ŋ ⁱ ʉ ɹɔᵓk
  b   ŋ ⁱ˅ᶾʉ˂ ᶾɹɔ ɹɔᶾᵓ k
65a   nɟʉ ɹɔ˅·ᵣk
  b   nɟʉ ᵘ˂ ɹɔ˅ᵊᵣk
  c   ŋ ⁱ ʉ ɹɔᶾᵓk
66a   ŋ ⁱ˅ᶾʉ ɹɔ˅ᵓk
  b   ŋ ⁱ ʉ ɹɔ˅ᵓk
67a   ŋ ⁱ˅ᶾʉ ɹɔᵊ k
  b   nᴵᶾ ʉ ɹɔ˂ᵊk
68a   ŋ ⁱ ʉ ɹɔæk
  b   ŋ ⁱ˅ᶾʉ ɹɔ˅ᵊk
69a   ŋ ⁱ˅ᶾu ɹɔᶾᵓk
  b   ŋ ⁱ ʉ ɹɔ˅ᵓ˅k
70a   nɟʉᶾʉ˃ ɹɔæᵣk
  b   ŋ ⁱ ʉ ɹɔ˂ᵊ·k
71a   ŋ ⁱ˅ᶾʉ ɹɔ·ᵊk
  b   nⁱ˅ᶾʉ ɹɔᶾᵊk
72ab   ŋ ⁱ ʉ ɹɔ˂ᵊ·k
73   ŋ ⁱ ʉ ɹɔ˂··ᵊk
74a   ŋ ⁱ˅ᶾʉ ɹɔ·ᵊk
  b   ŋ ⁱ ʉ˂·· ɹɔ˅ᵓk
75a   ŋ ⁱ˅ᶾʉ˃ ɹɔ˂ᵊᵣk
  b   nⁱ ʉ ɹɔ˂ᵊk

NORTH CAROLINA

1   ŋ ⁱ ʉ˂ʉ ɹɔᶾᵊk
2a   nⁱᶾᵊʉ ɹɔᵊᵊk
  b   ŋ ⁱ ʉ ɹɔæk
3a   ŋ ⁱ ʉ ɹɔ·ᵊk
  b   nᴵ^ ʉ ɹɔ·ᵊk
4a   ŋ ⁱ ʉ˂ ɹɔᶾᵓk
  b   ŋ ⁱ ʉ˂ ɹɔᶾᵓk
5a   ŋ ⁱ ʉ ɹɔæk

NC

5b   ŋ ⁱ ʉ˂ ɹɔ˅ᵊk, ŋ ⁱ Yᶾ ~
6   ŋ ⁱ ʉ˂ ɹɔᶾᵓk
7a   ŋ ⁱ ʉ ɹɔ·k
  b   ŋ ⁱ ʉ ɹɔ·ᵊk
N8   ŋ ⁱ ʉ˃ ɹɔᶾɔ^k
8a   ŋ ⁱ˅ ʉ ɹɔ˅·ᵊk
  b   ŋ ⁱ˅ ʉ ɹɔ˅·ᵊk
9ab   ŋ ⁱ ʉ˂ ɹɔ·ᵊk
10a   ---
  b   ŋ ⁱ ʉ˂ ɹɔ·ᵊk
  c   ŋ ᴵᶾ ʉ˂ ɹɔ^ᵊk
11a   ŋ ⁱ ʉ ɹɔ·ᵊk
  b   ŋ ⁱ ʉ˂ ɹɔ·ᵊk
12a   ŋ ⁱ˅ ʉ˂ ɹɔ·ᵊk
  b   ŋ ⁱ Y^ ʉ˂ ɹɔᶾᵓk
13a   ŋ ⁱ ʉ ɹɔ˅·ᵊk
  b   ŋ ⁱ Y^ ʉ˂ ɹɔ·ᵊk
N14   nuᶾ ɹɔ˅·k
14a   ŋ ⁱ ʉ ɹɔ˅:ᵊk
  b   nɟʉ· ɹɔᵊ·k
  c   ŋ ⁱ˅ ʉ˃ ɹɔ^ᵓ˅k
15a   ŋ ⁱ ʉ ɹɔæk
  b   ŋ ⁱ ʉ˂ ɹɔᶾᵓk (✓)
16a   ŋ ⁱ ʉ ɹɔ·ᵊk
  b   ŋ ⁱ Y^ ʉ˂ ɹɔ·ᵊk
17a   ŋ ⁱ ʉᶾ ɹɔ·ᵊ˅k
  b   ŋ ⁱ˅ ʉ ɹɔæ^k
18a   ŋ ⁱ ʉ ɹɔæk
  b   ŋ ⁱ˅ ʉ ɹɔ˅·ᵊk
19a   ŋ ⁱ ʉ· ɹɔæk, ~ ɹɔᵊk
  b   ŋ ⁱ ʉ ɹɔ·ᵊk
20a   nɟʉ ɹɔ^ᵊk
  b   ŋ ⁱ˅ ʉ ɹɔ^·ᵊk
  c   ŋ ⁱ ʉ ɹɔ·ᵊk
21a   ŋ ⁱ ʉ˃ ɹɔæk

NC

21b   ŋ ⁱ˅ ʉ˂ ɹɔ·ᵊk
22a   nᴶ ʉ ɹɔ·k
  b   ŋ ⁱ ʉ ɹɔ˅·ᵊk
23a   ŋ ᴵᶾ ʉ˃ ɹɔ˅·ᵊk
  b   ŋ ⁱ ʉ ɹɔᵊk
  c   nʉ ɹɔ˅ᵓk
  d   ---
N24   nu˂ ɹɔ·k
24a   ŋ ⁱ˅ ʉ ɹɔ˂ᵊk
  b   ŋ ⁱ˅ ʉ ɹɔᵊk
N25   nɟʉ˃ ɹɔ·ᵊk
25a   ŋ ⁱ˅ ʉ ɹɔ˂ᵊk
  b   ŋᴶ ʉ ɹɔ·k
26ab   ŋ ⁱ˅ ʉ ɹɔ˅ᵊk
  c   ŋ ⁱ˅ ʉ ɹɔ˅ᵊk
27a   ŋ ⁱ ʉ˃ ɹɔrk
  b   ŋ ⁱ ʉ ɹɔæk
28a   ŋ ⁱ ʉ ɹɔæk
  b   ŋ ⁱ˅ ʉ ɹɔæk
  c   ŋ ⁱ˅ ʉ ɹɔ˅ᵊk
29a   nɟʉ ɹɔ˂ᵊk
  b   ŋ ⁱ ʉ˂ ɹɔ˅·ᵊk
30a   ŋ ⁱ ʉ˂ ɹɔᶾᵓk
  b   ŋ ⁱ˅ ʉ˂ ɹɔᶾᵊk
31a   ŋ ⁱ ʉ ɹɔᶾ^k
  b   ŋ ⁱ ʉ˃ ɹɔᶾᵓk
32a   nɟʉ ɹɔᵊᵣk
  b   ŋ ᴵᶾ ʉ ɹɔ˅·ᵓk
33a   ŋ ⁱ ʉ˂ ɹɔ·ᵊk
  b   ŋ ⁱ ʉ˂ ɹɔ·ᵊk
34a   ŋ ⁱ ʉ· ɹɔ·ᵊk
  b   ŋ ⁱ˅ ʉ ɹɔ·ᵊk
35a   ŋ ⁱ ʉ˃ ɹɔ˅·k
  b   ŋ ⁱ˅ ʉᶾ ɹɔ˅·ᵊk,
      ŋ ⁱ˅Yᶾ ~

NC	NC	NC	SC
N36 ŋⁱˀ ɐ< ɟɔ:k	54b ŋⁱ ɐ ɟɔˢɘk	73b nⁱ ɐ ɟɐɔk	9b ˈnɟɐ· ˌɟɔᵛ·ək
36a ŋⁱ ɐ ɟɔᵛrk	55 ŋᴵˆ ɐ ɟɔ·ɘk	74ab ŋⁱˀ ɐ ɟɔˢɘk	c̲ nɟɐ· ɟɔˢ·ək
b ŋⁱ ɐ ɟɔ·ᵊk	56a nᴵˆ ɐᵛ ɟɔᵛᵊk	75a ŋⁱ ɐ> ɟɐɔk	d̲ cv ˈnɟɐ·ˌɟɔᵛ<·ək
37a ŋⁱ ɐ ɟɑᵛɔk	b̲ ŋᴵˆ ɐ ɟɔ^ɔᵛk	b ŋⁱ ɐ ɟɔᵛɘk	10a ---
b ŋⁱ ɐ ɟɔˢɔk	57a ŋᴵˆ ɐ> ɟɔᵛ·ɘ̨k		b̲ cv nu<· ɟɔ^·ɘ̆k
N38 ŋ ɐ> ɟɔᵛ·ᵊk	b ŋⁱᵛ ɐ ɟɔᵛɔk	**SOUTH CAROLINA**	c̲ ---
38a ŋⁱ ɐ ɟɔᵛɔ^k	58a ŋⁱ ɐ ɟɔᵛrk	1a ŋⁱˀ ɐ> ɟɔɘ̨k	N11 nɟɐ ɟɔˢ·ᵊk
b ŋⁱ ᵛɐ̲ ɟɔᵛɔk	b ŋⁱ ɐ ɟɔᵛ·ɘk	b ŋⁱ ɐ ɟɔ·ᵊk	11a nɟɐ<· ɟɔˢ·ɘk
39a ŋⁱ ɐ ɟɔ·k	59 ---	2ab ŋⁱ ɐ ɟɔ·ɘk	b ˈnᴵu< ˌɟɔ·ɘk
b̲ ŋⁱ ɐ ɟɔᵛ·k	60 ŋⁱ ɐ ɟɔ·ᵛɘ̨k	3a ŋᴶ ɐ ɟɔᵊk	cv ˈnᴵ ɐ· ~
40a nɟɐ ɟɔᵘk	61a nᴵu< ɟɔ·ɘk	b cv ˈnɟɐ·ˌɟɔ·ᵊ>k	c ˈnɟɐ<· ˌɟɔˢ·ᵊk
b ŋⁱˀ ɐ ɟɔᵛ·ᵊk	b ŋᴵˢ ɐ ɟɔᵛɘk	c̲ cv ˈnɟɐ·ˌɟɔ·ᵊk	d nɟɐ> ɟɔ<·ɘk
41 ŋⁱ ɐ ɟɔ^ɔᵛk	62ab ŋⁱˀ ɐ> ɟɔᵛɘk	4a ---	e cv nɟɐ ɟɔˢ·ᵊk,
42a ŋⁱˀ ɐ ɟɔɘ̨k	63a ŋⁱˀ ɐ ɟɐɔk	b ˈnɟɐ·ˌɟɔ^·ᵊk	ˈ~ ˌɟɔˢ·ᵊk ˈsɪ^ǂᵻˢ
b ŋⁱ ɐ ɟɔᵛ·ᵊk	b ŋⁱˀ ɐ ɟɔᵛɘk	c nɟɐ ɟɔ<·ᵊk	f ---
43a ŋⁱˀ ɐ ɟɔᵛɔk	64a ŋⁱ ɐ> ɟɔᵛɘk	5a *ˈnɐ< ˌɟɔ^·ɘk	g̲ nɐ^ ɟɔᵛ·ᵊk
b ŋⁱˀ ɐ ɟᵊk	b nᴵˢɐ^ ɟɐɔk	bc ---	2N11 ˈnɟɐ<· ɟɔˢɘk
44 nᴵˢ ɐ ɟɔᵛ·k	65a ŋⁱˀ ɐ ɟɔᵛ·ɘk	d̲ ˈnɟɐ·ˌɟɔ·ᵊk +	ˈsɪ>ǂᵻˢ
45 ŋⁱ ɐ ɟɑᵛᵛk	b nⁱ ɐ ɟɔ<ɘk	cv ˈnɐ· ~,	11h nɟɐ ɟɔ<·ᵊk
46a ŋᴵˢ ɐ> ɟɔᵛrk	66a ŋⁱˀ ɐ ɟɔᵛᵊk	nɟɐ ɟɔ<·ᵊk,	→ˈnɟɐ>· ˌ~
b ŋⁱˀ ɐ> ɟɔᵛɘ̨k	b ŋⁱ ɐ ɟɔɘk	ˈnɟɐ· ˌ~	i̲ nɟɐ> ɟɔ·ᵊk
c̲ nᴵˢ ɐ> ɟɔᵛɔk	67a ŋⁱˀu< ɟɔᵛᵣk	N6 ---	j̲ nɟɐ>· ɟɔˢ·ək
47 nⁱ ɐ ɟɔᵛɘk	b nⁱᵛ ɐ ɟɔɘk	6a nɟɐ> ɟɔ<ɘk	cv nɟɐ ɟɔˢ·ᵊk,
48 ŋⁱˀ ɐ ɟɔ·ɘk	68a ŋⁱˀ ɐ>· ɟɔ·ɘk	b ---	nɟɐ ɟɔˢ·ɘk
49 ŋᴵ ɐ> ɟɔɘk	b ŋⁱˀ ɐ ɟɔᵛɘk	c̲ ˈnɟɐ·ˌɟɔ·ɘk	12a ---
50a nᴵɐᵛ ɟɔ·ɘ̨k	69a ŋⁱˀ ɐ> ɟɔ·ɘk	N7-7a ---	b nɟɐ ɟɔ^·k
b̲ ŋⁱ ɐ ɟɔˢɔk	b nⁱˀ ɐ ɟɔɘk	7b cv ˈnᴶ ɐ ˌɟɔˢ·ɘk,	13 ---
51a ŋⁱˀ ɐ ɟɔ·ɘk	70a ŋⁱ ɐ ɟɑ̆ˢɘk	nᵛ ɟɔ<·ᵊk,	14a nɟɐ> ɟɔ·k
b ŋⁱˀ ɐ ɟɔᵛ·ɘ̨k	b ŋⁱ ɐ ɟɔᵛɘk	nə ɟɔ<·ɘk	b cv ˈnɟɐ·ˌɟɔ·ᵊk
N52 nɐ> ɟɔᵛ·ᵊk	71a ŋⁱ ɐ> ɟɔˢɘk	c̲ ---	15a ˈnɟɐ·ˌɟɔ<·ɘk
52a ŋⁱˀ ɐ ɟɔˢɘk	b nⁱˀ ɐ> ɟɔᵛɘk	d̲ ˈnɟɐ·ˌɟɔˢ·ɘ̆k	cv ˌ~ ˈɟɔˢ·ɘ̆k
b ŋⁱˀ ɐ ɟɔᵛɔk	c̲ nuˆu< ɟɔᵛk	8a ---	b ˈnɟɐ· ˌɟɔˢ·ɘ̆k
53a ŋⁱ ɐ ɟɔ·ɘk	72a ŋⁱ u ɟɔˢɘk	b cv ˈnɟɐ·ˌɟɔᵛ·ɘk	c cv ˈnɟɐ·ˌɟɔ<·ɘ̆k
b ŋⁱ ɐ< ɟɔ·ɘ̨k	b ŋⁱˀ ɐ ɟɔᵛɘk	c cv ˈnɟɐ·ˌɟɔ^·ᵊk	N16 ˈnɐ· ˌɟɔ·ɘk
54a nⁱ ɐ ɟɔᵛɘ̨k	73a ŋⁱ ɐ>· ɟɔᵛɘ̨k	9a cv ˈnɟɐ· ˌɟɔ·ɘk,	16-17c ---
		ˈnᵻ ɐ ˌɟɔ^·ɘk	

SC

17d cv ˈnᴶɐ·ˌcɹı·ɘˑek,
ˈnɟɐ·ˌcɹɔˆ·ɘk,
~ ˌcɹɔˇ·ᵊk,
ˈnɟɐˌᴶɔˆ·ɐk

N18 ˈn⁺ɐ<·ˌcɹɔɕ·ᵊk

18a cv nɟʏ>·ˌcɹ<·ɘk

b cv ˈn⁺ɐ<·ˌɔɕ·ᵊk

c ˈnɟʏ>ˌcɹ<·ᵊk

N19 ---

19a nɟʏ>·ˌɔɕ·k

b nᴵɐ ˌɔ·ɘk

c nɟʏ>·ˌɔ<·k

d nɐ ˌɔˆ·ɘk

20a nɟɐ·ˌcɹ ɐˌk

b ˈnɟɐ<·ˌcɹı·ɐk,

c ˈnɟɐ·ˌı·cɹ·ɔˆk

d cv ˈnɟɐ·ɐˌcɹı·ɔ·ɔˆk
ˈsteˆ·ɫ, ~ ˌɹɔˇɔk

21a ŋᴵɐ·cɹ·ɘk

b ŋᴵ⸲ɐˌcɹ ˌɔˇ·ᵊk

N22 ---

22a ˈnɟɐ·ˌcɹ·ɔˆ·ɐk

b ---

c ˈnɟɐ·ˌcɹ·ɐˇ·ᵊk

23a ˈnɟɐ·ˌcɹɔˇ·ᵊk

b ˈnɟɐ·ˌᴶɔˆ·ɐk
ˌsteˑᵊɫ

c ˈnɟɐ·ˌcɹɔˇ·ᵊk

de ---

N24 cv ˈnɟɐ·ˌɐˌɔˆ·ᵊk

24a ˈnᴵɐ·ˌcɹɔ·ɘk

b ---

c cv ˈnɟɐ·ˌcɹı·ᵊk

d cv nɟɐ·ˌcɹˇ·ᵊk

25a nɟɐ·ˌɔ<·k

SC

25b ˈnɟɐ·ˌᴶɔˇ·ɐk

c ˈnɟɐ·ˌcɹı·ᵊk

26a ˈnɟɐ·ˌᴶɔ<·ɐk

b ---

27a nᴵɐ·ˌɔ·ɐk

b ˈnɟɐ·ˌcɹ<·ɐk

28a ˈnɟɐ·ˌᴶɔ·ᵊk

b ---

c ˈnɟɐ·ˌcɹı·ɐ·ᵊk

d ˈnɟɐ·ˌcɹı·ᵊk

29a ˈnɟɐ·ˌɔˇ·ɐk

b ---

c nɟɐ·ˌɔ·ɐk

30a nᴵɐ·cɹ·ᵊk

b cv ˈnɟɐ<·ʷɐˌɔ·ɔˆ·ɔk

c ˈnɟɐ<·ˌɐ·ˆ·ᵊk

31a ˈnɟɐ·ˌcɹı·ᵊˆ·ɐk

b ˈnɟɐ·ˌcɹ·ᵊˆk

32a ˈnɟɐ<·ʷˌcɹı·ᵊˇ·ᵊk

cv ˈnɟɐ·ˌcɹı·ᵊˆ·ᵊk

b ---

c nɟɐ·cɹ·ᵊk

d ˈnɟɐ·ˌᴶᵊˇ·ᵊk

33a nᴵɐ·ˌcɔˆk

b ˈnɟɐ·ˌᴶɔ·ɔˆk

34a ˈnɟɐ<·ʷˌɔ·ɔˆ·ɔk

b cv ˈnɟɐ·ʷˌɔ·ɔˆk

c cv nɟɐ·ˌɔˆ·ɔk

35a cv ˈnɟɐ·ˌᴶɔˇ·ᵊk

b ---

c ˈnᴵɐ·ˌcɹɔˇ·ɔˆk,
~ ~ steˑᵗ

36a ---

b ˈnɟɐ·ʷˌcɔˇ·ᵊ>k

cv ˈnɟɐ·ɐˆˌᴶɔˇ·ᵊ>k

SC

36d nɟɐ·ˌɔˇ·ᵊk

37 nᴵɐ·cɹ·ᵊˇk,
ˈnᴵu·ˌ~ˌsteⱦ
cv ˈnᴵɐˆˌcɹı·ᵊk

38a cv ˈnɟɐ·ɐˌᴶɔˆ·ɔk

N38 nɟɐ·ʷᴶɔˆɔk

38b ˈnɟɐ<·ʷˌᴶɔˆɔk

c cv nɟɐ ᴶɔˆ·ɔk

d nɟɐ<·ᵘᴶɔˆ·ɔˆk

39a ˈnɟɐ<·uˌᴶɔˆɔk

b ˈnᵒɟɐ<·uˌᴶɔˆk

40a ˈnɟʏ>ɐˆˌcɹᵊˇɔk

b ˈnɟʏ>ɐɕˌᴶɔˆɔk

41a nᴵ ɐˌɔɕ<ɐk

b nɟʏ>ɐˆˌᴶɔɕ·ᵊk

cv nɟɐ nɕˌᴶɔˇɔk

42a nɟʏ>nɕˌɔɕ<ɔ<·ᵊk

N42 ˈnɟʏ>·ɐɕˌᴶɔˆɔˇk
cv ˈnɟʏ·ɐ ~

42b cv ˈnɟʏɕ·ɐˌcɹı·ɔɕˇk

c ˈnɟɐ<ɐɕˌᴶɔɕɔ<ᵊˇk

d ---

e ŋᴵɐˌɔˇɔk

43a ---

b ˈnɟɐɐˆˌᴶɔɕ·ᵊk

c ˈnɟʏuˌᴶᵊˇ·ᵊˆk

44a ˈnɟʏ>ɐˆˌᴶcɹ·ɔᵊˇk

cv ˈnɟɐ<ɐɕˌcɹı·ɔ<ɔᵊˇk

b *ˈnɟʏ>ɐˆˌᴶɔˇɔᵊˇk

GEORGIA

N1 ˌnᴵu<·ˈᴶcɹı·k·ˌsteˑᵗ

1a *ˈnᴶɐ·ˌcɹ<·ᵊˇk

b ˈɐɐˌcɹı·ᵊˇk

c cv ˈnɟɐ·ˌᴶɔɕ·ᵊˇk,
nɟɐ·ˌᴶɔ<·ᵊˇk,

GA

(1c) ˈnɟɐ<·ˌ~

d ---

e ˈnɟɐ·ˌcɹı·ᵊ<·ᵊˇk

f nɟuɕˌᴶɔ:k

g ---

h cv ˈn⁺<ɐ·ˌcɹı·ᵊ<·ᵊˇk

N2 ---

2a ˈnɟɐ·ˌᴶɔˇ<·ɐ>k

b ˈnɟɐ·ˌᴶɔˇ<·ɐ>k

3a nɟuɕ·ˌᴶɔ:k

b ---

N4 ɲuɕ·ˌɔ·k

4a ˈnɟɐ·ˌᴶɔˇ·ɘk

b ---

c n⁺ɐ ˌᴶɔˆ·ᵊˇk

5a ˈnɐ·ˌᴶɔˇ·ᵊˇk

b cv ˈnɐ>·ˌᴶɔɕ·ɘk

c cv nu ˌᴶɔˆ·ᵊˇk

d cv ˈnɐ>·ˌᴶɔˇᵊˇk,
ˈnɐ·ˌcɹˇk,
ˈnu<·ˌᴶɔˆk

e nɐ·ˌᴶɔˆ·ᵊˇk

6a cv ˈnu<·ˌᴶɔ·ᵊˇk

b ˈn⁺ɐ·ˌᴶɔˆ·ɘk

7 cv ˈnɟɐ·ˌᴶɔˇ·ɔk

8a nɟɐ·ˌᴶɔˇ·ᵊˇk

b nɟɐ·ˌᴶɔˆ·ɐk

9a cv ˈnᴵ<ɐˆˌᴶɔ·ɐk

b ---

10a nɟɐ>·ˌᴶɔɹk

b ˈnɟɐ·ˌcɹı·ᵊˇk

N11 n⁺ɐ ˌᴶɔɐk,
ɐɐ ~

12a ---

b ˈn⁺ɐ·ˌcɹı·ᵊˇk,

GA

(12b) ₁n^Iʉ ˈ~ ₁steᵗ,
      ~ ~ sɪ†ᵗ

13a njuʂ ɟɔʂ·ᵊk

b̲   ˈnjʉ· ₁cɟɪ·ʉˈ<·ᵊk

c̲v̲ nju<· ˈ~

14a njʉ ɟɔ<··ᵊk

b   ˈnjʉ<·· ₁cɟɪ<·ᵊk

c   ---

15a nⁱʉ> ɟɔ·k

b   ---

16a ˈnᴶʉ ₁cɟɪ<··ɚ̆k

b   ˈnjʉ ₁cɟɔˇ·k

     c̲v̲ ˈnjʉ· ₁cɟɔ^·ᵊk

c   ---

d̲   ˈnjʉ· ₁cɟɔ^·k

N17 n^Iʉ ɟɔˇ·ɚ̆k,
     ~ ˈɟɔˇ·ɔcˇk ₁steᵗ

17   n^Iʉ ɟɔˇ·ɚ̆k

18a ŋⁱʉ ɟɔ̧ɚk

b   ˈŋⁱʉ ₁cɟɔ·ɚk

19a **ˈnjʉ· ₁cɟɔˇ·ɚ>k

b   ˈnjʉ ₁cɟɔˇ·ɔk

20a njʉ ɟɔ̧^ɚk

b   ---

21a n^Iʉ ɟɔ·ɚk

b   ---

GA

22a njʉ· ɟɔ·ɚ̆k

b   ˈnjʉ· ₁cɟɔ^·ɚ̆k

23a ---

b   ˈnⁱʉ ₁cɟɔˇɔk

c   ˈn^ᵗʉʉ^ ₁cɟɔɚk

d̲   ---

e̲   n^Iʉ ɟɔɚk

     c̲v̲ nʉ ɟɔ·ɚk²

f̲   ˈn^ᵗʉ ₁cɟɔ·ɚk

N24 steᵗ ə ˈn^Iʉ
     ₁ɟɔˇɔk, ~ ~ steᵗ,
     ~ ~ sɪ†ᵗ^

24a nⁱʉ ɟɔ·ᵊk

b   njʉ· ɟɔ̧ɔk

N25 ˈnⁱʉ ₁cɟɔɔk

26   ˈn^Iʉ ₁cɟɔ^ɔ^k,
     ₁~ ˈɟɔ̆k ₁ste·t

27   nʉ ɟɔˇɚk

28   ˈn^Iʉ ₁cɟɔ̧ɚk

29a ˈnjʉ· ₁cɟɔˇ·ɚk

b   c̲v̲ ˈnjʉ· ₁cɟɔ·ᵊk

30a ---

b   c̲v̲ ˈnjʉ<·ʷ ₁cɟɔ^·ɔk

c̲   n^Iʉ ɟɔ̧ɚk

31   ₁n^Iʉ ˈɟɔ·ɚk

GA

(31) ₁steᵗ

32   ˈn^Iʉ ₁cɟɔɚk

33a ˈnᴶʉ ₁cɟɔɚk

b   nᵗʉ ɟɔ̧ɔk

N34 ˈnjʉ· ₁cɟɔˇɔk

34a ŋⁱʉ ɟɔ̧·ᵊk

b   ˈnᴶʉ ₁cɟɔˇ·ɚk

N35 n^Iʉʉ^ ɟɔ·ɚk,
     ~ ~ ˈsteᵗ

N36 n^{iˇ}ʉʉ^ ɟɔɚk

N37 ˈnʉ ₁cɟɔɚk,
     nʉ̆ ɟɔ·ɚk,
     steᵗ əv ˈn^Iʉ ₁~

37a nʉ<·ʉ ɟɔ̧·ɚk

b   ˈnjʉ· ₁cɟɔˇ·ɚ̆k
     ˈsɪ^†ɪ>i>

c   ˈn^Iʉ ₁cɟɔ·ɚk

2N37 n^Iʉ ɟɔˇ·ɚk

37d̲ n^Iʉ ɟɔ·ɚk

e̲   ˈn^Iʉ ₁cɟɔ·ɚk ˈsteᵗ

f̲   ---

g̲   ˈnjʉ· ₁cɟɔ^·ɚ̧^k

h̲   c̲v̲ ˈnʉ<·ʷ ₁cɟɔ·ɚ̆k,
     ~ ₁cɟɔ·ɚk ˈsɪ^†ᵗᶻ

i̲   nʉ· ɟɔ·ɚk,

GA

(37i̲) n^Iʉʉ^ ɟɔɚk

38   ---

39   ˈnʉ· ₁cɟɔ·ɚk

40   n^Iʉ ɟɔrk

41   ---

42a ˈnjʉ ₁cɟɔ<·ɚk

b   ---

43   nⁱʉ ɟɔ<ɚk

44ab ---

c   ˈnjʉ· ₁cɟɔˇ·ɚ̧k

d   ---

e   ˈnⁱʉ>ʉ̧ ₁cɟɔɚk

FLORIDA

1   ˈnʉ· ₁cɟɔˇ·ɚk
     ˈsteʌ·ᵊt

2a   ˈnʉ· ₁cɟɔˇ·ɚk

b   nʉ ɟɔ̧ɚk

c̲   ₁njʉ ˈɟɔˇ·ɚk
     ₁steʌ·ᵊt

3a   njʉ· ɟɔ·ɚ̆k

     c̲v̲ ˈ~ ₁cɟɔ·ɚk

b̲   c̲v̲ nə ɟɔˇ·ɚk

4   ˈn^Iʉ ₁cɟɔ^·ɚk

5a   ---

b   ˈnʉ<· ɟɔ̧^·ɚk

COMMENTARY

ONTARIO

6   [ʋ]: *sic*

10   cf. Yorkshire
     [ˈɟɔ<ɚkʃɪɚ]

NEW YORK

18c̲ [nu·]: *sic*

25a [₁ɟɔ̧ˇɚᵗk]: field record

NY

(25a) [₁ɟɔ̧ˇɚᵗk]; ð̧ɪᶻ
      ˈɛ^mₚɑ·ᵗɚ ₁steˇ·ᵗ<t

26b   ˈʌˇp steˇᵗ<t

27c   nə ɟɔ̧ɚkɚ^z

29c   York State shilling
      [ˈɟɔ̧k ₁steᵗ ˈʃɪlᵗŋ]=

NY

(29c) 12½¢

32a   *York State*: old

b   *York State*: by out of
      state people

33b   northern *New York*
      [ˈnɔ̧ɚðən ₁nuˇu ˈɟɔ̧k]

NY

47a ˈɪ̃ᵐpeˆɨɚ ˌsteᵛɨt;

ˈɹo̜꞉ɚkɚˆz

48d ðə ˈɛˆmpeɨɚ ˌsteᵛɨt

50a *York State*: by outsiders

55a ðɪ꞉ ˈɪᵛmˌpeᵛɨɚ ˈsteᵛɨt

58a western *New York*

[ˌwɛˆstɚˆn ˌ~ ˈ~]

63a ⊥: Michigan!

d †[ˈɹɔ<ɚk ˌsteᵛɨ̬tɚ]:

NY

(63d) "used in the west"

NEW JERSEY

17a [ɔᵛ·ᵊ]: *sic*

WEST VIRGINIA

3 [nᴵˆu·]: *sic*

DELAWARE

6a [ʊɚk]: *sic*

VIRGINIA

14b [nʉˆʉ]: modern only

VA

32 [nŭˆ]: in this name only

53a [nu꞉·]: *sic*

b [nʉ>·]: in this name only

59b no stress on [ŋⁱʉ]

NORTH CAROLINA

15b [ɔ꞉ɔ]: *sic*

SOUTH CAROLINA

32a cv [ɹɔˆ·ək] (SC)

7. NEW JERSEY

WS 86.2

New Jersey was systematically investigated only in the MAS. *Jersey* was sometimes recorded in addition to or instead of *New Jersey*. The stress patterns ~ ˈ~ and ˌ~ ˈ~ are not marked.

ONTARIO

1a	cv nu< dʒ³ɚzɨˆ
1b-2a	---
2b	nu꞉u< dʒɜˆɚzɪ꞉
3	---
4a	nʉ dʒɚzɨ
b	nᴵu꞉ᵘ< dʒɚzɨ^ˆ
5-8a	---
8b	nu꞉u< dʒɜ̜>ɚzɪ꞉
c	cv ŋu꞉u< dʒɜ̜>ɚzɪ꞉
d	nɹu꞉u< dʒɜ̜>ɚzɪ꞉
9-10	---

NEW YORK

1-2c	---
3a	nɨu< dʒɚ·zɨ꞉
b	nɨu< dʒɘɚzɨˆ
c	nu<· dʒɚzɨ꞉
3d	nɨu< dʒɵɨzɨˆ
4a	nu<· dʒɘɚzɨ꞉
b	dʒɵə̜zɨˆ
c	nu<· dʒɵɨˆzɨ꞉
5a	nu<· dʒɔ<ɨˆzɨˆ
b	nu<· dʒɵɨᵛzɨ꞉
c	dʒɵˆᵊ̣ˆzɨˆ, nu<· ~
d	nu<· dʒɵᵊ꞉zɨ꞉
e	dʒɵɨ̣ᵛzɨ꞉, nu<· ~
f	nŭ꞉ŭ dʒɵɨᵛzɨ꞉
g	nu< dʒɜɨzɨ꞉
h	nu< dʒɵˆɨᵛzɨ꞉
i	nᴶu< dʒɜˆɜ̜ˆzɨ꞉
6a	d̥ʒ̊ɵ>ɨᵛzɨˆ
b	nu< dʒɵˆ·ᵊˆzɨˆ
7a	dʒɵ·ᵊ꞉zɨ꞉
7b	nu· dʒɵ·ɨᵛzɨ꞉
c	nu<· dʒɵə̜ˆzɨˆ
d	dʒɵɨˆzɨ꞉, nu<· ~
e	nu<· dʒɵə̜꞉zɨ꞉,
	~ dʒɵɨˆ-
f	dʒɵə̤꞉ˆzɨ꞉, nu<· ~
g	nu<· dʒɵˆɨˆzɨ꞉
h	nu<· dʒɜᵊ꞉zɨ꞉
i	nu<· dʒɵ̱ɨzɨ꞉
j	nu< dʒɜˆ·zɨ꞉
k	nu· dʒɵˆ·ə꞉zɨ꞉
l	nu<· dʒɜˆ·zɨ꞉
m	nu<· dʒɜ꞉̆·zɨ꞉
8	nu· dʒɵɨ̣ᵛzɨˆ
9ab	nu<· dʒɚ·zɨˆ
c	nu<· dʒɜ̣·zɨ꞉
10a	dʒɚzɨˆ, nu<· ~
b	nu<· dʒɚzɨˆ
11	nu<· dʒɚ·zɨˆ
12a	nɨŭ< dʒɚzɨˆ
b	nu<· dʒɚzɨˆ
c	nu< dʒɵə̜ˆzɨˆ
13a	nu<· dʒɚzɨˆ
b	nu<· dʒɜɨᵛzɨˆ
14a	nu· dʒɚ·zɨˆ
b	nu<· dʒɚ·zɨˆ
15a	nɨu dʒɚzɨˆ
b	nɨu dʒɚ·zɨˆ
16a	nu· dʒɜɨzɨˆ
b	nu· dʒɚ·zɨˆ
17a	nɨu< dʒɚzɨˆ
b	nu· dʒɚzɨˆ

NY

18a	nɪu‹ dʒɚz‡·^
b	nu‹· dʒɚ·z‡^
c	nju· dʒʒ̧e›z‡^
19	nuʂ· dʒɚz‡^
20a	nɪu dʒɚz‡^
b	nu‹ dʒɚ·z‡^
21	nu· dʒɚ·z‡^
22	nu· dʒɚz‡^
23a	---
b	cv dʒʒ›ɚzɪ^ⁱ, nu‹· dʒʒ›ɚzɪ^
c	nuʂu dʒʒ›ɚzɪ̧
24a	nɪu‹ dʒɚ·z‡^
b	nu· dʒɚz‡^
25a	nu‹·ᵘ dʒʒ̧›ɚzɪ̧
b	dʒʒ›·ɚzɪ̧, nju^u ~
26a	nuˇ· dʒɚ›zɪ̧ cv dʒʒ›^ɚzɪ̧
b	nuˇ· dʒʒ›·ɚzɪ̧
c	---
27a	nᴶu^·u dʒʒ›·ɚzɪ̧
b	---
c	nu‹u dʒʒ›ɚzɪ̧
28a	nuˇ· dʒʒ›ɚʂɪ̧
b	nuˇ· dʒʒ›·ɚzɪ̧
29a	cv nuˇ dʒʒ̧›ɚzɪ̧
b	nᴶu‹ dʒʒ̧›ɚzɪ̧
c	nʉ· dʒɚzɪ̧zɪ›ⁱ›
30a	ˈnju‹· ˌdʒʒ̧›ɚ›zɪ̧
b	cv ˈnju‹· ˌdʒʒ̧›ɚzɪ̧
cd	---
e	nᴶʉ›· dʒʒ›ɚzɪ̧
31a	nuʂu dʒʒ›ɚzɪ̧
b	njʉ· ʉ·dʒɚ̧zeˇzɪ̧
32a	nju‹· dʒʒ̧›ɚzɪ̧

NY

32b	nju̧u‹ dʒʒ›·ɚzɪ̧
33a	---
b	nuˇu dʒʒ›·ɚzɪ̧, nᴶu·̌ ~
c	nuʂu dʒʒ›·ɚzɪ̧
34a	cv nʉʉ dʒʒ̧›ɚz‡‹
bc	---
d	nᴵʉʉ dʒʒ›·ɚz‡‹
35a	nɪu‹ dʒɚz‡^
b	nɪu dʒɚz‡^
c	---
36a–37a	nɪu dʒɚz‡^
37b	nu‹· dʒɚz‡^
c	nuʂ· dʒɚz‡^
38a	nɪu‹ dʒɚ·z‡^
b	nɪu›‹u dʒɚz‡^
39a	nɪu dʒɚz‡^
b	nɪu›u dʒɚ·z‡^
40a	nɪu›u dʒɚz‡^
b	nu· dʒɚ·z‡^
41	nu‹ dʒɚz‡^
42a	nɪu‹ dʒɚz‡^
b	nu‹ dʒɚz‡^
43a	nɪu‹ dʒɚz‡
b	nu‹ dʒɚz‡^
c	nu‹ʷ dʒɚ·z‡^
44a	nɪu‹ dʒɚz‡^
b	nu· dʒɚz‡^
45abc	---
d	cv nuʂu dʒ̊ʒ̧›ɚzɪ̧
46a	nʉˇʉ dʒʒ›ɚz‡‹
b	nᴵʉ dʒɚz‡^
c	nu‹ dʒɚz‡
47a	nʉʉ dʒʒ›·ɚzɪ̧
b	nuʷ dʒɚz‡^

NY

48a	nᴶʉ›· dʒʒ›·ɚz‡‹
b	cv nuʂu‹ dʒʒ̧›·ɚz‡‹
c	njʉ dʒʒˇ^ɚzɪ›
d	nʉʉ̧ dʒʒ̧›·ɚz‡̧
49ab	---
c	nᴵuʂu‹ dʒʒ°›ɚz‡^›‹ *nuʂu‹ ‡ʃ°ɚz‡^
d	nuʂu‹ dʒɚz‡^
50a	nju‹u dʒʒ̧›·ɚz‡‹
b	njʉʉ dʒʒ̧›ɚz‡‹
51a	njʉˇʉ dʒʒ›ɚzɪ̧
b	nuʂu‹ dʒʒ‡ˇɚz‡‹
c	nuʂu‹ dʒʒ›ɚzɪ̧
de	---
52a	nuʂu‹ dʒʒ›ɚzɪ̧
b	---
c	nᵻʉ dʒɚz‡^
53a	nᴶʉˇʉ dʒʒ›ɚzɪ̧
b	nju̧u‹ dʒʒ›‡zɪ̧
54a	nu‹· dʒɚz‡ cv dʒɚz‡^
b	nuʂu‹ dʒ°ʒɚz‡
55a	nʉ· dʒʒ̧›·ɚzɪ›ⁱ›
b	cv dʒʒ›^ɚzɪ̧, nuʂ dʒʒ›^ɚzɪ̧
56a	nᴶʉ dʒʒ̧›ɚzɪ̧, nʉˇʉ dʒʒ›ɚzɪ̧
b	nᴶʉ· dʒʒ›ɚzɪ̧
57a	nuʂu dʒʒ̧̧›ɚzɪ̧
b	---
c	nju‹ˇ dʒʒ̧›ɚzɪ›ⁱ›
58a	nuˇu dʒʒ̧›ɚzɪ̧
b	nu‹· dʒʒ̧›ɚzɪ̧
c	---
d	nuˇu dʒʒ›‡zɪ̧

NY

(58d)	‡dʒʒ›‡zɪ̧
58e	nᴶu‹ dʒʒ̧›ɚzɪ̧
f	---
59a	njʉ·ʉ dʒʒ›ɚzɪ̧
b	nɪu‹ dʒɚz‡^
60a	nʉˇʉ dʒʒ›ɚzɪ›ⁱ›
b	nᴶu‹· dʒʒ›^ɚzɪ̧
61a	nu‹ dʒʒ›ɚzɪ̧
b	nu‹ dʒʒ̧›ɚzɪ̧
62a	---
b	nu‹· dʒʒ›ɚzɪ̧
c	nu‹ dʒʒ̧›ɚzɪ̧
d	nu‹ dʒʒ›ɚzɪ̧
63a	nu‹· dʒʒ›ɚ̧zɪ̧
b	nᴶu‹· dʒʒ›^ɚzɪ̧
c	nᵻu dʒɚz‡^
d	ˈnʉ·ʉ ˌdʒʒ̧›^ɚzɪ›ⁱ›
64a	nᴶu‹ dʒɚ›zɪ̧
b	nʉ›· dʒʒ›^ɚzɪ̧›ⁱ›
c	cv nᴶʉ· dʒʒ›^ɚzɪ̧

NEW JERSEY

1a	---
b	nʉ›· dʒɚ·z‡^
2ab	---
3a	nʉ› dʒɚ·z‡‡^
b	nʉ· dʒɚz‡^
4a	---
b	nu‹· dʒɚz‡‡^
5a	---
b	nuʂ· dʒɚ·z‡‡^
6a	nʉ›· dʒɚz‡^
b	nʉ›· dʒɚz‡‡^
7a	---
b	nʉ›· dʒɚz‡̧
8a	nu‹· dʒɚ·z‡^

NJ		PA		PA		PA	
8b	nu‹· dӡɚ·z‡ꙅ	1g̲	nu‹ dӡɚz‡	16b	nu· dӡɚz‡^	36a	nu· dӡɚz‡^
9a	nuꙅu dӡᶿɚz‡‡^	h̲	---	c	---	b	nu‹ dӡɚz‡^
b	nʉ› dӡɚz‡ꙅ	2ab	nu‹· dӡɚz‡^	17a	nu· t̠ʃɚrs̠‡^	37a	nu‹ g̊ɚrs̠‡^
10a	nu‹· dӡɵz̦‡^	3a	nu‹· dӡɚz‡‡^	b	nu· g̊ɚrz‡^	b	nu‹ dӡɚz‡
b	nʉ›· dӡᶿɚz‡ꙅ	b	nŭ^ŭ‹ dӡɚz‡^	18ab	nu· dӡɚz‡^	38a	nʉꙅ dӡɚz‡
c	nʉ›· dӡɚz‡ꙅ	c	nu‹· dӡɚz‡^	19ab	dӡɚz‡	b	---
d̲	nu‹· dӡɚz‡^	4a	nu· dӡɚz‡^	20ab	nu‹· dӡɚz‡	39a	nu‹· dӡɚz‡^
11abc	nʉ›· dӡɚz‡ꙅ	b̲	nu‹· dӡɚz‡^	21a	nɪu‹ dӡɚz‡	b	---
12a	nʉ›·· dӡᶿɚz‡‡ꙅ	5a	nu‹· dӡɚz‡	b	nu· dӡɚz‡	40a	nu‹ dӡɚz‡^
b	nu‹· dӡɚz‡^	b	nu‹· dӡɚ·z‡^	22a	n‡u‹ dӡɚz‡	b	nu‹· dӡɚ·z‡^
13ab	nʉ›· dӡɚz‡^	c	nuu‹ dӡɚz‡	b	nu· dӡɚz‡	41a	nu‹· dӡɚz‡^
14ab	nu‹· dӡɚz‡ꙅ	de̲	---	23a	n‡u dӡɚz‡	b	nʉ›· dӡɚz‡^
15a	nu‹· dӡɚ·z‡^	6a	nu· t̠ʃӡꙅ·s̠‡	b	n‡u‹ dӡɚz‡	42a	nu‹· dӡɚz‡^
b	nŭ‹ dӡɚz‡ꙅ	b	nu· dӡӡꙅz‡	24ab	nu· dӡɚz‡	b	nu‹· dӡɚ·z‡^
16a	nu‹· dӡᶿɚz‡ꙅ	c	nu· dӡӡrz‡	25a	n‡ŭ‹ dӡɚz‡	43a	nu‹· dӡɚz‡^
b	nuꙅ· g̊ӡᶿɚz‡ꙅ	d̲	nu· dӡɚz‡^	b	nu· dӡɚz‡^	b	nu‹· dӡɚz‡
17a	dӡᶿɚz‡ꙅ	7ab	---	26a	n‡‹u‹ dӡɚz‡	44a	nu‹· dӡɚz‡^
b	nʉ›· dӡɚz‡ꙅ	c	nu· t̠ʃɚrs‡	b	nuᵂ dӡɚz‡	b	nu‹· dӡɚ·z‡^
18a	nu‹· dӡɵz̦‡^	d̲	nu‹· dӡɚz‡^	27a	*n‡u‹ dӡɚz‡‡^	45a	nu‹· dӡᵊrrz‡^
b	nu‹· dӡɵꙅz‡ꙅ	8ab	---	b	n‡u‹ dӡɚz‡	b	nu‹ dӡᵊrz̦‡
c̲	nu‹· dӡɚz‡ꙅ	c	nu‹· t̠ʃɚrs‡^	28a	nu dӡɚz‡^	46a	nʉ· dӡɚz‡^
d̲	nu dӡɚ·z‡^	d̲	nu‹ dӡɚz‡^	b̲	nu‹· dӡɚz‡^	b	nʉ̲ dӡɚz‡^
19a	nu‹· dӡɵz‡^	9a	nu‹· t̠ʃӡs̠‡	29a	nu‹ dӡɚz‡^	47a	nʉ›· dӡᵊrz̦‡^
b̲	nu· dӡɵˇz‡^	b	nu· dӡɚz‡^	b	nu· dӡɚz‡^	b	nʉ· dӡᵊrz̦‡^
20a	nu‹· dӡᵊrz‡^	c̲	nʉ›· dӡɚz‡ˇ‡	30ab	n‡u‹ dӡɚz‡	48a	nu‹· dӡᵊrz‡^
b	nu· dӡɵz̦‡^	10	nu· g̊ᵊrs̠‡^	31a	nu‹· dӡɚz‡^	b	nʉ· dӡᵊrz‡^
21a	nu‹· dӡɚz‡^	11a	nu· dӡɚz‡^	b	dӡɚz‡^, nu·~	c	nʉ· dӡɚz‡^
b	nu‹· dӡɚ·z‡ꙅ	b	nu· dӡɚz‡^	32a	nu· dӡɚ·z‡^	49ab	nʉ›· dӡᵊrz‡^
		12a	nu‹· dӡɚz‡^	b	---	50a	---
PENNSYLVANIA		b	nu dӡɚz‡	33a	nu‹· dӡᵊrz‡^	b	nʉ›· dӡᵊrz̦‡^
1a	nu‹· dӡɚ·z‡^	13ab	nu‹· dӡɚz‡^	33b-34a	nu‹· dӡɚz‡^	c̲	nʉ· dӡɚz‡^
b	nu· g̊ᵊrz‡^	14a	nu‹· t̠ʃɚrs̠‡ꙅ	34b	nu‹· dӡɚz‡	51ab	nʉ›· dӡᵊrz‡^
c	nuꙅ dӡɚz‡^	b	nu‹· dӡɚz‡ꙅ	c	*nu‹ dӡɚz‡^	52a	nu‹· dӡᵊrz‡
d	nu‹· dӡɚz‡^	15abc̲	nu· dӡɚz‡	35a	nu‹· dӡɚ·z‡^	b̲	nʉ dӡɚz‡
e̲	nu· dӡɚz‡	16a	nu· t̠ʃɚrs̠‡^	b	---	53a	nuu‹ dӡᵊrz‡ꙅ
f̲	nʉ›· dӡɚ·z‡^						

PA

53b nu^u< dʒɚzɨ^
54a nu<· dʒɚrzɨ^
b nʉ· dʒɚzɨ^
55a nu· dʒɚ·zɨ^
b nʉ>· dʒɚzɨ^
56a nu<· dʒɚzɨ^
b nʉ>· dʒɚrzɨ^
57a nʉ>· dʒɚ̆rzɨ^
b nʉ>· dʒɚrzɨ^
58a nu<· dʒɚzɨ^
b nʉ>· dʒɚzɨ^
59a nu<· dʒɚṛzɨ^
b nu< dʒɚ̆ṛzɨ^
60a nʉ· dʒɚrzɨ^
b nʉ· dʒɚ̆rzɨ^
61a nu<· dʒɚ̆rzɨ^
b nʉ· dʒɚ̆rzɨ^
62a nu< dʒɚrzɨ^
b nu< dʒɚ̆rzɨ^
63a nu<· dʒɚ̆rzɨ^
b nu<· dʒɚ̣·zɨ^
64a nɨw dʒɚ·zɨ^
64b-65a nɨu dʒɚzɨ^
65b nu<· dʒɚzɨ^
66a nu· dʒɚzɨ^
b nɨu< dʒɚzɨ
67ab nɨu< dʒɚzɨ^

WEST VIRGINIA

1-7b ---
8a nʉ dʒɚzɨ^
b ɲjʉ· dʒɚzɨ^
9a nu< dʒᵊɚzɨ^
b nu<· dʒɚzɨ^
10a ɲʲʉ· dʒᵊɚzɨ^
b nu< dʒɚ̆rzɨ^

WVA

10c ---
11ab nʉ· dʒɚzɨ^
12a-13a nu<· dʒɚzɨ^
13b nu<· dʒᵊɚzɨ^
14a nu< dʒɚzɨ^
14b-15a nu< dʒᵊɚzɨ^
15b nu< dʒɚzɨ^
16a nⁱʉ dʒᵊɚzɨ^
b nu<· dʒᵊɚzɨ^
17a ---
b nu<· dʒᵊɚzɨ^
c nu<· dʒɚzɨ^
18a njʉ dʒᵊɚzɨ^
b nu< dʒɚzɨ^
19a njʉ>· dʒɚrzɨ^
b ɲⁱʉ dʒɚzɨ^
20a nⁱʉ dʒɚ̆ṛṛzɨ^
b nⁱʉ dʒɚ̆ṛzɨ^
21a ɲⁱʉ dʒᵊɚzɨ^
b nʉ dʒɚzɨ^
22a njʉ dʒɚzɨ^
b ɲⁱʉ dʒᵊɚzɨ^
23a ɲjʉ dʒɚzɨ^
b njʉ dʒɚzɨ^
24ab ɲjʉ dʒɚzɨ^
25a ɲjʉ· dʒɚzɨ^
25b-26a ɲjʉ dʒɚzɨ^
26b ɲjʉ· dʒɚzɨ^
27a ɲjʉ· dʒᵊɚzɨ^
b ɲjʉ dʒᵊɚzɨ^
28a ɲjʉ· dʒᵊɚzɨ^
b ɲjʉ dʒᵊɚzɨ^
29ab ɲjʉ· dʒᵊɚzɨ^
30a ɲⁱʉ dʒᵊɚzɨ
b ɲjʉ dʒɚ·zɨ^

WVA

31a ɲjʉ dʒᵊɚ̆zɨ^
b ɲⁱʉ dʒᵊɚzɨ^
32ab njʉ dʒɚzɨ^
33a njʉ dʒɚ̆ṛzɨ^
b ɲⁱʉ dʒᵊɚzɨ^
34a njʉ dʒɚzɨ^
b nu<· dʒᵊɚzɨ^
35a njʉ dʒɚzɨ^
b njʉ dʒɚ·zɨ^
36a nu< dʒᵊɚzɨ^
b nʲʉ dʒᵊɚzɨ^
37a nu< dʒɚzɨ^
b nʉ> dʒɚzɨ^
38a nu<· dʒɚzɨ^
b nʉ>· dʒᵊɚzɨ^
39a nʲʉ dʒᵊɚzɨ^
bc nu< dʒɚzɨ^
40a nⁱʉ dʒᵊɚzɨ^
b ɲⁱʉ dʒᵊɚzɨ^
41a nⁱʉ dʒɚzɨ^
b nⁱʉ dʒᵊɚzɨ^
42a nʉ· dʒɚzɨ^
42b-43a nu<· dʒɚzɨ^
43b nʉ>· dʒɚzɨ^
44a nu< dʒɚzɨ^
b nu<· dʒɚzɨ^
45a nu<· dʒᵊɚzɨ^
b nʉ> dʒɚzɨ^
46a nʉ>· dʒɚ̆ṛzɨ^
b nʉ> dʒɚzɨ^
47a nu<· dʒᵊɚzɨ^
b nʉ> dʒɚ·zɨ^
48a nʉ dʒɚzɨ^
bc ---
d nʉ> dʒɚzɨ^

WVA

49a nʉ>· dʒɚ̆ṛṛzɨ^
b nʉ>· dʒɚ·zɨ^
50a nu< dʒɚ̆rzɨ^
b nu<· dʒɚ·zɨ^
51a nu<· dʒᵊɚzɨ^
b nu<· dʒɚ̆ṛzɨ^
52a nʉ>· dʒɚzɨ^
b nu<· dʒɚ·zɨ^
c nu̧ dʒɚzɨ^
53a nu<· dʒɚzɨ^
b ---
c nu<· dʒɚzɨ^
54ab nʉ· dʒɚrzɨ^

OHIO

1a nɨu dʒᵊɚzɨ
b nɨu< dʒɚzɨ
c nu<· dʒɚzɨ^
2a nu< dʒɚzɨ^
b nu<· dʒɚ·zɨ^
3a nu<· dʒɚzɨ^
b nu< dʒɚzɨ^
4a nu< dʒɚ̆ṛzɨ^
b nu<· dʒɚzɨ^
5a ---
b nu< dʒɚzɨ^
c nu<· dʒɚ·zɨ^
6a nu̧ dʒɚzɨ^
6b-7a nu<· dʒɚzɨ^
7b nu<· dʒɚ·zɨ^
8a nu· dʒɚzɨ^
b ---
c nu<· dʒɚzɨ^
d ---
e nju< dʒɚ̣·zɨ
9a nu<· dʒᵊɚzɨ^

OHIO		OHIO		SOUTH CAROLINA		SC	
9b	---	12a	ŋ̩ᶦʉ dʒɚ̌ɽz‡ˆ	11b	nᴵu< dʒɜ̧ˑᵊˣz‡	42e̲	ŋ̩ᴵ̆ʉ dʒɜ>ᵊz‡ˣ
c	nu<· dʒɚz‡ˆ	b	nʉˀ̧ dʒᵊᶿ·z‡ˆ	14b	cv dʒɜ̧ˣ·‡z‡ˣ	GEORGIA	
d	---	12c–18 ---		19b	nᴵʉ dʒɜ>·ᵊz‡ˆ	17	nᴵʉ dʒɜˆ·z‡
10a	nʉ>· dʒɚz‡ˆ	KENTUCKY		27a	nᴵʉ dʒɜ>‡z‡	N25	nʉ dʒɜ>s‡
b	nu<· dʒɚz‡ˆ	2a	ŋ̩ᴵʉ dʒɜ>ɚz‡	35c	nᴵʉ dʒɜ̧ˣ‡z‡ˆ	27	nᴵʉ dʒɜ‡z‡
11a	nu<· dʒɚ̌ɽz‡ˆ	3a	ŋ̩‡ʉ dʒɜ>ɚz‡	37	nᴵʉ dʒɜ̧ˣɚz‡ˆ		cv ˈnʉ· ˌdʒɜˆ‡z‡
b	nu<· dʒɚz‡ˆ					37d̲	nᴵʉ dʒɜ>ɚz‡ˆ

8. PENNSYLVANIA

WS 86.2

Pennsylvania was systematically investigated only in the
MAS and NCS. The usual stress pattern, -ˈv- or ˌ-ˈv-,
is unmarked.

ONTARIO		NY		NY	
1a	pɛntsɫve‡n‡ˆə	3a	pɛ>ntsɫveˇ‡nɟə	7b	pɛ>ntsɫveˇ‡nɟə
1b–2a	---	b	pɛntsɫveˇ‡nɟə	c	pʰɛ>nsɫveˇ‡nɟə
b	ˈpɛˆⁿsɫˌveˇ‡nɟə	3c–4a	pɛntsɫveˇ‡n‡ˆə	d	pʰɛ>ntsɫveˇ‡nɟə
3̲	ˈpɛˆntsɫˌveˇ‡<nɪ̧ə	b	pɛntsɫveˇ‡nɟə	e	pʰɛ>ntsɫveˆ‡nɟə
4a	pɛnzɫve‡nɟə	c	pʰɛntsɫveˇ‡n‡̧ə	f	pɛnsɫveˇ‡nɟə, -ə̧
b	pɪˇntsɫveˇ‡nɟəˆ	5a	pɛntsɫveˇ‡n‡ˆə	g	pʰɛntsɫveˇ‡nɟə
5	---	b	pʰɛntsɫveˇ‡nɟə	h	pɛntsɫveˆ‡nɟə
6̲	pɛnsɫve‡nɟə	c	pɛntsɫve‡nɟə	i	pɛntsɫve‡n‡ˆə
7	ˈpɛntsəɫˌve‡nɟə̌,	d	pɛ>ntsɫveˇ‡n‡ˆə	j̲	pɛntsɫveˇ‡nɟə
	ˈpʿɛntsɫˌve‡nɟə	e	pʰɛntsɫveˇ‡n‡ˆə	k̲	pɛntsɫveˇ‡nɟə
8ab	---	f	pɛ>ntsɫveˇ‡nɟə	l̲	pɛntsɫveˇ‡nɟə
c	cv ˈpɛˆntsɫˌveˇ‡<nɟə	g	pʰɛntsɫveˆ‡nɟə	m̲	pʰɛntsɫveˇ‡nɟə
d	cv pɛˆntsɫveˇ‡nɟə	h̲	pɛntsɫve‡nɟə	8	pɛntsɫve‡nɟə
9̲	cv ˈpɪˇnzɫˌveˇ‡nɟə (√)	i̲	pɛntsɫveˇ‡ˇnɟə	9a	pɛntsɫveˇ‡nɟə
10	cv pɛˆnsɫveˇ·‡nɟə	6a	pʰɛ>ntsɫveˆ‡n‡ˆə	b	pɛntsɫveˇ‡n‡ˆə
NEW YORK		b	pɛntsɫve‡nɟə	9c–10b̲	pɛntsɫveˇ‡nɟə
1–2c	---	7a	pɛntsɫve‡ˇnɟə̌	11	pʰɛntsɫveˇ‡nɟə

NY

12a	pɛntsɫve‡n‡
bc	pɛntsɫveˇ‡nJə
13a	pɛntsɫve‡n‡^
b	pɛntsɫve‡n‡^ə
14a	pɛntsɫve‡nJə
b	pɛntsɫveˇ‡n‡^ə
15a	pɛntsɫve‡n‡^
b	pɛntsɫve‡nJə
16a	pɛntsɫve‡n‡^ə
b	pɛntsɫveˇ‡nJə
17a	pɛntsɫve·‡n‡
b	pɛntsɫveˇ‡n‡^ə
18a	pɛntsɫve‡n‡^
b	pɛntsɫveˇ‡n‡^ə
c	pɛntsɫve‡n‡^ə
19	pɛntsɫve‡nJə
20a	pɛntsɫveˇ‡n‡^
b	pɛntsɫve‡nJə
21	pæ^·ntsɫve·‡ˇn‡^
22	pɛntsɫve·‡nJə
23a	---
b	cv pɛ^ntsɫveˇɪ>nJə
c	pɛ^ntsɫveˇ‡nJə
24ab	pɛntsɫveˇ‡n‡^ə
25a	pɛ>ntsɫveˇ‡nɪɹ-ə
b	pɛ^ntsɫveˇ‡nJə
26a	pɛ^ntsɫveˇ‡<nJə
b	p‘ɛ^ntsɫveˇ·‡nJə
c	---
27a	pɪ^ˇntsɫveˇ·‡nJə
b	---
c	pɛ^ntsɫveˇ‡nJə
28a	pɪ^ˇtsɫveˇ‡nJə
b	p‘ɛ^ntsɫveˇ·‡nɪɹə
29a	---

29b	pɪ^ˇntsɫve·‡nJə
c	pɛntsɫve·‡nJə
30a	'pɪntsɫˌveˇ‡nJə
b	p‘ɛ^ntsɫveˇ·ᵊnɪɹ
cd	---
e	pɛ^nsɫve·‡nJə
31a	pɛ^ntsɫveˇ·‡ŋJə
b	pɛ^ntsɫveˇ·ŋJə (√)
	cv '-ˌveˇ‡<n‡<,
	p‘ɛ^ntsɫveˇ·‡nJə
32a	cv pɪ^ˇntsɫveˇ·‡nJə,
	-səveˇ‡-, pɛ^ntsɫve·‡-
b	pɛ̃^sɫveˇ‡ŋJə
33a	---
b	'pɛ^ntsɫˌveˇ‡nɪɹə
c	pɛ^ntsɫveˇ‡nJə
34a	cv pɛ^ntsɫveˇ‡nJə,
	'-səˌveˇ‡n‡ə
bc	---
d	pɪ^ˇntsɫveˇ‡n‡<ə
35a	pɛntsɫve·‡ˇn‡^
b	pɛntsɫve‡n‡^ə
c	---
36a	pɛntsɫve·‡ˇn‡^ə
36b-37a	pɛntsɫve‡n‡^
37bc	pɛntsɫve·‡ˇn‡^ə
38ab	pɛntsɫve‡n‡^
39a	pɛntsɫveˇ·‡n‡^
b	pɛntsɫve·‡n‡^
40a	pɛntsɫveˇ·‡ˇn‡^
b	pɛntsɫve‡nJə
41	pɛntsɫve‡n‡^ə
42a	pɛntsɫve‡n‡^
b	pɛntsɫve‡nJə
43a	pɛntsɫve·‡n‡^

43b	pɛntsɫve·‡n‡^ə
c	pɛntsɫveˇ‡n‡^ə
44ab	pɛntsɫve‡nJə
45a	cv pɛ^ntsɫveˇ‡ŋJə,
	'-ˌve·ŋJə
b	---
c	cv pɛ^ntsɫveˇ‡<ŋJə
d	cv pɛ^ntsəveˇ·‡ŋJə,
	-sɫ-, -veˇ·‡-, -ve·‡-
46a	cv pɛ^ntsɫveˇ‡ŋJə
b	pɛntsɫve‡n‡^ cv -n‡ɹ,
	-n‡^, -vɛ^‡n‡ˇ
c	pɛnsɫve‡nJə
47a	pɪ^ˇntsəveˇ·ŋJə
	cv 'pɛ^ntsəˌveˇ‡-
b	pɛntsɫve·‡nJə
48a	pɛ^ntsɫveˇ‡<ŋJə cv -sə-
b	---
c	cv pɛ^ntsɫveˇ‡<ŋJə
d	'pɪ^ˇntsɫˌveˇ‡<ŋJə
49a	cv pɛ^ntsɫveˇ‡<ŋJə
b	---
c	pɛntsəve‡ŋJə, -sɫ-
	cv '-ˌve‡n‡ə
	*'pɛnsɫˌve‡nJə
d	pɛntsəve‡ŋJə cv '-sɫˌ-
50a	pɪ^ˇntsɫveˇ‡<ŋJə
b	cv 'pɛ^ntsɫˌveˇ‡<ŋJə
51a	cv pɛ^ntsəve·‡ŋJə,
	-sɫ-, -veˇ‡-
b	pɛ^ntsɫveˇ‡ŋJə,
	pɛnsɫveˇ‡ŋᴶə
c	cv pɛ^ntsɫveˇ‡ŋJə
de	---
52a	pɛ^nsəveˇ‡ŋJə

NY

52b	cv	pɪˀntsəveˇɨ‹ŋɹə
c		pɛntsəveɨŋɹə
53a	cv	pɛˆntsɫveˇɨŋɹə
b		pɛˆntsɫveˇɨnɹə
	cv	pɪˇntsɫveˇɨŋɹə
54a		pɛntsəveɨŋɹə
b		ˈpɛntsəˌveɨŋɹə
55a		pˈɛˆntsɫveˇ·ŋɹə
	cv	ˈpɛˆntsɫˌveˇ·ɨ‑
b		pɛˆntsɫveˇ·ɨŋɹə
56a		pɛˆntsɫveˇɨŋɨ cv ‑ŋɹə
b		pɛˆntsɫveˇɨŋɹə
	cv	‑nɨ‹, ˈ‑ˌveˇɨŋɹə
57a		pɛˆntsɫveˇɨŋɹə
b		cv pɛˆntsəveˇ·ɨŋɹə
c		pɛ̃ˆnsɫveˇɨŋɹə
58a		cv pɛˆntsɫve·ɨŋɹə
b		cv ˈpɛˆntsɫˌveˇɨŋɹə
c		‑‑‑
d		pɛˆntsəveˇɨnɹə›
e		pɛˆntsɫveˇɨnɪˀə
f		‑‑‑
59a		pɛˆntsɫveˇɨŋɹə
	cv	pɪ̃ntsɫveˇɨ‑
b		pɛntsɫveɨŋɹə
60a		cv pɛˆntsɫveˇɨŋɹə
b		ˈpɛˆntsɫˌveˇɨŋɨ
61a		pɛˆntsɫve·nɪˀə
b		pɛˆntsɫveˇɨŋɹə
62a		‑‑‑
b		pɛˆntsɫve·ɨnɪˀ
c		ˈpɛˆntsɫˌve·ɨŋɹə
d		cv ˈpɛˆntsɫˌve·ɪˀŋɹə
63a		ˈpˈɛˆntsɫˌveˇɨŋɹə
	cv	pɛ̃ˆnsɫveˇ·ɨ‑

NY

63b		pɛˆntsɫveˇɨŋɹə
c		pɛntsɫveɨŋɹə
d		pɛˆntsɫveˇ·ɨŋɹə
64a		pɛˆntsɫveˇ·ɨŋɹə
	cv	ˈ‑ˌve·ɨ‑
b		pɛˆntsɫve·ɨnɹə
c		cv pɛˆntsɫveˇ·ɨnɹə

NEW JERSEY

1a‑5b		‑‑‑
6a		pʰɛntsɫveˆɨnɹə
6b‑7a		‑‑‑
b		pɛntsɫveɨŋɹə
8a		pɛntsɫveˆɨnɨˆ
b		pɛntsɫveˇɨnɹə
9a		pɛntsɫweɨnɨɨˆ
b		pɛntsɫveˆɨnɹə
10a		pɛntsɫve›ɨnɹə
b		pɛntsɫveɨnɨˆə
c		pɛntsɫveɨɨˆnɹə
d		pɛ›ntsɫveˇɨnɹə
11ab		pɛntsɫveɨŋɹə
c		pɛntsɫveˆɨnɨˀ
12a		pɛntsɫve›ɨnɹə
b		pɛntsɫveɨnɨˆ
13a‑15a		pɛntsɫveɨnɹə
15b		pɛntsɫveɨnɹɨ‹
16a		pɛntsɫveɨnɹə
b		pɛ›ntsɫveɨnɹə
17a		pɛntsɫveˇɨnɹə
b		pɛntsɫveˇɨnɨˆə
18a		pʰɛntsɫveˇɨnɹə
b		pʰɛ›ntsɫveˀnɹə
c		pɛnsɫveˇɨnɹə
d		pɛntsɫveɨnɹə
19a		pʰɛ›ntsɫveˇɨnɹə

NJ

19b		pɛntsɫveˇɨnɹə
20a		pɛntsɫveˇɨnɹə
b		pʰɛntsɫveɨnɹə
21a		pɛntsɫveˇɨnɹə
b		pʰɛntsɫveˇɨnɹə

PENNSYLVANIA

1a		pɛntsɫveˀɨnɹə
bc		pɛntsɫveɨnɹə
d		pɛntsɫveˆɨnɹə
e		pɛntsɫve›ɨnɹə
f		pɛntsɫveˇɨnɹə
g		pɛntsɫveɨnɹə
h		‑‑‑
2ab		pɛntsɫveɨnɹə
3a		pɛntsɫveˇɨnɹə
b		pɛntsɫveɨnɹə
c		pɛntsɫveˇɨnɹə
4a		pɛntsɫveˇɨnɨ
b		pɛntsɫveˆɨnɹə
5a		pɛntsɫveˆɨnɨ
b		pɛntsɫveɨnɹə
c		pɛntsɫveˆɨnɨˆə
d		pɛntsɫveɨˇnɹə
e		pɛntsɫveɨnɹə
6a		pɛnsɹve·nɨ
b		pɛntsɹveɨˇnɹə
c		pɛnsɹve·nɹə
d		pɛntsɹve·nɹə
7a		pɛntsɫveɨnɨˆ
b		pɛntsɫveɨnɹə
c		pɛnsɹve·nɨˆə
d		pɛntsɫveˇɨnɹə
8a		pɛntsɫveɨˇnɨˆ
b		‑‑‑
c		pɛnsəɹve·nɹə

PA

8d̲	pɛntsɫveɫnjə
9a	pɛntsɪʋe·nɫ
b	pɛntsɫweˇɫnɫ (√)
c̲	pɛntsɫvɛɫnjə
10	pɛntsə̆lʋe·njə
11ab	pɛntsɫveˇɫnjə
12a	pɛntsɫveˇ·ɫˇnɫˆ
b	pɛntsɫveɫnjə
13a	pɛntsɫveɫnɫˆ
b	pɛntsɫveɫnjə
14a	pɛnsəlʋe·njə
b	pɛntsɪveɫnjə
15ab	pɛntsɫveˇɫnjə
c̲	pɛntsɫvɛɫnɫˆə
16a	p̄ɛnnsɪʋe·njə
b	pɛntsɫveɫnjə
c	---
17a	pɛnnsɪʋe·nɫˆ
b	pɛntsɪʋe·njə
18a	pɛntsɫveɫnjə
b̲	pɛntsɫveˇɫnjə
19a	pɛntsɫveˇɫnɫ
b	pɛntsɫveˇɫnjə
20a	pɛntsɫveˇɫnɫ
b	pɛntsɫveˇɫnjə
21a	pɛntsɫve·ɫˇnɫ
b	pɛntsɫveɫnjə
22a	pɛntsɫveɫˇnɪɫ
22b–23a	pɛntsɫve·ɫˇnjə
23b–24a	pɛntsɫveɫnjə
24b	pɛntsɫve·ɫˇnjə
25a	pɛntsɫveɫnɪɫ
b	pɛntsɫveɫnjə
26a	pɛntsɫveˇ·ɫnɫ
b	pɛntsɫveɫnjə

PA

27a	*pɛntsɫveɫnjə
b	pɛntsɫveɫnjə
28a	pɛntsɫve·ɫnɫˆ
b̲	pɛntsɫveˇɫnjə
29a	pɛnsɫweˇnjə
b	pɛntsɫveɫnjə
30a	pɛntsɫve·ɫˇnɫ
b	pɛntsɫveˇɫnjə
31a–32b	pɛntsɫveˇɫnjə
33a	pɛntsɫveˇɫnɫˆ
b	pɛntsɫveˆɫnjə
34a	pɛntsɫveˇɫnɫ
b	pɛntsɫveˇɫnjə
c̲	*pɛntsɫvɛɫnjə
35a	pɛntsɫveˆɫnɫˆ
b	pɛntsɫveˇɫnjə
36a	pɛntsɫveɫnə
b	pɛntsɫve·ɫˇnjə
37a	pɛnsɪʋe·nɫˆ
b	pɛntsə̆lweɫnjə
38a	pɛntsɫveɣɫnjə
b	pɛntsɫveˇɫnjə
39a	pɛˈntsɫveɫnjə
b	pɛntsɫveˇɫnjə
40a	pɛntsɫveˆɫnjə
b	pɛntsɫvɛɫnjə
41ab	pɛntsɫveɫnjə
42a	pɛntsɫveˇɫnɫˆ
42b–45b	pɛntsɫveˇɫnjə
46a	pɛntsɫveˇɫnɫˆ
b	pɛntsɫveˇɫnjə
47ab	pɛntsɫvɛɫnjə
48a	pɛntsɫvɛɫnɫˆ
bc	pɛntsɫvɛɫnjə
49a	pɛntsɫvɛˆɫnjə

PA

49b	pɛntsɫveˇɫnjə
50a	---
b	pɛntsɫveɫnjə
c̲	pɛntsɫvɛɫnjə
51ab	pɛntsɫveˇɫnjə
52a	pɛntsɫveɫnɫ
b̲	pɛntsɫvɛɫnjə
53a	pɛntsɫveˈɫnjə
53b–55b	pɛntsɫveɫnjə
56a	pɛntsɫveɫnjə
b	pɛntsɫveɫnjə
57ab	pɛntsɫveˇɫnjə
58ab	pɛntsɫvɛɫnjə
59a	pɛntsɫveˇɫnɫˆ
59b–60a	pɛntsɫveˇɫnjə
60b	pɛntsɫveˈɫnjə
61a	pɛntsɫveˇɫnɫˆ
b	pɛntsɫvɛɣɫnjə
62a	pɛntsɫveˇɫˇnɫ
62b–63a	pɛntsɫveˇɫnɫˆ
63b–64a	pɛntsɫveɫnjə
64b	pɛntsɫveˇɫnjə
65a	pɛntsɫvɛɫnɫɫˆ
b	pɛntsɫvɛˆɫnjə
66a	pɛntsɫvɛˆɫnɪɫ
b	pɛntsɫveˇɫnɫˆ
67ab	pɛntsɫveˇɫnjə

WEST VIRGINIA

1̲–7b	---
8a	pɛntsɫveɫnɫˆ
b	pɛntsɫveɫnjə
9a	pɛntsɫveˇɫnɫˆ
b	pɛntsɫveˇɫnɫ
10a	pɛntsɫvɛɫnɫˆ
b	pɛntsɫveˇɫnɫˆ

WVA

10c	pɛntsɫveˀɨnjə
11a	pɛntsɫveˇɨnjɨˆ
b	pɛntsɫveɨnjə
12a–13a	pɛntsɫveˇɨnjə
13b	pɛˆntsɫveˆɨnjɨˆ
14a	pɛntsɫvɛˆɨnjə
b	pɛntsɫveˇɨnjɨˆ
15a	pɛntsɫvɛˆɨnɨˆ
b	ˈpɛntsɫˈveˇɨnjə
16a	pɛntsɫveˇɨnɨˆ
b	pɛntsɫveˇɨnjɨˆ
17a	---
17b–18a	pɛntsɫveˇɨnjə
18b	pɛntsɫvɛˆɨnjə
19a	pɛntsɫveɨnjə
b	pɛntsɫveˇɨnjə
20a	pɛntsɫveɨnɨˆ
b	pɛntsɫveɨnjɨˆ
21a	pɛntsɫveɨnɨˆ
21b–22a	pɛntsɫveɨnjɨˆ
22b–23a	pɛntsɫveɨnjə
23b	pɛntsɫveɨnjə
24a	pɛntsɫveɨnɨˆ
b	pɛntsɫveˇɨnjə
25a	pɛntsɫveɨnjə
b	pɛntsɫveˇɨnjə
26a	pɛntsɫveɨnɨ
b	pɛntsɫveɨnjə
27ab	pɛntsɫvɛˆɨnjə
28ab	pɛntsɫveˇɨnjə
29a	pɛntsɫveˇɨnɨˆ
b	pɛntsɫvɛˆɨnjə
30a	pɛntsɫveˇɨnɨˆ
b	pɛntsɫvɛˆɨnjə
31ab	pɛntsɫveɨnjə

WVA

32ab	pɛntsɫveˇɨnɨˆ
33a	pɛntsɫveˇɨnjə
b	pɛntsɫveɨnjə
34a	pɛntsɫveɨnɨˆ
b	pɛntsɫvɛˆɨnjə
35a	pɛntsɫveˇɨnɨˆ
b	pɛntsɫveˇɨnjə
36a	pɛntsɫvɛˆɨnɨˆ
b	pɛntsɫvɛˆɨnjɨˆ
37a	pɛntsɫveˇɨnɨˆ
b	pɛntsɫveɨnjə
38a	pɛntsɫvɛˆɨnɨˆ
b	pɛntsɫvɛˆɨnjə
39a	pɛntsɫveˇɨnjɨˆ
bc	pɛntsɫveˇɨnjə
40a	pɛntsɫveɨnjɨ
b	pɛntsɫvɛˆɨnjə
41a	pɛntsɫveɨnɨˆ
41b–42a	pɛntsɫveˇɨnɨˆ
42b	pɛntsɫveˇɨnjɨˆ
43a	pɛntsɫveɨnjɨˆ
b	pɛntsɫvɛˆɨnjə
44a	pɛntsɫveˇɨnjɨˆ
b	pɛntsɫvɛˆɨnjə
45a	pɛntsɫvɛˆɨnjɨˆ
b	pɛntsɫveˇɨnjə
46a	pɛntsɫveɨnɨˆ
b	pɛntsɫveˇɨnjə
47ab	pɛntsɫvɛˆɨnjə
48a	pɛntsɫveˇɨnjə
bc	---
d	pɛntsɫvɛˆɨnjə
49a	pɛntsɫveˇɨnjɨˆ
b	pɛntsɫvɛˆɨnjə
50a–51a	pɛntsɫveˇɨnjə

WVA

51b	pɛntsɫveˇɨnɨˆ
52a	pɛntsɫveˆɨnɨˆ
bc	pɛntsɫveˆɨnjə
53a	pɛntsɫvɛˆɨnjɨˆ
b	---
c	pɛntsɫveɨnjə
54a	pɛntsɫveˇɨnjə
b	pɛntsɫveˇɨnɨˆ

OHIO

1a	pɛntsɫveɨnɨ
bc	pɛntsɫveɨnjə
2ab	pɛntsɫveˇɨnjə
3a	pɛntsɫveɨnɨˆə
3b–4b	pɛntsɫveˇɨnjə
5a	pɛnsɪveɪnjə
b	pɛntsɫveˇɨnjɨˆ
c	pɛntsɫveˇɨnjə
6a	pɛntsɫveˇɨnɨˆ
6b–7a	pɛntsɫveˇɨnjə
b	pɛntsɫveɨnjə
8a	pɛntsɫveˇɨnɨˆ
b	pɛnsɪveɪnjə
c	pɛntsɫveˇɨnjə
d	pɛnsəˑɪveɪniə
e	pɛntsɨɫveˇɨnjə
9a	pɛntsɫveˇɨnjɨˆ
b	pɛnsɪlveɪniˇ
c	pɛntsɫveˇɨnjə
d	pɛnsɪlveɪniə
10a	pɛntsɫveˇɨnɨˆ
b	pɛntsɫveˇɨnjɨˆ
11a	pɛnntsɫveˇɨnɨˆ
b	pɛntsɫveˇɨnjə
12a	pɛntsɫveˇɨnjɨˆ
b	pɛntsɫveˇɨnjə

OHIO

12c-13a   ---

13b   pɛnsəveˇ‡nJə

c   pə‹nsɪlveɪniˇə

14   <u>cv</u> pɛˆntslve‡ŋJə

15a   ˈpɛnsəˌveˇ‡nJə

b   pɛnsəve‡nJə

16a   pɛnsɫvɛˆ‡ŋJ‡

b   pɪˇnsɫvɛˆ‡ŋJə,

   pɛntsɫvɛ‡-

c   pɛˆnᵗsɫvɛˆ‡ŋJə

17   <u>cv</u> pɛˆntsɫvɛˆ‡ŋJə,

   ˈ-ˌveˇ‡ŋJ‡

18   *pɛˆntsɫvɛˆ‡nJə

KENTUCKY

la   pɪˇntsɫveˇ‡n‡

b   <u>cv</u> pɛˆntsɫvɛˆ‡ŋJəˆ

2a   pɪntsɫve·‡n‡‡ˆ

b   ---

c   pɛntsɫve·‡ŋ‡‡ˇ

3a   pɪˇntsɫve·‡ŋJ‡

KY

3bcd   ---

e   ˈpɛˆntsɫˌve·‡n‡

4a   pɛˆntsɫve·‡ᵢJ‡

b   ˈpˈɛntsɫˌve·‡ŋJ‡

c   pˈɪntsɫve·‡ŋJəˆ

5a   pɛˆntsɫve·‡n‡

b   pɛˆntsɫve·‡ŋJə

6a   pɛˆntsIve‡ŋJə

b   ---

c   ˈpɪntsəɫˌve·‡ŋJə

7a   pɛˆntsɫve·‡ŋJ‡

b   pɪntsɫve·‡ŋJə

SOUTH CAROLINA

llb   pɛnsIve·ᵊnJə

19b   pɛnᵗsəlve·ŋJə

20d   <u>cv</u> ˈpɛˆntsəˌve·‡ŋJə

24a   ˈpɛntsIˌve·nᶦə

27a   ˈpɪnᵗsəlˌve·nJə

35c   <u>s</u> ˈpɪntsɫˌveˇ‡ŋJ‡

37   p‡ɕntsɫve·‡nJə

SC

38b   ˈpˈɛˆntsɫˌve·ᶦnJə

42<u>e</u>   p‡ntsɫve‡ŋJə

GEORGIA

N1   pɛnts‡venJə

1b   ˈpɛntsIˌve·nJə

N11   pɪntsIve·nJə

17   pɛnsəlveᶦnJə

22a   pɛntsəˡve·‡ŋJə,

   ˈpɪ›ntsɫˌ-

23<u>f</u>   pɪntsIve·nJə

<u>27</u>   ˈpˈᛒnts‡Ive‡nJə

28   pɛnsɫve‡ŋJəˆ

29b   <u>cv</u> pɪˇntsIve·ˆ·ŋJə

30<u>c</u>   <u>cv</u> ˈpˈɛˆntsɫˌve‡ŋJə

37<u>d</u>   pɛntsɫve‡ŋJə,

   pɪˇntsɫve·‡-

<u>i</u>   <u>cv</u> ˈpɛntsIˌve‡nJə

FLORIDA

4   <u>cv</u> pɛntsɫveˇ‡ŋJə, -sə-

COMMENTARY

ONTARIO

7   *Pennsylvania* Dutch

   [ˈpˈ- ˈdʌ‹t∫]

8c   <u>cv</u> pɛˆntsɫve·‡‹ŋJəˆnz

9   [z]: *sic*; *Pennsylvania*

   Dutch <u>cv</u> [~ ˈdʌˆt∫]

NEW YORK

27c, 28b   [ɫ]: strongly velarized

31b   [eˇ·]: *sic*

34a   *Pennsylvania* Dutch

   <u>cv</u> [ˈ~ ˈdʌˆt∫]

PENNSYLVANIA

8c   [pɪnsəlfɔˆ·n‡]:

PA

(8c)   Pa. German form

9b   [w]: *sic*

16a   [p̄ensɭfɔˆ·n‡ˆ]:

   Pa. German form

17a   [pɛnnsɭfɔˇ·n‡ˆ]:

   Pa. German form

9. OHIO

WS 86.2

Ohio was systematically investigated in the MAS and NCS, and for the preliminary SAS survey. The regular stress pattern, ˌ-ˈh- or -ˈ-, is unmarked.

ONTARIO

1a	əha^ǂə
b	ˌo^{U}ˈhɑ^ǂˌo^{U}
2a	---
b	ɔ<̭u<hɑ^ǂə̮^{ʉ}
3	o<̬u<hɑ<̭ǂə̮^{ʉ}
4a	ˌɔ^uˈhɑ^ǂˌoˇ$^{U<}$
b	ˌo^{U}ˈhɐˇǂˌo<$^{U<}$
5	---
6	əhɑ<ǂɔ̆^^{U}
7	cv o<̬u<ˈhɐǂˌo<$^{U<}$
8a	---
b	ˌɵu<ˈhɐˇ·ǂˌo<̬u<
c	ˌɵ>u<ˈhɐˇǂˌɵ>u<
d	o<̬u<hɑ^ǂə̮^{ʉ}
9	ɵu<hɑ^ǂə̮
10	o<u<hɐǂɔ̆^ŭ

NEW YORK

1-2c	---
3a	o<̬uhɑ^ǂ>ɞu
b	ɞ̆>ŭha>ǂ>ŏŭ
c	o<̬uhaǂo<̬u
d	ˌo<uˈha>ǂˌo<u
4a	ɞuha>ǂɞu
b	o<uha>̭ǂo<u
c	ɞ>uha>ǂɞ̆>ŭ^
5a	o<̬uha>ǂər̮
b	o<̬uhaǂŏ<̬ŭ
c	ŏ<̬ŭhaǂŏ<̬ŭ
de	ɞ>uhaǂɞ>u
f	ɞ>uhaǂɞ̆ŭ

NY

5g	ɞ>uha>ǂɞ>u
h	ɞ>uhaǂɞu
i	ɞuhaǂɞu
6a	o<̬uhɑ^ǂoˇu
b	o<̬uhaǂo<̬u
7a	ŏ<ŭhaǂə
b	o<̬uhaǂo<̬u
c	o<̬uhɑ<ǂə
d	ɞ>uhaǂɞ>u
e	ɞuha·ǂɞu
f	o<̬uhaǂo<̬u
g	o<̬uhaǂə
h	ɞ>̭uhaǂɞ>̭u
i	ɞ>uha>ǂɞ>u
j	o<̬uhaǂə
k	o<̬uhaǂo<̬u
l	ɞuhaǂɞu
m	o<̬uhaǂo<̬u
8	o<uhaǂou
9a	oˇuhaǂŏ<̬ŭ
b	ouhɐǂou
c	o<̬uhaǂo<̬u
10a	o<uhaǂ<ou
b	o<uhaǂə
11	o<̬uha>ǂə
12a	ouhɐǂou
b	oˇuhaǂoˇu
c	ŏ<̬ŭhaǂŏ<̬ŭ
13a	o^{U}haǂo^{U}
b	o<uhaǂŏ<ŭ

NY

14a	o<̬uhaǂou
b	o<̬uhaǂo<̬u
15a	oˇ·^{Uˇ}ha>ǂoˇ^{Uˇ}
b	o^{U}ha>̭ǂo^{U}
16a	o^{U}ha>ǂo^{U}
b	o<̬uhaǂə
17a	ouhɐˇǂou
b	oˇuhaǂoˇu
18a	o^{U}hɐǂo^{U}
b	o<̬uha>̭ǂou
c	ouha>ǂou
19	o>̬^{U}ˈha>ǂˌo<̬u
20a	oˇuha>̭ǂo<̬u
b	oˇuhaǂou
21	o^{U}ha>̭ǂə
22	oˇ·^{Uˇ}ha>ǂə
23a	---
b	ɔ^uhɑ·ǂo<̬$^{U<}$
c	o<·u<hɑ·ǂɵ^{ʉ}
24a	o<̬uha>̭ǂo<̬u
b	ɵˇuha>̭ǂə
25a	ˈo<·u<ˌhɑ·ǂo<̬^{U}
b	ˌɔ^uˈhɑ·ǂˌɵ^{U}
26a	---
b	oˇhɐ·ɪ>ə̮
c	---
27a	ˌɔ^^{U}ˈhɑ·ǂˌo<·$^{U<}$
b	---
c	o<u<hɐ>ǂə̮
28a	ˌo<·u<ˈhɑ·ǂˌo<u<

NY

28b	o<u<hɑ·ǂə̮
29a	---
b	o<u<hɑ·ǂə̮
c	o<u<hɑ<̭·ǂɵ^{ʉ}
30a	ˌo<u<ˈhɐ·ǂˌo<·u<
b	o<u<hɑ·ǂə̮
cd	---
e	ˌo<u<ˈhɐ·ǂ<ˌɵ^{ʉ}
31a	o<̬u<ɦɐ·ǂo<̬u<
b	o<̬uˈhɐ·ǂˌɵʉ>
32a	o<̬u<hɐ·ǂə̮
b	o<̬u<ˈhɐ·ǂˌɔ<̭u
33a	---
b	o<u<hɑ^·ǂə
c	o<u<ˈhɑ·ǂˌo<u<
34a	o<̬u<hɐ·ǂə̮^{ʉ}
bc	---
d	ˌo<̬u<ˈhɑ<̭ǂˌo<̬u<
35a	o^{U}hɐˇǂə
b	o^{U}hɐˇǂo^{U}
c	---
36a	o^{U}ha>̭ǂo^{U}
b	o^{U}hɐˇǂə
37a	əha>̭ǂo<̬^{U}
37b-38a	o^{U}ha>̭ǂo^{U}
38b	o^{U}hɐˇǂə
39a	o^{U}ha>̭ǂo<̬u
b	o^{U}hɐˇǂə
40a	o^{U}ha>̭ǂo^{U}
b	o^{U}ha>̭ǂə

NY		NY		NEW JERSEY		PENNSYLVANIA	
41	oᵁheˇɫə	(54a)	o·ᵁheɫoᵁ	1a-5b	---	1a	oʂᵁhaɫə
42a	oᵁhaʐɫoᵁ	54b	oʂuhaˆɫo<ᵁ<	6a	ɞˆuhɑ<ɫə	b	oʂuha>ɫə
b	oᵁha>ɫˇŏᵁ	55a	oʂ·u<heˇɫo<ᵁ<	6b-7a	---	c	oʂᵁha>ɫoʂu
43a	oᵁheˇɫoᵁ		cv ᵢo<u<ˈhe·ɫᵢo<ᵁ<	7b	ɞ>uhaɫɞu	d	oᵁhaɫə
b	oᵁheˇɫə	b	ᵢoʂ·ᵁheʐ·ɫᵢeᵁ	8a	o<uha>ɫo<u	e	ouhaɫou
c	oʂuhaɫoʂu	56a	cv oʂu<ˈhe·ɫᵢo<ᵁ<,	b	o<uha>ɫə	f	ɞuhaɫ·ŏŭ
44a	oᵁheʂɫoᵁ		-ˈheˆ·ɫ-,	9a	ɞ>uhaʂɫə	g	oʂuha>ɫoʂu
b	ouheɫə		ᵢeʉ>ˈheˇɪ-	b	o<uhɑ<ɫə	h	---
45abc	---	b	e<ᵁhe·ɫə	10a	oʂuhɑ<ɫə	2a	oʂuhaɫə
d	oʂu<ˈhaˆɫᵢoʂu<	57a	oʂu<ˈha·ɫᵢo<u<	b	ɞ>uhaɫə	b	oʂuha>ɫo<ᵁ
46a	ᵢoʂu<ˈheˇɫᵢo<ŭ<	b	---	c	ɞ>uha>ɫˆə	3a	oʂuha>ɫə
b	oᵁheɫˆŏᵁ	c	oʂu<haʂ·ɫə	d	oʂuha>ɫoʂu	b	ŏʂŭha>ɫə
c	oᵁhaˆɫəᵝ	58a	ᵢo<u<ˈhaˆɫᵢo<ᵁ<	11a	ɞ>uhɑ<ɫə	c	oʂuhaɫə
47a	o<u<heˇɫo<ᵁ<	b	ɔˆŭhɑ·ɫə	b	ɞ>uhaɫɞ>u	4a	oʂᵁha>ɫə
b	oᵁhaʐɫoᵁ	c	---	c	oʂuha>ɫə	b	oᵁha>ɫə
48a	eᵁheˇɫə	d	o<ᵁ<ˈhe·ɫᵢo<u<	12a	ɞ>uhaɫə	5a	o<uha>ɫə
b	---	e	ᵢe>u<ˈhaˆɫᵢo<ᵁ<	b	əha>ɫə	b	oʂuha>ɫə
c	oʂu<heɫəᵝ	f	---	13a	ɞ>uha>ɫə	c	ɞ>uhɑ<ɫə
d	oʂu<haʂɫə	59a	oʂu<hɑˆ·ɫo<ᵁ<	b	ɞ>uhɑ<ɫə	d	oʂuhaɫə
49ab	---	b	oᵁheɫoᵁ	14a	oʂuhɑ<ɫoʂu	e	o<uhaɫˇə
c	oᵁˈha>ɫᵢoᵁ	60a	oʂu<ˈheˆ·ɫᵢo<ᵁ<	b	ɞ>uha>ɫɞu	6a	o·haɫə
d	ᵢoᵁˈhaɫᵢou	b	ˈo<u<ᵢhaˆɫə	15ab	oʂuha>ɫə	bc	o·haɫo<
50a	ᵢoʂu<ˈhaˆɫᵢoʂu<	61a	o<ᵁhɑ·ɫə	16a	ɞʂuha>ɫə	d	oᵁhaɫə
b	ɔˆuhɑˆɫə	b	o<u<heˇ·ɫə	b	oʂuhɑ·ɫoʂu	7ab	ɵ>uhaɫə
51a	o<ᵁ<heˇ·ɫə	62a	---	17a	ɞ>uhɑˆɫə	c	o·haɫə
	cv ᵢeᵝ>ˈhaˆɫᵢo<ᵁ<	b	o<uhaʂɫə	b	o<uha<ɫŏ<ŭ	d	oʂuhaɫə
b	oʂu<ha>ɫəᵝ	c	o<u<he·ɫo<ᵁ<	18a	ɞ>uha·ɫɞ>u	8a	əɦa>ɫə
c	oʂu<ˈheˇ·ɫᵢoʂᵁ<	d	o<u<hɑˆ·ɫə	b	ɞ>uhaɫɞu	b	---
de	---	63a	o<ŭ<hɑˆɫə	c	ɞʂuhaɫɞʐu	c	oˆ·ˈhaɫᵢoˆ
52a	ᵢoʂu<ˈhaˆ·ɫᵢoʂu<	b	o<uˇhaʂɫə	d	ɞuhaɫɞu	d	o·ha·ɫˇə
b	---	c	oˇᵁhaʐɫˆɑᵁ	19ab	oʂuhaɫoʂu	9a	o·haɫə
c	oʂᵁheɫŏ<ᵁ	d	---	20a	oˇᵁhaɫoᵁ	b	oᵁha>ɫə
53a	ᵢɔˆuˈheˇ·ɫᵢoʂᵁ<	64a	ᵢo<u<ˈheˇɫᵢo·ᵁ<	20b-21a	o<uha>ɫo<u	c	oʂuhaɫə
b	oʂu<heʂɫə	b	o<··ŭ<he<··ɫeᵝ>	21b	ɞ>uha>ɫɞ>u	10	o·haɫə
54a	o<ᵁ<heɫo·ᵁ,	c	---			11a	oᵁhaɫə

PA

11b o‹uhaɫə
12a oᵁhaɫə
b o·ᵁhaɫə
13ab oᵁhaɫə
14a ŏhaɫə
b oᵁhaɫə
15a oᵁha›ɫoᵁ
b ouhaʑɫə
c oᵁha›ɫou
16a o·haɫo‹
b oᵁhaɫŏ‹
c ---
17a o·haɫə
b o·ha›ɫŏ
18a oᵁhaɫə
b oˇuhaɫə
19a ouha›ɫoᵁ
b oʂuha›ɫə
20a ouha›ɫoᵁ
b ouha›ɫŏ‹ᵁ
21a oᵁheˇɫoᵁ
b oᵁhaʑɫoᵁ
22a oˇᵁˇhaʑɫoˇᵁˇ
b oˇᵁhaʑɫə
23a oᵁˇhaʑɫə
b oᵁhaɫə
24a oˇᵁha›ɫoˇᵁ
b oˇᵁˇhaʑɫə
25a oᵁhaɫoᵁ
b oᵁhaɫŏᵁ
26a o·ᵁˇhaʑɫoᵁ
b oᵁhaʑɫə
27a *oˇuhaɫə
b oᵁhaʑɫə
28ab oᵁhaɫə

PA

29a oʑᵁhaɫ^ə
b oᵁhaɫə
30a oᵁhaʑɫə
b oᵁhaɫoᵁ
31a oˇuhaʑɫoˇu
b ouhaʑɫə
32a oᵁha›ɫə
b o‹ha›ɫə
33a ɢʑuhaɫə
33b-34a o‹uhaɫə
34b o‹ha›ɫə
c *oʂuhaɫə
35a oʂuha·ɫə
b o‹uha›ɫə
36a əᵁhaɫoᵁ
b o·ᵁhaɫə
37a o·haɫə
b oᵁhaɫə
38a oʂuɦaɫə
b o‹ᵁhaɫə
39a oᵁhaɫə
b o‹uhaɫə
40a o‹uha›ɫə
b ɢ›uhaɫə
41a o·haɫ^ə
b oʑ·ha·ɫˇə
42ab o‹uhaɫə
43a o‹uhaʑɫə
b o‹ᵁhɑ‹ɫˇə
44ab o‹uhaɫə
45a əhaɫə
b o‹uhaɫə
46a əhaɫə
b ɢ^u^haɫˇə
47a o‹uhaɫə

PA

47b ɢʑuhaɫˇə
48a əhaɫə
b ɢ›uhaɫə
48c-49b ɢuhaɫə
50a ---
bc ɢ›uhaɫə
51a əhaɫə
51b-52a oʂuhaɫə
52b ouhaɫou
53a əhaɫə
b ɢ›uhaɫə
54a əhaɫə
b ɢ›uhaɫə
55a o‹ᵁhaɫŏ‹ᵁ
b ɢ^uhaɫɢ^u
56ab əhaɫə
57a ɢuhaɫ^ə
b ɢʑuhaɫə
58ab əhaɫə
59a ouhaɫə
b ɢ›uhaɫə
60a ɢuhaɫə
b ɢ›uhaɫə
61a o‹uhaɫə
b ɢ^uhaɫə
62a o‹uhaɫə
b oᵁhaɫə
63a o·haɫə
b o‹uhaɫə
64a oˇuhaʑɫə
b ouheˇɫoˇu
65a oᵁhaɫoᵁ
b eˇᵁhaɫə
66a əhaɫə
b oˇuhaɫoˇu

PA

67ab ouheˇɫə

WEST VIRGINIA

1-4a ---
4b oᵁha›ɛ›ə
5-7b ---
8a əha·ɛu
b oᵁha›·ɛə
9a o‹uhaɛ^o‹u
b əha›ɫˇə
10a əhaʑɫə
b əɦa›·ɫˇə
c o‹uha›·ɛə
11a əhaɫə
b o‹uhaɫo‹u
12a əhaɫə
b əhaɛ^ə
13a əha·ɫˇə
b oᵁha›·ɛ›ə
14a əhaɫə
b o‹uha›ɛə
15a əha›ɫˇə
b əhaɫə
16a ---
b əha›·ɫˇə
17a ---
b əhaɫˇə
c əhaɫə
18a əhaɫˇə
b ɢuhaɛ^ə
19a əhaɫə
b o‹uhaɛə
20a əha›·ɛə
b o‹u^haɛo‹u
21a ouha·ɛə
b ɢ›uhaɛə

WVA		WVA		OHIO		OHIO	
22a	ouhaɨˇə	39c	ouhaɛə	1a	əheɨə	(13b)	cv ŏhaɨə
b	o<uhaɨˇo<ʊ	40a	əha>·ɨˇə	b	oˇuhaʑɨə	13c	ouhɑɪoŭˇ
23a	oᵁha·ɛoᵁ	b	əha>ɛə	c	oˇuhaʑɨə, -oˇʊ	14	cv əha>·ɨə,
b	o<ᵁha·ɛə	41a	oᵁha·ɛ>oᵁ	2a	eˇuhaʑɨə		əha>ɨə
24a	oᵁha·ɛə	b	əha>·ɛ>ou	b	oʂuhaʑɨə	15a	---
b	əᵁha·ɛoᵁ	42a	əhaɨˇə	3a	ŏ<ŭhaʑɨ^ə	b	ouhaɨə, əha·ɨə
25a	oᵁhaɨə	b	o<uhaɨə	b	o<uhaɨo<ʊ,	16a	eˇᵁhaʑ·-ə
b	əha·ɛə	43a	əhaɨˇə		əhaʑɨə		cv əha>ɨə
26a	əˈha>·ɛ^ˌo<ᵁ	b	əha>·ɛə	4a	əhaɨə	b	əhaʑ·ə
b	o·ᵁha·ɛə	44a	əhaɨə	b	ɜ>uhaɨ^ə	c	ɔʑu<ha>ɨə
27a	o·ᵁha·ɛoᵁ	b	ouhaɨə	5a	əhɑᴵə	17	cv o<ᵁ<ha>ɨə,
b	o<uha·ɛə	45a	oˇuhaɨou	b	ŏʂuhaɨə		-ha>ɹə
28a	əha·ɨˇou	b	əha>ɨˇə	c	ŏ<uhaɨə	18	*o<ᵁ<haʑ-o<ᵁ<
b	o<uha·ɛə	46a	ɜuhaɨə	6a	əhaɨə		
29a	oᵁha·ɛə	b	əhɑ<·ɨˇə	b	o<uhaɛ^o<ʊ,	**KENTUCKY**	
b	o<ᵁha·ɛə	47a	əhɑ<·ɛə		əha·ɛə	1a	cv o<ᵁ<haʑ-ə
30a	əˈha·ɛˌoᵁ	b	əhɑ<·ɨˇə	7a	o<ᵁhaɨə	b	o<ᵁ<haʑ·-ə +
30b-31a	əha·ɛə	48a	əha>ɨˇə	b	ɜuhaɨə	2a	cv əhaʑ·-ə
31b	əˈhaɛˌoᵁ	bc	---	8a	əhaɨə	b	---
32a	əha>·ɛə	d	əhaɨˇə	b	oheᴵo	2c-3a	əhaʑ·-ə
b	o<uha>·ɛə	49a	ɜʑuha·ɛə	c	o>uhaɨə	3b	---
33a	əˈhɑ<·ɛˌou	b	əha>·ɨˇə	d	oˇuhɑɪou	c	cv əhaʑ·-ə
b	oᵁhaɛoᵁ	50a	o<uhaɨə	e	oˇuhaɨoˇʊ	d	---
34a	əha·ɛo<ʊ	b	əhaɨə	9a	o<uhaɨˇou	e	cv o<ᵁ<haʑ·-ə
b	əhaɛə	51a	ɜ>uhaɨɜu	b	ouhɑ·ɪə	4a	o<ᵁ<haʑ·-ə
35a	əha·ɛou	b	ɜ>uhaɨˇə	c	ɜ>uhaɨə	b	o<ᵁ<haʑ·-ə
b	əha·ɛə	52a	əha·ɨə	d	ouhɑ·ɪoʂŭ	c	cv o<ᵁ<haʑ·-o<ᵁ<
36a	ŏŭhaɛ^ŏŭ	b	ɜ>uha·ɨə	10a	əha·ɨə	5a	o<··ᵁ<haʑ·-o<··ᵁ<
b	əha>·ɛ^ə	c	əhaɨoʑu	b	əha·ɨˇə		cv ˌo<ᵁ<ˈhɑˌo<ᵁ<
37a	əhaɛ^o<ʊ	53a	əha>·ɨə	11a	əha>·ɨˇə	b	o<ᵁ<ha>·ə
b	əha·ɛə	b	---	11b-12a	əhaɨə	6a	o<ᵁ<haʑ·-ŏ
38a	əha>·ɛə	c	oᵁhaɨə	12b	əha·ɨˇə	b	---
b	əhaɛ^ə	54a	ɜ>uhaɨə	cd	---	c	o<ᵁ<haʑ·-o<ᵁ<
39a	o<uha·ɛə	b	əhaɨə	13a	ŏhaɛŏ<	7a	cv o<ᵁ<ha>·ə,
b	oʑuˈhaɨˌoʑu			b	ohaɨoᵁ		əhaʑ·-ə
						b	o<ᵁ<haʑ·-ə

DELAWARE

2a o˛uhɑ<ε>ə

5a ouɦɑ‡ˇoᵁ

MARYLAND

4c ouhɑ<ε>ŏ˛ᵁ

N9 oᵁhɑε>ə

13e o·ᵁhɑ<ε>oᵁ

16 oᵁhɑ<ε>ə

20a oᵁha>ε>o<

22a oᵁha‡ˇə

DISTRICT OF COLUMBIA

1a oˇᵁˇha>ε>ɵ

VIRGINIA

8a oᵁhɑ<ε>ə

14a o<ᵁhɑε>ə

23b oᵁha>ε>ə

30c oˇha>ε>oˇᵁ

34a oˇuha>ε>oᵁ

38 oˇᵁhaεə

45a oᵁha>ε>ə

46a oha>ε>o

54a o<ᵁha>ε>ə

55a oᵁha>ε>ə

N59 o^·ha>‡ˇo^

61a *o˛uha‡ˇŏ˛

VA

65a o˛uha>εŏ˛

b o˛uha>ε>ə

70a o˛uhaε>ŏ˛ŭ

NORTH CAROLINA

2a ɵuhɑ·‡ˇŏᵁ

7a oᵁha>·ε>oᵁ

14b oˇuha>ε>oᵁ

20a o˛ᵁhɑ<‡o˛ᵁ

22a o˛ᵁhɑ<ε>ŏ˛

N25 o^hɑε>ŏ^

25b oᵁhɑ^‡ˇo^

29a o^ha·ε>ə

32a oᵁha>ε>oᵁ

35a o^ha>ε>o^

40a o<ᵁhaε>ŏᵁ

47 oᵁhaεoᵁ

54a oᵁhɑ<ε>oᵁ

65b oᵁhɑε>o

67b oᵁhaε>oᵁ

69b oᵁha>ə<oᵁ

73b ˌoᵁˈhɑ·ε>ˌoᵁ

SOUTH CAROLINA

3a o^hɑ<·ε>o^

6a oˈha>ε>ˌo·

SC

N11 oha‡o

11b o·həˇ‡<o<·

i oha‡o

12b o^ha>‡o^

14a oha‡o

19b o·ha>‡o<·, o·ə-

cv o·ˈhe‡ˌo·

24d cv ˈo˛·ʷˌɑ˛·ɹo˛·

25a o·hɑ·ε>o

27a ˌo·ˈhe‡ˌo·

30a ˌoᵁhɑ<ε>ˈoᵁ

c cv o<ha˛·ɹo˛·u

33a oᵁha>ə<oᵁ

35c ˌo<u<ˈha˛·ˌo<ᵁ<

37 oᵁwa˛·o<ᵁ

r ˌo<ᵁˈɦa˛·ˌo<ᵁ<

41a oᵁha>ε>oᵁ

42e o<ᵁ<ha˛·ə

GEORGIA

1f o^ha>·‡ˇo^

3a o^ha‡o^

N4 o^ha>‡o^

9b oᵁˈha˛·ˌoᵁ,

-ˈha˛·ə-

GA

10a o·ha·ε>o·

N11 ˌoˈha˛·ˌo·

13a o^ha˛·‡o^

15a oᵁha>ε>oᵁ

16b cv o<·ha˛·ɹə

17 oᵁha·‡ə (?)

22a o<ha˛·əɵ̆ʉ,

əha˛·əɵʉ

23c cv ˌoᵁˈha˛·əˌo·

N24 cv o<ᵁ<ha˛·-ə

24a ˌoᵁhɑ<ε>ˈo·ᵁ

27 oᵁha‡oᵁ

28 ˌo<ᵁ<ˈha˛‡ˌo<ᵁ<

30c o<ᵁ<ˈha˛·əˌo·ᵁ<

34a oᵁˈha>ε>ˌoᵁ

N35 oᵁha˛·-ə

37d ˌo<ᵁ<ˈha˛·ˌo<u<

cv -ˈha˛·əˌo<ᵁ<

i cv o<ᵁ<ha˛‡ŏ<ᵁ<

43 oᵁha>·ε>o

FLORIDA

2c cv o·hɑ·‡ə

COMMENTARY

NEW YORK

5a *Ohio*, isn't it

[~ ɪznt̬ ə^t]

OHIO

3b [əha˛‡ə]: quick pron.

GEORGIA

17 [‡]: doubtful

10. MARYLAND

WS 86.3

In *Maryland* the regular stress pattern ˈ‿ is unmarked. Stress
is marked where secondary stress was recorded on the last syllable.

ONTARIO		NY		NY		NY	
1a	ˈmɛɚɬˌɫæˆnd	7ef	mɛrələnd	20ab	mɛrələnd	34a	mɛˆɚɬləˆn
b	mɛˆɚələˆn	g	mɛ̆ɾ̥ələnd	21	mɛɚəɬənd	bc	---
2a	---	h	mɛrələnd	22	mɛˀɚəɬənd	d	mɛɚələˆnd
b	cv mȝˆɚɬləˆn	i	mɛrələnᵈ	23a	---	35ab	mɛɚəɬənd
3	ˈmɛɚɪ̣ˌlæ·nd	j	mɛˀrələnᵈ	b	mɛ·ɚələˇn	c	---
4a	ˈmeˀᵊɚɬˆˌlæˆ·nd	k	mɛrələnd	c	m̥ɛ̣ɚŏˀl̩n	36a	mɛɚələnd
b	ˈmeˇɚɬˌɫæˆ·nd	l	mɛɾ̣ələnd	24a	mɛɚələnd	36b–37a	mɛɚəɬənd
5–8a	---	7m–8	mɛrələnd	b	mɛrəɬənd	37b	mɛˀɚəɬənd
8b	m̥ɛ̣ɚələˆnd	9a	mɛɚələnd	25a	m̥ɛ̣ɚələˆn	c	mɛɚəɬənd
c	mɛɚələˆnd	b	mɛˀɚŏlənd	b	m̥ɛ·ɚəl̩n	38a	mɛˆɚŏɬənd
d	m̥ɛ̣ɚələˆn	c	mɛrələnd	26a	mɛ·ɚəl̩n	b	mɛɚŏɬənd
9–10	---	10ab	mɛɚəɬənd	b	mɛɚəl̩nd	39a	mɛɚlənd
NEW YORK		11	mæᵊrələnd	26c–27b	---	b	mɛɚəɬən
1–2c	---	12a	mɛˆɚələnd	27c	mɛ·ɚɬˀləˆn	40a–41	mɛɚələnd
3a	mɛˀrələnd	b	mɛɚələnd	28a	mɛɚəɬn̩d	42a	mɛˆɚələnᵈ
b	mɛrələnd	c	mɛ·rələnd	b	mɛˆɚŏl̩n	b	mɛɚŏlŏnᵈ
c	mɛɚələnd	13a	mɛˆrələnd	29a	---	43a	mɛˆɚŏɬənd
d	mɛˀrələnd	b	mɛrələnd	b	m̥ɛ̣ɚəl̩n	b	mɛˆɚŏlənᵈ
4a	mɛɚəɬənd	14a	mɛˆɚələnd	c	mɛɚələˆnᵗ (✓)	c	mɛrələnd
b	mɛrələnd	b	mɛɚəɬənd	30a	mɛ·ɚələˇn	44a	mɛˆɚələnd
c	mɛˀrələnd̥	15a	mɛˆɚəɬənd	b	mɛɚələˆn	b	m̥ɛ̣ɚəɬənd
5a–g	mɛrələnd	b	mɛɚəɬənd	cd	---	45abc	---
5h	mɛɾ̥ələnd	16a	mɛˀrələnd	e	m̥ɛ·ɚəl̩n	d	mɛɚələˆn
i	mɛɚələnd	b	mɛrələnd	31a	ˈmɛɚŏˌləˆn	46a	mɛɚɬl̩n
6a	mɛrələnd	17a	mɛɚələnd	b	mɛˆɚɬlŏˆn	b	---
b	mɛrəɬənd	b	mɛɚŏɬənd	32a	mȝˀɚəˆləˆn	c	mɛɚəɬənd cv -ən
7a	mɛˀɾ̥ələnd	18a	mɛɚələnd	b	mɛɚələˆn	47a	mɛɚələˆn
b	mɛrɬɣlənᵈ	b	mæˆɚələnd	33a	---	b	mɛɚəɬənd
c	mɛrələnd	c	mɛrələnd	b	m̥ɛ̣ɚələˇn	48a	mɛˆɚŏˆləˆn
d	mɛˀɾ̥ələnd	19	mɛɚəɬənd	c	mɛ·ɚəl̩n	b	---

NY

48c	mɛ̞ɚələ^n
	c͟v mɛ̞ɚələn
d	mɛˑɚələ^n
49ab	---
c	mɛɚ‡ɫə^n
d	mɛˇɚəɫə^n
50a	mɛɚ‡<ln
b	mɛ̞ɚələ^n
51a	c͟v mɛ̞ɚələ^nd
b	mæ^ɚəln
cd͟e	---
52ab	mɛ̞ɚələ^n
c	mɛɚələ^n
53a	c͟v mɛ̞ɚələ^n
b͟	mɛɚ‡lnd
54a	mɛ^ɚələ^n
b	mɛɚəɫə^n
55a	mɛ̞ɚ‡<lə^nd
b	mɛ̞ɚələ^n
56a	mɛ̞ɚəln
b	mɛ̞ɚə^lə^nd
57a	mɛˑɚəlnd
b	---
c͟	meˇɚ‡lə^nd
58a	mɛ^ɚ‡lə^n
b	meˇɚə^ln
c	---
d͟	mɛˑɹələ^n
e͟	mɛ̞ɚələ^nd
f͟	---
59a	mɛˑɚələ^nd
b	mɛˑɚəɫə^nd
60a	mɛ̞ɚ‡ln, -lnd
b͟	mɛ̞ɚəln
61a	mɛ̞^ˑɚəɫn

NY

61b	mɛ̞ɚələ^n
62a	---
b	mɛ̞ɚələ^nd
c	mɛ̞ɚəln
d͟	c͟v mɛ̞ɚəln
63a	mɛ̞ɚələ^n
b	mɛ̞ɚəln
c	mɛɚə̆lənd
d͟	mɛ̞ɚəlnd c͟v -ln
64a	mɛˑɚ̆lə^n
b	mɛˇˑɚəlnd
c͟	---

NEW JERSEY

1a	mɛɚəɫən^d
b	mɛ^ɚəɫən^d
2a	mɛɚəɫən^d
b	mɛɚə̆lən^d
3a	mɛɚəɫən^‡
b	mɛ^ɚələn^d
4a	mɛɚə̆ɫənd
b	mɛ^ɚələn^d
5ab	mɛɚəɫən^d
6a	mɛɹələnd
b	mɛˑˑɚəɫən^d
7a	mɛ^ɚəɫən^d
b͟	mɛɚə̆lənd
8a	mɛɚlən
b	mɛɚələnd
9a	mɛɚə̆lən^d
b	mɛɚələnd
10a	mɛɹəɫənd
b	mɛɚə̆ln
c	mɛɚələn^d
d͟	mɛɹəɫənd
11a	mɛɚəɫən^d

NJ

11b	mɛɚə̆ɫənd
c	mɛɚə̆ɫənd
12a	mɛɚə̆ɫən^d
b	mɛɚəlend
13a	mɛɚələn^d
b	mɛɚəlend
14a	mɛ^ɚə̆lənd
b	mɛɚə̆ɫənd
15a	mɛɚələnd
b	mɛɚə̆lənd
16a	mɛɹələnd
b	mɛˑ^rələnd
17a	mɛɚə̆lənd
b	mɛɚə̆ɫənd
18abc͟	mɛɹələnd
d͟	mɛɚələnd
19a	mɛɹələnd
b͟	mɛˑrələnd
20a	mɛɹələnd
b	mɛˑrələnd
21ab	mɛɹələnd

PENNSYLVANIA

1a	mɛˑrələnd
b	mɛˑɚələnd
c-g͟	mɛɚələnd
h͟	mɛɚə̆lən^d
2a	mɛɚələnd
b	mɛ^ɚələnd
3a	mɛɚələnd
b	mɛɚə̆lən^d
c	mɛɚələnd
4a	mɛɚə̆lənd
b͟	mɛɚələnd
5a	mɛɚələn^d
bc	mɛɚələnd

PA

5d	mɛɚələn^d
e͟	mɛɚələnd
6a	mɛɹ‡læn‡
b	mɛɹələnd
c	mɛrɪlæn‡
6d͟-7b	mɛɚələn^d
7c	mɛɹələn̥d
d͟	mɛɚələnd
8ab	mɛɚələn^d
c	mɛrələn‡
d͟	mɛɚələnd
9a	mɛ^ɚələn‡
b	mɛɚələnd
c͟	meˇɚələnd
10	mɛrələn‡
11a	mɛɚə̆lən^d
b	mɛɚəɫənd
12ab	mɛɚələn^d
13a	mɛɚə̆lən^d
b	mɛˑɚələn^d
14a	mɛrələn‡
b	mɛ^rələnd
15a	mɛɚ̆lənd
b	mɛɚələnd
c͟	mɛrɪ^lən^d
16a	mɛˑrələn‡
b	mɛrələnd
c	---
17a	mɛrələn‡
b	mɛrələn°^d
18a	mɛ^ɚələnd
b͟	mɛrələnd
19a	mɛɚələn^d
19b-20a	mɛɚələnd
20b	mɛrələnd

An inventory of the phonetic symbols and diacritics appears in Vol. I, pp. 2-3. A fuller description of the following labels and substitute symbols appears on pp. 3-5. A complete description of all these will be found in Chapter IV of the *LAMSAS Handbook*. See also Chapter IV of the *LANE Handbook*.

LABELS

(a) Labels preceding the forms:

c̲v̲	observed in unguarded conversation
s̲	suggested by the field worker and recognized as natural
f̲	forced, secured by repeated questioning
c̲r̲	offered as a spontaneous correction
r̲	repeated at the field worker's request
:	a hesitating response
?	doubt as to the pronunciation, meaning, or naturalness
!	uttered with signs of amusement
⊥	reported as heard from others
N	judged as Negro usage
†	judged as old, out of date, obsolete
→	judged as recently introduced

(b) Labels following the forms:

(?)	doubt on the part of the field worker
(√)	certainty on the part of the field worker

SUBSTITUTE SYMBOLS

~	replaces a word repeated without change
-	replaces part of a word repeated without change
+	following a form indicates that an identical response was recorded from the informant's unguarded conversation
=	used after a semicolon to indicate that all the forms preceding the semicolon in the entry are to be repeated after it
---	indicates that no response was secured
Δ	indicates a cross-reference to another list

Additional copies of the base map issued with the first fascicle
may be obtained through the secretary of the American Dialect
Society, whose address can be found in the *Newsletter of the
American Dialect Society,* in the annual directory in *Publications
of the Modern Language Association,* or from the editor of *American
Speech.*